From Johnson's Kids to Lemonade Opera

Advisor in Music to Northeastern University Press
GUNTHER SCHULLER

From Johnson's Kids to Lemonade Opera

The American Classical Singer Comes of Age

Victoria Etnier Villamil

Northeastern University Press
Boston

Northeastern University Press

Copyright 2004 by Victoria Etnier Villamil

Library of Congress Cataloging-in-Publication Data

Villamil, Victoria Etnier.
From Johnson's kids to Lemonade Opera : the American classical singer comes
of age / Victoria Etnier Villamil.
p. cm.
Includes bibliographical references and index.
ISBN 1-55553-635-2 (cl : alk. paper)
1. Singers—United States—Biography. 2. Opera—United States—20th
century. I. Title.
ML400.V56 2004
782.06'8'0973—dc22   2004006204

Designed by Joyce C. Weston

Composed in Sabon by Wellington Graphics, Bridgewater, Massachusetts.
Printed and bound by Sheridan Books, Ann Arbor, Michigan. The paper is
House Natural, an acid-free stock.

MANUFACTURED IN THE UNITED STATES OF AMERICA
08 07 06 05 04   5 4 3 2 1

To the memory of Puli Toro
1940–2002

For my grandchildren
Anna, Lena, Cyprjan, and Sirius

Contents

Illustrations

Preface

WHEN I BEGAN TO STUDY singing in the mid-1950s, vestiges of the momentous events and sweeping cultural changes the previous decade had witnessed still lingered. Moreover, many of the singers whose careers had been formed in those earlier, complicated days were still singing— some in their prime.

I remember my very first voice lesson with my very first teacher in 1956. Lotte Leonard had been an important concert singer in Germany. She had gone to Paris in 1933 and when the Nazis marched in fled to America. She taught at Mannes and Juilliard, but she also had a private studio on the Upper West Side of Manhattan, which is where I went. It was quite a first lesson. One of her students, Mattiwilda Dobbs, already a star in Europe, had made a triumphant debut at the Metropolitan Opera the night before, only the third black singer to achieve that honor, and the phone never stopped ringing. Mme. Leonard apologized, but she needn't have. For a sixteen-year-old whose every free moment was spent at the opera, it was very exciting—as it is in retrospect. For now, a half century later, I realize that a palpable piece of my heritage as an American singer was in the room that day, and that I, in fact, was one of the first generation to benefit fully from the story I am about to tell.

It is the story of a generation of classically trained American singers who saw their profession, their image, and their art transformed by the extraordinary times in which they lived; it is about the obstacles they overcame, the breakthroughs they made, and the legacy they left. American singers once suffered from a terrible feeling of inferiority. Lawrence Tibbett and other singers spoke of the problem often, and it was regularly discussed in editorials and other writings of the period. Now they stand without apology on any international stage. This is the story of the brief period in which they made that journey.

"I think Richard, as great as he was, felt very deeply that the American artist was not received in his own country like the European was," Jerome Hines once wrote as part of a tribute to his colleague the tenor Richard

Tucker. "The mood was pervasive—we American singers were treated much better in Buenos Aires and in Europe than we were here. . . . I think that prejudice has pretty well left us in America today, and the American singer is now received as a first-rank star at the Metropolitan and throughout this country. That took an awful lot of doing, and there were a lot of pioneers who were *bloodied* in the process."[1]

Though correcting the record where subsequent scholarship has shown the need, I have written *From Johnson's Kids to Lemonade Opera* as much as possible from the point of view of those who lived the story. All quotations are therefore either from period writings or from autobiographies and interviews with the singers and others involved. Of course, one cannot believe everything one reads in the press, but the periodicals and newspapers of the period followed cultural developments with avid interest in those days, and I used them not only to better understand what people were thinking at the time but for color, mood, and information about singers, events, and companies that otherwise might easily have passed me by. The Lemonade Opera, for example, does not appear in any history or reference work, but the enterprising little company fascinated the contemporary press.

But as I turned my research into a story, one worry and one regret have stayed with me that must be mentioned. My worry is that I may have made a mistake of fact. (Though some may think my opinions are mistaken, they are only opinions, solely mine, and do not adversely affect the recording of history.) I found few sources I felt I could totally depend on, including the singers themselves, who, human like the rest of us, do not always remember even their own stories accurately. As discrepancies as to specifics and facts cropped up everywhere, it often required a great deal of detective work to make a decision as to what to believe. Though I try to make it clear to my readers either in the text or in a footnote if I have any doubts about a fact, I still worry that I might have unwittingly perpetuated some kind of error in the historical record. If so, I can only apologize and hope that someone down the line will find a good place to correct it.

My regret is that in writing first and foremost the story of an era and a profession, I have not been able to allot more space to the singers individually, or to include everyone. The book is neither an encyclopedia nor even a comprehensive history. To include too many dates and places of birth, teachers, roles, and so forth would have impeded the narrative, and therefore both the quantity and kind of information included about each singer as well as the selection of the singers themselves were determined wholly by the appropriateness for the narrative. To solve at least part of the problem, however, I have included a biographical appendix, which supplies additional data on most of the American singers. In this way, readers can learn more about singers who particularly interest them and I can relax in the knowledge that almost every singer from the period mentioned in the book is more suitably identified for posterity.

It touched me that many of the lesser-known singers I interviewed were so pleased to be found. So often they would begin by saying, "I can't imagine why on earth you would want to talk with me," and end with "That was fun talking about the good old days." Even Frank Guarrera, whom I think of as being famous, having sung nothing but leading roles at the Metropolitan Opera (among other important places) for almost three decades, often said, as he did when the members of a small opera club rose to their feet with prolonged applause to welcome him, "It's so nice to be remembered."

But it is more than just "nice" for a singer to be remembered; it is imperative to the recording of the history of a great art. And at no time was this made clearer to me than the day I played a compilation of singers I had just bought on CD (*The Record of Singing*, volume 4, EMI) and was staggered to hear as beautiful a rendering of Handel's "Care selve" as I could ever have imagined. The singer was someone by the name of Florence Quartararo. The liner notes told me she was an American who had sung at the Met for four seasons, married the Italian bass Italo Tajo, and stopped singing. But where did she come from, what happened to her, and how was it possible I had never heard of her? Clearly I had to find the answers. Clearly, such a great artist should never be forgotten.

May those readers fortunate enough to have heard Quartararo and the other singers in my book enjoy being reacquainted with them; may those who have not be glad of the introduction. And may all my readers come away moved by this singularly vital chapter of our history.

Acknowledgments

B ECAUSE I HAD ORIGINALLY planned to end the book in 1955 and realized that 1950 was a more appropriate cutoff date only after I had conducted most of my interviews, I first want to apologize to those singers who gave me interviews but for that reason are not included. Yet I express my gratitude to each and every one—some extremely articulate and many with a great deal to say—because all informed my thinking about the era and so contributed to this book. In alphabetical order, they are Adele Addison, Licia Albanese (for a foreigner's perspective), Thelma Altman, Rose Bampton (who as my first interview kindly let me practice on her several times), Bethany Beardslee, Adelaide Bishop, Ann Blyth, Helen Boatwright, Natalie Bodanya, Fausto Bozzo (the son of Mina Cravi), Lucielle Browning, Margaret Carson (publicist), Nadine Conner, Marilyn Cotlow, Mary Curtis-Verna, Vivian Della Chiesa, Maria di Gerlando, Thea Dispeaker (manager), Dorothy Dow, Todd Duncan, Alice Esty, Ellen Faull, Richard Flusser (founder and director of the After Dinner Opera Theater), Reva Freidberg Fox (secretary to Johnson and Bing), Frances Greer, Frank Guarrera, Josephine Guido, Carla Hackett Quijano (daughter of Charles Hackett), Margaret Harshaw, Thomas Hayward, Mary Henderson, Vicky Hillebrand (secretary to Dorothy Kirsten), Jerome Hines, Alice Howland, Lois Hunt, Helen Jepson, Irene Jordan, Ruth Kobart, Gloria Lane, Brenda Lewis, Martha Lipton, David Lloyd, Robert Merrill, Patrice Munsel, Russell Oberlin, Marguerite Piazza, Guido Salmaggi (the son of Alfredo), Jane Stuart Smith, Risë Stevens, Blanche Thebom, Richard Torigi, Theodor Uppman, Jess Walters, Dorothy Warenskjold, Camilla Williams, Dino Yannapoulos (stage director), and Francis Yeend. I am also grateful to the soprano Marguerite Willauer and the pianist James Benner, who contributed to my interviews with their spouses, Dino Yannapoulos and Frances Yeend, respectively, and to those who spoke to me informally: Elaine Malbin, James Christe, and Kinney Frelinghuysen (about Suzy Morris), Nancy Kendall-Stitt (about the Lemonade Opera), Carol Poppenger (student and friend of Galli-Campi), Marie Quartararo (sister of Florence Quartararo), Heddy Reid (niece of

Janet Fairbank), Vivian Warren (sister of Leonard Warren), Victoria Kirk (granddaughter of Alice Howland), Barbara Ziemba (daughter of Winifred Heidt), Robert Fisher (friend of Winifred Heidt), and Marjorie Melton Nutt (daughter of James Melton).

It was an adventure finding many of the singers. I knew some and had connections to others. John Pennino of the Metropolitan Opera Archives kindly forwarded my letters of inquiry to those the Met still knew how to contact. But after that it was a matter of either a great variety of people (too numerous to list, but thank you all), who both wracked their brains and sometimes did actual legwork to help me track down my most elusive subjects, or, as in several truly delightful instances, pure serendipity.

In addition to those I interviewed I want to express my gratitude and appreciation to the staffs of the Library of Congress, the New York Public Library for the Performing Arts, and the Free Library of Philadelphia; to Margaret Kulis at the Newberry Library, regarding Janet Fairbank; to Howard Hook, who generously provided me with a private history of the early auditions to which I constantly referred; to the staff at AGMA, who allowed me to rummage in their files; and to Robert Tuggle, archivist, and John Pennino, assistant archivist of the Metropolitan Opera Archives, for the help they gave me in a great variety of ways. I thank Doris Coleman, Harriet Pattison, Sybil Baldwin, and Stephanie Doane, who read early parts of the manuscript and spurred me on at that critical juncture. And I am indebted to Harold Bruder, who read the entire manuscript and assisted me in every way imaginable way, from providing advice, support, and always just the right answer to a question to helping me find a good publisher.

For it was Harold who introduced me to Charles Mintzer, biographer of Rosa Raisa, to whom I am indebted in turn for leading me to his publisher, the excellent Northeastern University Press, where I found a wonderfully conscientious and efficient staff. I thank them all, most especially Sarah Rowley and Ann Twombly.

Once again, my heartfelt gratitude goes out to my husband, who read the manuscript and gave me his insightful opinion whenever I suddenly felt the need for it, who humored me through such desperate moments as computer breakdowns and the loss of whole chapters, who always seemed to know just how and how much to help, and who never wavered in his faith that I could do the job. Last, I thank Rose Hirschorn. Rose not only helped me find singers and read and commented on the entire manuscript, but, most important, provided the kind of support she knew our treasured mutual friend Puli would have given were she still with us. Puli Toro, to whose memory I dedicate this book, was a superb mezzo, an artist of the highest order, a prized teacher, and an unflagging champion of the music of her native Puerto Rico. She was also the best and truest of friends. Happily she was able to read the first chapters of my manuscript before she died, and the enthusiasm she expressed for it was all I needed to know I wasn't wasting my time. Still, though I imagine her looking over my shoulder as I write, I miss Puli terribly.

Prologue: Epiphany

I N THE LAST DAYS OF 1924 the Metropolitan Opera was preparing a gala revival of Giuseppe Verdi's masterpiece *Falstaff* to celebrate Antonio Scotti's twenty-fifth season with the company. The great Tullio Serafin, recently arrived from Italy, was to conduct, and the company's general manager, Giulio Gatti-Casazza, had surrounded the Italian baritone, who was singing the title role, with an all-star international cast that included Frances Alda, Lucrezia Bori, Beniamino Gigli, Marion Telva, and in the role of the jealous husband, Ford, a little-known American by the name of Lawrence Tibbett. Engaged the previous season for minor roles, the young Californian seemingly had done well enough in occasional performances of supporting roles to interest Gatti in trying him for bigger things.[1]

Tibbett worked hard to learn Ford, but rehearsals went badly. A gangly greenhorn in a complicated ensemble opera, "surrounded by a horde of the greatest names in grand opera, I was at first a stumbling incompetent," he later admitted. "I balled up stage directions which, in Italian, had to be translated for me. At one time I was so bad that somebody went to Gatti and said I would never do." But then one day Tibbett decided to stop apologizing; he would "do or die."[2] "'You know, Grace,'" he told his wife, "'I've worked Ford to the *death*. If I don't hit the bell this time, we might as well pack up and head back to California.'"[3]

The great night arrived, January 2. *Falstaff* had not been heard at the Metropolitan since 1910 and Scotti was a favorite. But if few gave much thought to the obscure native, the story of how in one "furious effort to make the audience pay some attention to [him],"[4] "behind his boscage of beard," as Oscar Thompson would remember it, "the young Tibbett took fire . . . [and] sang like one possessed," is now legend.[5] Indeed, as Lawrence Gilman of the *Herald Tribune* reported it, the American's "magnetic and authoritative performance in the Inn scene of the second act took the audience completely captive. After the curtain had fallen on the scene they kept up a tornado of applause, shouts, whistles and catcalls, paying no attention whatsoever to the fact that Mr. Serafin was impatient to get on with the next

Lawrence Tibbett as Ford in Falstaff, *about 1925. Photo by Mishkin*

scene, and that the modest Mr. Tibbett quite evidently did not want to get between the limelight and Mr. Scotti and take a curtain call alone. But his compatriots would not let him off. . . . Finally, Mr. Tibbett showed himself alone before the yellow curtains, the audience split the roof and then the show proceeded."[6]

After the performance, over a bowl of soup the modest baritone told his wife and teacher he hoped the reviews would say more than that he was "adequate." Back at his office, Olin Downes, the critic for the *New York Times,* told his editor what had happened. "You have exactly forty minutes to write a story for Page One"[7] was the response. And the next morning, Saturday, there it was, page 1: "AMERICAN BARITONE STIRS OPERA HOUSE."

Though over the years some have suggested that Scotti was jealous and tried to prevent his young colleague from taking a solo bow, Tibbett always maintained just the opposite—that he "was perhaps naturally a little timid myself and . . . held back."[8] But, as Downes believed, what mattered was that "the audience, justly or unjustly, had gained the impression that Mr. Tibbett was not allowed to come before them and receive their appreciation and had determined that the performance should go no further until he had done so."[9]

The next day, while the Metropolitan "buzzed . . . with echoes of an American audience's pointed ovation to a native singer," the chairman of the board, Otto Kahn, wrote Tibbett a letter on behalf of the company. "It is a particular gratification to see so gifted and serious a young American come into his own by so spontaneous and hearty a public recognition. The occasion was not only a great and well-deserved tribute to yourself, but also an expression of pride in the artistic achievements of an American."[10] A week later a popular columnist for *Musical America,* still riding high, exclaimed:

> Here's new heart for every American artist! The most remarkable individual demonstration of years, and perhaps in the entire history of the Metropolitan Opera House, has been accorded an American artist. . . .
>
> What makes me fling my cap in the air is simply this—*it happened!* And when I read that Giulio Gatti-Casazza had wrung the young man's hand, and that Otto H. Kahn, as chairman of the board of directors, had sent him a letter of felicitation, I think I could have eaten my newspaper and put my omelet in my overcoat pocket, so eager was I to shout three cheers for the American artist.[11]

Chapter One

1935

WHEN MARCELLA SEMBRICH DIED after a brief illness at her home in New York City, her family announced her wish that the funeral service be simple; no eulogy for the legendary diva, only a few musical numbers and the usual prayers. Nevertheless, Sunday afternoon, January 13, 1935, found majestic Saint Patrick's Cathedral filled with seven carloads of flowers and more than thirty-five hundred mourners spilling onto the icy sidewalks.[1]

After all, the stocky little coloratura from Galicia was among the world's most celebrated and beloved artists—an authentic luminary in an authentic golden age of singing and a prodigious musician who excelled as well on the piano and violin. When as a young girl Sembrich had auditioned her several gifts for Franz Liszt, the old master advised: "God has given you three pairs of wings with which to fly through the country of music . . . but sing, sing for the world, for you have the voice of an angel."[2] And so, she had honed her technique in Italy under the great Lampertis, father and son, and then, just nineteen years old, embarked on her fabulous career, making her American debut as Lucia di Lammermoor on the second night of the Metropolitan Opera's inaugural season in 1883.

Others filling the great nave included such notables from the world of music as Sergei Rachmaninoff, Josef Hoffmann, and Antonio Scotti. There was as well a phalanx of her many students; for after her retirement from the Metropolitan, Sembrich had settled in America to concertize and teach. In her recitals she had introduced a new kind of programming, which rendered in chronological order and in more than one language a quality and variety of repertoire hitherto unknown in America. And, it being her fervent wish to pass on to her adopted country the great vocal precepts of bel canto she had learned at their Italian source, she had taught extensively in private and as head of the voice departments of the prestigious Juilliard School and Curtis Institute. Her students, primarily young American women, included Dusolina Giannin , ..ow world-famous; Josephine Antoine, on the threshold of a solid Metropolitan career; and Queena Mario, a Met favorite, who was already teaching the Sembrich legacy to the next generation.[3]

Giulio Gatti-Casazza too was there, an honorary pallbearer. The former director of La Scala had become the manager of the Metropolitan Opera at the beginning of the 1908–09 season, the very one in which Sembrich had said farewell to the company with a great gala performance. Now, more than a quarter century later, having left a legacy of his own to America, Gatti himself was about to retire.

Although many possible successors to Gatti had been discussed, the month after the funeral found the field narrowed to two: Edward Johnson, a Canadian-born tenor, and Herbert Witherspoon, a bass from Buffalo. If nothing else, after years of dealing with an employer who barely spoke English, American singers would now be able to conduct business freely in their native tongue and, better yet, with an experienced singer.

Though still actively performing with the Met, the popular Johnson had been anticipating retiring from singing, after which he planned to found a junior opera company. The staid Witherspoon since leaving the company in 1916 had written a popular book on singing, founded the American Academy of Teachers of Singing, headed both the Chicago Musical College and the Cincinnati Conservatory of Music, served as artistic director of the Chicago Civic Opera, and was preparing to join the Juilliard faculty—an impressive résumé. But because Witherspoon had been away from the Metropolitan for a long time, was newly married, and had assured his wife he would not accept the position, and because Gatti had made known his preference for Johnson, the odds seemed to favor the tenor.

Nevertheless, in early March Witherspoon got the nod, and Johnson was named an assistant manager who would also be in charge of a new supplementary season of opera: it would take place in the spring after the company finished touring and the works would be sung in English. As the performances were to feature younger singers, especially Americans, the plan appealed to the tenor. And indeed, everyone seemed pleased with the new arrangements, even if some minded the large role the Juilliard Musical Foundation had played in making them.

For when at his death in 1919 the philanthropist Augustus Juilliard had left twelve million dollars to music, he had stipulated that part of it go to the Metropolitan Opera, if ever needed, which at the time seemed highly unlikely. Wealthy patrons easily sustained the company and Gatti had even built up a surplus. Indeed, the idea of a stock market crash so devastating that the patrons would have to withdraw their support and a depression so profound that the nest egg would be reduced to nothing was unimaginable. But that is what had happened, and with the company on the verge of extinction, a desperate board had had to swallow its pride and accept the foundation's substantial offer of $150,000, even though it meant answering to a coterie of high-powered representatives from Juilliard in exchange.

On March 19 the company mounted a gala farewell to its retiring chief. Gatti, who throughout his tenure had remained a remote figure to the public, emerged long enough to greet Mr. and Mrs. Witherspoon and, to everyone's delight, his former friend Arturo Toscanini, with whom he had recently reconciled.[4] Then, withdrawing to the safe confines of his office, he listened through speakers as a galaxy of the stars he had brought to the Metropolitan showed their appreciation in scenes from six operas.

On the last day of March the company frolicked though the annual Grand Operatic Surprise Party. Mostly fun and highjinks, it included Tibbett, dressed as a dragon, singing "Der Wurm Turns," Lily Pons and Lauritz Melchior (the tenor in pink tights) performing an acrobatic stunt, and Johnson and Gladys Swarthout dancing a waltz. After the annual tour, which this year economics dictated be brief and confined to the Northeast, the company tacked on two performances of *Parsifal* in New York with Kirsten Flagstad as Kundry. Since her unheralded but spectacular debut as Sieglinde in February, the indefatigable Norwegian had satisfied America's insatiable appetite for the great Wagnerian dramas[5] by performing seven of the leading roles (including two Brünnhildes) some eighteen times (often with no rehearsal). Indeed, with Frida Leider, said to be pressured by her country's führer to remain in Berlin, unable to fulfill her contract, the fair Flagstad had proved a savior.

On April 27 Rosa Ponselle hosted a farewell luncheon for the company and friends on board the ocean liner *Rex* in honor of the departing Gatti and his second wife, the ballerina Rosina Galli. Then, after murmured goodbyes, everyone gathered on the pier and, choking back tears, sang "Auld

Lang Syne" to their beloved old boss, who wearily waved a large white hand-kerchief as the liner slipped out of its berth and headed out to sea, bound for Italy.[6]

May 7 found Edward Johnson, now an assistant manager, in Detroit, winding down his singing career performing *La Rondine* opposite his favor-ite leading lady, Lucrezia Bori. In New York, Herbert Witherspoon, who had been working like a house afire ever since his appointment, prepared to sail on the eleventh for a scouting tour of Europe. But on the tenth, after a day signing contracts, Witherspoon was just finishing a late afternoon meeting with his assistant manager, Edward Ziegler, and the treasurer, Earle Lewis, when, smiling over a favorable advance ticket sales report, he stepped out of Ziegler's office to advise his waiting wife that the meeting was almost over, slumped to the floor, and died of a heart attack. On the sixteenth the board announced that Johnson would replace Witherspoon.

Edward Johnson assumed the position of general manager at a time of omi-nous developments abroad, from civil war in Spain to Italy's invasion of Ethiopia and Adolf Hitler's renunciation of the Versailles Treaty and increas-ing repression of the Jews. But under President Franklin D. Roosevelt the American economy at least appeared to be recovering. Inflation stood at 1 percent; unemployment was down to 20 percent; and the new Social Secu-rity system and Works Progress Administration would soon be up and run-ning. The WPA promised funds for projects involving musicians ranging from the building of civic auditoriums to the support of civic music associa-tions; its offshoot, the Federal Music Project, was poised to provide jobs in arts relief programs to eighteen thousand musicians, as well as to sponsor concerts for performers, research for scholars, and commissions for com-posers.

With concerts and solo recitals on a notable upswing, stars, especially those with radio or motion picture celebrity like Tibbett and Swarthout, crisscrossed the nation, performing several times a week. They still traveled mostly by rail, but improvements in air travel, such as the new twenty-one-passenger DC-3 that boasted heated cabins and flew coast-to-coast in fifteen hours, now made it possible to accept more engagements.

In the spring the Russian bass Feodor Chaliapin, long absent from American opera stages, returned for a concert tour; in an interview he criti-cized Americans for still not singing concert and opera in their own language, as every other country did.[7] Mary Garden, now sixty-one, gave a New York recital followed by master classes in Chicago. In addition to the annual recitals of favorites Lotte Lehmann, Elisabeth Rethberg, John Charles Thomas, and Roland Hayes, Manhattan's fall season brought the return of Povla Frijsh and Paul Robeson, and the recital debuts of Flagstad and a new soprano from Brazil, Bidù Sayão. The radio singer Winifred Cecil, on the threshold of a notable career abroad, also gave a highly acclaimed recital. Though marriage to the president of the Turin opera, who during the war would act as a liaison with the Partisans, would later keep the Sembrich protégée detained in Italy, now the esteemed critic Leonard Liebling wrote: "This reviewer left the recital wondering why those responsible glorify foreign, worn-out singers so blaringly and profitably when there is available one of our own young artists as gifted as Miss Cecil. What is the matter with us Americans, anyway?"[8]

Popular Town Hall was the venue for virtually all these occasions, as it was on the penultimate day of the year, when the audience arrived to be met with the unusual sight of a closed curtain. The artist, it seems, had broken her foot on her ocean voyage home from Europe and did not want to be seen entering in a wheelchair. Because she had been away for four years, everything had to be just right, she insisted: and so it was. "Let it be said at the outset," declared Howard Taubman of the *New York Times* the next day, "Marian Anderson has returned to her native land one of the great singers of our time."[9]

But not of opera; for with rare exception, opera was not an option for singers of Anderson's color, unless, of course, the company was itself black, or the opera was written expressly for them, like George Gershwin's *Porgy and Bess,* which was currently playing on Broadway.

Warmer weather brought music festivals just as popular, if rarely as sophisticated, as their European prototypes, though, now in its second season, the Berkshire Music Festival in western Massachusetts known as Tanglewood had such aspirations. "It is high time that America had its own Salzburg, and we are taking a step in that direction,"[10] Gertrude Robinson Smith, its enthusiastic cofounder, proclaimed. But since neither the programming nor soloists had yet come close to evoking the famous Austrian festival, which that summer boasted Bruno Walter and Arturo Toscanini, the Vienna Philharmonic, and such illustrious singers as Pinza, Lehmann, Mariano Stabile,

and the American Dusolina Giannini, that fall the board named as Tanglewood's new director the Russian-born conductor of the Boston Symphony
Orchestra, Serge Koussevitzky.

As was the custom, the 1935 summer season opened in May with festivals
in Ann Arbor, Cincinnati, and Bethlehem, Pennsylvania, this year all celebrating the 250th birthdays of Handel and Bach, and closed in October at
Worcester, Massachusetts. In between, Americans enjoyed a veritable feast of
music making, especially in the urban areas. The Depression had silenced
Chicago's Ravinia Festival, but Philadelphia's determined citizenry had won
its fight to save the Robin Hood Dell, which that summer introduced Margaret Harshaw, a local contralto with a day job as stenographer for the Bell
Telephone Company, in excerpts from De Falla's *El Amor Brujo*. And in
Washington, D.C., performing on a barge anchored at the Watergate on the
Potomac, the National Symphony inaugurated a new summer series of concerts with Winifred Cecil among the soloists and Antonia Brico, a rare
woman conductor.

In St. Louis, the Municipal Opera, charging two dollars at most,
mounted a new operetta every week of twelve; Lewisohn Stadium in New
York included concert versions of the standard operas amid its usual potpourri of offerings; and the Hollywood Bowl in Los Angeles showed off the
marvels of its acoustics with an unheard-of four operas, including *Lohengrin*,
its first Wagner production. In addition, the sixty-second season of the
Chautauqua Institute presented twelve fully staged productions; the Cincinnati Opera, now in its fifteenth season, extended its season from five to
six weeks; and the Steel Pier Opera in Atlantic City embarked on its eighth
season.

Americans who aspired to singing careers but declined the presumed advantage of going to Europe found private teaching at home, thanks to an end-
less stream of émigrés bearing Europe's great vocal traditions, at least as good
as on the Continent, but they found opportunities for training in opera
severely wanting. Opera workshops were virtually unknown, and though
several of the country's many music schools advertised impressive vocal fac-
ulties, few offered opera programs. Exceptions were Philadelphia's Curtis
Institute, an all-scholarship school, and New York's Juilliard School of Music, where productions in 1935 included *Orfeo ed Euridice* and the world pre-

miere of Robert Russell Bennett's *Maria Malibran* with students Risë Stevens and Josephine Antoine in respective title roles. A few blocks from Curtis, the newly formed School for Vocal Scholarships, soon to be renamed the Academy of Vocal Arts, addressed the specific needs of the young singer in the grip of the Depression by similarly offering tuition-free education. In New York the new High School of Music and Art announced auditions.

There were few competitions. But on December 22 the Metropolitan Opera announced what it hoped would be an annual radio contest for aspirants. Heretofore, it had been the company's policy to grant any singer's request to be heard. "You had only to write a letter," Helen Noble, a secretary said. "A date would be set; and when you arrived the top men of the Opera House were waiting to hear you."[11] Mary Moore, who had performed only once in public and had to be told to remove the cough drop from her mouth before she sang for management, had done just that and received a contract to perform that very spring.[12] As it turned out, bronchitis thwarted her scheduled debut as Gilda; Lily Pons graciously filled in. But the pretty Irish American was reassigned to a Sunday evening concert, coincidentally on St. Patrick's Day, and did well. In fact, the critics, who rarely covered these weekly operatic potpourris but were curious about the girl with the nonexistent résumé, were kind, even enthusiastic, about her *Lucia* selections. "Here is a young American who has the material with which to build," the *Times* said.[13] And at the Cincinnati May Festival, where she sang next, another critic predicted she would be "one of the world's most eminent coloratura sopranos."[14] But like so many talented but woefully ill-prepared and ill-advised young Americans, Mary Moore would never realize her promise.

By mid-decade opera production across the country, which had been sent into a tailspin by the Depression, was making something of a comeback. Performances by the symphony orchestras of Philadelphia, Cleveland, and Boston were especially newsworthy. Boston, under Koussevitzky, offered the American premieres of excerpts from Alban Berg's *Lulu* with the Russian refugee Olga Averino and Igor Stravinsky's *Perséphone,* conducted by the composer with the "ultra-modern" Canadian Eva Gauthier doing vocal honors. Cleveland under Artur Rodzinski performed six operas, including *Lady Macbeth of the Mtsensk District* by a young composer from the Soviet Union, Dimitri Shostakovich. The singers, White Russians and a few Americans, came from a group known as the Art of Musical Russia Inc., which had been making news with its series of Russian operas at various New York sites. And the Philadelphia Orchestra under the direction of Fritz Reiner and Alexander Smallens mounted ten full productions in its first and only year of opera production.

Otherwise, Pierre Key's *1935 Music Year Book* lists a total of thirty-four professional opera companies in the country, including festivals and touring troupes. Regional opera was barely more than a concept, but that fall the St. Louis Grand Opera opened its new hall in spectacular fashion with Maria Jeritza as Turandot, and the San Francisco Opera proudly offered its first performance of Wagner's complete *Ring* featuring Flagstad, Melchior, Rethberg, and Friedrich Schorr. The Chicago Grand Opera Company, a sad successor to the once-prestigious Chicago Civic, which had gone under in 1932, offered a spotty season at best, but opened auspiciously with the American premiere of Boito's *Mefistofele.* Pinza led the cast as the Devil; Edith Mason, a Chicago favorite, was Margherita, and—after four years singing in Italy under the exotic name of Franco Foresta-Hayek—Minnesota-born Frank Forest was Faust. Because that same night the touring San Carlo was playing *Carmen* across town, it was estimated that on November 2, 1935, some seven thousand Chicagoans heard opera.

Back in New York City, the impresario Alfredo Salmaggi fulfilled a lifelong dream and, in addition to his usual standard fare, gave the American premiere of Rossini's *Mosè in Egitto.* And Fortune Gallo's popular San Carlo Opera celebrated its silver anniversary with a Jubilee Tour, which crisscrossed North America for some thirty-five weeks, once again providing its singers with the most regular work for their instrument in America—with the exception of radio.

Indeed, now in its golden age, radio offered a veritable feast for singers. Programs were usually known by their sponsors, and in a typical week in 1935 lovers of the vocal art could hear, in addition to the offerings of countless lesser-known soloists, those of such upcoming stars as Rose Bampton (Smith Brothers cough drops) and Helen Jepson (Kraft cheese), and such celebrities as Tibbett (Packard automobiles), Nelson Eddy or Richard Crooks (Firestone tires), Lily Pons (Chesterfield cigarettes), Gladys Swarthout (Palmolive soap), Grace Moore (Vicks Chemical), and the beguiling Jessica Dragonette, who still headlined the great *Cities Service Concerts.* Saturday, of course, meant the broadcast of an entire opera live from the Met, and on Sunday, in addition to the *General Motors Hour* and Radio City Music Hall's weekly opera presentation, wonderful symphonic programs were broadcast live, many with famous singers as featured soloists.

The nation also appeared to be renewing its love affair with the phonograph record, which in recent years had taken a backseat to radio. In May the country's first magazine devoted to recording, the *American Music Lover* (soon to be renamed the *American Record Guide*) made its first appearance. A twelve-inch 78-rpm domestic recording cost about a dollar and a half, though one had to buy twenty or more to get a complete opera.

But if every singer coveted a recording contract, the bigger prize was an invitation to the West Coast, where the Hollywood musical was reaching its heyday. In 1935, only days after giving a well-received Town Hall recital, Nelson Eddy saw his star go into the stratosphere with the opening of his first major motion picture, *Naughty Marietta;* Lawrence Tibbett starred in a film about opera singers called *Metropolitan;* the radio tenor James Melton sang his way to a fictional Met debut in *Stars over Broadway;* and, after picking up a gold medal from the Society of Arts and Sciences for her 1934 hit, *One Night of Love,* Grace Moore opened in *Love Me Forever,* yet another film in which a pretty young soprano makes good. Foreigners also got in on the act. The chic Lily Pons virtually played herself—a girl from the French provinces who becomes a famous singer—in *I Dream Too Much,* and the sleek Italian tenor Nino Martini offered up songs and arias in *Here's to Romance.* But if Hollywood seemed preoccupied with opera, the Marx brothers kept perspective with their newest riot of laughs, *A Night at the Opera.*

Meanwhile, a variety of excellent periodicals kept music lovers abreast of all the activity. *Musical Courier* and the equally popular *Musical America* appeared biweekly (monthly in the summer). A year's subscription cost three dollars. Both teemed with news, reviews, articles, chitchat, and wonderful photographs. Chicago's *Musical Leader* and Pierre Key's *Musical Digest* used similar formats but were not as substantial. *Etude,* which included actual sheet music appropriate for amateurs along with its generally more pedagogical articles, was all but obligatory in any home that had a piano. And though the monthly *Musician* had stopped including sheet music during the Depression because it was too costly, improving economic conditions would soon allow for its return. *Billboard* and *Variety* focused on show business but kept tabs on classical music. And though no periodical devoting itself to opera had ever survived more than a few years, this would change in 1936 when the new Metropolitan Opera Guild introduced a newsletter it called *Opera News.*

If that weren't enough, in New York City, which was rapidly becoming one of the world's greatest centers for classical music, eight newspapers (down from a pre-Depression high of thirteen) sent such stellar critics as Pitts Sanborn, Lawrence Gilman, Leonard Liebling, Samuel Chotzinoff, Francis Perkins, William J. Henderson, Carleton Smith, Howard Taubman, and Olin Downes to cover events. That several of them believed the American singer to be coming into his own (Oscar Thompson, an editor for *Musical America,* was writing the first book on the subject) was a new development that some found heartening.

With public relations now all but required for a performer to succeed in America, Constance Hope, a former pianist and singer, opened a firm to provide counsel on promotion to such celebrities as Pons, Pinza, Lehmann, and Melchior. Though Americans had once thought opera singers glamorous by virtue of the mystery that surrounded their private lives, in recent years they had come to prefer them as next-door neighbors. A master at both the publicity stunt and the human-interest story, Hope, who would title her memoirs *Publicity Is Broccoli,* managed to keep her clients dignified even in aprons and undershirts, while turning public relations into a virtual art form.

In December all eyes turned back to the Met, where, after a summer of scouting and signing singers abroad, Johnson had settled into Gatti's vacated office. During his absence the company had announced the formation of a Metropolitan Opera Guild. But the other good news, that before his death Witherspoon had already engaged nine new singers, including six Americans, was overshadowed by rumors that top stars Tibbett, Pons, and Ponselle had not yet re-signed. Their reluctance to forfeit the lucrative fees of radio, film, and concert for the relative pittance offered by the beleaguered opera company was apparently at the root of the problem. But the new manager, in a test of the diplomatic skills for which he would soon be known, smoothly talked his old colleagues back.

The jockeying for opening night tickets, which ranged from one and a half to ten dollars, recalled the boom days of the 1920s, and, in fact, everything pointed to a revitalized company. There were new subscribers, new seats, new carpets, new paint, a new lighting system, and a new, modernized bar and lounge in the capable hands of the popular restaurateur Louis Sherry. George Balanchine's American Ballet Company was now in residence, and hired applauders—the claque—were officially banned. On December 16 society showed up in pre-Depression splendor with orchids, tiaras, gowns of velvet and satin, and furs of ermine and mink that reflected the economic optimism. As always, the press meticulously noted the occupants of every box, from titled Europeans to the president's mother and the cast's family members.

Tried and true *La Traviata* was the opera of choice—a sensible one for the company's new captain, whose first task was to guide the foundering ship into safer waters. Under the Argentinean conductor Ettore Panizza, the Spaniard Lucrezia Bori (who the next day would announce her retirement at the end of the season) and the Americans Lawrence Tibbett and Richard Crooks led the cast. Cleveland-born Thelma Votipka, in the small role of Flora, was the evening's only debutante.

With opening night behind him, Johnson kept attention on the company by introducing a dozen new singers in the first fortnight alone, among them the Australian Marjorie Lawrence, the Chilean Carlo Morelli, the Swede Gertrude Wettergren, and a hefty handful of lesser-known Americans. Nothing, however, compared to the excitement of two veteran stars taking on challenging new roles: on December 27, Ponselle as Carmen— "And if that's not news I'll bite the dog!" Johnson said in making the announcement—and less than twenty-four hours later, Tibbett as Rigoletto.[15]

Yet unknown to the world at large, a splendid quartet of future operatic greats tried out their vocal cords for the first time in 1935. Italy saw the births of the soprano Mirella Freni, the mezzo Fiorenza Cossotto, and the tenor Luciano Pavarotti—soprano and tenor sharing both the same hometown of Modena and the same wet nurse—while Downers Grove, Illinois, greeted the baritone Sherrill Milnes. And in Tupelo, Mississippi, it must be reported—for it would one day affect them all—a baritone of another ilk, Elvis Presley, began his rocket ride to rock-and-roll fame.

As the year drew to an end, two untimely deaths affected the singing community in disparate ways. On December 21, the much-loved American contralto Sophie Braslau died in her New York apartment at the age of forty-three. And at just about the same time Sergei Rachmaninoff and Jasha Heifetz were playing at her Christmas Eve funeral service, Alban Berg, only fifty, died in Vienna of complications from a bee sting, leaving his new opera, *Lulu,* incomplete.

Despite snow and freezing temperatures, New York was just one American city that saw 1935 out in more carefree fashion than it had permitted itself for many years. With liquor store sales booming and signs of increasing prosperity everywhere, the beleaguered Stock Exchange went so far as to revive a custom it had dropped five years earlier and engaged two orchestras to accompany the day's buying and selling; then, just before the final gong, strains of "Auld Lang Syne" wafted from the gallery to bring trading to a halt. That night Tibbett sang a special program of arias and songs on the radio, while at the Metropolitan Opera Pons fired off Lucia's pyrotechnics for a capacity audience, some of whom perhaps recalled the company's first unfortunate bride of Lammermoor, the late Marcella Sembrich.

Chapter Two

Microphone Metamorphosis

SHELLAC, CELLULOID, WAVES OF AIR. By such arcane mediums America's singers found their art reaching untold millions as the nation entered the century's second quarter. Since the beginning of time performer and listener had of necessity shared the same space, but now audiences were a vast, unseen populace. Mechanized music was upon the land, and the singer standing before the microphone cautiously adjusted as it recast his world.

It had all happened with startling celerity. Only twenty-five years separated the first primitive squawks recorded on tinfoil in Thomas Edison's laboratory from the glorious tenor of one Enrico Caruso, as engraved on shiny black discs of shellac in a Milan hotel room in 1902. These recordings, by virtue of their extraordinary commercial success, would not only jump-start the career of the young tenor but also go a long way to acquaint a young nation, timid about its cultural worth, with the pleasures of opera and classical singing.

For as the era's great singers hurried to the recording studio to cash in on the phenomenon, Americans bought their latest releases to play at home on their new phonographs. Not only the machine but often the music and performers themselves, the likes of which many had never heard, amazed them; some young listeners, overwhelmed by the singing of a Titta Ruffo or an Amelita Galli-Curci as it emanated from the family's windup victrola, dreamed of making such sounds themselves.

The phonograph would not stand dispensing its music in isolated splendor for long, however. By the 1920s radio, purveying everything from baseball scores to classical music, had also taken its place on store shelves, and the older industry was not happy to see it. After all, if with just the turn of a dial one could listen to music continuously, why would one spend money on records that had to be changed every few minutes? For that matter, if one could hear an artist for free, why would one buy his records? To protect themselves, the recording companies, essentially Victor, Columbia, and Brunswick, prohibited their artists from performing on radio. But as sales declined anyway, Victor decided to try a little reverse psychology: the company would sponsor its own series of radio programs, it announced late in 1924, with no less than its finest artists performing the same music they had already recorded on its prestigious Red Seal label. Tune in at 9 P.M. sharp on New Year's night to hear the great John McCormack and Lucrezia Bori.[1] It would be the beginning of a new era in broadcasting, Victor said, for international artists of such stature had never before sung on the radio in America.

Indeed, opera singers were for the most part terrified of radio. Bori herself confessed to being "scared to death"[2] at the thought of singing for so many people she couldn't see. But while six million listeners within reach of the transmission drew close to their Atwater-Kents or, donning earphones, crouched over homemade sets, for one hour the beloved Spanish soprano and the popular Irish tenor stoically rendered their arias and songs into the dreaded microphone—McCormack even introduced a new Irving Berlin ballad. Before the week was out sales of Bori and McCormack recordings were reportedly back on track; the sheet music for Berlin's "All Alone" sat on more than a hundred thousand piano racks; McCormack's upcoming recital was sold out; and Radio Corporation of America's stock was up thirteen points. Victor had made its point: listen to the radio and learn what you want to hear; buy phonograph records and hear what you want when you want.[3]

Statistics show that by 1938 radio was a fixture in five of every six American homes, with the average set in use a total of four hours daily. It was the nation's favorite pastime, the number one dispenser of entertainment, and the single most powerful factor in shaping public taste. And though only 5 of the 62 percent of airtime allotted to music was devoted to classical repertoire, it was a precious share, which those in charge recognized they must fill to the best of their ability.[4] They must find the best talent, and they must learn not only what the public wanted to hear but also what it might want to hear if given the chance: for example, when Giulio Gatti-Casazza, who had previously resisted all overtures from radio to broadcast performances from the Met, changed his mind, the results were surprising and wonderful. Indeed, for the Metropolitan Opera itself, the live broadcasts, which began on Christmas day of 1931, provided the link with the nation the company so badly needed; for lovers of good singing who counted themselves lucky to hear an aria, let alone a complete opera, they were a dream come true; for those who dismissed opera as a dalliance of the wealthy they were a revelation; for the artists who performed them they were invaluable exposure; for young American singers they were palpable, exquisite inspiration.

"[American radio] is commercialized," the German soprano Lotte Lehmann explained to European readers of her autobiography in 1938, "but on account of the tremendous competition, it offers much more than a state system ever could. The most famous orchestras with their eminent conductors and world-stars as soloists are presented to the public and radio-listening does not cost them a cent. Everything is run on a basis of 'advertisement.'. . . One soon gets used to thinking it not funny that between two symphonies there should be talks on motor tires."[5]

Certainly, the *Atwater-Kent Hour* (1925–31) broadcast from New York, the *Standard Oil Hour* (1925–53) from San Francisco, and the *General Motors Concerts* (1929–37) from Detroit set a formidable precedent for quality classical music dependent on this commercial system. But for longevity and sheer popularity—even if a major cut below in quality and sophistication of programming—first prize had to go to *Voice of Firestone* (1928–54). The first commercial program to be heard coast-to-coast, Firestone's wholesome blend of classical and semiclassical music performed by famous artists made it a favorite cultural outlet for the general public and consequently the model for countless other shows. Tibbett set the pace on early shows; other featured regulars included Richard Crooks, Eleanor Steber, and Risë Stevens. But virtually every singing star from Ezio Pinza to Roberta Peters, as well as many renowned instrumentalists, appeared at one time or other, all, in addition to their chosen potpourri of selections, obliging as well by dutifully opening and closing the program with "In My Garden" and "If I Could Tell You" by Idabelle Firestone, widow of Harvey, the great tire and rubber company's founder.

Led by the Atwater-Kent National Radio Auditions, established in 1927 with the purpose of discovering unknown talent, radio competitions of all kinds also became popular. Beside cash and scholarships, the famous radio manufacturer's contest offered valuable exposure, and many of its winners and runners-up went on to important careers, among them Agnes Davis, Josephine Antoine, Genevieve Rowe, Julius Huehn, Lucine Amara, Rosa Tentoni, Margaret Harshaw, and Theodor Uppman.

But a radio competition of quite another ilk, and one that clearly low-ered the bar for the category, was *Major Bowes Original Amateur Hour,* which began in 1934 and became a veritable craze as every week thousands of amateurs from accordion players to opera singers requested auditions. Lis-teners were urged to telephone in their vote for the best of the sixteen who appeared on each program, but the Major, as he was known, had only to personally strike a gong, even in the middle of a performance, to eliminate a contestant. In fact, having entered the competition under a pseudonym for the sole purpose of promoting a friend's song, Eileen Farrell, already a popu-lar radio singer, never even got to the gong stage, because Bowes simply did not like her voice in her audition. "So there I was, at age twenty-two," she would recall, "the star of my own show and a Major Bowes reject, all at once."[6]

Yet Bowes did get it right sometimes. Winners included Merrill Miller (Robert Merrill), Mimi Benzell, Jess Walters, Regina Resnik, Russell Ober-lin, Frank Sinatra, and Belle Silverman (Beverly Sills), who, having won the competition singing Verdi's "Caro Nome" at the age of seven, also became a regular on Bowes's long-running *Capitol Family.*

Adaptations and abridgments of operetta and opera, usually in English translation, were also successful in radio's early years. Most used established opera singers for leads, young unknowns for supporting roles, and actors for the narration and dialogue that connected the selected scenes. And because opera requires all kinds of voice types, lower voices, both male and female, which had been thought to vibrate too much for the delicate technology, finally got their chance. Devora Nadworney, a New Yorker of Russian par-ents, for example, made a fine career as the contralto for countless studio op-eras, boasting, as early as 1928, over one hundred roles on radio—a good indication in itself of how much opera there was.

In addition, live opera from the Chicago and Metropolitan companies, Radio City, and the NBC Light Opera Company and rebroadcasts of Euro-pean performances were all regular radio fare. So sincere in fact were the net-works that they even commissioned radio operas: among them were Vittorio Giannini's *Beauty and the Beast* (1938), starring the coloratura Genevieve Rowe as Beauty, and Gian Carlo Menotti's delightful *Old Maid and the Thief* (1939) with Robert Weede, Dorothy Sarnoff, and Margaret Daum.

In the early days of radio, program directors searched endlessly for talent to fill the hours. Celebrities were preferred, but microphone compatibility was essential. As a result, many of the first radio singers came virtually off the street. This fact gave rise to a plethora of Cinderella stories and, in turn, a stampede of young hopefuls requesting to be heard. Sopranos led the way; not far behind were the tenors. But a voice suitable for radio was a rare commodity, and less than 1 percent of those who auditioned ever went on the air. "Proportionately, more people succeed in auditions for the Metropolitan Opera Company, than for the great radio networks," Gladys Swarthout warned aspirants in 1934.[7]

To accommodate the exacting nature of the microphone some employed a new style of singing known as "crooning." Though Rudy Vallee was the best known of the early crooners, the style may have originated with Vaughn DeLeath, whose high notes had literally burst the delicate tubes of the transmitters on an experimental broadcast in 1919. To rein in her huge voice the former concert singer had evolved a sliding and scooping style that resulted in a deliciously mellow kind of vocalism that captivated proponents but offended purists. "The most abnormal expression of sound produced by a human being," "demoralizing," "made me sick at my tummy," they complained to *Musical America* in 1932.[8] But whether they crooned or not, early radio preferred well-produced, smaller voices—easily amplified if necessary by the man in the booth. Any other was dangerous to the equipment and worrisome to the engineer.

The acclaimed teacher Estelle Liebling took radio very seriously. Herself a student of the great Mathilde Marchesi, with credits ranging from a brief Met career to many hundreds of appearances with John Philip Sousa's band, Liebling made an exhaustive study of what her students might gain from it. Comparing a singer's sound in the studio with what she heard in the control room not only sharpened her concerns about intonation, diction, and vibrato, but also fortified her belief that radio actually developed good singers. Liebling added classes in radio singing to her schedule and ran a school for radio singing every summer. Her studio, already popular with those aspiring to everything from vaudeville to opera, and frequented by such divas as Frieda Hempel, Amelita Galli-Curci, and Maria Jeritza, now became a mecca for radio singers as well: Jessica Dragonette, Beatrice Belkin, Lucille Manners, Lucy Monroe, Rose Dirman, Rosemarie Brancato, and a very young Sills, to name but a few.

It was Dragonette who first alerted Liebling to radio's potential. Born in Calcutta, India, to American parents of French and Italian decent, but orphaned as a child, Dragonette had grown up in a Catholic convent in New Jersey, where she had spent much of her time hoping to unravel the secrets of singing by listening to recordings of great artists, especially her favorite, Galli-Curci. And when she had written the famous coloratura asking with whom she should study, the answer had been unequivocal: Estelle Liebling.

In addition to being an excellent teacher, Liebling cared for her students as though they were her children and often used her considerable influence to find them work. Knowing Dragonette was badly in need of money, she recommended her for the role of the unseen, ethereal voice in a play, *The Miracle,* directed by the great Max Reinhardt. (One can hardly imagine a more apt and prophetic role for the sweet-voiced, diminutive blonde, just out of the convent, who would devote her entire career to the unseen listeners of radio.) Then, on the strength of that success, she told her about auditions being held at a radio station.

Engaged by WEAF for a new show featuring operetta, Dragonette initially recoiled at the cold ambience. In 1926 there were as yet no live audiences. But when fan letters, many speculating about her looks and personality, began pouring in from across the country, her dismay turned to astonishment and then delight. "I began to see the microphone in a new light," she would write. "I began to regard it as the most alive audience I had ever known. In a rush of fervor I wanted to dedicate myself to wooing it." She was young; radio was young; they would grow together, she decided.

When taken all together—the small size, purity, and "velvet-pansy quality" (Liebling's description) of her high soprano, her impeccably clear diction, and her enormous repertoire embracing everything from imposing operatic arias to the latest popular song—Dragonette was tailor-made for early radio, and no one worked harder to serve it. Even before there were studio audiences, she dressed to complement the number she was going to sing, changing, if need be, during the broadcast, so certain was she that somehow it all came over the airwaves. To be sure, devoutly religious and reclusive in private life, Jessica Dragonette fervently believed that "radio had given the world a second pair of eyes—eyes of the spirit."[9]

In 1930 the National Broadcasting Company, the country's first coast-to-coast network, made Dragonette the star of its big new show, *The Cities Service Hour,* and "the girl with the dimple in her voice" quickly became so popular that, seven years later, on finding she had been terminated, her myriad fans unleashed a storm of protest. That her radio career would continue on other networks was assured. But it was all enough to persuade the "Garbo of Radio" (yet another of her many sobriquets) that the time had come to show herself, and in 1938 Dragonette launched a concert tour that took her

Jessica Dragonette, the "Queen of Radio"

from Maine to Hawaii. The press covered it all as though it were a historic event; her fans came out in droves to finally see as well as hear her; and with a technique from Liebling that allowed her voice to penetrate the deepest reaches of any of the huge auditoriums they filled, the "Queen of Radio," as they had so often voted her, fulfilled their every expectation.

As it turned out, Lucille Manners, Dragonette's replacement on *Cities Service,* had a Cinderella story of her own. A stenographer for NBC who every Friday evening listened to her idol, Dragonette, Manners had occasionally sung small parts for the network but only dreamed of radio stardom for herself. It was, therefore, a complete surprise when, after giving her a new hairstyle, wardrobe, and lessons in everything from makeup to graceful walking, the network announced she would be its new featured singer. But if some, like Dragonette, would make their careers almost entirely on radio, Manners, who sang frequently in concert and opera in the 1940s, including leading roles at the New York City Opera, typified the classically trained singer who used her radio celebrity to help her build a career in other mediums as well.

To be sure, two other radio nightingales from this period even made it to the Metropolitan—albeit briefly: Lucy Monroe, who sang a Musetta in the 1937 Spring Season (we will meet her again during the war), and Jean Dickenson, a protégée of Lily Pons, who introduced the pretty brunette on the radio, where she was an instant success. With both Pons and radio celebrity recommending her, Dickenson made a much ballyhooed Met debut as Philine in *Mignon* early in 1940. But, if one can believe the critics, neither her ultralight instrument nor her technique stood the trial, and, though she continued to perform concert and opera around the country, she is best remembered as the "Nightingale of the Airwaves."

Margaret Speaks also used recognition won on the airwaves to build a substantial concert career. For though the Ohio-born soprano had worked in musical comedy and vaudeville and given recitals accompanied by her uncle Oley Speaks, the composer of such popular concert ballads as "Sylvia" and "On the Road to Mandalay," it was her occasional partnering of Richard Crooks and Nelson Eddy and appearances as a featured soloist on *Voice of Firestone* that suddenly enabled her to line up the concert tours she so ardently wanted at home and abroad.

But probably no one owed as much to radio as the Bowes reject Eileen Farrell, who, born into show business (her parents, both of Irish heritage, were the Singing O'Farrells of vaudeville renown), worked her way up from chorus and assisting other artists to her own show. Indeed, for six years *Eileen Farrell Sings* aired live, usually on Friday nights from 11:30 to midnight, while its star rendered everything from Wagner to Gershwin and learned to build "interpretations that would convey the full meaning and spirit of the songs through tone alone."[10] The soprano's career in opera and concert in the late 1950s and early 1960s would one day overshadow her years in front of the microphone, but the experience, not only on her own show but as a guest on a vast number of others, clearly shaped the Farrell art and made the Farrell name.

Of the classically trained male singers who appeared on early radio, most were tenors with light, honeyed voices to complement the dulcet sopranos and evoke the style and repertoire of the still-active and ever-popular McCormack.

Though he could not read music and was essentially a ballad singer, Frank Munn, who began on radio in 1923, out-pioneering even Dragonette, deserves first mention, as for more than two decades, unapologetically imitating McCormack recordings, he made the rounds of the biggest shows. Known as the "Golden Voice of Radio," Munn is probably best remembered for the popular *Palmolive Hour,* which also featured the famous Revelers male quartet and Virginia Rea, a sparkling coloratura. As Paul Oliver and Olive Palmer—a pseudonym gimmick of the sponsors—Munn and Rea were radio's highest-paid performers during the program's heyday. Rea, who had prior experience in classical music in Europe and reportedly a four-octave range, used the show to expand her career to include some opera and even a Town Hall recital of art song. Munn, however, stuck to radio.

Though loosely referred to as crooners, Lanny Ross, Frank Parker, and Kenny Baker, with voices à la McCormack and serious classical training, also used their success on the air to explore other avenues. Ross, who had studied at Juilliard, for example, easily balanced a lucrative and high-profile job as host of Maxwell House's popular variety show, *Show Boat,* with a nice second career in concert. And radio was behind the opera and concert careers of Felix Knight and Conrad Thibault as well. Knight, in fact, went from radio and such film credits as Tom-Tom in the Laurel and Hardy version of *Babes in Toyland* to singing leading roles at the Met. Thibault, who was a student at Curtis when his appearances on the *Curtis Hour* brought him to the attention of NBC, was both one of radio's first important baritones and a successful concert singer.

In other words, whereas it had once taken years to build a national reputation, radio could bring singers national celebrity virtually overnight, and with it fans who followed their every move in radio magazines, voted for them in annual radio polls, attended their live concerts, and filled their mailboxes with their ardor. Yet most worked as hard as any other artists, continually polishing their instruments and building repertoires that ranged from ballads and show tunes to art songs and operatic arias. Dragonette herself sang in five languages, memorized two new songs a day, and sang for six months before she allowed herself to repeat a number.

As the microphone grew better able to accommodate bigger voices, radio singers, once almost a breed apart, had to give more and more of their classical share of airtime to opera singers, who happily filled their pockets in a half hour's time with more money than they could earn in weeks spent in the opera house. Meanwhile, some worried about radio's effect on the nation's vocal estate. Radio is "a Frankenstein as well as a boon," Giovanni Martinelli warned. "It has provided an immensely lucrative field for an enormous quantity of mediocre talent, and what is more, pays lucrative prices for little work. America today moves fast . . . [and] the contemporary young singer is too impatient."[11]

But if radio could accelerate a young singer's career, the new sound pictures—more difficult to break into, more time-consuming, but unbeatable when it came to exposure and money—could put it in high gear. Indeed, even in the days when no sound emanated from the silver screen, opera stars the likes of Mary Garden and Geraldine Farrar had been more than glad to lend their glamour to the art, and the new industry had been more than glad to have them for that very reason. Opera singers had been right there as well in 1926, when Vitaphone first demonstrated the technology that united sound with moving pictures. Martinelli's electrifying delivery of "Vesti la giubba" was even said to have played a large part in convincing the specially invited audience of the new medium's possibilities.[12]

And so it was not so strange that the fledgling industry would want to nab opera's dashing new star Lawrence Tibbett for a film; nor was it so

strange that, even as his friends warned him movies would damage his reputation as an artist, the young baritone would be unable to resist the big
money it offered.[13] And when his first movie, *The Rogue Song,* which opened
in New York in 1930, was a hit, and its opera star in the role of a swashbuck-
ling cossack bandit an even bigger one, it was not so strange either that one
particularly intrepid colleague would conclude she too must go west.

As it was, neither Grace Moore nor her first films were very successful
and the pretty soprano was soon on her way back east. But in 1934, with
prospects for the industry improving as the Depression receded, Moore returned to Hollywood, hoping to land the lead in a remake of *The Merry
Widow;* she signed instead with an unknown studio to star in a low-budget
film about an American girl studying opera in Italy who overcomes a complicated relationship with her teacher to make it all the way to the Met.

A box-office bonanza, *One Night of Love* put Columbia Pictures on the
map and sent Moore soaring to international stardom on wings of "celluloid
fame."[14] And before the decade was out, opera singers, foreign and domestic,
from Pons, Swarthout, and James Melton to Miliza Korjus, Nino Martini,
and even Kirsten Flagstad, were seeing their names on movie marquees
across the land, even as their days as movie stars dwindled.[15] For there would
be no more hits on the level of *One Night of Love.* Try as Hollywood might,
the very premise—a singer's triumph over all obstacles—could be rehashed
in only so many ways, and without it there was little else for an opera singer
to do. Operetta, which was moribund in Hollywood in the 1930s, might
have been a possibility, but what little there was of it had a lock, a lock with
the names Jeanette MacDonald and Nelson Eddy.

In their different ways, had it not been for the new technology, either one of
the famous team might have enjoyed a traditional career in classical music.
Even as a child growing up in Philadelphia Jeanette MacDonald had fancied
herself an opera singer, and her lovely soprano clearly had operatic potential.
But the beautiful redhead, lured by show business, had at the age of sixteen
instead gone to New York City, where she rose quickly from chorus girl to
Broadway musical star; and by the time Hollywood came courting in 1929
Verdi and Puccini were remote figures.

For Eddy, on the other hand, to make movies was to turn his back on an
opera career already well under way. The handsome baritone had made his

Nelson Eddy and Jeanette MacDonald

operatic debut in 1924 as Tonio in *Pagliacci* with the Philadelphia Civic Opera. He had studied abroad and even refused a contract to sing with the Dresden Opera in Germany. He wanted to make his operatic career in his own country, he said, which, bolstered by concert and radio, he had clearly begun to do. But a contract with MGM, offered after a scout from the studio heard him in a concert in California, and the staggering success of his first film with Jeanette MacDonald, who, already on her thirteenth, was by then a screen idol, had put an abrupt end to the high road. "It's ter-rific," the columnist Ed Sullivan crowed after *Naughty Marietta* opened in New York in March 1935. "MacDonald and Eddy are the new team sensation for the industry."[16] The following November Eddy sang Amonasro in *Aida* with Rethberg and Martinelli in San Francisco, then closed the book on opera.

And so, for the next seven years—historically the Golden Age of the Hollywood musical—the good-looking pair held sway over all comers in anything resembling operetta. MacDonald, a vivacious actress, invariably lit up the screen, while Eddy, a diffident heartthrob, worked to catch up as an actor. ("Movies are curing grounds for operatic hams," he would say.)[17] But mostly the pair just sang—very well. "It is not too much to say that in tone, formation, attack, equality of scale, breath control, intonation, and diction [MacDonald and Eddy] hold their own with any other artists of their day," the eminent critic W. J. Henderson wrote after hearing them in *Rose Marie*. "Young persons studying voice ought to listen to them and consider carefully how they do it."[18]

In 1942, after nine films, MGM decided it could milk the duo no more. Going their separate ways, Eddy and MacDonald found new partners and studios, and while both sang more radio and concert than ever, MacDonald now took the time as well to revisit her dream, making her operatic debut as Gounod's Juliette in Montreal in 1943, then essaying both Juliette and Marguerite in *Faust* in Chicago and Cincinnati. Skepticism that the movie star could sing opera ran high, but MacDonald's performances, few as they were, were authentic successes, and when she returned to Chicago for more in 1945, the insulting microphones they had installed on her first visit were gone. Lotte Lehmann, who helped MacDonald prepare and believed she could have developed into a "serious and successful lieder singer if time would have allowed it," urged her to study Mimì.[19] But, except for some performances several years later in Philadelphia, the movie star now put the dream to rest.

Over the years, Moore, Tibbett, Eddy, MacDonald, and such others as Susanna Foster, Deanna Durbin, and Allan Jones, who, in a happy blur of highbrow and lowbrow, bridged the gap between classical singing and movies, would ignite the dreams of countless young people. "I never missed a movie musical," Eleanor Steber would recall of her girlhood in West Virginia. "We drove all the way to Pittsburgh to see 'One Night of Love.' That movie—Grace Moore herself, and the part she played—stirred something earthshaking deep inside of me, some recognition, some inner urge, which fired my imagination beyond my ability to express."[20]

"The radio has already finished the concert in America and sooner or later the talking movies are going to finish opera,"[21] Mary Garden had lamented in 1927. But if on the contrary radio and the talkies may ultimately have even fueled enthusiasm for live performance, the new technologies did turn topsy-turvy the values and emphases of the American singing career. "Those two Frankensteins of the Machine Age . . . first isolated living music from its great public and then returned it with a vigor and robustness unprecedented in musical history," Moore would write from the perspective of two decades. "Making good at the Met is still the peak achievement of any singing career, but there are a thousand other ways to make good from coast to coast without even a peek-a-boo at the gold-flake horseshoe."[22]

Confronted, therefore, with options their predecessors had never known, classically trained singers now had to make hard decisions regarding their artistic principles. "We are singing today not only for an opera and concert public but for a movie audience," the soprano Helen Jepson freely admitted. "The soprano today, to be tops, has got to be an eyeful as well as an earful. . . . Subdued Westian curves, and a face that's easy on an audience's eyes are more important than a perfect B Flat."[23]

To be sure, it had taken only one film for the mezzo Gladys Swarthout to see her fee for a single radio appearance go from one thousand to three thousand dollars and her prestige in concert and opera soar. Accustomed to singing the small role of Frédéric in *Mignon* at the Met, she was now Mignon herself; directors suddenly clamored for her Carmen; and Town Hall was no longer large enough for all her fans—only Carnegie Hall would do. On the other side of the coin, if Nelson Eddy still included Schubert and Debussy in his concerts, he made sure that semiclassics and popular numbers constituted the far greater portion of his programming. Elitist critics complained, but Eddy, reportedly the highest-paid musician in the United States at approximately three thousand dollars for a single concert, walked a fine line.

Meanwhile, opera managements could only watch as movies, radio, and concerts kept their artists running after the easy money and exposure. Fortunately, Hollywood was a long way from the East Coast and had few openings for opera singers. But everyone did radio and, for that matter, treated it as sacrosanct above all other obligations. Swarthout once canceled a matinee of *Carmen* in Chicago because it would make her late for an evening radio broadcast in New York, and in the same city Josephine Antoine kept a *Rigoletto* on hold for an hour to complete a radio obligation, forcing management to bring on the ballet to entertain the audience in the interim.[24]

It was a state of affairs so far removed from the revered operatic traditions of his native land that Giulio Gatti-Casazza had all but lost patience and was only too happy to be leaving the problem to someone else. That Edward Johnson, a singer whose prime performing years had paralleled the new technologies, was taking the helm at such a pivotal time in the nation's cultural life was probably a good thing.

Chapter Three

Edward Johnson and the Gatti Legacy

T HE INCUMBENT IS A MAN IN HIS FORTIES," the reporter wrote. "His reddish brown hair is just beginning to be touched with gray."[1] In truth, Edward Johnson was fifty-seven years old and his hair totally gray. In his career as a tenor, his trim figure and chiseled features had clearly been an asset, and he had done well in retaining the all-important illusion of a romantic leading man. "Our John Barrymore," a secretary called him.[2] But now, his performing days behind him, the new general manager of the Metropolitan Opera was about to forgo the chore of coloring his hair. Gray, after all, befitted his new role of authority. ("Tenor in Power," *Time* called him.) Besides, gray went well with full dress—the white tie, white gloves, top hat, and tails that were his trademark attire and that by the end of his fifteen-year tenure would become so shiny with use that "you could almost comb your hair looking at his back."[3]

Had he noted it, the reporter might have gotten Johnson's nationality wrong as well, for the press, like everyone, feeling a little chauvinistic about the matter, seemed determined to claim nothing less than American citizenship—North American was not good enough—for the new chief. But in fact, despite spending the greater part of his life in the United States, Johnson, born in the town of Guelph in the province of Ontario in 1878, would die there in 1959 without ever relinquishing his Canadian citizenship.[4]

Of Irish and Welsh ancestry, Eddie, as he was called throughout his life, had grown up singing in church, playing flute and piano, and dreaming of becoming a prizefighter. But as his voice had made him a local celebrity, he had gone first to New York to study and sing concert and light opera, and then on to Europe to pursue the bigger dream of a career in opera. Settling in Florence with his wife, Beatrice d'Arneirio, a Portuguese viscountess and musician he had met on an earlier visit, Johnson had studied with Vincenzo Lombardi, Caruso's principal teacher, and welcomed the arrival of his only child, his daughter, Fiorenza. In 1912, under the name Eduardo di Giovanni, he had made his Italian debut as Andrea Chénier in Padua, two years later bowed at La Scala as Italy's first Parsifal, and in 1919 created Luigi in *Il Tabarro* and Rinuccio in *Gianni Schicchi* in the Italian premiere of *Il Trittico* at the Teatro Costanzi in Rome. It was by any account an important Italian career. But the sudden death of Beatrice on the day of the Florence premiere of the Puccini had brought it to a poignant end.

Dropping the Italianization of his name, Johnson had sung with the Chicago Opera from 1919 until 1922, then made a strong debut as Avito in Montemezzi's *L'Amore dei Tre Re* with the Metropolitan, where over the next thirteen years he sang twenty-three leading roles ranging from Roméo and Canio to Peter Ibbetson, a role he created, and Pelléas, a role in which that great discerner of voices W. J. Henderson found him "unsurpassed."[5] If some critics thought his voice unexceptional, nary a one failed to praise his musicality, diction, erudition, intelligence, and, of course, good looks.

Already forty-three years old at the time of his Met debut, by 1935 Johnson, now fifty-seven, was ready to retire from performing and looked forward to his new job as assistant manager of the Metropolitan under Witherspoon. That spring he sang his last performance for the company, an *Ibbetson* on tour in Boston, then traveled to Detroit to honor a final contract. With the news of Witherspoon's death he returned to New York for the funeral, but made it back to Detroit in time for a final *Ibbetson*. And it was there that, just as he was leaving for the theater, he was handed the telegram. "Hope you will accept appointment as general manager Metropolitan," the Met board had written. "We are all agreed upon you and you will have loyal backing."[6]

Notwithstanding the "loyal backing," many problems awaited the new manager, not the least of which were the demands—most specifically from the Juilliard board—that the nation's preeminent opera company engage more native singers. Such demands were nothing new. Gatti had repeatedly heard them and in his memoirs would state, "It was from the beginning my intention and my manifest duty to do my utmost for American artists and American art."[7] And indeed, despite early concerns that the Italian would be

*Edward Johnson, soon to become general manager
of the Metropolitan Opera. Photo by Gretchen Dick*

"partisan and sectarian,"[8] in his twenty-seven seasons at the helm Gatti had
not only presented the Metropolitan's first American opera and followed it
with some fifteen more, but also engaged some 125 American singers.
Granted, he had proceeded slowly, but of his final roster of 101 singers, 44
were Americans, and of these almost half sang leading roles at least occasion-

ally. This is an impressive statistic when one considers that of the 34 singers on the Metropolitan's first roster, probably only 2, notably Alwina Valleria of Baltimore, were American,[9] and that of the 77 singers on the last roster of Gatti's predecessor, Heinrich Conreid, 9 sang leading roles[10] and an additional 6 to 9 (approximately) sang secondary roles.[11]

But now it was Johnson's turn, and as he moved to make up his first roster, he was glad to be re-signing a fair number of Gatti's Americans, including, for leading roles, four sopranos, two mezzos, five tenors,[12] and three baritones, though the higher number of men is misleading. For if one looks at Gatti's last roster in its entirety, Americans constitute close to three-fifths of all the women, and only one-quarter of the men. For one thing, Gatti believed American men did not understand the subtleties of the small character roles (of which there are many more for men than for women) and so made a point of importing foreigners to fill them. For another, singing opera had until recently been considered inappropriate as a profession for American males—a concern of which Europeans, born into the tradition, knew nothing.

Times were changing, though; the American men Johnson now inherited—only a little younger than Johnson himself—had been born in the last years of the nineteenth century. They had begun their careers at the end of the Great War (in most cases having served their country in it) and come to artistic maturity as the last vestiges of Victorianism dropped away. Virtually all family men, they took an aggressive and businesslike approach in the management of their careers and plied their art with an eye to making money—as would men in any profession. But they also took it seriously and resented that Gatti, with a stable of golden-voiced imports at his disposal, paid natives less and seemed to appreciate them only for their reliability and versatility.

To be sure, if an American was to survive, he had to be ready for anything at anytime. As one of Gatti's oldest bequests to Johnson, Paul Althouse, once warned a new soprano, "If you fail in an emergency, your goose is cooked."[13] After auditioning for Gatti, the tenor, only twenty-two and with no experience in opera, had been hired on the spot and, after some feet-wetting performances as a guard in *Die Zauberflöte,* officially introduced as Grigory in the American premiere of *Boris Godunov.* "A valuable addition," W. J. Henderson had called him.[14] And Althouse, the first American-born, American-trained male to sing leading roles with the company, had stayed seven seasons, appearing regularly in a wide-ranging repertoire, before moving on to capitalize on his growing reputation in the more lucrative mediums of concert and oratorio. But then, having retrained as a Heldentenor, Althouse had returned as Siegmund in *Die Walküre*. It was February 3, 1934, a matinee, noted only because, quite by coincidence, that very evening another native from the company's past also rejoined the tenor wing.

Only a month older than Althouse—perhaps too old to be reintroduced as Roméo but still tall and handsome—Charles Hackett, unlike Althouse, had followed the more tried-and-true path and launched his career in Italy. The Italian press had raved over Carlo Hackett's "distinctly pure, delicate, truly tenor organ."[15] And in response *Musical America* had warned, "If there is any longer delay . . . in bringing over a native artist who has made a greater instantaneous success [in Italy], the Metropolitan must find a valid excuse or it will be forced to admit that its much advertised interest in native artists is, as a matter of fact, rather lukewarm."[16] So Hackett had made his Met debut as Almaviva in *Il Barbiere di Siviglia* in 1919 but, after finding neither the money nor the opportunity sufficient for a man with a growing family, had left after just three seasons. He had spent the next years commuting—opera primarily abroad, concert at home—but now, longing to finally give his family a permanent home, he had similarly welcomed Gatti's offer to return.

Despite his successful debut as Cavaradossi in 1920, Mario Chamlee would also grow tired of feeling utilitarian. Perhaps it was the two hundred dollars a week he earned singing leading roles when the Europeans were getting a thousand dollars or more a performance. In any case, after eight seasons the California tenor had left the Met, returned to Europe, and enjoyed such a success there as the cobbler Mârouf in Rabaud's comic opera of that name that he had switched to a lighter repertoire—a repertoire that, as it turned out, Johnson would invite him back to essay in 1936.

Gatti did leave his successor one native tenor happy to call the Metropolitan home, however—happy even to be so utilitarian as to be known as the Metropolitan Minuteman. For a Christian Scientist who himself never canceled, Frederick Jagel's rescues of those who did were legion and legendary. Indeed, so indefatigable was the upbeat tenor from Brooklyn that between 1924, when, under the name Federico Jeghelli, he launched his career as Rodolfo in Italy, and 1927, when, discovered there by Gatti, he returned for a Met debut as Radamès, he had notched almost two hundred performances of leading roles on the Italian circuit.

But if Jagel was the happiest and most useful of the native tenors Johnson inherited, without question the most popular was Richard Crooks, as the almost unprecedented thirty-seven curtain calls he received for his debut as Massenet's Des Grieux in 1933 confirmed. Best known for his tasteful, dulcet renderings of ballads and standard repertoire regularly heard on radio and recordings, Crooks, once renowned in his hometown of Trenton, New Jersey, for his beautiful boy soprano, was, in fact, sometimes called the "American McCormack." Moreover, with his melting pianissimi, magical head tones, and legato to match any foreigner's, he was one of the most admired Americans singing in Europe.

Similarly, the baritone John Charles Thomas not only enjoyed an enviable reputation in opera and concert abroad, but also was enormously popular at home for his recordings, concerts, and radio broadcasts. Indeed, some complained that Gatti's slowness in engaging Thomas, who was virtually a household name by the time of his sensational Met debut as Germont in *La Traviata* in 1934, had been a slight to Americans. But if Gatti had felt the pressure, the easygoing Thomas, who had once allowed the flip of a coin to decide whether to study medicine or music, had not been particularly concerned, and after just two performances was gone, not to return until his friend Eddie took charge.

Far more valuable to the baritone wing from Gatti's and Johnson's points of view had to have been Richard Bonelli, who had cut short a notable European career to join the Chicago Opera in 1925 and then been swept up by the Met when that company folded. Of Bonelli's debut as Germont in 1932, the *Times* had reported: "After his initial exit . . . he was recalled by long applause. But this did not satisfy the audience. Miss Ponselle had to go offstage to bring him back before the opera could continue."[17] Here were shades of a certain *Falstaff* performance as another American audience insisted on proper recognition for one of its own. But in this case Bonelli, mature, experienced, and known, immediately settled in as a leading baritone; Lawrence Tibbett, even after his epiphanic performance as Ford, still had dues to pay.

Indeed, for all the history Tibbett had made on that second night in January 1925, his Met star had not shot into orbit the next day, or even the next month. For one thing, he knew few major roles; for another, Gatti already commanded a veritable army of premier baritones. Nonetheless, over the next two seasons, while discreetly mixing them in equal parts with small character roles, Gatti had assigned Tibbett increasingly important roles. And if it is difficult to pinpoint just which one secured his star, it is fair to say that the baritone's portrayal of King Eadgar in the world premiere of Deems Taylor's *The King's Henchman* in 1927 established him not only as an artist of distinction but as an artist who could do much for American opera.

For Tibbett, the quintessential American singer whose father, a sheriff, had been killed in a shoot-out with an outlaw, and whose training and experience had been solely American, would go on to create leading roles in half a dozen American operas and almost single-handedly give the genre the jump-start it so badly needed. His teacher in Los Angeles, the former Met bass Basil Ruysdale, had instilled in him that diction and acting must be natural—a simple principle, to be sure, but one that would in time pay huge dividends for a new generation of native artist seeking a sound and expression to call his own.

In any case, already a star of radio and opera, in 1930 Tibbett had added film star to his credits, and as each medium tied into and played off the other, his celebrity had gone into the stratosphere. "Idol of Millions," his two-page ads proclaimed. And so he was when Johnson moved into the executive offices of the Metropolitan Opera.

The Americans who made up Gatti's distaff legacy to Johnson were as a group younger than the men. Born right around, even on, the century mark, this half-generation difference meant that they had begun their studies with the improved conditions of post–World War America already in place. Excellent new teachers who had left war-torn Europe to take up residence in America had somewhat reduced the need for study abroad; radio, recording, and sound pictures offered new ways to gain experience and recognition; new freedoms for their sex provided both the means and the courage to break with the past. Though all would marry, only one (Helen Jepson) would have children. Indeed, with the notable exception of Louise Homer, who with six children was clearly an anomaly, there was so little precedent for combining motherhood and career that the notion was rarely entertained. After all, as Mary Garden declared on her return from France in 1918, "War has set women free."[18]

And so this very particular generation, whose lives would run in tandem with the century, had left it to their parents to uphold the morals and manners of Victorianism and taken on the Roaring Twenties with all the high spirits of their own twenties. Cutting their hair, painting their faces, trashing their corsets, and raising their skirts, with a no-thank-you to chaperones and with the right to vote in their pockets, they had headed to the cities to flaunt their freedom and make their dreams come true.

Such was certainly the impulse of eighteen-year-old Rosa Ponzillo, when in 1915 the Connecticut-born daughter of Italian immigrants packed her bags to join her older sister, Carmela, in New York City and form a vaude-ville act. But the dream was to sing opera. And after a few heady years as the Tailored Italian Girls, the sisters had begun to study voice seriously, then—on Caruso's recommendation—sung for Gatti-Casazza of the Metropolitan Opera. That Rosa had never stepped foot on an operatic stage, knew not a single operatic role, and fainted dead away during her audition, seem to have been only small concerns for the manager. With the war stranding so many singers in Europe, Gatti desperately needed a leading soprano for the up-coming Metropolitan premiere of Verdi's *La Forza del Destino*.[19] "Either she will succeed magnificently, or she will fail abysmally," he had reportedly told Caruso on engaging her. "If she is a success, the doors of the Metropolitan will be opened to other American singers because she will have made it possible."[20]

Was Gatti forgetting such eminent Americans as Lillian Nordica, Emma Eames, Geraldine Farrar, Louise Homer? Did he view Ponselle differently because she had not prepared abroad? Was he truly planning changes for Americans if she succeeded? No matter: on November 15, 1918, Rosa Ponselle—her name "internationalized" on Gatti's orders[21]—succeeded mag-nificently but changed little.

In the case of twenty-one-year-old Grace Moore of Jellico, Tennessee, whose father refused to let her go on the stage, going for her dream was as much a matter of defiance and determination as impulse. But obsessed with becoming a star, the girl with "the lion's heart . . . nobody could put . . . down"[22] had, in fact, run away from school; after establishing herself as a leading lady in musicals on Broadway, she had gone on to study in Paris—the only one of the female legacy to go abroad. It had taken her a decade and many auditions to win a contract of seventy-five dollars a week for the honor of singing at the Met. But that had been the ultimate goal. And when the former musical-comedy star finally made her Metropolitan debut on Febru-ary 7, 1928—her first opera on any stage—her performance as Mimì (oppo-site Johnson) earned her not only a huge ovation from the celebrity-studded, sold-out audience but a spot (à la Tibbett) on the front page of the *New York Times*—as good as the dream could get.

Yet another plucky soprano, Queena Mario, was only sixteen when in

1912 she left the comforts of a New Jersey home for New York to write for the city's newspapers,[23] study with Marcella Sembrich, and ultimately audition for the fledgling San Carlo Opera. Caruso told the company's director he would "pay my salary should I turn out to be a failure,"[24] she would recall. But the tenor's wallet was safe. Mario sang three years for Fortune Gallo, then signed on with Scotti's touring company. Scotti, she knew, would give her entrée to the Metropolitan.

Mario had made her debut as Micaela in 1922 and with a voice routinely described as silvery and girlish settled into a steady diet of ingénue roles. Her greatest happiness, however, turned out to be teaching, and it follows that one of Mario's first students was one of Gatti's last Americans, a soprano the manager had chanced to hear singing arias and show tunes on Paul Whiteman's radio program. And so it was that in the winter of 1935 Helen Jepson both made her Metropolitan Opera debut in the premiere of John Seymour's one-act *In the Pasha's Garden* (*Bohème,* with her teacher as Mimì, filled out the odd evening), and—in an ultimate sign of the times—won the award as the most important new radio personality of 1934.

Though the Metropolitan boasted a plethora of world-class voices in the early and mid-1930s, it lacked low-voiced women for its French and Italian repertory. The lovely Missourian Marion Telva, who might have capitalized on the situation, retired in 1933, and the Russian-born Ina Bourskaya and Irra Petina, except for occasional Carmens, were generally treated as secondary singers. Maine-born Doris Doe, who had made an inauspicious debut with the company as Brangäne in 1932, stayed on to contribute some routine Ortrudes but fared better in smaller roles. And the Philadelphian Kathryn Meisle, after bowing as Amneris early in 1935, would sing just thirteen performances over three seasons before devoting the better part of her distinguished career to oratorio, where her true contralto shone. Rose Bampton and Gladys Swarthout might have filled the void, but, as we shall see, neither would evolve quite as Gatti probably imagined.

Aside from their Midwestern roots and stunning looks, the two had little in common. Swarthout, essentially a lyric mezzo, fared best in French roles; Bampton's repertoire was primarily Italian and German, her more dramatic voice from the beginning suggesting the full-throated soprano she would become on Johnson's beat. Swarthout, a star of radio and the silver screen, was continually in the public spotlight; Bampton, despite a weekly fifteen-minute radio show, stayed closer to the opera and concert world, where she was admired more than adulated. Swarthout, supremely confident, was equivocal about her career; Bampton, filled with self-doubt, was ambitious and determined.

Born in the town of Deepwater, Missouri, on the first Christmas of the century, Gladys Swarthout had made her operatic debut in 1924 as the off-stage voice of the shepherd in *Tosca* with the Chicago Civic Opera, then set-tled into a routine of performing a small role almost every other day for the company. Introduced as La Cieca in *Gioconda* at the Met in 1929, she had continued in secondary roles, but in 1931 made the most of a chance to sing Adalgisa to Ponselle's Norma, and immediately moved into leading roles.

For Ohio-born Bampton, beset as she was by doubts as to her true vocal range, it was never so clear-cut. Though she had entered Curtis as a high so-prano, a doctor examining her for laryngitis there had decreed her vocal cords were those of a contralto. Bampton had made the change, and for a while, at least, it seemed the right thing. Indeed, she enjoyed such a success as Waldtove in the American premiere of Arnold Schoenberg's *Gurrelieder* under Stokowski that the Met asked to hear her in person. She had made her debut as Laura to Ponselle's Gioconda in 1932. "The vocal range was gener-ous, the quality unusually warm, smooth and even, marked by a duskiness of hue in middle and lower notes," one critic wrote. "Her top notes proved full and resonant."[25]

An impressive group, Gatti's American legacy to Johnson: Ponselle, of course, lives with the immortals and Tibbett stands tall with the great; Crooks and Thomas are world-class by any count; the names Moore and Swarthout, by virtue of their celebrity, come easily to the tongue even today; Bampton, Bonelli, and Hackett, if overlooked, command the highest respect in the circles that mattered most to them, and neither Althouse, Chamlee, Jagel, Mario, nor Jepson is ever dismissed out of hand. Sadly, however, in the years ahead these same singers would see more than their share of truncated careers and even real tragedy. Only a small handful would give Johnson un-swerving service; only three would see him through his tenure.

With the Met's roster rife with fine tenors, Althouse, Chamlee, and Hackett would all soon turn to teaching, though Hackett would die tragically on January 1, 1942, from complications following elective surgery inexplicably scheduled for New Year's Eve. Mario too, fascinated by teaching since filling in for Sembrich at Curtis, would make the leap from stage to studio. Performing got in the way, she explained, making no mention of the fact that her eleven-year marriage to Wilfrid Pelletier, the Met coach and conductor with whom she shared an avid interest in young singers, had ended, and that Pelletier had married one of her students, Bampton.

But it was Ponselle whose untimely departure would be felt most keenly. Ponselle had started at the top and never left it. She had never sung a small role, nor ever had the benefit of trying out a role under less stressful conditions, and she had routinely sung under the unrelenting scrutiny of the most powerful critics. And yet, for nineteen seasons Ponselle had distinguished herself in one great dramatic role after another on one of the world's most prestigious operatic stages. Now, still in her thirties, she was worn down by the pressures of her greatness and burned out by her struggles with an almost pathological stage fright. Recently married, she craved rest and personal happiness, and the critics' blistering attacks on her Carmen, which she performed for the first time early in Johnson's tenure, only compounded the matter.

Ripe for confrontation, Ponselle got it during Johnson's second season by uncharacteristically delivering an ultimatum: mount *Adriana Lecouvreur* for her or she would not return. But Johnson refused her, insisting that even with the Ponselle name the Cilea opera would not make it at the box office. Ponselle gave her last operatic performance, a 1937 broadcast matinee of *Carmen* while the company was on tour in Cleveland. Settling into a luxurious mansion outside Baltimore, she concertized a little and flirted with Hollywood. It would take her some time to adjust, but in later years Ponselle would provide valuable counsel to young singers and prove instrumental in helping Baltimore found its own company.

In summarizing Ponselle's career in light of the American singer's story, certain points should be made. First, essentially all of it—not only the training—was made on American shores. The only exceptions were some performances at London's Covent Garden and Florence's Maggio Musicale. Second, primarily because she started so young and came to artistic maturity at a time when singers still tended to belong to a single opera house, her loyalty to the Metropolitan was paramount. Though most of the other women of the Johnson inheritance were by and large of the same generation, they had started their Metropolitan careers just that little bit later, when companies were beginning to share singers and improvements in transportation made moving around the country more palatable. Ponselle never sang with the prestigious companies of Chicago or even San Francisco. And though she, too, lined her pockets with huge fees from radio and concerts, nothing in her eyes, "regardless of the pay involved, could take the honorific place of the Metropolitan Opera House."[26]

Finally, all-American as was her career, Ponselle's personality neither inclined to nor suited the role of popular icon or champion of a cause. Despite her accomplishments, unlike Tibbett and Moore, she never lit fires under the starry-eyed or beat the drum for the native artist. Her legacy to the American singer is her example and her art.

From the oldest, Bonelli, born in 1887, to the youngest, Bampton, born two decades later, the Americans who passed from Gatti to Johnson belonged to a singular generation of performers: the last to grow up without radio and sound pictures, the first to use them to further their careers. And so as Johnson was sharpening his pencil to fill in the casts for a new era at the Metropolitan, Swarthout, for one, was hitting her stride in movies and radio and using her popularity in those mediums to further her career in concert. Leading roles in the standard repertoire for a lyric mezzo of her status at this time usually meant only Mignon and Carmen, and she now took to singing the latter to the exclusion of all other roles, even though critics often decried her portrayal as too ladylike; or as one correctly pointed out, "It is not the fault of Miss Swarthout. . . . She just isn't the type."[27]

In any case, with her classical features, big brown eyes, and svelte figure clad almost exclusively in Valentina originals, Gladys Swarthout was the stuff of magazine covers and the prototype of modernity—her streamlined career the work of both the new publicity machines and her second husband, Frank Chapman, a baritone who gave up his own career to manage hers. Ambitious for his wife, who herself disliked celebrity and its trappings, Chapman was so successful, in fact, that ultimately the image he manufactured for Swarthout overshadowed her art. Nevertheless, when she dropped off the roster in 1945, the popular mezzo continued to concertize and was again Carmen in the first grand opera produced just for television in 1950. But in 1954 open-heart surgery ended a career clearly on the wane.

Image also helped sustain the brief but starry career of "pretty Helen Jepson," as *Time* liked to call the soprano. If, however, her voluptuous figure, luxuriant blonde hair, and exuberant personality evoked a cross between a Jeritza and a Moore, the brilliant vocalism of the former and charisma of the latter were absent in the Pennsylvania native. Jepson nevertheless was a popular concert artist and radio personality who clearly enjoyed her generation's fast pace. The Met cast her when she was there, especially as Violetta and Marguerite, and inexplicably revived *Pelléas and Mélisande, L'Amore dei Tre Re,* and *Thaïs* specifically for her—roles too mysterious and nuanced for her wholesome persona. But Jepson never stayed long, and in the mid-1940s a throat problem first slowed and then ended her singing career.[28]

As for Moore, the buoyant diva flew so high on her "celluloid wings" that in Johnson's first season she could muster only two Mimìs. Moreover, lack of discipline would keep her from learning more than a few roles, just as it would keep serious musicians from taking her seriously. Critics were hard on Moore, repeatedly taking her to task for faulty technique, intonation, and pronunciation. But her voice—mellifluous, personal, with a little flutter—had authentic appeal and her exuberance and wholesome loveliness were irresistible. Moore might have continued to dance in and out of the Metropolitan for a while longer had fate not intervened. But on January 26, 1947, the Stockholm-bound airplane carrying the soprano and twenty-one others, including the son of the crown prince of Sweden, crashed just after takeoff from Copenhagen, where she had given a recital the previous night. There were no survivors.

Nor would Johnson see much of Thomas or Crooks, whose high-powered radio and concert careers left little time for opera. In nine seasons with the company Crooks would sing just ninety performances before being slowed by illness. Like the tenor's, the baritone's sound was ravishing, his singing reflecting his natural optimism and self-confidence. And if his philosophy of entertaining at all costs—such as suddenly launching into "Home on the Range" during curtain calls, as he did one night during a Chicago *Aida*—did not sit well with critics and opera managers, he was an audience favorite. Johnson struggled therefore to accommodate him. But in 1943, fed up with the demands and small recompense, Thomas just quit.

Bonelli, on the other hand, gave Johnson many good seasons before retiring in 1945. The possessor of a dark, virile, but inherently lyric baritone, he might have sung premieres and opening nights had he not been squeezed out of public and critical consciousness by Tibbett, Thomas, and the beginnings of a long line of great American baritones. As it was, he was the ideal "house" baritone.

And so only Jagel, Bampton, and Tibbett would see the decade through to depart with their former colleague at the mid-century mark. By then, Jagel had invested an uninterrupted thirty years with the company. If his singing was neither warm nor beautiful it was, as the critics were wont to write, invariably solid, resonant, and earnest—pluses in any house—though "constricted" joined the list later. And if his expression was prosaic, his acting stiff, and his physique hardly that of the romantic lover, Jagel could boast some thirty-five roles with the Met and sixty-three all told, an impressive number for a leading tenor.

Bequeathed to Johnson as a mezzo, Bampton was glad to be his new soprano two years later. As doubts as to her true vocal category continued to plague her, she had retrained and then taken Tullio Serafin's advice to retry the higher realms as Leonora in *Il Trovatore* abroad before unveiling her new repertoire in the Met's 1937 spring season. Ultimately, Bampton's voice—vibrant, wide-ranging, with dramatic power and flexibility—was a spinto. But with such luminaries as Rethberg, Lehmann, and Zinka Milanov on hand for her varied repertoire, in her eighteen seasons with the company she would be cast only a little over one hundred times, most often as Sieglinde. Even so, the tall, willowy brunette with the dreamy eyes sang across America, and in London and Buenos Aires. A favorite of conductors and composers—Toscanini's choice for Leonore in *Fidelio*—she sang with most of the great American orchestras and explored (far more than the average opera singer) the contemporary repertoire. But in 1950 Bampton, only forty-three, and Pelletier, whom she had married in 1937, left with Johnson.

At the peak of his fame and capabilities Tibbett added some eight new roles during Johnson's first three seasons, made his European debut at Covent Garden, concertized around the world, and at home kept up a whirlwind schedule of radio, film, and concerts, in addition to helping found and serving as president of the American Guild of Musical Artists. But around 1940 a throat ailment, possibly aggravated by excessive drinking, began to take its toll.[29] Tibbett stopped singing for a few months, but when he returned the voice was as in a visor, unable to respond to the great communicator's commands. While Johnson loyally continued to cast him, Tibbett, true to his character and to his art, tried to reapply himself, but only glimmers of the old refulgence were ever heard.

Fully cognizant that his sad vocal estate could not survive the new regime, Tibbett appeared briefly on Broadway, directed some opera for television, and continued to fight for artists' rights. And when he died in 1960—the same year that saw the deaths of the American baritones John Charles Thomas, Mack Harrell, and Leonard Warren—his familiar image once again appeared on front pages across the nation. "Tibbett is more than an artist," a critic once wrote, "he is a chapter of history. He is the symbol of full opportunity for the American singer."[30]

Chapter Four

Johnson Opens the Floodgates

I F THE REPORTER from the *New York Post* was mistaken as to his age and hair color, his description of Edward Johnson's easy smile and "shrewd and kindly [eyes] . . . full of humorous sparkle" was on the mark. Compared to the "bearded Milanese sphinx," Giulio Gatti-Casazza, the genial new manager seemed an open book. What is more, he had cheered the place up: bright flowery curtains on the barred windows, a tapestry on the wall, a bowl of roses, and a graceful Queen Anne chair in place of the "huge, old swivel" affair from which the portly Italian had conducted business. His trim successor hoped the reporter noticed "the freer, happier spirit." After all, having been a singer himself, he had "a double slant on things" and understood that even if there was no money for new sets, new costumes, or any of the serious physical renovation the house so desperately needed, there were conceptual changes he could effect for the company itself. "My policy," he told the reporter "may be expressed in a little twist of the Golden Rule: I am doing unto others as I have wished, for a long time, to be done by."[1]

And, in fact, with social reform a reality of daily life and "organize" the rallying cry of the times, a "little twist" from one of their own in the executive branch was just what singers under contract to the Metropolitan Opera needed. For years they had complained of management abuses—the restrictions it put on their working outside the house and the excessive commissions and fees it routinely took from their earnings. The idea of forming a union was hardly new: in 1923 John McCormack and Johnson himself had even tried to organize one. But clearly, given the new environment, the time had come for singers to put aside the facade of glamour and mystery that traditionally attended their profession and show themselves as working people who needed protection like everyone else. And it was in that spirit that on March 11, 1936, eleven would join eight other prominent musicians to inaugurate the American Guild of Musical Artists (AGMA), elect Tibbett their president, and begin the process of righting wrongs. These were wrongs the Met's new chief had experienced firsthand and, "now in the position of a member of the Labor Party who is suddenly elevated to the post of Premiere,"[2] as he had told the reporter, could do something about.

For, on the face of it, Edward Johnson was both a consummate diplomat and a caring boss, even if underneath a sadness and tension (in part derived from the untimely loss of his beloved wife and the stress of being a single parent) rendered him a man of many contradictions. Indeed, smiling, compassionate, and approachable on the one hand, cold and inscrutable on the other, Johnson sometimes left his artists wondering where they stood; hating to displease, refuse, or fire any of them, he compounded matters by leaving any unpleasant tasks to Edward Ziegler, his assistant manager and, unquestionably, the second most powerful man in the house. To be sure, Earle Lewis, the box-office manager, also wielded power, but less overtly. For if Lewis did not involve himself with the artists directly, years of selling tickets and talking with patrons gave him insight into which operas and which singers would fly, and ultimately, of course, it was all about box office. Often seen prowling the halls together, Johnson, Lewis, and Ziegler came to be known as the Triumvirate or Troika; not surprisingly, given the new egalitarian impulse, the names Ziegler and Lewis soon joined Johnson's own in equal-size letters on the cover of the opera programs.

But if there were shortcomings in Johnson's character, he generally kept them in check. The public loved its attractive new manager, who in turn made every effort to make it feel as though opera belonged as much to them as to the wealthy elite, and the great majority of his artists believed he could do no wrong. He said he wanted his company to be "just one big happy family,"[3] and for the most part it was. "Congeniality permeated the atmosphere while he ran the Met," said Steber,[4] who, like so many of the young Americans Johnson brought into the company, thought of him as a father figure and herself as one of "Johnson's kids."[5]

Certainly, it was not easy for many of these young singers, left as they were to fend for themselves in a high-powered company that had no time to give them the special attention they too often badly needed. Management told them which roles they were responsible for, but little about when (or even if) they would actually perform them. And because roles were only loosely "covered," many, either hoping for the big break or afraid to say no, said yes to replacing an ailing colleague even at the last minute—even when it meant exposing themselves without a rehearsal.

For rehearsal time on the stage or with the orchestra was a rarity for the young Americans. The policy was that first casts rehearsed and anyone involved in a later performance learned by watching. This meant that Europeans, who by virtue of their experience generally formed the first cast, got all the rehearsal, while Americans, who by virtue of their lack of it generally formed the second, performed almost cold. "I thought the Europeans were rather selfish," Nadine Conner would say. "But, happy to be singing at all, I sang for four years without either a stage or an orchestra rehearsal."[6]

The matter of salaries and fees was also a bone of contention. For whereas a foreigner such as the Italian Licia Albanese, who arrived with years of experience and full name recognition, might receive $300 a performance for leading roles, an American such as Steber, who had little experience and no name recognition but sang many of the same kinds of roles, earned between $75 and $150 a week. (Every artist, it should be noted, preferred a per-performance fee to a weekly salary. Europeans routinely received it; Americans, even principals, worked their way up to it.) Humble in such august company and, like Conner, happy just to be there, Steber accepted the disparity at the time, but thought it a different matter altogether when a few years later she too was a star and nothing changed.

Even so, it was one of the new manager's highest priorities that more young Americans sing with what many viewed as the national company, and on December 19, 1935, with his first season just under way, the following brief announcement informing singers of a possible new route to the Metropolitan Opera appeared (buried deep) in the *New York Times* and in short order in papers and periodicals around the country:

Auditions for the Metropolitan Opera, which hitherto have been conducted privately, will be broadcast over a nation-wide network in a series of thirteen weekly radio programs starting Dec. 22. While the Metropolitan committee on auditions headed by Edward Johnson, general manager, will act as judges, the radio audience will be invited to comment on the merits of the candidates. Mr. Johnson and the Metropolitan Orchestra under the direction of Wilfrid Pelletier will participate in the broadcasts each Sunday at 3:30 PM over the WEAF network. It is expected that at least thirty-six singers will be heard in the series.[7]

So there it was: a chance to be heard nationwide, and, better yet, as they would soon learn, a chance for a Metropolitan Opera contract. Never had the door of 1417 Broadway been opened so wide. In the first season alone some seven hundred hopefuls requested preliminary auditions, of which forty-eight sang on the radio broadcasts.

Over the next few years, Wilfrid Pelletier, the competition's passionate, compassionate, and indefatigable director, would, in fact, hear an average of fifty aspirants a week in New York; and at other times, so that out-of-towners would not make the trip unnecessarily, he would personally scour the country for the best candidates—a practice he dropped only after written applications for determining eligibility were added in 1944. He might even hear someone extemporaneously, as he did for example the young coloratura Patrice Munsel, whose coach simply informed her one morning that she was ready for the Met, picked up the phone, and sent her to audition that very afternoon. Just seventeen years old at the time, Munsel would recall that she had sung the Queen of the Night wearing bobby socks and saddle shoes with her hat and glasses still on; that Pelly, as he was affectionately known, had asked her to remove the hat and glasses before tackling Lucia and Lakmé; and that, the marathon audition concluded, he had said the preliminary rounds were over, but that he would like her to sing in the following Sunday's broadcast anyway. And so it had gone until the next thing Munsel knew, she had won.[8]

Sponsored by the Sherwin-Williams Paint Company, the Auditions broadcasts took place before an audience in NBC's studio 8H. Pelletier conducted; Johnson usually presided. The format varied over the years, and though initially as many as four contestants sang on one program, usually there were two, who sang a duet and two arias each (or an aria and a song), which were interspersed with orchestral numbers. Winners received contracts; runners-up received cash awards and the company's option on their services. For the first eight seasons, NBC broadcast the award ceremonies from the studio, but in 1944 the scene moved to the Met stage, where contestants sang their prizewinning arias for a live radio audience and an in-house audience of agents, managers, press, singers, fans, friends, and family.

The public loved it all, rooted for their favorites, and sometimes even bought tickets to see the winners in their debuts. Of the almost five hundred contestants who went airborne in the Johnson era—not forgetting two years when, for want of a new sponsor, there was no competition—some twenty-eight received immediate contracts: among them were Munsel, Resnik, Steber, Marilyn Cotlow, Frank Guarrera, Leonard Warren, Robert Merrill, Mack Harrell, Margaret Harshaw, Lois Hunt, Anna Kaskas, Arthur Kent, Maxine Stellman, William Hargrave, Hugh Thompson, Emery Darcy, Thomas Hayward, Annamary Dickey, and Christine Johnson. There were also several runners-up who walked away with contracts despite not winning, notably Christina Carroll, Lucielle Browning, Emery Darcy, Winifred Heidt, Gertrude Ribla, and Anne Bollinger. And any number, including Richard Tucker, Risë Stevens, Martha Lipton, Florence Kirk, Walter Cassel, and Kenneth Schon, competed but found their way to the Met by other means.

In fact, one just never knew what might happen, as Marie Wilkins, who had been a semifinalist the previous year, found out in 1942 when she visited Pelletier to ask his advice about trying again. If she didn't win she would settle for being a housewife, she told him. But no, the director said, not only should she try again, she should also learn Lakmè. Lily Pons, it seems, was not feeling well. And indeed when two weeks later the diva finally succumbed, giving just a few hours' official notice, the former Auditions runner-up went on. The press reported a splintered high E, but the audience applauded the heroics, and, though ultimately the Met left her to carve out a small freelance career, it first rewarded her with a few concerts and a Queen of the Night.

The program did not exclude foreigners, but it made no effort to look for candidates outside the United States. Arthur Carron, a winner the first year, and Thomas L. Thomas, the second, were English and Welsh respectively, and several Canadians did well over the years, but most contestants were American-born.

Anna Kaskas, a Connecticut native of Lithuanian descent, who had some European credentials, won the first Auditions. Earle Lewis had heard the attractive blonde in a lesson with Enrico Rosati, and recommended her

Anna Kaskas, first winner of the Metropolitan
Auditions of the Air. Photo by Bruno

to Pelletier. Kaskas appeared with three male contestants on the first Auditions broadcast, moved on to the semifinals, and then the finals, at which time she showed off her solid, wide-ranging mezzo with Fidès's aria from Meyerbeer's *Le Prophète*. Summoned to an office soon after, she found the tenor Carron and a telegram declaring them both winners. And then, she recalled, she made her way to Rosati's studio, where she burst into tears.

Kaskas would give the company a decade of solid service in secondary roles—an auspicious beginning for the new competition.

No question about it, though: by introducing in his first fortnight eight Americans versus four foreigners in casts already heavily favoring the home-grown from the Gatti legacy, Johnson was making a statement. But how would they fare? As the critics sharpened their pencils to consider Johnson's "Americanization of the Met," they were pleased to have so many nice things to write, at least for the first week.

Certainly everyone agreed that the debuts of Charlotte Symons, Helen Olheim, and Thelma Votipka boded well for natives in the comprimario department. The Ohio-born Votipka, the possessor of an "outstanding voice, large, warm, well used and of beautiful quality,"[9] as *Musical America* wrote after hearing her as the Countess Almaviva with the American Opera Company in 1928, might even have essayed leading roles had she so wanted. Helen Noble would recall hearing "a voice so beautiful and resonant and full" practicing behind a closed door that she was first riveted and then amazed to see Tippy, as the soprano was affectionately called, emerge.[10] But Tippy preferred making little roles big—forty-two of them—and, as one who once performed two weeks in a row without a night off, she would log in almost fifteen hundred performances for the company before officially retiring in 1963.

Happy too were the critics with Connecticut-born Charles Kullman, who bowed as Faust three nights into the season—the first of Johnson's Americans to essay a leading role. A former Juilliard student who had come to singing only after financial difficulties made it impossible to complete his medical studies at Yale, Kullman, of German descent, had been a leading tenor at the Berlin Opera until 1934, when, released by the company for singing in Salzburg in defiance of Hitler's ban on the festival, he had joined the roster of the Vienna State Opera. And that summer he had sung at Covent Garden, where Johnson heard him.

Versatility was Kullman's middle name. From Parsifal to Don Basilio in *Nozze di Figaro,* the number and variety of his roles were astonishing. But when Howard Taubman wrote, "Mr. Kullman made an effective debut, if not a sensational one,"[11] he bespoke the tenor's entire career. Kullman quickly became a workhorse at the Met—in the space of just six days that January he added Alfredo, Don José, and the Duke to his credits—and with

*Charles Kullman returning
from Europe, about 1935*

the decades his not-large instrument, having to cope so often in the huge theater, lost its sheen. Nonetheless, always an intelligent and interesting artist who looked good and acted convincingly, Kullman would ultimately give the company twenty-one solid consecutive seasons.

And finally, rounding out the first week, Chase Baromeo and Julius Huehn commanded the stage as Ramfis in *Aida* and the Herald in *Lohengrin* respectively. But if Baromeo's sonorous bass and wide experience, including seasons at La Scala and Chicago, might have led New Yorkers to expect important things for him at the Met, as it turned out the slender, aristocratic-looking basso would sing only three seasons of secondary roles for Johnson before retiring to teach in Texas. Though cut from quite another cloth it would seem, the brawny six-foot-four Huehn, a former riveter in his father's steel mill in Pittsburgh and recent Juilliard graduate, would serve the company well and often in a wide range of baritone roles from Kurwenal to Gianni Schicchi until 1944, when service to his country became the bigger issue.

So far so good, then; thus far the natives had not disappointed. But now the critics grew testy. "So rapidly is the principle of the Monroe Doctrine penetrating the walls of the Metropolitan that we may soon be faced with the astonishing condition of an American opera house, manned by American artists," Samuel Chotzinoff quipped on hearing Susanne Fisher as Madama Butterfly, adding, "I would hesitate to say that Miss Fisher possesses a first-string voice."[12]

An exchange student from the Juilliard Graduate School when she first went abroad, the soprano from West Virginia had, in fact, worked her way up from small to leading roles at the Staatsoper in Berlin and sung with the Opéra-Comique in Paris. But such credentials did not impress Olin Downes either, who protested, "Audiences in the Metropolitan Opera House have the right to hear the great roles sung in great fashion, with an effect commensurate to the traditions of the organizations and the proportions of the theater."[13] And if Hilda Burke, a soprano who had been singing leading roles at the Chicago Opera since 1928, was lucky in that the next night the critics had so much vitriol to spill on Ponselle's first Carmen, there was little space for the new Micaela, Downes still managed to slip in that her singing simply did "not rank with the traditions of the Metropolitan."[14]

And there was more. Though Johnson had promised no special consideration would be given Juilliard students despite the Juilliard Foundation's financial guarantee, thus far critics counted half of his eight new Americans with ties to the school. So when Colorado-born Josephine Antoine, a protégée of Sembrich at Juilliard, where she had fairly triumphed as Zerbinetta in *Ariadne auf Naxos* and as Maria Malibran in Robert Russell Bennett's opera of that name, made her debut as Philine in *Mignon,* it was all Chotzinoff could do to contain himself. "The newest debutante from Claremont Avenue [Juilliard] . . . like all the other recruits from New York's biggest conservatory . . . has a nice, respectable voice . . . but without distinction. Naturally, it is too much to expect vocal style and polish from a young lady who goes from a music school straight into a stellar role at the Metropolitan."[15]

But this time he got it wrong. Not only did Johnson desperately need a

Josephine Antoine, about 1937. Photo by De Bellis

coloratura to spell Pons, but Antoine was the genuine article. Critics developed respect for the tenacious coloratura, whose smooth pyrotechnics and clear, expressive singing routinely impressed. Antoine developed a following across the country and, until the arrivals of Patrice Munsel and Mimi Benzell in the early 1940s, was indispensable to the company.

Besides, everyone could relax now, for the arrival of Joseph Benton the following week brought the Juilliard run to a happy end. Moreover, the story of how the new tenor had auditioned for Johnson on Wednesday and just happened to be conferring with the manager on Thursday when Richard Crooks called in sick for Friday's *Manon* made good copy. With Hackett, the company's other Des Grieux, out of town, why not Benton, Johnson figured, as he turned to the tenor before him. The Oklahoma native was, after all, a seasoned performer with a decade's experience abroad; he had just sung the role in Chicago; and he was highly intelligent.

For that matter, Benton not only had three degrees from the University of Oklahoma, but also had turned down a Rhodes scholarship to pursue singing. He had studied with Oscar Saenger at the Chicago Musical College and with Jean de Reszke in France, where he had made his operatic debut as Don Ottavio in a de Reszke production of *Don Giovanni* in 1924. He had taken on the name Giuseppe Bentonelli, on the orders of a Fascist judge who said Benton sounded too French, when he made his Italian debut in *La Traviata* in 1928. Thereafter he had sung in North Africa and the Netherlands and performed throughout Italy until 1934, when, weary of the restrictions imposed on foreigners and wary of being voted one of the country's four favorite tenors by the Italian Fascist Society of Musicians, he had returned home for a Chicago debut as Cavaradossi.

The New York critics liked this American: they praised his tall, slim physique, his tasteful acting, and his pleasing lyric tenor; they found his style elegant and his French superlative. Benton would stay only two seasons, however, and then, not even forty years old—in a move unexplained in his charming volume of anecdotes about his career—return to Oklahoma to teach.

But if Benton's debut was unexpected, no debut was more eagerly awaited than that of Johnson's last new American of the season, Dusolina Giannini. For years it had been rumored that Gatti-Casazza would engage the Philadelphia soprano: years in which her reputation had grown by leaps and bounds, years in which demands had grown ever louder to hear her on a stage to which she had every right to lay claim. Yet, reportedly owing to a feud with Gatti, that right had been denied her. But now in February Johnson welcomed the "Aïda from Philadelphia,"[16] as *Time* magazine headed its story. Just as it was altogether appropriate that the Metropolitan be the venue for her first professional opera in her native land, it was altogether appropriate that she, Giannini, be Johnson's first authentic native star.

The Giannini family had put down deep roots in the musical life of its adopted country. Dusolina's father, Ferruccio, a tenor who had studied with Francesco Lamperti and the first singer to record opera on flat disc, had founded a successful theater in Philadelphia. His wife played several instruments; the children, in addition to Dusolina, included Vittorio, a noted composer, and Eufemia, or Madame Gregory, as the renowned teacher of the Lamperti method would be known at the Curtis Institute for over a quarter of a century.

Naturally Dusolina had also learned the Lamperti method, first from her father, who used his own company to launch his eleven-year-old daughter as La Cieca in *La Gioconda,* and then from Sembrich, who oversaw her change from mezzo to dramatic soprano. Giannini made her operatic debut as Aida in Hamburg in 1925, and thereafter alternated a highly successful career abroad with periods of concertizing in the United States. Never abandoning the great traditions of bel canto on which she had honed her gleaming instrument, Giannini could sing opera with smoldering expressivity and still easily temper her instrument for the intimacy of song—her profound interpretations of lieder and inimitable renditions of her brother's arrangements of Italian folk songs are but two examples of her richly varied recital fare.

But while critics generally embraced this vibrant artist in her long-awaited Met debut, the annals show that over six seasons she would sing just twenty-two times. Was her acting too verismo for Met audiences, or, as Downes suggested, was her voice "no longer in its best estate"?[17] In a 1942 article called "Among the Missing," the critic Robert Lawrence was at a loss to explain "The Great Giannini Mystery."[18]

Recapping Johnson's first season in the *Times,* Downes gave an approving nod to Giannini and Kullman, expressed interest in Huehn and Bentonelli, but summed up the new manager's efforts to Americanize the Metropolitan Opera with these hard words:

It would be a pleasure to say that among the young Americans some new potentialities of world-shaking capacity were revealed. Unfortunately that is not the case. . . . On the contrary, singers whose appearance in principal parts were justified neither by voice nor achievement were repeatedly given leading roles, which in former years at the Metropolitan would only have been bestowed upon those indubitably worthy of the honor. It is very much to be hoped that this departure on the part of the new management will be looked upon as an experiment tried but not approved, and rejected as unsuccessful experiments should be. Our well-meaning theorists to the contrary, the American public will not welcome a further decline of Metropolitan standards through which the quality of the casts is brought down to the level of immaturity or mediocrity or both, instead of insistence upon the artist rising to the level of the best Metropolitan tradition. No other course than the latter will pay—pay either the Metropolitan Association or the institution which now influences its artistic procedure [the Juilliard]. This should be clear by the results of the Winter.[19]

Perhaps, then, Johnson's best hope for finding American singers lay with the spring. The aims for the new Spring Season, as the supplementary series was called, were simple enough: make opera accessible to a wider audience by charging popular prices and performing the operas in English; provide a place for young American singers to get real experience while the Metropolitan considered them for advancement into the parent company.

But as it turned out, the Spring Season that got under way in May 1936 almost immediately lost sight of its aims. True, tickets were modestly priced; but only one of the ten productions was in English, and many of the best roles went to foreigners and established Met artists. The opening night *Carmen,* for example, was sung in French, and three of the four leading roles were sung by established foreigners;[20] only Natalie Bodanya as Micaela supplied an inexperienced American. But *The Bartered Bride* was a big success in its English translation, and at the end of the season Johnson announced the entire production would be performed in the winter season and several of the large cast retained for other roles as well. And so it was that Lucielle Browning, a lovely strawberry-blonde from Juilliard, came to anchor the mezzo comprimario roster for the entire Johnson tenure; George Rasely, a veteran of concert, radio, and musicals, to provide the company with wonderful primarily comic cameos for eight seasons; the petite Bodanya, a Sembrich student at Curtis and Juilliard, to sing a variety of roles both small and secondary until 1942; and Norman Cordon, a six-foot-four bass, who already boasted experience with several American companies, to give yeoman service in roles of all sizes and styles for a decade. Indeed, Helen Noble once ventured that had his voice been larger and had the big guns from Europe (Pinza, Schorr, Lazzari, List, and Kipnis) not provided such formidable competition, Cordon might have gone even further.

Sidney Rayner, a major talent with a major résumé, also stayed on. The strapping tenor from New Orleans, once a leading lyric at the Opéra-Comique in Paris, had just completed a season with the Chicago Opera and was appearing with Salmaggi at the Hippodrome when the Met approached him for the Spring Season and immediately put him to the grindstone in dramatic roles. At one point, in fact, Rayner essayed *Carmen, Aida,* and *Cavalleria* for the junior company without a day's rest. But on being signed with the parent company, with its plethora of fine tenors, for his Italian and French repertoire,[21] Rayner, whose early recordings reveal a beautiful lyric voice, suddenly found himself with little to do. And it is regrettable that he is probably best remembered at the Met as the hapless tenor who replaced Richard Crooks as Des Grieux when Bidù Sayão made her debut as Massenet's Manon. "Onstage I waited at the inn for des Grieux," the soprano would recall, "and imagine my surprise when it turned out to be a man I had never seen before."[22] Management, it seems, thinking the change of leading men at the last moment might upset the tiny debutante, had chosen not to tell her. (That Rayner himself had never sung the role at the Metropolitan was apparently not a concern.) In any case, Rayner would leave the Metropolitan after three seasons and, with the threat of war making it unwise to return to Europe, tour extensively with America's popular San Carlo Opera before closing out his singing career on Broadway in a small role in Kurt Weill's *Street Scene.*

Hoping to improve on the first Spring Season, Johnson made some changes in its leadership for the second, only to have it prove just as desultory. Highlights were a revival of Rabaud's *Mârouf;* a *Trovatore* mounted for Rose Bampton to try her new soprano voice; a *Pagliacci* with the popular Radio City baritone Robert Weede; and a *Mignon* with Jennie Tourel, a Russian-born mezzo. Walter Damrosch's *Man without a Country* received its world premiere and was also performed once in the winter season. But in this case not one of the production's singers stayed on, including the soprano Helen Traubel, who had impressed in the opera's only female role. And though Donald Dickson, who, *Musical Courier* said, had "the potentialities of a Lawrence Tibbett,"[23] sang a single Silvio with the parent company on tour, the big baritone told *Opera News* he wanted to work out the kinks abroad. But war clouds would keep Dickson at home as well and he would ultimately make the better part of his career in radio.

And so, the Spring Season for which there had been so much hope folded unceremoniously. Though the official explanation was that the company would not have the time for it the following season because it had to participate in the 1939 World's Fair, it was no secret that it had been a financial loss and that management was discouraged in its search for American talent. In any case, Johnson, having flung open the floodgates to Americans, now temporarily slammed them shut—with the exception of the two short-lived sopranos whose curious experiences round out this part of the story.

Indeed, it is fair to say that the debut of Franca Somigli as Madama Butterfly in 1937 was awaited almost as eagerly as that of Dusolina Giannini. Not only had the New York soprano, whose real name was Marion Bruce Clark, studied with Rosina Storchio, the first Cio-Cio-San, but ever since her bow in Rovigo as Mimì in 1927, she had been a veritable star in Italy. Johnson had heard her singing Mistress Ford under Toscanini in Salzburg in 1936, and though she had been negatively received in Chicago in 1934, he had been glad to engage her for the Met.

But New York, it seems, disliked Somigli as much as Chicago had, and she would stay long enough to entertain only two Mimìs and two Butterflies before returning to Italy, where she would make her home. "In both her singing and her acting were characteristics more likely to meet immediate approval in Milan or Naples than in this country," *Musical America* theorized.[24] To be sure, as Anna Hamlin once mused, "It is an odd thing how some artists find one country so appreciative of their gifts, while in another part of the world, they are almost nobody."[25]

The Metropolitan career of Amri Galli-Campi, or Irmengard Gallenkamp, as she was born in Pennsylvania, was even more fleeting. The coloratura had auditioned for Johnson after considerable experience in Europe, and her debut as Gilda with the company on tour in Cleveland was by all accounts an unqualified success. The audience awarded her a four-minute ovation after her aria, and the *Times* reported that Johnson called her debut "the first of importance ever made outside New York."[26] But whether because her own manager caused a problem for the Met or because Lily Pons saw her as a threat—two theories she believed—Galli-Campi never sang again for the Metropolitan.[27]

Doubtless because he felt responsible to the Juilliard board, as well as to the public, the press, and the singers, Johnson had been overzealous in his efforts to bring natives into the Metropolitan Opera. The Auditions of the Air would quietly continue and soon become the single most effective tool in achieving that goal, but the well-intentioned manager now put all other efforts on hold, while the press, which had routinely yet pointedly counted how many new Americans were on each roster, now refrained from remarking on their total absence. For those aspiring to a career in opera the silence could only have been deafening. Europe was all but closed, and the American operascape of the 1930s was barely a work in progress.

Chapter Five

Not Much Else

OR AMERICA'S OPERATIC ASPIRANTS emerging from their
teachers' studios, scales smooth, high notes centered, roles memorized, the overriding question was: Where does one go from here? The answer had always been Europe. "The student who wants to sing in opera will
find in Europe ten opportunities for gaining experience for one here," the
baritone Reinald Werrenrath had said in 1921.[1] To be sure, Europe offered
any number of small, year-round companies ideal for cutting artistic teeth.
The idea that "so rich and enterprising a country" as America could not provide the same was "almost unbelievable" to a visitor such as the German
soprano Frida Leider.[2] But, with the notable exception of symphony orchestras, which had sprouted up everywhere, Americans seemed to have little interest in their cultural institutions, and their government even less.

Now, however, with the threat of war taking the European option off the
table, the problem was out front for all to see, and the call for native companies—especially ones with seasons long enough to provide their artists with
some financial security—resounded with new urgency. It is a "vicious circle,"
William Brady, a teacher, said in 1937. "No extensive system of American operatic houses with resident companies can be established until we have
American-trained singers in sufficient quantity to equip them, and we cannot have such a quota of routined singers until we have the houses in which
they can accumulate the needed experience."[3]

The sad truth was that the United States, a country of some three million square miles and 130 million inhabitants, could count but three resident
companies, aside from the Metropolitan, that presented professional opera
for more than a week at a time, for a grand combined total of fourteen weeks
or approximately one hundred performances of opera—annually. The
Salmaggi Opera in New York and the touring San Carlo Opera operated

steadily and for long periods of time, but, as we shall see, the former was pickup opera that barely paid its singers, and the latter was always on the road. What was needed were resident repertory companies, such as were commonly found throughout Central Europe and Italy.

Johnson could plead for "bush-league opera houses in which to season some of [the Metropolitan's] discoveries."[4] Such had been the hope for its Spring Season. But the "experiment" had failed; no bush-league system was in sight. And even as late as 1945, when a reporter asked young Blanche Thebom if her eye had always been on the Metropolitan (where she had just sung her first operatic performance on any stage), the answer was: "There isn't much else, is there?"[5]

Of course, there was a time the mezzo might have tried Chicago, home to some of the greatest opera the country had ever known. Much like the Met, Chicago's resident company had once mounted seasons of opera lasting three months or more with rosters that teemed with both international stars and qualified Americans. If many who sang in Chicago never sang with the Met, it was primarily only because of the rival status of the two great companies.

But the 1930s had found opera in the Windy City a shadow of its former self. The stock market collapse coming only weeks after the opening of the new twenty-million-dollar opera house had taken a terrible toll. There was no season in 1932, and if the new company that opened the following fall hoped to evoke the glory days by calling itself the Chicago Grand Opera Company, the illusion would be short-lived. Indeed, with the Depression at its nadir, Paul Longone and Gennaro Papi, its two Neapolitan-born directors, were forced to impose drastic cost-cutting measures. And as one of these was to hire more Americans—natives, after all, came cheaper than imports (cheaper still if they were local)—for the first time in its distinguished history Chicago opera smacked of provincialism. To be sure, though it is unlikely Longone often took money from singers in exchange for letting them perform with the company, as Papi charged on announcing his resignation from the company and as several corroborated in the press, the situation was desperate. And the annals show not only an inordinate number of singers, primarily sopranos, who appeared just once or twice in leading roles not to be heard from again, but also several who continued to perform with the company despite talent that was clearly below its standards.

One wonders, for example, about Jean Tennyson, who made her debut as Mimì in 1934 and sang frequently with the company for three seasons. A curvaceous blonde who had performed with the Earl Carroll Vanities before training as an opera singer, Tennyson was also the wife of Camille Dreyfus, founder and chairman of the Celanese Corporation of America, the sponsor of the radio show that later made her nationally known. She was certainly competent, as in fact the court ruled after one Celanese stockholder sued, claiming it cost the company a million dollars to present the president's wife, but it is clear from listening to recordings taken from broadcasts of *Great Moments in Music* that she should not have been singing leading roles in Chicago, given the level of singing the city had come to expect.

Let it be said, however, that Tennyson had a big heart and did many good things. She put on a good radio show, engaging as guests not only established artists but such talented novices as the yet-to-be-discovered Mario Lanza and once even devoting an entire show to Broadway understudies. And she put her money to good use as well, establishing, for example, a foundation that annually distributed some twenty thousand dollars to young musicians, and once awarded six young singers, including Beverly Sills, scholarships to study the French repertoire with Tennyson's former teacher, Mary Garden—a great diva, Tennyson explained, who was simply "down on her luck."[6]

But if in a scorching article in 1935 called "Chicago's Worst," *Time* included Tennyson as one of the opera company's "blatantly unqualified" singers, it was Virginia Pemberton it singled out as having given "the season's most inept performance."[7] To be sure, the city did not suffer this other Illinois girl of means long, and Pemberton soon moved on to finance (or so it was rumored) performances in other cities.[8] But when she passed through Chicago with the San Carlo Opera in 1949, Pemberton sang a Violetta so "catastrophic" that some customers demanded their money back while others cheered the heroine's demise. *Musical America* took the opportunity to remind its readers that her "ineptness" should not have surprised anyone old enough to recall her history in the Longone era.[9]

Of course, not all Longone's Americans were suspect. Bentonelli, Lucille Meusel, and Vivian Della Chiesa, for example, were certainly distinguished recruits. Betty Jaynes and Rosemarie Brancato might have raised suspicion because of the fuss made over their ages; but, in fact, Jaynes, though only fifteen when she was introduced as Mimì opposite Giovanni Martinelli, an event deemed so extraordinary that it was covered by the national press, not only kept her composure, but, clearly talented, was soon on her way to a brief career in Hollywood. The twenty-one-year-old Brancato, a Liebling student, survived the tremendous ballyhoo that accompanied her sudden debut as Gilda, replacing the former prodigy Marion Talley, and later enjoyed a nice career in radio and opera.

Still, there seemed no end to Longone's problems, and when the helpless impresario began raiding the once off-limits Metropolitan, only to have most of its American wing descend on Chicago, the virtual cloning of the old rival did not sit well with the critics either. After Longone's death, in 1939, a variety of managements struggled to keep opera alive in Chicago, but the economics proved too much for them all, and at the close of the 1946 season the decision was made not to try again.

But while opera floundered by the lake, it flourished by the bay. In fact, thanks primarily to the vision, energy, and boundless enthusiasm of its founder, Gaetano Merola, the San Francisco Opera Company, having introduced itself with a week of performances in various facilities in 1923, could be found a decade later performing for a month in the first municipally owned opera theater in the United States, a theater the dapper conductor from Naples had convinced San Franciscans their opera company simply had to have.

Moreover, the casts were invariably star-studded; for Merola, who put great singing above all else, not only combed the globe to get the best, sometimes even convincing world-class singers to make American debuts under his aegis, but also had no qualms about importing Met singers. And the Met singers in turn had no qualms about singing in San Francisco both because it was prestigious and because it conveniently preceded the New York season. In deference to the city that had adopted him, however, Merola also made a point of using local talent whenever possible, talent that ranged from George Stinson, a local cop he prepped to sing Canio, to Jerome Hines, America's first great bass, who made his company debut in the small role of Monterone in *Rigoletto.* And for many years San Francisco program covers boasted, "World Famous Principals and Leading California Artists."[10]

Indeed, the brief career of Josephine Tuminia from the city's Marina district all but began and ended with the company. Just twenty-two when in 1935 she bowed as Rosina in a *Barbieri* cast that included Schipa, Bonelli, and Pinza, the perky coloratura, who sang swing with Tommy Dorsey on the side, would go on to perform opera in Europe and in 1941 make her debut at the Met as Gilda, only to see her career fade quickly thereafter. For if the composer Virgil Thomson, the *Herald Tribune*'s newest critic, thought her "sensational," declaring hers, "a vocal technique such as has not been heard here for many years,"[11] for some reason Tuminia sang just two seasons for the Met for a total of twelve performances. In 1942 she substituted for Lily Pons in Chicago and drew an eight-minute ovation for her Lucia Mad Scene. But then her trail disappears—until, that is, another sudden Pons indisposition in 1947 forced Merola to track her down, a housewife in San Mateo who gamely donned Lucia's wedding dress once again to save a performance for the man who had launched her career only a dozen years before.

But the best place outside New York for an opera singer to find work may well have been just ninety miles south, in Philadelphia. Although none of its opera companies lasted long enough to compete with San Francisco or with Chicago in its glory days, from the early 1920s to the early 1940s the City of Brotherly Love was often unsurpassed when it came to—if not always the quality—the quantity, vitality, and scope of its offerings.

To be sure, in matters operatic Philadelphia had a great deal to recommend it. Its proximity to New York made it easy not only for the Met to perform, which it did every Tuesday of the season, but also for all the great foreign artists who regularly visited that metropolis to do so. Moreover, the city boasted excellent music schools, most notably the new Curtis Institute, a world-renowned orchestra, which attracted world-renowned musicians, including many who took up residence, and a large Italian population, which, proud of the city's century of opera giving, avidly filled its many excellent theaters, including Oscar Hammerstein's mammoth Metropolitan Opera House and the beautiful Academy of Music.

If Philadelphia had a problem it was only its inability to rally round any single company long enough for it to become permanent. The city's opera companies sparkled, then sputtered; thrived, died, revived; changed their names; and came and went with head-spinning frequency. And they tended to be either categorically traditional or determinedly innovative. The traditional routinely presented old-fashioned opera the old-fashioned way; often products of the Italian community, they were generally run by local impresarios on the order of a Merola, but without the vision. The singers either came from the community or had connections to someone in it; all others stayed on the periphery unless their services were requested.

Francesco Pelosi oversaw some of the best of these companies, and, like Merola, was a Neapolitan who put great singing first. "Toscanini, he is a musical god. But I coulda have alla Toscaninis I want, anda without a Caruso I coulda no fill my opera house," the effusive impresario once told an interviewer.[12] But in addition to presenting such world-renowned Italians as Ruffo and Martinelli, Pelosi used his keen ear to discover young Americans, some of whom—Jan Peerce, James Melton, Dorothy Kirsten—the Metropolitan itself had not yet heard. His most important company, the Philadelphia La Scala, lasted well into the 1950s and probably came closest to providing the city with a conventional resident company.

The innovative companies were likely to be fostered by émigrés associated with the orchestra and Curtis. The Philadelphia Civic under Alexander Smallens made it a policy not only to essay unusual repertoire but also to cast Americans whenever possible. Among its many achievements was the 1928 American premiere of Richard Strauss's *Ariadne auf Naxos* with the Philadelphia soprano Irene Williams as the Composer, a much-touted but soon forgotten tenor from Brooklyn, Judson House, as Bacchus, and Eddy and Jepson in secondary roles.

For a few years the Philadelphia Grand under Artur Rodzinski overlapped with the Civic and the city rocked with great opera. But when the stock market crashed, it took with it the Civic, and the Grand was left to hold down the fort. Affiliating itself with Curtis, it engaged such stars as Mary Garden and John Charles Thomas and supported them with such quality Curtis students as Bampton, Jepson, and Conrad Thibault. Its production of Strauss's rarely heard *Elektra* and first American performance of Berg's *Wozzeck* put Philadelphia on the operatic map again. But then in 1934 the Grand too fell to the Depression, the Met suspended its visits, and to fill the void and ensure that the city get its fill of opera, someone (not Stokowski, who wanted nothing to do with it) persuaded the Philadelphia Orchestra itself to enter the risky business of opera production.

With Smallens and Fritz Reiner dividing up the conducting and with Herbert Graf, newly arrived from Austria, directing, in its first and only season in the business (1934–35) Philadelphia's great orchestra mounted productions ranging from *Tristan und Isolde* and *Carmen* to first American performances of Gluck's *Iphigénie en Aulide* and Stravinsky's *Mavra*—ten in all. And though Reiner said he had come up short after examining some "500 pounds" of opera scores by Americans, the Hungarian-born conductor did reassure the press: "We are working on the principle that no foreigner is used if an American is available. We aim for opera in English with predominantly

American casts, thus tying up opera with the life and experience of this country."[13] Consequently, though an occasional international star such as Emanuel List or Lotte Lehmann was imported to ensure an audience, most roles went to promising young Americans, especially those affiliated with Curtis and the nearby Juilliard—the two schools providing, for example, the greater part of the casts of *Le Nozze di Figaro* and *Falstaff.* In fact, Julius Huehn's portrayals of Falstaff and other major roles in Philadelphia are said to have been what convinced the Met to engage the Juilliard student the following fall. And Agnes Davis's highly touted Alice Ford may well have resulted in the Colorado soprano's getting a chance in its Spring Season, even though nothing further came of it.

Indeed, Davis, the first winner of the Atwater Kent competition, was a particular favorite at Curtis, and excerpts of her Brünnhilde recorded under Stokowski give every indication that her gleaming soprano had authentic dramatic potential. Why the critics were so indifferent to her Elsa in *Lohengrin* at the Met or why that company dropped her after just one performance is difficult to understand. But at least the unhappy experience did not collapse her career, for Davis did continue to perform, if primarily as an orchestral soloist, well into the late 1940s.

In any case, despite a generally excellent press, the Philadelphia experiment folded after just one season, the victim of poor attendance, poor management, and serious overspending. But the Metropolitan soon resumed its visits; Pelosi's La Scala got under way; and then in 1939 an experiment of another kind announced itself.

Describing the Philadelphia Opera as "a resident non-profit organization," the new company's founder, artistic director, and conductor, Sylvan Levin, declared its aim was to "present well-rehearsed operas with casts entirely composed of singers living or studying in the Philadelphia area." There were to be no stars; members would sing both leading and minor roles; all productions would be in English.[14]

Though offering only a handful of performances a season, the new company held close to those lofty goals, and fairly captivated the city with its fresh young talent and imaginative, often innovative, always wonderfully integrated productions. Sometimes it even attracted a national press, as when tenors sang the trouser roles traditionally performed by mezzo-sopranos. *Faust* even had William Hess, a former ticket seller at the Met, singing Siebel on one occasion and Faust on another. And it was very big news when, for reasons that are not clear, Maurice Maeterlinck attended the company's *Pelléas and Mélisande,* for it was common knowledge that the opera's librettist, having feuded with Debussy, had vowed never to see the opera. But now pictures of the great poet and the company's Mélisande, Frances Greer, appeared in the press across the country.

Chosen from the more than 350 singers Levin first auditioned, Greer was more experienced than most members of the company. A native of Arkansas, she had sung leading roles in the opera department headed by Pasquale Amato at Louisiana State University; and, though inexplicably rejected by Curtis, where she had hoped to continue her studies, she had won a Philadelphia Orchestra Youth Award. Greer sang small roles and even did her bit in the chorus for Levin, but from the beginning it was clear she was a star. "Miss Frances Greer's Musetta was as fine an impersonation of this elusive character as may be seen on any opera stage anywhere," Henry Pleasants wrote of her debut in the company's inaugural performance.[15] Pretty and vivacious, Greer would go on to win the 1942 Metropolitan Auditions of the Air and, after making her debut with that company (again as Musetta), win favor through the decade in soubrette roles from Susanna to Oscar.

Unlike Greer, Brenda Lewis arrived with little formal training and no experience whatsoever, not having seriously entertained the idea of becoming a singer until studying pre-med at college. Initially, Levin cast the eighteen-year-old Pennsylvania native (another Curtis reject) in small roles. But as he also told her to understudy all female roles, the next thing Lewis knew, with only one week to learn the part, she was suddenly performing the Marschallin (opposite the Octavian of the tenor David Brooks) in the *Rose Cavalier.*

Dorothy Sarnoff, Alice Howland, Mario Berini, Leonard Treash, James Pease, Robert Gay, and Howard Vandenburg were others who enjoyed early experience with the Philadelphia Opera. But in 1942, soon after the company began touring under the auspices of Sol Hurok, Levin resigned, surely taking the heart out of the company, which in 1944 announced it was suspending its plans for the upcoming season because of the shortage of male singers due to the war. The Philadelphia Opera never resurfaced, but Lewis, who would become one of America's finest singer-actors, has made the point that because the basis of its work was theater, the company was "the root of what we now take for granted."[16]

In contrast to Europe, where opera festivals were big summertime music attractions, in America orchestral music dominated warm-weather perfor-

*Frances Greer as Musetta. Photo by
J. Abresch, courtesy of Frances Greer*

mance. Even the Hollywood Bowl, which had opened in 1922 with an ambitious production of *Carmen,* starring Marguerita Sylva and Edward Johnson, had not added opera to its regular schedule until the mid-1930s, and then only one or two productions a season. Otherwise, the St. Louis Municipal Opera, the Atlantic City Steel Pier Opera, and Chautauqua in New York offered some steady work for opera singers in the summer;

Randall's Island and Jones Beach in New York City and the Paper Mill Playhouse in New Jersey mounted operettas and some opera; and in the late 1930s Central City in the Rocky Mountains began adding opera to its festival.

But for those willing to sweat that extra bit for their art, nothing topped the experience at Cincinnati's Zoological Gardens. For the Zoo Opera, as it became known, was almost as famous for the encounters between the venue's full-time residents and the visiting singers as for the performances themselves—there was, for example, the peacock that burst out singing every time he caught sight of a certain flamboyantly costumed tenor in *Lucia*. Everybody, including foreigners—though it has been called "the cradle of American singers"—loved the relaxed atmosphere, not to mention the six or more weeks of solid work the festival provided. And many thought it the best place to try out a new role or to make an operatic debut.

It was in Cincinnati that, for example, Swarthout and Stevens essayed their first Carmens, Robert Weede and Robert Merrill their first Rigolettos, Kirsten her first Tosca, Martinelli his first and last Tristan. And it was in Cincinnati that, singing their first opera anywhere, Nan Merriman was La Cieca in *Gioconda* and Melton was Pinkerton to Rosa Tentoni's Butterfly. A Minnesotan of Italian parentage, Tentoni had herself received a warm reception for her operatic debut as Nedda at the Zoo in 1933 and subsequently become a Cincinnati favorite. The lovely soprano would also sing in the Met's Spring Season, in San Francisco, and with the Philadelphia Orchestra, but not much more. One can only wonder why this was so, in light of her consistently excellent reviews, the compelling personal expression and distinctive crystalline timbre one hears on a tantalizing recorded excerpt of her Mimì, and her great popularity in Cincinnati.

What the country really needed, though, as Richard Crooks once said, were the "Salmaggis and Fortune Gallos where a young artist can learn and get kicked around a bit and prove himself before he gets to the big time."[17] To be sure, of all the mustachioed Italian immigrants seeking to purvey the lyric art to Americans, either of these colorful impresarios could have taken the prize for quantity of opera produced and number of singers employed. The difference was only that Fortune Gallo had artistic standards; Alfredo Salmaggi, by most accounts, did not.

Tall and handsome, Salmaggi had come to America from his native

Abruzzi in 1910 to be an assistant conductor for the Boston Opera Company. The company's early demise had forced him to turn to singing and teaching to earn a living. But in 1918 he had switched professions again after a performance of *Pagliacci* he mounted for his students, with himself as Canio, sold out at the Brooklyn Academy of Music, grossed over seven thousand dollars, and drew an audience that included the likes of Geraldine Farrar, Pasquale Amato, and Gatti-Casazza. For, as the illustrious visitors told him after the performance, though his singing wasn't much, he clearly had the makings of a great impresario.

And so, after a few years' practice here, there, and everywhere, Salmaggi opera became a New York institution. And a rare night it was that one of his popular-priced productions was not playing somewhere in the city, all of which meant work for a great many singers, even if it meant putting up with a lot. For to sing with the "greatest producer of second-rate opera in the U.S."[18] was to be pinned into a costume that probably did not fit; to be sent on a stage with scenery you had never seen; and to sing with an orchestra you had never heard and with singers you met for the first time onstage—all in front of a large and very vocal audience and for probably the lowest paycheck in all opera.

But if Salmaggi was the first person every Italian just off the boat called, the majority of his singers were more likely to be either Italian Americans or Americans who had Italianized their names. Who knew, for instance, that the soprano Annunciata Garrotto, who sang more than one hundred performances of leading roles for his various companies, was from Omaha, Nebraska? Salmaggi liked and encouraged Americans. He found them generally more ambitious and hard-working than Europeans, and he admired their musicality, their ability to sing in several languages, and their concern for acting.[19]

Because he made so many claims, it is difficult to be certain just who did sing for Salmaggi, but we do know that he provided Herva Nelli, Norina Greco, Marie Powers, Richard Tucker, and Eugene Conley with early experience; that he brought Anne Jeffreys from Hollywood to sing her first operatic role, Tosca; that he introduced Bruna Castagna to America; that he gave Astrid Varnay's mother work after her husband died; and, as we shall see, that he presented the first black ever to sing with a white company in America.

Though Alfredo Salmaggi went on mounting opera until he was eighty-five, Guido, one of his nine children, essentially took over for his father in the 1950s. He balanced the books, rehearsed, and saw to it that choristers no longer wore brown shoes with evening dress. He gave the actor José Ferrer the chance to sing Gianni Schicchi, Skitch Henderson the chance to conduct *La Traviata,* and a whole new generation of young singers the chance to be heard. But the title "P. T. Barnum of bargain opera"[20] he left to his father.[21]

Unlike Salmaggi, seventeen-year-old Fortune Gallo had no job awaiting him on his arrival in America in 1895. Worse yet, having lost all his money playing craps on the voyage over, he was "as clean of cash as a freshly plucked hen—or rooster," albeit a Lucky Rooster, as his name translated into English, and as he later titled his autobiography. For Immigration officials would have sent the boy back to Italy had one of them not seen "'the makings of a first-class citizen,'" given him three dollars, and let him stay.[22]

And so Gallo had made his way from bank clerk and dance band manager to founder of the San Carlo Opera, which he named for the opera house in Naples, where he had heard his first opera the night before he left for America. But the idea for the company, he said, came from his friend Caruso, who once told him: "This America of yours is a great country populated by many people. . . . The larger cities they may hear opera. But in the smaller towns they have only the records we make for their phonographs. That is wrong. Destiny some day will appoint someone to bring opera to them."[23]

A well-oiled machine comprising chorus, orchestra, scenery, and as many as seventy-five soloists, the San Carlo traveled (mostly by rail) an average of some twenty thousand miles a season, sometimes for as long as nine months at a time. It performed quality opera at affordable prices, and, except for its first year, never lost money or required financial backing of any kind, surviving very nicely instead on ticket sales. For along the San Carlo trail, as it became known, the company built up huge audiences of passionate fans who eagerly awaited its return each year. For one opera fan, Tom Durrie, growing up in Portland, Oregon, a San Carlo visit was "a five-day orgy of operagoing."[24] For the young Patrice Munsel, who attended a San Carlo performance of *Madama Butterfly* in Spokane and afterwards told a friend she would one day sing at the Metropolitan Opera, it was inspiration.

Gallo found his singers everywhere and anywhere, and he engaged the best available. Singers trusted him and knew a tour with the San Carlo was a respectable way to make a living with the voice. And though many left the San Carlo for the Met, conversely, others who had been let go by that company prolonged their careers with Gallo. Cardell Bishop, who wrote something akin to a biography of the San Carlo, lists a lifetime roster of approximately seven hundred singers, and it is especially interesting to note some of the many Americans who got early experience with it, such as Jerome Hines, James Melton, Elaine Malbin, David Poleri, Dorothy Kirsten, Jean Madeira, and Eugene Conley.

The soprano Mary Henderson, who sang both for Gallo and briefly for the Met, has suggested that association with the former could stigmatize a singer in the eyes of the latter. Be that as it may, there were many whose names were made by and still resonate because of the San Carlo. Lucille Meusel, for instance, a lyric coloratura who had been with the Chicago Civic in its heyday and also sang in Belgium, is certainly best remembered for the seasons between 1934 and 1943 when she sang regularly for Gallo. And though Bishop called Meusel "the company's finest artist from every viewpoint,"[25] Mina Cravi, who joined in 1945 and sang many of the same roles, is said to have maintained Meusel's high standards. Of Cravi one critic wrote, "She sang with such pathos and so beautiful a lyric line and acted so simply and movingly [as Mimì] that it is hard to imagine why the Metropolitan has not become interested in her."[26]

There was also the elegant lyric soprano Mobley Lushanya, an American Indian, and the dramatic soprano Selma Kaye, the daughter of an opera soprano from Czarist Russia, both of whom were enormously successful, especially singing Verdi. "The glory of that voice—plangent, glistening, spectacular in range and volume," Claudia Cassidy wrote of Kaye, "is going to explode over opera some of these days with international impact."[27]

And "Who could forget Coe Glade's dusky-voiced Carmen?"[28] It has been said that some two thousand audiences witnessed Glade's gypsy, mostly in her appearances with the San Carlo. As the Chicago native has told it, she was visiting relatives in Asheville, North Carolina, when the company came to town and she decided to audition. She had little vocal training and even less experience, but Gallo, needing an Amneris for the following week, engaged her on the spot and introduced her at the Century Theater in New York on September 14, 1926.[29] And though *Musical America* wrote that "she used a rich toned voice acceptably, but has yet to acquire operatic routine,"[30] apparently she acquired it quickly. For after only a year with Gallo, Glade signed with the Chicago Opera, and in her first season there sang Amneris,

Coe Glade as Carmen. Photo by Maurice Seymour

Carmen, Dulcinea in Massenet's *Don Quichotte,* and Adalgisa. But if there-after engagements with practically every company in the country but the Metropolitan kept her busy elsewhere, Glade would return to star with the San Carlo from 1936 to 1948.

What was it about Coe Glade? Her looks for one thing: her large, haunt-ing eyes and slight figure, made slighter still by the mass of long, sable-colored tresses it bore. Dorothy Kirsten, who made her debut in Chicago as Micaela opposite Glade, remembered being "mesmerized by her long, bejeweled eyelashes" and "incredible flamboyance . . . a trait which the pub-lic absolutely adored."[31] "Glade," the eminent Chicago critic Edward Moore once wrote, "is the kind of a Carmen that makes the lights seem to be turned up a bit when she comes on the stage and the music to sound a little more golden."[32]

In the late 1940s the San Carlo would begin to slow down, as the 221 per-formances it had boasted in the last year of the war were cut almost by half just two years later. With the rising costs of travel and the growing power of unions, the nation's foremost barnstormer would for the first time have trou-ble making opera pay. And the San Carlo productions in fact looked a little tired compared to the more streamlined offerings of the new itinerant troupes that now shared the road. But the company had accomplished what its indefatigable leader had always wanted for it. And on the principle of "Get them once. They'll come back for more,"[33] Fortune Gallo probably did more than any other individual to develop an audience for opera in America and to provide its singers with steady work.[34]

Chapter Six

"Aida without Makeup"

IN THE SUMMER OF 1933 the intrepid Alfredo Salmaggi engaged the first person of color ever to sing with an all-white opera company in America and in so doing succeeded in making what he liked best: news and money. "The Hippodrome was sold out days in advance, standees were thick in the aisles," *Time* reported under the headline "Aïda without Makeup." "Tall and good-looking, dark enough to need no makeup in the role of an Ethiopian slave, [Caterina] Jarboro revealed the husky voice of her race, rich in texture, not perfectly schooled."

Actually, the handsome "Negress," the magazine said, was only part Negro, her mother being Native American. But as a little girl in North Carolina, Catherine Yarborough, as she was born, had both "moaned the throaty melodies of her race [and sung] Gregorian chants in Latin in a Catholic choir."[1] On the death of her parents, Jarboro had gone to live with her aunt in Brooklyn, then, after a brief career in show business, gone abroad to study and, she hoped, sing opera. Blacks, merely curiosities to Europeans, had been singing with white opera companies on the Continent for several years; some, such as the lovely Lillian Evanti, had even essayed the so-called "white" roles that in the United States they could sing with only all-black companies. In any event, in 1930, three years after Florence Cole Talbert from Detroit became Europe's first Aida *senza trucco* (without makeup), Jarboro had made her operatic debut in the same role at the Puccini Theater in Milan and thereafter made the rounds of the provincial theaters.

Back in America, Jarboro sang just two Aidas and a Sélika in *L'Africaine* (another role designated as dark-skinned) for Salmaggi, then toured as a concert singer. But when her career at home did not do as well as hoped she returned to Europe to sing concert and opera, adding now Tosca and the title role in Gounod's rarely heard *La Reine de Saba* to her résumé, across the

Continent, North Africa, and even in Russia. Caught in France when war broke out, Jarboro worked for the French Red Cross before making it back to the United States in 1942. Of her Town Hall recital that same year, Virgil Thomson (after pointing out how much higher expectations for the black artist always were) wrote, "No soprano at the Metropolitan Opera House is doing that kind of dramatic singing today and few concert artists of any kind are putting out the solid musicianship. . . . I had thought the species extinct, but there it is, a diva, no less, grand and glamorous and beautiful and a thoroughgoing professional."[2]

For Jarboro's second performance, "to darken the stage yet more,"[3] Salmaggi cast the black baritone Jules Bledsoe in the role of Aida's father, Amonasro, creating (possibly for the first time on either side of the Atlantic) an *Aida* with all principals of the appropriate skin color. Known for his work in show business, the Texas native had portrayed Joe in the original production of Jerome Kern's *Show Boat* as well as in the first film version. His opera credits included a Boris Godunov, which he had performed abroad, and an Amonasro in a pickup performance in Cleveland.[4] But Bledsoe's greatest love was the recital stage, where his erudition, consummate artistry, and honeyed high baritone shone in a repertoire ranging from Bach and Beethoven to his own compositions and arrangements of black spirituals. "There is the great certainty, the never failing artistic insight, the tenderness and the vehemence of a true lieder singer," a critic in the Netherlands wrote in 1937.[5]

As it was, Bledsoe, who would die suddenly of a cerebral hemorrhage at the age of forty-two, would remain under the long shadow of the era's other great black baritone, Paul Robeson. Almost the same age, the two had much in common. Both had excelled in college sports; both were intellectually inclined and had special interests in philosophy, history, and languages; both had studied at Columbia University for careers that had nothing to do with music. (Robeson graduated with a law degree; Bledsoe studied medicine.) Both were well known in Harlem, where a fervently artistic black community had grown up in the aftermath of World War I. Both had massive builds and commanding stage presences. And both were versatile singer-actors who had career-making successes in the role of Joe in *Show Boat*.

But there the similarities end, for while Robeson was better looking and more charismatic and had the superior instrument, he, unlike Bledsoe, had little formal training in either music or vocal technique. Perhaps because so much of his career was devoted to the legitimate theater, perhaps because he wanted his music to be accessible to the masses, the Princeton, New Jersey, native simply never applied himself to the study of these areas and so eschewed opera and art song in favor of a more popular and folk repertoire. Historically, the beauty of his instrument and the impact of his personage and influence invariably link Robeson with the great black concert artists Anderson and Hayes, but, in reality, he remains a peripheral figure on the classical scene.

Despite his success in introducing Jarboro and Bledsoe, Salmaggi would make no further move to engage blacks, and for twelve years no impresario chose to follow his lead. Yet in that time an extraordinary confluence of personages and events would bring the black singer to the fore of classical music just the same. It was not for the first time, it should be said, but, happily, it was not as the curiosity and novelty he had once been.

For there had been a time when blacks astonished white audiences with their phenomenal singing of classical repertoire from operatic arias to German lieder. That few had much training was only because there had been neither precedent in their race for such singing nor inclination by whites to teach it to them. But in the mid-nineteenth century Elizabeth Taylor-Greenfield, a former slave with only a modicum of training, was said to have had a voice of such extraordinary range, power, and flexibility that some even dared compare her to her contemporary Jenny Lind, the "Swedish Nightingale." Herself known as "the Black Swan," Taylor-Greenfield had sung for huge, primarily white audiences and for crowned heads around the world. And there had been many others like her; all with the sobriquets that enabled managers with an eye on the box office to promote them not as artists but as acts and attractions. We remember, for example, Marie Selika ("The Queen of Staccato"), Thomas Bowers ("The American Mario"), Lloyd D. Gibbs ("The Black de Reszke"), Flora Batson ("The Double-Voiced Queen of Song" or "The Colored Jenny Lind"), and, arguably the most famous, Sissieretta Jones ("The Black Patti").

As the novelty wore off early in the twentieth century, however, whites began to forget about this area of black prowess, and it would not be until 1917 that, coinciding with a resurgence of interest in black culture that emanated primarily from Harlem, a black singer surprised them again—although this time, for quite other reasons. For it was in that last year of the Great War that a diminutive but determined son of a former slave named

Roland Hayes rented Symphony Hall in Boston to give a concert—not as a performer of an act but as an artist.

Georgia-born, Hayes had arrived in Boston by way of Chattanooga, Tennessee, where he had grown up after the death of his father, and where his beautiful singing in church had so moved one listener that he had played recordings of Caruso for the young tenor to inspire him to try singing himself as a profession. "The beauty of what could be done with the voice just overwhelmed me,"[6] Hayes would recall of the experience. And so he had gotten himself to Fisk University and, while touring as a soloist with the famous Fisk Jubilee Singers, discovered Boston. There, under cloak of night, at his teacher's home so that the white students would not know, Hayes had studied voice with Arthur Hubbard, and though everyone, even his own mother, told him a black man could not make a career in classical music, he had hustled to prove them wrong. He had toured with his own group, booked his own recitals, rented Symphony Hall—to everyone's amazement, actually sold it out—and by 1920 saved enough money to try his luck abroad.

In London, Hayes had rented the best halls and given acclaimed recitals. And after Buckingham Palace called for a command performance, he had become something of a celebrity, patronized by Dame Nellie Melba, entertained in aristocratic circles. And then in 1923, bearing the coveted rubber stamp of European acceptance, he had returned home to sing Mozart, Berlioz, and spirituals with the Boston Symphony—the first of his race to sing with a major orchestra—and electrify New York in a recital at Carnegie Hall—the first of his race to perform music other than spirituals on that most venerated stage. In his first year back Hayes sang 30 concerts; in the second, 125.

As time went on, finding his personal vocal color preoccupied Hayes. In his early years, like most black singers, he had tried to imitate the white sound. One critic in London had even urged him to "apply the same outlook he has as regards the Spirituals to the music of the white writers in order to become a more admirable singer."[7] Ultimately, however, there would emerge no finer prototype for the black aspiring to sing classical music. Hayes's pure tenor, like "fine, spun silk,"[8] his polished phrasing, gossamer pianos, crystal clear (if somewhat stilted to modern ears) diction, and his liquid vocal emission all gave his singing—echoing his persona—an almost aristocratic aura. But his expression remained deeply profound and profoundly elemental.

Hayes sang with nearly every major symphony orchestra, sometimes even operatic arias—Mozart and "Le Rêve" from *Manon* were considered ideal—but, of course, never a role. In recital he sang a repertoire that extended from the fourteenth to the twentieth centuries, as well as the "primitive African airs," as one early critic had called the black spirituals that were growing ever more popular.[9] The black baritone Harry Burleigh, who had been the first to arrange the old plantation melodies in a manner appropriate for the concert stage, had often sung them himself, but it was Hayes who, in light of his elevated status, brought them to the nation's attention. Indeed, Hayes regarded the spiritual as having the same universal appeal as the German lied and, imbuing it with the same profundity, programmed the two side by side.

For a time Roland Hayes stood alone at the frontier. His direct descendants, Robeson, Bledsoe, and Marian Anderson, would make New York recital debuts shortly after his historic 1923 concerts, but, a decade or more younger (though Hayes would sing the longest), they would not have a full impact on the scene until the mid-1930s. Of the three, Anderson followed the Hayes example most closely. Fortunately, she had many opportunities to learn from her idol; for on tour Hayes often performed at the Union Baptist Church in South Philadelphia, where Anderson enjoyed a second home and where her phenomenal range had her singing whatever was needed from bass to soprano.

The "baby contralto," as the choir liked to call Anderson, was in fact the eldest of three daughters. Her father, a coal and ice salesman, had died when she was nine, and her mother, formerly a teacher in Virginia, did laundry. Marian helped out, earning a few dollars by singing to her own accompaniments at clubs and other churches. A local soprano gave her free lessons, then recommended she study with a more experienced teacher. But after standing in line for hours to apply to a local music school only to be told, "We don't take colored," Marian Anderson had then and there resolved never to pursue a formal musical education.

And so, with funds raised by her church, Anderson had studied with Giuseppe Boghetti, a Philadelphia tenor with some singing experience abroad whose real name was Joe Bogash. And she had begun to tour, giving concerts sponsored by black churches and colleges. Venturing into the South, she steeled herself for Jim Crow: the segregated trains, restaurants, hotels, restrooms, drinking fountains. At her concerts she tolerated blacks sitting on one side of the hall and whites on the other but refused to sing when blacks were relegated to the back.

Slowly her fees went up and even the white press began noting her activities. In 1923 Anderson gave a recital at New York's Town Hall, but the critics said she had more to learn: her interpretations were superficial; and, in truth, she had sung the foreign languages phonetically. She went back to work, briefly coached with Frank La Forge, and then in 1925 entered a competition, taking first place over some three hundred contestants. The prize was an appearance at Lewisohn Stadium. The first black to perform at the famed summer concerts, Anderson sang the aria "O, mio Fernando" from *La Favorita* and two spirituals. Notices were good and brought more work, better fees, and management with Arthur Judson; white people began to appear in her audiences. But acceptance was extremely slow. She was, after all, black, female, and American—a hard sell even for Judson; she would go abroad.

With a grant from the Julius Rosenwald Fund, Anderson, like Hayes, settled in London and, in 1930, made a recital debut at Wigmore Hall. Unlike Hayes, she did not make an impression; Buckingham Palace did not call. But on her second trip, a Swedish agent caught up with her. Blacks were virtually unknown in Scandinavia and Anderson was a popular Swedish name, he said. He was sure that with the help of the Finnish pianist Kosti Vehanen as her accompanist he could arrange a tour that would be successful. He was right. The love affair between the "chocolate" contralto and the people of Scandinavia lasted three years and might have gone on forever had not word of her triumphs in the north wafted south.

In 1934 Anderson's three highly acclaimed recitals in Paris caught the attention of Sol Hurok, who convinced her to let him take over her management. It was a pivotal moment; and there was another pivotal one the following summer when, at the urging of the contralto Madame Charles Cahier, with whom she had taken some lessons, she sang for a private audience during the famous Salzburg festival. For, as the great journalist Vincent Sheean recalled, whereas her "phenomenal singing . . . beyond the range of art" left most of her listeners "in a kind of thoughtful daze,"[10] it sent Arturo Toscanini to her dressing room to express himself directly. "Yours is a voice such as one hears once in a hundred years," he told her. And though Anderson would say she did not remember the words because she had been so awed to see the great man, Cahier and Vehanen, who stood nearby, knew just what they had heard.[11] And so it was that expectations were high on that penultimate night of 1935, when the capacity audience filled Town Hall in New York City to hear the black American contralto who had conquered not only Europe and Hurok but Toscanini.

But if, as we remember, the recital was a triumph and offers poured in, the concert trail at home now became a daily fending against racial slights for Anderson. Hurok tried to shield her from them; she tried to pay them no mind. But in 1939, refused permission to perform in historic Constitution Hall by its keepers, the Daughters of the American Revolution—the repugnance of their action compelled First Lady Eleanor Roosevelt to resign her membership—Anderson suddenly found herself at the center of a controversy she had no choice but to address. Asked at the request of the president to sing at the Lincoln Memorial as a response to the DAR's actions, she reluctantly agreed, for, as she would write, "I had become, whether I liked it or not, a symbol representing my people. I had to appear."[12]

And so, in the shadow of the Great Emancipator on a chilly Easter Sunday in April, Marian Anderson stood tall in her fur coat against the cold and injustice. Her heart was beating madly, she would remember, but she sang—her eyes closed much of the time, as was her wont—"My Country 'tis of Thee," Schubert's "Ave Maria," the aria "O, mio Fernando," a few spirituals, and as an encore "Nobody Knows de Trouble I've Seen." Seventy-five thousand men, women, and children of all races and creeds listened, hushed and stirred, and when she had finished they cheered. The moment, of course, belongs more to the history of civil rights than to a history of the American singer. But Anderson was now the conscience of the nation, and by that daunting status would henceforth be measured.

On an August morning four months later Serge Koussevitzky called for a break during an orchestra rehearsal at Tanglewood and, at the request of a friend, while his musicians went outside to relax, grumpily settled himself to listen to a "brown, bosomy, 28-year-old Negro soprano."[13] The conductor was not happy about the intrusion. But as the first phrases of "Oh, Sleep Why Dost Thou Leave Me?" wafted out into the festival's music shed, and the musicians drew near to better hear, it is said that he smiled ever so slightly, and that by the time she had finished "Ach, Ich fühl's," he was on his feet and shouting, "It is a musical revelation. The world must hear her!"[14]

It was a stunning endorsement for young Dorothy Maynor, whose goal had been only to teach, and who had sung for three years in the Hampton Institute Choir before her voice was even noticed by Nathaniel Dett, its famous director. But even then she had pursued a degree in choir directing at Westminster Choir College before beginning intensive vocal study in New York, courtesy of some wealthy admirers—one of whom had recommended her to Koussevitzky.

In any event, the next day, at the conductor's request, Maynor sang a private recital for the festival's "awed music makers,"[15] and then returned to Manhattan to prepare for her previously scheduled New York debut recital. The story of her success at Tanglewood was all over the press—"the discovery of the decade," the *New Yorker* ventured.[16] And on November 19, before she had sung even a note, the capacity audience, studded with celebrities from Roland Hayes to Jessica Dragonette, greeted the cherubic-faced minister's daughter in her first appearance at Town Hall with a tumultuous ovation.

Maynor, of course, survived the tumult, and she survived again a year later when Virgil Thomson called her "immature vocally and immature emotionally."[17] For even as critics agreed she must deepen her interpretations, the public loved the "native Kirsten Flagstad," as Koussevitzky dubbed her; loved the wondrous beauty of her bell-like lyric, the miracle of her long, sustained lines and floating pianissimi; loved the ingratiating smile and unassuming manner. Within months of her first recital, Dorothy Maynor was making recordings and filling concert halls across America.

In the mid-1930s, while Hayes and Anderson were smoothing the way for black singers in concert, two curious by-products of the post–World War black American renaissance provided important points of entry for those inclined to the lyric theater. To Jerome Kern's Joe and Verdi's Aida and Amonasro, Virgil Thomson and George Gershwin now added not only new characters for blacks to essay but whole casts, and because the composers were themselves white, the black performers now got to show their stuff for white audiences in white theaters.

Thomson and his librettist Gertrude Stein had had no particular singers in mind when they collaborated on *Four Saints in Three Acts*. But struck by the impeccable enunciation of a black entertainer he heard on a visit to Harlem, and remembering "how whites just hate to move their lips,"[18] and how Stein's words—nonsensical and difficult to declaim convincingly—must be understood to rationalize the simplicity of his music, Thomson decided to cast his opera exclusively with blacks. After all, the plot—what there was of one—was about Spanish saints, so it hardly mattered what color they were.

Other than Edward Matthews, a professional, in the role of Saint Ignatius, the approximately forty black performers who now materialized on the Great White Way lacked important or even trained voices. Most had come from church choirs and had no interest in pursuing careers on the stage. Indeed, though many thought Beatrice Robinson Wayne from the Harlem choir had quite a beautiful voice and real potential, the soprano who created the important role of Saint Teresa I preferred to stay with teaching. In any case, because of the declamatory nature of the vocal writing, the level of vocal quality and training made little difference anyway. And, except to praise the singers' musicality, intelligibility, theatricality, and enunciation—or, as in a very few instances, to make condescending remarks that their lack of sophistication made it easier for them to make something of Stein's inane text—the press made little of the unusual casting.[19] But if *Four Saints* was not conceived for blacks, had nothing to do with them, and offered them little opportunity to show their voices, *Porgy and Bess* was just the opposite.

Of the large *Porgy* cast, Abby Mitchell was the only known name. Classically trained, a former student of Jean de Reszke in France, the soprano had starred in everything from vaudeville to straight theater, toured Europe with "Abby Mitchell and Her Full Harmonic Quartet," and given art song recitals in Paris, Vienna, and Berlin. Now at the end of her impressive career, she introduced "Summertime" to the world.

By contrast, the opportunity to play the dramatic, difficult role of Serena would be the highlight of the all-too-brief career of the petite Ruby Elzy, who had worked her way out of extreme poverty in her native Mississippi to make it all the way to Juilliard. Like Mitchell, Elzy oozed talent. Before *Porgy and Bess,* she had appeared in a small, nonsinging role in the screen version of O'Neill's *Emperor Jones,* starring Paul Robeson; after, she would embark on a concert career. She had, *Musical America* wrote after her first New York recital in 1937, "a voice of great beauty."[20] But in 1943, soon after rejoining many of her colleagues from the original cast for the first revival of *Porgy and Bess,* the very gifted soprano would die following routine surgery.

For the role of Porgy, Gershwin had wanted Paul Robeson, but the great singer-actor, reaching the peak of his career, was unavailable and someone recommended a young baritone who had recently sung Alfio in *Cavalleria Rusticana* with the all-black Aeolian Opera. Tired of auditioning baritones, the composer was skeptical when the college professor from Howard University with a masters degree from Columbia University (like Bledsoe and Robeson) arrived at his penthouse apartment prepared to sing nothing but classical music. But, as Todd Duncan would remember it, he had sung no more than twelve measures of the eighteenth-century Italian aria "Lungi del caro bene," when Gershwin looked up and asked, "Will you be my Porgy?"[21]

For the role of Bess, virtually a streetwalker, the light-skinned, highly educated Anne Wiggins Brown was perhaps an even more curious choice. But the first black singer to attend Juilliard had read in the paper about *Porgy*, as it was then called, and written to Gershwin requesting an audition. She had sung Brahms, Massenet, Schubert, and even his own "The Man I Love" for the composer but grown defensive when he asked for a spiritual. Why, she demanded to know, do whites always expect blacks to sing spirituals? Then, seeing that he understood she had sung without accompaniment but with great emotion the plaintive "City Called Heaven," and when she finished they had hugged. And so it was that Gershwin composed more and more music for the character of Bess until one day shortly before it opened for a trial run in Boston, he told Brown his opera would no longer be called just *Porgy* but "henceforth and forever" *Porgy and Bess*.[22]

Porgy and Bess opened at Broadway's Alvin Theater on October 10, 1935. Reviews were mixed; there was no run on the box office, but the singers were generally praised. A recording was made only days after the opening using the Met stars Jepson and Tibbett for the title roles: Duncan and Brown were not well enough known, Victor said. But to many black singers, the far greater affront was the stereotypical and demeaning way their race had been depicted. Over the years *Porgy and Bess* would launch the careers of countless blacks, but there would always be a few who refused that particular opportunity.

Just the same, from art song to opera America was learning that whites did not hold a patent on classical singing. Blacks were just as full-throated; could just as easily put their tongue around a foreign language; could just as idiomatically interpret European art music. Indeed, as the venerable W. J. Henderson wrote after Bledsoe's 1924 recital, "Colored men and women have discovered that music may be pursued as a general art and not cultivated by them merely as a specialty confined to performances addressed to their own people."[23]

Chapter Seven

Clouds and Kids

I T WAS MARCH 1938, and the "boiling political pot" Leonard Stocker had at first found "exciting" had become ugly. The American tenor had been happy studying German song in Vienna, but with the Nazis in the city and having taken over the country seemingly overnight, he was worried. "I should certainly hate to go," Stocker wrote home, "but if Hitler tries to go on to Czechoslovakia, it could mean war. . . . It looks as if my well-laid plans for the future are kaput."[1]

In the throes of planning a recital in the city, Alice Tully too had been growing uneasy. Not only had an official asked her if Ernest Chausson, whose music she had programmed, might be a Jew, but the soprano had "had to go through seven [accompanists] before one was approved because he was not Jewish."[2] Seeing her colleagues suddenly start executing the Nazi salute at the Opera, where she was preparing for a guest appearance, Risë Stevens hurried to the manager's office. What, she demanded to know, was going on?

Later that summer, while Hitler announced his plans for Czechoslovakia for anyone willing to listen, Stevens, a leading mezzo with the German Opera Company, joined the soprano Harriet Henders back in Prague in an al fresco performance of Mozart's *La Finta Giardiniera*. Henders, the only other American in the company, was going home. Stevens, recently engaged to a popular Hungarian actor, planned to return for another season, but she first had important debuts to make in Buenos Aires and New York—career moves for which she was clearly ready.

Born in the Bronx in New York City in 1913, the daughter of a Norwegian salesman and a Jewish-American homemaker who wanted only that her daughter be a star, Stevens had been in show business since the age of ten, when she began appearing on the radio. At sixteen, she had joined the short-

Risë Stevens, about 1938. Photo by Annemarie Heinrich

lived Opéra-Comique of New York, and so impressed Mme. Anna Schoen-René in a performance that the famous teacher had offered her a full scholarship to study with her at Juilliard.

Given its close ties with Juilliard, the Met soon heard about Stevens. Johnson saw her as Gluck's Orfeo with the opera department, urged her to enter the new Metropolitan Auditions of the Air, and, when she finished a runner-up to Anna Kaskas, urged her to be Orfeo in the company's new Spring Season just the same. But Stevens declined, opting instead for a second visit to Europe, where the conductor George Szell heard her and recommended she audition for the German Opera Company in Prague. The salary was meager and everything was sung in German, but she would get real experience.

Stevens scored solid successes in Prague; word spread, and Johnson, after making a special trip to hear her again, offered her a full Metropolitan contract for the 1938–39 season. She would earn only a hundred and fifty dollars a week, but she would enter as a principal. And so that fall, after first singing in Buenos Aires, Stevens headed home to garner reviews so favorable for her Metropolitan debuts as Octavian in Philadelphia and Mignon in New York that *Time* said, "Even the morosest critic prophesied an expansive future."[3]

With the arrival of Stevens and, five days later, Leonard Warren, another Bronx native—the two setting off a run of important singers born to Jewish-Russian immigrants in a New York borough[4]—Johnson's American policy appeared to be making a comeback. Because of growing international tensions, Warren had also returned from Europe earlier than he had planned. Twenty-seven years old but a novice in matters operatic, the baritone had been in Italy, sent by the Met to learn roles. Now in its review of his debut, in which he sang selections from *La Traviata* and *Pagliacci* in a Sunday night concert, the *Times* wrote, "His voice is good-sized, round, healthy, and altogether one of the most attractive of the company's younger set"[5]—high praise for the burly baritone, whose road to the Metropolitan Opera had been (unlike that of Stevens) as implausible as one finds among the many motley stories that chart the progress of the American singer.

Indeed, Leonard Warren might well have ended up in business of some kind, most likely his father's wholesale fur business in Manhattan's Lower East Side. He had, after all, taken night classes in business at Columbia University. But with a voice that could not be ignored, the big baritone had also taken some music classes and auditioned for Radio City Music Hall, imagining himself a soloist like the up-and-coming Robert Weede and Jan Peerce. But instead, assigned to the Male Glee Club, he had gone nowhere for three years.[6] And in the spring of 1938 Warren had decided to try out for the Metropolitan Auditions of the Air. He could barely read music, had studied voice for only a year, and knew but one aria, "Largo al Factotum," sufficiently well to perform. Nevertheless, sitting in the control room so as not to be influenced by how the singers looked, Wilfrid Pelletier heard such an amazing voice coming through the speakers that he thought someone had substituted a recording as a joke.

Warren won the Auditions, of course, but Pelly, recognizing the huge gaps in his training, insisted that before the Met could honor any contract he must first study in Milan. Warren spent the spring and summer in Italy, learning roles, imbibing the culture, and courting a young Juilliard soprano from his pensione. The two would marry in 1941, at which time Warren would convert to Catholicism. But by October 1938 it was clear that, given the speed with which clouds were gathering over Europe, it would be enough just to get home.

By engaging a host of new foreigners for the 1938–39 season—the last to see the world officially at peace before the coming conflagration—it was almost as if Johnson had known time was running out. And it was. On September 3, 1939, Britain's and France's declarations of war on Germany sent musicians scrambling to reach their destinations before borders were sealed and the opera world in short order turned on its head.

"Opera Season Opens Gayly Despite Shadow of War," the *New York Times* headlined its coverage of the opening night *Simon Boccanegra*, which starred Tibbett, Rethberg, Martinelli, and Pinza. But inside the paper reported Johnson's concern over the detention of so many of his foreign artists: Maria Caniglia, Mafalda Favero, Galliano Masini, Hans Hermann Nissen, Lina Aimaro, Giuseppe de Luca, and Erich Witte, who were all scheduled to return, and Ebe Stignani, Alessandro Ziliani, Salvatore Baccaloni, and Herman Wiedemann, who were to make their debuts. These important artists were not being allowed to leave Europe. And though Italy would release de Luca in time for the end of the season, it would soon add Lauri-Volpi and

Gina Cigna to the list. "It is amusing to think that we were considered national treasures," Caniglia would say in retrospect, "but at the time it was far from being a joke."[7]

Newly arrived from Europe were only the Italian sopranos Licia Albanese and Hilde Reggiani, the Russian bass Alexander Kipnis, and a Czech soprano, Jarmila Novotna, who on her arrival rushed to help out in San Francisco, where artist cancellations had caused particular havoc for that company's October opening. Americans would have "a greater opportunity to work their way into the high places of the Metropolitan casts,"[8] Johnson told reporters, as always putting the best face on things, while *Musical America* somberly announced, "The days of predominantly American casts are upon us."[9]

Having engaged Americans right and left in his first two seasons, a stance from which he had retreated in the 1937–38 season, Johnson now became mired in another unsettling approach. "Why," one editorial asked after the 1938–39 season, "does the [Metropolitan] management give such a poor chance to many of the native artists it engages? It certainly is a dash to hopes when, after long work to perfect themselves in repertoire, they finally land in the company's roster—only to find that one performance is hastily given them somewhere near the end of the season in an inconspicuous part."[10] And indeed, of the nine new Americans engaged for following season (1939–40) only three—Mack Harrell, Annamary Dickey, and Helen Traubel—would be able to make anything of the opportunity (four if we include the tenor Anthony Marlowe, who, though he initially stayed only one season, returned in 1944 for several solid years as a comprimario).

Winifred Heidt, as we shall see, had a personal problem; Jean Dickenson, as we know, disappointed; and Edith Herlick sang only the smallest roles. But what, one wonders, of the two who came proven stars from Europe: the soprano Henders, who, as Sophie opposite the Octavian of her friend from Prague, bowed and said farewell all in the same night, and the tenor Eyvind Laholm, who did Henders only one performance better? In preparing its readers for Henders's arrival, *Opera News* reported that in addition to having some forty-five roles to her credit, the Ohio native had been an overnight success in Germany, a leading soprano in Prague, the first American ever to sing Richard Strauss's Arabella, and Toscanini's choice to

sing Marzelline *(Fidelio)* in Salzburg. With such a résumé, why would Johnson drop her after just one performance? But there it was; and, unable to re-
sume her career abroad because of the war, Henders, after some concert
work, turned to teaching and domesticity.

It was much the same for Laholm. Born Edwin Johnson in Eau Claire,
Wisconsin, but changing his name so as not to be confused with the tenor
who would so briefly become his boss,[11] the six-foot tenor had made his German operatic debut in 1927 as Canio in *Pagliacci,* then built a reputation as a
Wagnerian in guest appearances from Vienna to Verona. Hitler apparently
liked him enough to invite him to sing privately for the duke of Windsor
and Benito Mussolini in Berlin. It was a concert appearance with Flagstad
and the New York Philharmonic, however, that alerted the Met. Reviews
were mixed for Laholm's debut as Siegmund; some said the voice was too
small for the house. Yet, judging from a few recordings, including a *Tannhäuser* broadcast that he sang with a cold a few days later, Laholm had much
to recommend, and, with a repertoire of some ninety roles, one would have
thought him at least useful to keep around.

But if European experience was not necessarily the ticket, there was still
the Juilliard connection and the Metropolitan Auditions of the Air, both of
which Annamary Dickey and Mack Harrell could claim. Texas-born Harrell,
a victim of polio as a child, had been a serious student of violin before his
voice was discovered, with the result that he received a scholarship to study
at Juilliard with Schoen-René. He had impressed Pelletier with his singing of
Amfortas in a concert version of *Parsifal* and entered the 1938–39 Auditions
on the conductor's recommendation. Dickey, a Sembrich student at Juilliard, had also entered that year, and both would win contracts. The soprano
from Decatur, Illinois, after five seasons of small roles and hard-edged
Musettas, would move on to star in Broadway musicals; Harrell would
imbue roles large and small with his distinctive artistry for over thirteen
seasons.

Although American hysteria during World War I had made it necessary
for the Metropolitan to ban virtually everything Teutonic, this time around
it saw no reason for such drastic measures. Because of the sensitive nature of
the story, it would take *Madama Butterfly* out of the repertoire following the
Japanese attack on Pearl Harbor, but otherwise continue to offer all ten of
the great Wagnerian dramas, even as the singers who sang them—namely,
the sopranos Flagstad, Lawrence, Lehmann, and Rethberg—slipped away.

The importance to the company of the new soprano who bowed late in 1939 as Sieglinde, therefore, cannot be overstated—even if she was already forty years old and had, in fact, graced that stage before.

The daughter of Germans, born and raised in the German section of St. Louis, Helen Traubel had grown up in a home filled with music and from the age of thirteen studied voice with Lulu Vetta-Karst, a tough, chain-smoking former singer who for eighteen years kept a tight rein on her prize student, and may in part have been responsible for her slow-developing career. For as over and over Traubel emerged to make a big impression with her singing, over and over she declined the offers she received as a result with the excuse that she was not ready.

But in 1937, after finally allowing Walter Damrosch to add a role for her in the all-male opera he was writing for the Metropolitan, Traubel had made her debut there in the premiere of *The Man without a Country* in the new Spring Season. And though in this instance her performance had not resulted in the company's offering her anything further, after her triumphant Town Hall debut recital and two appearances with the New York Philharmonic, in the fall of 1939 the Metropolitan, goaded by the press, had been forced to change its mind.

As described in Traubel's notoriously unreliable autobiography, *St. Louis Woman,* the negotiations that ensued seem comical in retrospect, with Johnson first offering and then insisting the soprano make her debut as Venus in *Tannhäuser,* and Traubel refusing and countering with Sieglinde (the only role she knew, she later admitted, but did not tell the infuriated manager), until things got so bad the Met called in a mediator. Nevertheless, on December 28, 1939, it all ended happily when a very excited sell-out audience "heard one of the finest Wagnerian voices ever to turn up at the Metropolitan"[12] make her official debut—as Sieglinde.

"Metropolitan Rings Up Curtain with 50 Per Cent Native Songsters," *Musical Courier* declared as the 1940–41 season got under way—the last before America too joined the ever-widening hostilities. With the exception of the native-free bass department, all other vocal categories were divided almost equally between domestic and imported. Never had the company had so many American singers; all that was needed now, the magazine said, was "a native conductor and an American opera to make it more nearly American than it has ever been in its history."[13]

New imports were but four: Alexander Sved, Margit Bokor, Stella Roman, and Salvatore Baccaloni; with Hitler now in Holland, Denmark, and France, the announced debuts by the French soprano Germaine Lubin and the Swedish baritone Joel Berglund had been postponed. Lubin's letter of cancellation, bearing the postmark of the Vichy government, had taken eighty days to reach him, Johnson reported. Clearly, with such delays in communication it would be all but impossible to make plans involving European artists.

As it was, Italians available for leading roles were so few that nary a one appeared in the opening night *Ballo in Maschera;* rather, the cast comprised three Scandinavians, two Balkans, and, in small roles, a Greek, a Russian, and two Americans. Tibbett was to have sung Renato, but a throat ailment had forced him to cancel all engagements until midseason, leaving the role to Alexander Sved; Stella Roman, scheduled to make her debut as Amelia, was held up in Europe, and Zinka Milanov replaced her. And when the Romanian was also too late for *Trovatore* in December, jump-starting a trend about to gather speed, this time an American, albeit Italian-born, took over in her absence.

She was Norina Greco, and she had come to the United States as a young child and grown up in Brooklyn. New Yorkers knew her from her performances with Alfredo Salmaggi, but she had also toured with Gallo's troupe and sung in Cincinnati and Rio de Janeiro. She seems to have made a good impression in her debut. *Musical Courier* was particularly enthusiastic, calling her "a discovery" and praising "her smoothly produced voice and genuine temperament."[14] As it turned out, though, Greco would stay only two seasons. With Milanov and finally Roman available, perhaps there was no need for her distinctive spinto, arresting on a broadcast *Trovatore,* but also technically insecure.

Greco brings to mind, however, another daughter of Italian immigrants in town at the time who certainly might have sung at the Metropolitan. The Manhattan-born, San Francisco–raised coloratura Lina Pagliughi was acclaimed around the world for her beautiful soprano leggiero and brilliant pyrotechnics. In Milan, where her mentor, the great Luisa Tetrazzini, had sent her for study and experience twelve years earlier, she was a star of the first magnitude. Now she was in New York for her American debut, which she planned to follow with a tour of her homeland. "Florid vocalism as scintillant as that put forth by Lina Pagliughi, 28-year-old American coloratura soprano, at her recital last night in Carnegie Hall, has not been heard here-

abouts since the days of Luisa Tetrazzini,"[15] the *Times* decreed. But the Met
was not biting. Perhaps it was her looks: five feet tall, overweight, and
homely—a "nightingale in the body of a tank,"[16] Elena Nicolai would say. As
it was, Pagliughi had only just begun her tour when Mussolini decided her
husband, an Italian tenor, could not join her, and back to Italy she went.

The Metropolitan tended to cast its new natives in clusters early in the season, and the first weekend of December 1940 produced an especially gen-
erous one. Though the *Samson et Dalila* on the Friday was notable for
Stevens's essaying her first seductress, it also found the baritone Arthur Kent
and the tenor Emery Darcy making bows in small roles. Kent, a winner of
the 1940 Auditions and the brother of the baritone Alfred Drake, himself
soon to be lifted to stardom in the Broadway musical *Oklahoma!,* would
enjoy only a brief career singing small parts before going into the military. Darcy would kick around—or be kicked around—right into the next
decade.

Though Darcy had studied as a baritone, the handsome Chicago native
had, on the advice of Johnson, who heard him compete in the 1939 Auditions of the Air, restudied as a tenor and reentered the Auditions the following year. Though he had not won, he had nonetheless received a contract
and was soon essaying a large repertoire of small roles, at one time singing
both Melot and the Sailor's Voice in the same performance of *Tristan*. Then
in 1944 he got a big break when Melchior suddenly canceled a Parsifal. But if
Newsweek thought Darcy "sang and acted the part . . . with such a credibility
and distinction" that he might be a possible successor to the great Dane,[17] he
would in fact sing a total of three Parsifals and Siegmunds each for Johnson
before returning to his usual beat as messengers and guards. In 1950 Rudolf
Bing gave Darcy a one-line role in the *Don Carlos* that opened his regime,
and three seasons later awarded him a single Parsifal—probably a last-
minute substitution. But when Darcy left the company at the end of 1953, it
was as he came: as the *Samson* messenger.

At the other end of the weekend, Monday was notable for the new baritone bowing as Enrico in *Lucia*. Though born Francis Valentine Dinhaupt
in New York, Francesco Valentino (ultimately modified to Frank Valentino)
had grown up in Denver and studied at the conservatory there before building a busy career in Italy. The conductor Fritz Busch had heard Valentino at
the Maggio Musicale in Florence, called his "the most beautiful baritone

Frank Valentino, about 1937. Photo by Vaghi

voice I have heard for years,"[18] and engaged him to portray Verdi's Macbeth in the June opera festival in Glyndebourne, England, in 1938 and 1939. But the festival was dark in June of 1940; and just as the British were engaging in a desperate effort to rescue more than three hundred thousand of their troops stranded in Dunkirk, France, Valentino had hustled his family out of Italy with the intention of returning alone to fulfill engagements. But when four days out at sea word came that Italy too had entered the war, the baritone, with no other option but to remain in America, had approached the Met.

Of his debut in *Lucia*, the *Times* wrote that Valentino "disclosed a light, soundly schooled voice, which lacks sensuousness but is used to good effect. He knows the routine, and should take his place as a valuable member of the company."[19] And that is exactly what he did. By the end of the season Valentino had sung seven of his eventual twenty-eight roles in twenty-one consecutive seasons with the company.

But the centerpiece of that December weekend—possibly even of the season—came on the Saturday night when from the bouquet of native offerings *Der Rosenkavalier* yielded one exquisite bloom. "Eleanor was the most beautiful Sofie I ever sang with," recalled Stevens, who, just twenty-four hours after portraying a sultry Dalila, was glad to present the silver rose to the radiant newcomer. "Vocally, she was absolutely superb. Of the other fifty Sofie's I sang with, her phrasing and beauty of tone surpassed them all."[20] Truly, no debut that season held more promise than that of the tall, slender, blue-eyed blonde from West Virginia.

Of German stock, Eleanor Steber had studied voice and piano first with her mother and then, her mother having found enough money for a year's tuition, at the New England Conservatory of Music in Boston. Because in the midst of a depression a job teaching piano was thought easier to find than one teaching voice, the plan had been for Eleanor to major in piano and minor in voice. But when the year was up, her voice teacher, knowing a far bigger future awaited his prize student, helped her secure a full scholarship and insisted she change her major.

Himself a disciple of the famous Luigi Vannuccini, William L. Whitney clearly deserves much credit for Eleanor Steber's superlative technique. Indeed, in her autobiography the soprano has given a glowing account of how through first exercises, then Mozart, and later Haydn, Handel, Rossini, and Bellini, the kindly taskmaster somehow instilled in his ebullient student such great bel canto disciplines as floating the tone, mounting the breath— Steber did not sing phrases; she sang sentences, someone once said—and messa di voce. At the same time, outside the studio, she gleaned enviable performing experience, singing oratorios for the WPA Choral Symphony, Senta in the *Flying Dutchman* and Jack's Mother in Louis Gruenberg's *Jack and the Beanstalk* for the WPA Opera Project, and light classics as the featured singer on a program with the unlikely name of *I. J. Fox Fur Trappers Radio Show*. Whitney worked with Steber for five years, then announced he had no more to teach her: it was time to go to New York.

Making do in a tiny walk-up apartment, Steber studied, auditioned, and, because it was "routine in those days," entered herself in the Metropolitan

Auditions of the Air. She had little thought of winning. She had placed only second in the Federation of Women's Clubs' competition and not at all in two attempts at the Naumberg. Yet, as she would happily recall, "People who heard the . . . broadcasts can't understand why I ever doubted the outcome."[21]

It seemed then that Edward Johnson was finding the resources for the Metropolitan's survival right in his own backyard. It seemed too that being responsible for the valuable commodity was bringing his paternal instincts to the fore. By virtue of her age, her temperament, and her history with the boss, Traubel, of course, would have none of being a "kid." What is more, it hardly mattered what he said; her own inclination was to go slowly—Wagnerian heroine by Wagnerian heroine, usually one a year.

Conversely, in light of her experience abroad as well as her early success in leading roles in the house, Stevens—though she would later describe herself as one of Johnson's "babies"—was in no mood to be held back. She had not performed much since her debut, and, with the exception of Dalila, had not been given any more leading roles. She was star material, her husband, Walter Surovy, insisted. (She had married the Hungarian actor, an ardent anti-Nazi, who on Hitler's arrival in Prague had escaped to New York to claim his bride and then taken over her management.) An offer from Louis B. Mayer, who had seen Stevens performing at the opera in San Francisco, therefore, seemed the ticket. She would go to Hollywood.

It would take a while; for if *The Chocolate Soldier*, in which Stevens starred opposite Nelson Eddy (his first film without MacDonald), proved she was no interloper as a movie actress, it did nothing to change her status at the Met. But two years later, offered a secondary role in a film called *Going My Way*, Stevens had the vehicle to get management's attention, and, better yet, to show what a perfect Carmen she made. Indeed, in the role of an opera singer, Stevens tore into the "Habanera" in her one big scene, and then with the film's release launched an intensive promotional campaign that included everything from advertising Chesterfield cigarettes in her Carmen costume—flower clenched in teeth—to making her first recording of the role. If it was, as has been reported, all a ploy masterminded by her husband; it worked. The Met would now pay Stevens a per-performance fee of five hundred dollars—an unheard-of amount for an American mezzo—and offer her essentially the pick of the mezzo repertoire, including Carmen.

Eleanor Steber in the early 1940s. Photo by Valente

Unlike Stevens, Leonard Warren initially had no problem with management's carefully considered building of his career. But as he painstakingly worked his way up from Sunday concerts and his first complete role, Paolo in *Simon Boccanegra,* to Valentin, Amonasro, and Barnaba in *La Gioconda,* critics complained that he always sang loudly, that his singing lacked refinement. Fearing he might end up a house baritone, Warren heeded the criticisms, and for the first time began to apply himself to the study of color, style, and interpretation. In 1943 his back-to-back first performances of Renato in *Ballo in Maschera* and Rigoletto the very next afternoon (because of the sudden indisposition of Tibbett) caught the critics' attention, and that spring he added Falstaff and Iago to his credits. And as he continued to probe his art, studying even with the great Giuseppe de Luca, suddenly it became clear that by dint of hard work, sheer will, and intense introspection Warren had transformed himself into a serious and very important artist.

Though Steber too initially tread water, even regressed to singing Flower Maidens, Rhine Maidens, and Forest Birds after her debut as Sophie, for the moment she was happy just to be at the Met. That her arrival there coincided with Bruno Walter's own proved particularly fortuitous. Above all, the great refugee conductor's presence gave Johnson new incentive to continue the Mozart revival he had proudly initiated in 1940, when he returned *Le Nozze di Figaro* to the repertoire after an absence of twenty-three seasons. At that time, the production, conducted by Ettore Panizza, had boasted an all-star international cast—Stevens in the role of Cherubino had been the only American—and included the German soprano Elisabeth Rethberg as the Countess Almaviva.

Walter first heard Steber in a private audition and, deeply moved, asked, "Child, where did you learn to sing Mozart like that?"[22] He chose her to be his First Lady in the new English-language production of *The Magic Flute* and then in the fall of 1942 his Countess Almaviva—the latter an impersonation the tough critic B. H. Haggin would call "one of the finest I have ever seen on the operatic stage."[23] In her old age, recalling the preparation for the role that would first reveal her as the great Mozartian singer she became, Steber reflected, "How could I imagine that this single role would change my life?"[24]

Chapter Eight

Star-Spangled Banner Time

ON THE AFTERNOON OF DECEMBER 6, 1941, opera lovers across America tuned their radios to the live Saturday matinee broadcast from the Metropolitan Opera. Forty-two-year-old Helen Traubel would be essaying her first ever Brünnhilde in Wagner's *Die Walküre,* and a twenty-three-year-old Swedish-American by the name of Astrid Varnay was to make her debut as Sieglinde, a last-minute replacement for a suddenly indisposed Lotte Lehmann. Thousands of miles to the west, the Japanese carrier *Striking Force* slipped into position. In just under twenty-four hours its planes would lift off, make their fateful run south, and drop their deadly payload on the just-waking island of Oahu.

Late the next afternoon, back from Connecticut, where they had gone to relax after the performance, Traubel and her husband were just sitting down to dinner at the Plaza Hotel when their lawyer told them the news. Eleanor Steber heard it when CBS suddenly canceled her appearance on *The Pause That Refreshes on the Air, Coca Cola,* scheduled for 5:30. We do not know how Leonard Warren learned; and Risë Stevens would later say she did not remember, for, like many, she had never heard of Pearl Harbor. But we do know that that night, while the baritone kept his appointment to sing excerpts from *Cavalleria* at the Metropolitan, the mezzo kept hers to sing on a new late-night radio program under Morton Gould, adding to her previously scheduled arias "The Star-Spangled Banner."

In the frenetic week that followed, which saw the United States declare war on Japan, and Italy and Germany declare war on the United States, at the opera house, only six days after her unexpected debut in *Walküre,* Varnay stepped in again—but not as Sieglinde. With Bampton available and Traubel the one indisposed, this time the intrepid soprano was Brünnhilde herself. Only the week before *Musical Courier* had noted that with Europe "barred and bolted," Flagstad trapped in Norway, and Marjorie Lawrence recently stricken by polio, "Over here new Isoldes and Brünnhildes do not grow on trees and the excellent Helen Traubel, we may depend on it, has her hands full."[1] But now, just as America joined the horror, the tree, it seemed, had put out another bud.

With America's entrance into the war, its opera companies, which had just been getting used to losing European singers, prepared to lose males. At the Met the comprimario tenor John Carter, a cowinner of the 1938 Auditions of the Air, joined the navy almost immediately, and the tenor Elwood Gary and the baritone Clifford Harvuot were drafted before they could even try out their spanking new contracts as winners of the 1942 Auditions. Their cowinners, Frances Greer and Margaret Harshaw, went right to work, but Gary would not get his chance until he was released from the armed forces in 1943, and Harvuot would have to wait till 1947. The baritone would later tell *Opera News,* "After all, you have lost nothing, but rather have gained in maturity both as an artist and as a person."[2] Unfortunately, the philosophy did not fit everyone; Arthur Kent and Julius Huehn would return to sing again, but would never quite pick up the pieces.

A few were fortunate to keep their vocal cords oiled in entertainment units. Eugene Conley and Mario Lanza, for example, performed in various air force shows, notably the popular musical *Winged Victory,* which toured the country and became a film. William Warfield, recently graduated from the Eastman School of Music and known as "the big black sergeant who sings opera,"[3] not only got to sing for the troops but also was able to use the languages he had learned for singing for military intelligence work. And overseas, Theodor Uppman, having landed in France just twelve days after the Allied invasion began, was about to join the fighting when someone, discovering that he was a singer, asked if he would like to audition for the first all-GI special service entertainment unit in France. Thereafter the baritone and a small orchestra followed the front, performing everything from pop to opera for the soldiers, even as battles raged nearby.

Meanwhile, singers not in uniform mobilized to entertain those who were. Most, after making their way through a bewildering number of agencies, landed in the Concert Talent Pool, which provided entertainers for Camp Shows Inc. under the auspices of the United Service Organization (USO). Though variety shows, swing bands, and pop singers were obviously most popular, to everyone's surprise the concern that servicemen would not appreciate classical music proved groundless. "The more than 1,000 men who crowded into the building were as enthusiastic a group as I have ever seen," an officer reported to the USO after a recital by the Met mezzo Doris Doe in Texas. "Frankly, I was concerned lest a voice concert be over their heads, but the way they ate it up soon dispelled my fears. The applause was terrific and the demands for encores so insistent that the concert was closed with difficulty."[4]

Singers went wherever they were asked, even when that meant being driven in secret without being told where they were going. The English soprano Muriel Dickson recalled singing for men "sitting at attention in full military regalia . . . with their helmets on,"[5] knowing only that she was somewhere in America. And they sang everything from operatic arias to the latest popular tunes, though as the show wound down they always encouraged the troops to join them in old favorites. The women learned the audiences liked to see them in evening wear; the male singers found that removing their coats and ties made them appear more accessible. Talking, not just singing, was also important; the key was to be natural.

In 1943 the Met baritone Lansing Hatfield and Edwin McArthur, who learned to play the accordion in case a piano was not available, performed for six months in the South Pacific. And that same summer, a quintet (Camp Show Unit #264) comprising the violinist Isaac Stern, the pianist Alexander Akin, and the singers Frederick Jagel, Robert Weede, and Polyna Stoska traveled some twenty thousand miles entertaining the troops on the islands. Stoska, the one female, was naturally a particular attraction. "Five 'long-haired' musicians from the Metropolitan and concert stage came out here to entertain us . . . the best show I've seen out here," a soldier wrote *Opera News*. "The gal . . . really held them spell-bound."[6]

Even Lily Pons decided it was not enough just to pour tea in her New York apartment for servicemen, and in 1944 she announced a leave of absence from the Met to tour with the USO. With her husband, Andre Kostelanetz, the soprano flew thousands of miles to sing almost daily, sometimes twice a day, for the troops. Debilitating stage fright had always plagued the delicate coloratura, but in war's arena, where the audience was there to enjoy, not judge, it vanished for the first time, and her effect on the troops was electric. Of one Pons appearance in 120-degree heat in Persia, a soldier wrote, "The audience nearly tore the place down with their applause.

We all felt very proud and possessive of her. . . . It's the best way to bring music off its high remote perch."[7]

In the European theater, the soprano Frances Cassard, who that fall would sing Tosca with the fledgling New York City Opera, arrived in Rome in the spring of 1944 just five days after the Germans surrendered the city. Heading north, she sang for the troops as they moved south on the road, sometimes standing in the rain to sing through the open doors of ambulances; in Corsica she climbed over sandbags in her evening dress to reach the GIs; in Persia she sang to them "with dust protectors over my mouth and eyes."[8]

At home the stage door canteens, where soldiers and sailors went for relaxation, always needed entertainment, and performers of all kinds were glad to provide it. On one occasion Helen Traubel appeared unannounced at a Philadelphia canteen, introduced herself as Mrs. Helen Bass, and sang for the men without ever letting on she had just come from singing Wagner with the Philadelphia Orchestra. "'Where have you been, ma'am?' one asked. 'With a voice like that, you should try to get yourself a job in opera!'"[9] The soprano also contributed to the Knitting for Victory Brigade, joined the American Women's Voluntary Services, and led a scrap metal drive to which she donated her own costume armor.

Indeed, contemporary periodicals abound with photographs of singers rallying to the cause: selling defense bonds; visiting hospitals to cheer the convalescent; collecting tin, rubber, books, records; and volunteering their services to the many music programs that were radio's way of answering the call. Some sang on armed forces radio; Steber and Frank Parker sang old favorites on *Your Home Front Reporter,* a program directed at families separated by war; and many of the biggest stars appeared on the music programs sponsored by the United States Treasury Department.

But probably nothing kept singers busier than the national anthem, which opened and often closed every public event. Though she also sang radio, concert, and opera—even a Musetta in the Met Spring Season—Lucy Monroe, in fact, is remembered for little else. By the Fourth of July 1941, "The Star-Spangled Soprano," as she was dubbed, could claim some 1,000 performances (often of both verses) with the 1,776th time conveniently falling on the Fourth a year later. But lest anyone think that was all she did for the war effort, to the contrary: dressed in red, white, and blue, Monroe (a descendant of the fifth president) traveled thousands of miles conducting community sings for the Treasury Department's War Bond Drive at army camps and industrial plants. Later she served as director of patriotic music for RCA Victor.

For those foreign artists who had already become naturalized citizens, American involvement in the war offered no problems. For those who hadn't, it made life very difficult, especially at the outset, when the State Department not only put citizenship for Austrian, Italian, and German refugees on hold but also clamped down on all alien movement. Even Toscanini, because he was still an Italian citizen, needed permission to conduct outside New York City. And though the German tenor John Garris was released after being questioned by the FBI, the popular Italian basso Ezio Pinza, though married to an American, was actually incarcerated for three months, accused of being a spy.

"Music Maintains Morale" was the watchword; but given all the restrictions, it was not easy to keep it going. Transportation, especially, was a constant headache, with the result that just getting to a concert was often a major problem. Automobile factories had converted to war production, so few people owned cars, and those who did faced severe tire and gas rationing; a rationing of just two pairs of new shoes a year made even walking questionable; and public transportation, where available, was unreliable. But even if the audience showed up, what about the performer, who often had to come great distances? Trains were crowded, slow, and, invariably late, causing many a missed connection; troops and war matériel had priority (even over celebrities); and with sleeping accommodations difficult to obtain, an artist might have to sit up all night before a performance.

Blackouts and dimouts posed other problems. Summer concerts were moved to an earlier hour or the lighting of the orchestra shell was adjusted so that the audience was in pitch darkness. Should the enemy be spotted during a concert at the Hollywood Bowl, however, there was a single switch to plunge everything into darkness and a loudspeaker system to give emergency directions.

But with the war machine in full operation money at least was not scarce, and if only they could get to it, people were better able to afford live music than they had been for some time. Touring companies reported staggering turnouts, as did the Met, which even added performances to its season. Moreover, in a move the consequences of which it could not have imagined at the time, the company gave large blocks of seats to servicemen, including many who had never seen an opera before and, delighted with what they saw, promised to come back when it was all over.

On October 14, 1941, the New Opera Company introduced itself at the 44th Street Theater in New York with much ballyhoo and Mozart's rarely heard *Così Fan Tutte.* The production was essentially the same as that given at Glyndebourne in 1935 in that it had Fritz Busch conducting, Colorado-born Ina Souez as Fiordiligi, and the rest of the all-American cast[10] performing Carl Ebert's original staging as taught to them by Busch's son, Hans. That it was also sung in Italian, as it had been in Glyndebourne, however, meant the company broke right from the top one of its stated purposes: to popularize opera in America by performing it in the vernacular.

The idea of making opera palatable to Americans by presenting tasteful, theatrically sound, well-rehearsed productions, sung by attractive young natives in the vernacular, was certainly not new. Jeanette Thurber's American Opera Company in 1885, George Hamlin's Society of American Singers after the Great War, Vladimir Rosing's American Opera Company in the late 1920s, and, most recently, the American Lyric Theater and the Philadelphia Opera Company had already made sterling, if fleeting, contributions to the cause. But hopes were high for the New Opera Company, which appeared to have a great deal going for it: notably, the artistic leadership of Busch; a staff that included such enlightened conductors and stage directors as Erich Korngold, Herman Adler, Antal Dorati, and Lothar Wallerstein; the financial backing of the wealthy socialite Mrs. Lytle Hull and her circle; and, above all, the managerial skills of the world's only female impresario, Yolanda Merö-Irion, whose idea it had all been and who had solid experience.

The Art of Musical Russia, a company this Hungarian-born former pianist had founded and directed during the Depression, had in fact not only mounted important productions of Russian operas rarely heard in America but also kept some 150 musicians employed in the process. Merö-Irion ardently wanted the same for the New Opera; and, indeed, with over 700 singers auditioning the first year, and more than twice that many when it was at the height of its activity two years later, the company would ultimately employ more than 450 performers.

In its first month the New Opera Company gave twenty-nine performances of four rarely heard operas, but it was *Macbeth,* another Busch production at Glyndebourne sung in Italian, that received the lion's share of the interest. Though New York had first heard the early Verdi opera in 1850, the Met had never mounted it; moreover, in the roles of Macbeth and his Lady the company had two exciting unknowns, Jess Walters and Florence Kirk.

Born in Brooklyn of Latvian parents, Walters, whose plans to be a farmer had been thwarted by the Depression, had made his operatic debut singing Silvio *(Pagliacci)* for Salmaggi in 1935, sung with various other local opera companies, and been a semifinalist in the 1937 Metropolitan Auditions of the Air. Given such experience and recognition, it seems strange that he would have auditioned for the chorus and been engaged for the title role only because (after six auditions) Busch and Dorati saw his potential, as Merö-Irion would tell *Opera News.*[11] In any case, there was no question that, with his rich voice and strong acting skills, Jess Walters was, as one critic said, "a real find."[12]

At the same time, Florence Kirk, whose sporadic credits included an Aida with the Philadelphia Civic Opera in 1938, was found to be an exciting actress who had the raw instrument for the formidable role of Lady Macbeth, if possibly not the technique. And she was temperamental. On one occasion, in fact, she became so angry in a dispute with Busch over her costume that she canceled,[13] not knowing Busch had—just in case—lined up a cover: an unknown twenty-year-old by the name of Regina Resnik, who reportedly sailed through the terrifying role with virtually no rehearsal or problem. At any rate, interest in Kirk was tremendous; *Variety* wrote that she "gave promise of being about the best American dramatic soprano since the days of Rosa Ponselle";[14] and she was soon on her way to the Met.

Nevertheless, by the end of the first season, the New Opera was already in trouble, having lost a staggering $153,000—more even than the Met had in its far longer season—despite well-received productions of Tchaikovsky's *Pique Dame* and Offenbach's *La Vie Parisienne* in addition to the *Così* and *Macbeth.* And though a double bill—Walter Damrosch's *The Cloak* (a gesture toward native opera) and Mussorgsky's *The Fair of Sorochinsk*—officially opened the second season, the rest of the its repertoire comprised primarily operas from the first, with the important exception of *Rosalinda,* an Americanized version of Strauss's *Die Fledermaus,* which the company mounted on Broadway as a side venture.

Conducted by Erich Korngold, *Rosalinda* would keep many singers happily employed for some time, among them Ralph Herbert, Dorothy Sarnoff, and Virginia MacWatters. But it also augured a change in direction for the

Jess Walters. Courtesy of Jeff Walters

New Opera, which in its third and fourth seasons added Broadway runs and tours of Lehár's *The Merry Widow,* starring Jan Kiepura and his wife, Marta Eggereth, and *Helen Goes to Troy,* an adaptation of various Offenbach operettas, with the Met star Jarmila Novotna. Someone, it seems, had concluded that light fare and big names were necessary for the company to stay afloat.

Though the mezzo Martha Lipton, who alternated with Pauline Pierce as Dorabella and sang the Lady-in-Waiting to Kirk's Lady Macbeth, has described the New Opera productions as wonderfully prepared and beautifully mounted, with no expense spared, the company clearly could not continue to heap its plate so high, spread itself so thin, and expect its wealthy patrons still to support it. And though by 1945 it had launched a host of fine American singers under optimum conditions,[15] the New Opera, with its lifespan virtually identical to that of the war, seems to have ended when a tour of *Tosca,* announced for that fall, never got off the ground.[16]

Six weeks after the New Opera's inaugural *Così,* for the first time in its history the Metropolitan Opera also opened its season with Mozart, though, with the exception of Stevens, only a smattering of Americans in small roles could be found in the star-studded cast of *Le Nozze di Figaro.* Strained as it was from dealing with the ramifications of the war in Europe, the Met, with some twenty countries represented on its roster, was still wholly international, and Europeans, such as the French mezzo Lily Djanel, who had escaped Paris the day Hitler marched in, still trickled in. But if, with so few new foreigners to look forward to, critics seemed singularly uninterested in the new season, the 1941–42 season would soon find them recharged as Johnson, to stay on top of the changing world situation, began to extemporize in new and sometimes unexpected ways.

Certainly the last-minute acquisition and debut, less than a week into the season, of the popular radio tenor Jan Peerce was something to write about. "Peerce's Met Debut Socks," *Variety* crowed as one of their own bowed in a matinee broadcast of *Traviata*—a performance of heightened drama, especially for the tenor, since the conductor Gennaro Papi had been found dead in his bedroom only an hour before performance time; and, fearing he might be upset by the news, no one had told the debutant someone else would be on the podium. "If Alfredo Germont looked a trifle flustered right after he made his entrance that afternoon, it wasn't debut nerves," Peerce would write. "It was surprise at perceiving, as soon as I sang my first word ("Marchese!"), that Papi was not conducting. . . . Well, this was the Met, I decided."[17] But, in fact, this debutant had seen enough in his thirty-seven years to be ready for anything.

Born Jacob Pincus Perelmuth on the lower East side of Manhattan, the son of Orthodox Jews from Russia, as a boy Peerce had sung in the synagogue choir and played the violin, and as a young man performed with a jazz group. He had started his own Pinky Pearl and His Society Dance Band, which played in restaurants and hotels in Manhattan, and Jack "Pinky" Pearl and His Society Dance Orchestra, which played resorts in the Catskill Mountains. But when Samuel "Roxy" Rothafel heard him, the great entrepreneur, known for his string of theaters and nose for talent, saw a bigger future for the funny-looking little violinist with the big nose and beautiful voice. Throw away your fiddle; think handsome; change your name; and be a singer. And with that he had hired tall, good-looking John Pierce to sing from behind a curtain in his new theater, the Radio City Music Hall.

Accompanied by the Music Hall's famous organ, "the Phantom Voice," as the tenor was dubbed before Roxy moved him in front of the curtain, sang everything from operatic arias to show tunes and his signature song, "The Bluebird of Paradise." In addition, he became a regular on radio: the *Radio City Music Hall of the Air,* the *A&P Gypsies,* the *Chevrolet Hour,* and— as Jascha Pearl—*Forverts,* a Jewish program. On Sundays he juggled two radio programs, two rehearsals, and four stage shows at Radio City. John Pierce was busy and happy and had just one problem: he didn't like his name. So one night Roxy discussed it with him on a live broadcast, figured out it was only the spelling that bothered him, and, with several million listeners as witnesses, settled the matter once and for all with a little adjustment of the letters.

In 1938 Jan Peerce made his operatic debut in the role of the Duke in *Rigoletto* with the touring Columbia Opera Company; the same year he appeared on the radio with the most famous conductor of the day. Arturo Toscanini, an inveterate radio listener, had heard Peerce perform the first act of *Die Walküre* in a broadcast from Radio City and, impressed to hear Wagner sung so lyrically, after a private audition, engaged him to sing in Beethoven's Ninth Symphony. As it turned out, it was just the beginning of a long association. For, from the Beethoven in 1938 to Verdi's *Ballo in Maschera* in 1954, Peerce would sing fourteen different broadcasts with the maestro and earn himself yet another appellation: "Toscanini's favorite tenor."

But now in the fall of 1941, Jan Peerce was singing at the Met, having only weeks before, flush from notable debuts at the San Francisco Opera and Hollywood Bowl, swallowed his pride to audition for a management desperate to solve the problems of a roster suddenly bereft of such foreign stars as Jussi Björling and Tito Schipa.

With the unexpected debuts of Peerce and Varnay so early in the season, things were heating up at the Metropolitan, where the Americans, as everyone had hoped, seemed to be pulling their weight.

"I asked myself, 'Am I nervous?' And I found I wasn't," Astrid Varnay told a reporter after being rushed into her premature bow when Lehmann called in sick. The fledgling soprano had, after all, been born into a family steeped in the ways of music and the theater. At the time of her birth, her Swedish-Hungarian father, formerly a dramatic tenor, was the regisseur for the Stockholm and Oslo operas, where her Hungarian-French-German mother, Maria Yavor, a coloratura of some renown, was performing. A colleague, Kirsten Flagstad, had even helped rig up a drawer in the dressing room to serve as a crib. When Varnay was four, the family had emigrated to Argentina for her father to direct the opera and then to New York, where he died soon after.

Growing up in New Jersey, Varnay, though aspiring to be a pianist, had studied voice with her mother, and, on the recommendation of their now-famous friend Flagstad, coached with Hermann Weigert of the Metropolitan Opera. Considerably older, the Jewish refugee from Germany would eventually marry his student. But first he helped her learn thirteen leading roles, primarily Wagnerian, in eighteen months, and then recommended her to Edward Johnson. How to use someone so young in such a repertoire was a problem. But with Flagstad and Lawrence gone, and Traubel slow to learn new roles, the Wagnerian wing cried out for sopranos, and Johnson scheduled Varnay for a debut in January as Elsa in *Lohengrin*.

It is hard to imagine a feat to surpass performing both Sieglinde and Brünnhilde in under a week's time when you are just twenty-three years old, have never appeared on an operatic stage in your life, and have had virtually no rehearsal. But that is what Varnay did that week of America's entrance in the war. And though some thought the Met thereafter took advantage, pushing her remarkable instrument into an early maturity, the soprano apparently thought otherwise. "Edward Johnson . . . who fathered my career . . . made sure I never had to do more than about a dozen performances a season," she would write, adding, "These included all the evenings I took over from other sopranos."[18]

Astrid Varnay as Sieglinde, the role of her debut

It has been said that Astrid Varnay was one of the "*very* strong ladies" of the era, and that Margaret Harshaw, who arrived singing small mezzo roles the same season, was another.[19] But if Varnay and Harshaw each had an iron constitution and an unwavering appreciation of Johnson, and they eventually shared many of the same Wagnerian roles, there the similarities end.

Born in Philadelphia of Scottish and English ancestry, Harshaw, though her voice was certainly recognized at an early age, had not even begun to study singing seriously until she was twenty; she was already twenty-six when she won a scholarship to work with Anna Schoen-René at Juilliard, and thirty when she essayed Purcell's Dido for the school.[20] "A voluminous contralto, of wide range and rich color, it would appear to have unusual possibilities," the critic for *Musical America* had written, while backstage Walter Damrosch prophesied, "My child, one day you will be Brünnhilde."[21] But in the meantime no one had seemed to know quite what to do with her.

A winner of the 1942 Auditions of the Air (competing when she was six months pregnant with her second child), after a debut as the Second Norn in *Die Götterdämmerung*—she would sing all three Norns, Waltraute, and Brünnhilde in the same opera within a decade—Harshaw settled into secondary roles, with rare essayals of Azucena, Amneris, and Ulrica that mostly brought yawns from the critics. Indeed, eschewing publicity and, unlike Varnay, manifesting only the mildest temperament, throughout the 1940s Harshaw was a singer adrift—her strong portrayal of Ortrud in *Lohengrin* providing perhaps the only glimpse of where her true potential lay.

On December 22, 1941, the Met's new English-language version of Mozart's *Die Zauberflöte* welcomed a new Pamina. The thirty-four-year-old[22] mother of two needed big shoes to replace the much admired Jarmila Novotna, who had sung the first performance of Johnson's second Mozart revival. But wearing her mother's silver sandals for good luck, Nadine Conner in fact "sang and played as if she belonged on that stage and in that company."[23]

The youngest of seven children, all of whom sang, Conner had grown up on a farm outside Los Angeles, where her parents directed and produced shows of every kind in a theater they had built themselves. Nadine had studied piano and voice, won an opera scholarship to the University of Southern California, and from there gone into radio. Moving up the ladder from staff vocalist for a local radio station to Nelson Eddy's partner in *Vicks Open House,* Conner had ultimately hosted her own show for Coca Cola, but at her husband's urging had also sung leading roles with the Southern California Opera Association,[24] where Earle Lewis and Bruno Walter of the Metropolitan Opera heard her.

The new production of *Die Zauberflöte* was a perfect first showcase for the very pretty Conner, whose experience on radio probably contributed to her convincing delivery of the English translation. It was as well for the pixie

James Melton

Lillian Raymondi, a protégée of Frances Alda, who after her debut as Papagena went on to virtually own the role during her decade with the company, and for the boyishly handsome James Melton, who bowed as Tamino.

Melton, a native of Georgia, was another Roxy discovery. The story goes that he had simply planted himself outside the big-hearted showman's door and burst into song, whereupon the discerning entrepreneur had awarded him a spot with Roxy's famous "radio gang." Thereafter, Melton had proceeded to radio stardom first as the most prominent member of a popular male quartet, the Revelers, and then as a radio personality in his own right. In the mid-1930s he had toured with George Gershwin (inexplicably singing spirituals and cowboy songs) and appeared in *Stars over Broadway,* the first of four feature films. But Melton wanted more from his singing; and in 1937 the tenor, who had once joked he "couldn't even pronounce Mozart,"[25] had begun a methodical study of the classical repertoire and in 1938 made his operatic debut as Pinkerton in Cincinnati.

If there were rumors that the Met signed Melton because the Texas Company sponsored both the company's broadcasts and the tenor's radio show, they were put to rest with the first reviews. "Mr. Melton acted and sang with the poise a singer gains only from years of appearing in public," Taubman wrote. "He sang as if the Metropolitan Opera were his domain. It is."[26]

Over the next eight seasons, without ever disrupting his concert and radio schedule, Melton lent his pleasing tenor to such lyric roles as Pinkerton and Wilhelm Meister. Reviews suggest neither costumes nor makeup could help him convey a character, but he always looked good, sang assertively, and, like Peerce, brought the company new fans from radio.

Despite engaging them in record numbers, in 1943 Johnson complained, "Young American singers, perhaps because they can now have a contract at the Metropolitan before winning their spurs, lack a certain humility."[27] Certainly he was not referring to Varnay, who, in all likelihood, had only emboldened him; but he may have been sweating the upcoming debut of the coloratura being touted as the youngest person ever to sing with the company.

To be sure, since winning the previous spring's Auditions of the Air and immediately signing a big-money contract with Sol Hurok, pretty, plucky, eighteen-year-old Patrice Munsel had been an object of fascination with the press. For opera lovers with long enough memories, it was all too much shades of Marion Talley, previously the youngest to sing with the company. Indeed, ever since the police had been called to keep order before her debut as Gilda in 1926, the Missouri coloratura's story had become synonymous with untimely vocal burnout due to grotesque overpromotion. Could the stage be set for a possible rerun? Talley at least had had some stage experience in her pocket; the even younger Munsel, though scrupulously well trained, had none.

Patrice Munsel, the youngest to sing a leading role at the Metropolitan Opera

A dentist's daughter from Spokane, Washington, Munsel in school had excelled in athletics, theater, dance, and artistic whistling. "She could have had a real career in whistling if she'd kept on," her whistling teacher of seven years said. "She did beautiful bird work. Her chirps were sure and fine."[28] But Munsel had decided to cultivate the cords, not the lips, and, with her mother in tow, had gotten herself to New York, found a top-notch teacher, and was just finishing two years of intensive study when her fateful audition for Pelletier and the Metropolitan Auditions sent her straight to the top.

On December 4, 1943, a jam-packed house "applauded vociferously" for the young prizewinner making her debut in the challenging role of the courtesan Philine in *Mignon,* but the next day the critics opted for a wait-and-see approach. "Miss Munsel will find it advisable to go slow before imposing upon [the voice] burdens which, if prematurely undertaken, can bring her disaster instead of ultimate success," Olin Downes warned.[29] But with Lily Pons about to absent herself to entertain the soldiers, Johnson's newest recruit would soon find herself deep in the great coloratura repertoire singing everything from Lucia to Lakmé. Moreover, with the Hurok machine now in high gear, she would soon be named not only Gladys Swarthout's replacement on the hugely popular *Prudential Hour,* but also the best female vocalist on the air; within ten years she would be honored once by *Time* and twice by *Life* with cover stories. But if Princess Pat, as some would dub her, was good copy, she was also an icon for young girls; so many were now trying out for the Auditions of the Air that Rossini's light "Una voce poco fa" overtook Verdi's dramatic "Pace, mio Dio" as the most popular audition aria; and so many were seeking out her teacher, William Herman, he would call his new house "the house that Pat built."[30]

Why did Munsel not go the way of Talley, as so many predicted? "They had no knowledge of my grounding," she would say. "I had an absolute sense of values, of who I was and what I wanted out of my life. This is what I had worked for eight hours a day."[31] Indeed, like Varnay and Harshaw, Munsel, despite her age, was one of those "*very* strong ladies." And the war would see to it that there were others. "We [young Americans] were rushed into big roles, making debuts that were more like auditions," Blanche Thebom, who would do exactly that the next year, has said. "You survived if you had guts and discipline."[32]

Chapter Nine

Meccas and Milestones

THERE WERE NO GALA TRIMMINGS for the first performance of the New York City Center Opera Company on February 21, 1944. The world was mired in a grim war, and the "latest entrant in the Manhattan operatic stakes"[1] was to be the people's opera. "Rhinestone Horseshoe," *Time* headlined the story, to make the point that in lieu of the Astors and Vanderbilts who regularly peopled the Metropolitan's "diamond horseshoe" of boxes, the best seats had gone to an ex-police commissioner and the president of the American Federation of Musicians for a top price of $2.20. But even without the trimmings, for the music-loving trio of the company's founders, Newbold Morris, Morton Baum, and, above all, Fiorello LaGuardia, the city's popular mayor, the evening was the culmination of a dream.

For years New Yorkers unable to afford the Metropolitan had depended on the annual visits of the San Carlo Opera and the perfunctory offerings of Alfredo Salmaggi for their only regular opera. And for years LaGuardia had wanted better for these constituents, many of whom had sacrificed a daily diet of the genre to emigrate to the New World. The Metropolitan's Spring Season and the New Opera had failed in their efforts to provide grand opera at popular prices, but now a viable solution seemed at hand.

For the city had a new theater, wonderfully situated on West Fifty-fifth Street, with a seating capacity of almost three thousand and a sizable stage, to boot. And it came virtually free. Built in 1925, the "massive masterpiece of Turkish bath rococo"[2] known as the Mecca Temple had been the home of the Ancient Order of Nobles of the Mystic Shrine. But when the Order stopped paying taxes during the Depression, the property had fallen into the city's hands; and though the city itself had neither the means nor the machinery to turn it into the municipal arts center it so badly needed, Morris, the president of City Council, and Baum, a lawyer, had determined that, for a nominal rent of just one dollar, a nonprofit corporation could. And so it was that in the spring of 1943 New Yorkers had learned their city was to have a City Center of Music and Drama, and now, less then a year later, they attended its first opera.

To lead the city's new company LaGuardia had selected a thirty-eight-year-old conductor of Hungarian birth by the name of Laszlo Halasz. Since coming to the United States to assist Toscanini with the new NBC Symphony, Halasz had headed the German wing of the Philadelphia Civic Grand Opera and reportedly accomplished miracles as musical director of the Saint Louis Grand Opera. Friends had told him not to bother applying for the New York job because he didn't have any political connection. But when LaGuardia interviewed the handsome Hungarian, he liked him; liked his passion for opera; liked his intense dislike of the star system; liked, in fact, that he was without political connections.[3]

Getting right to work, Halasz had chosen *Tosca, Carmen,* and as a novelty Flotow's *Martha* as the operas for his first season, then engaged Dusolina Giannini and Jennie Tourel to portray Tosca and Carmen, respectively. If at cross-purposes with both his avowed dislike of stars and his wish to "create a place where young talented unknowns could have a chance,"[4] the idea was to ensure an audience and media attention. Though in recent years Giannini's career had slowed, she had a large following of fans who were disgusted with the Met for not having made better use of her considerable gifts. And Tourel, who had sung Carmen in Paris some two hundred times, was the talk of the city as a result of her appearances with the New York Philharmonic and her recent Town Hall recital debut. His stars thus penciled in, Halasz had set to work auditioning the better part of the thousand singers who had applied in response to the ad he had put in the paper looking for chorus and principals to fill out the company's first roster.

And so just four months after his appointment, Halasz had launched the New York City Center Opera with a performance of *Tosca,* and the next morning Olin Downes described it as "of the most refreshing sincerity, competence, and dramatic impact." The scenery was "inadequate" and the orchestra "too small," but he preferred Giannini and the Polish baritone George Czaplicki to the celebrities who sang the same roles at the Metropolitan, and he found much to like as well in "the manly voice and communicative ardor" of the Russian-born, San Francisco–raised tenor Mario Berini, the Cavaradossi.[5] A veteran of Merola's chorus and Radio City Music Hall,

Berini would later sing a handful of performances at the Met, but in his one year with the nascent City Opera he appears to have been indispensable. The baritone Emile Renan, who sang the Sacristan, would also prove indispensable, appearing six times in the inaugural week alone and essaying some thirty-four character roles with the company before retiring in 1959 to become a stage director.

A total of nine performances in one week sung by two dozen singers constituted the New York City Opera's first season. The productions were shabby: the lighting, *Newsweek* complained, was "atrocious"; the sets "left much to be desired"; the gun had failed to go off in *Tosca*, and Cavaradossi was left to fall in silence; and a soldier in *Carmen* had tried to put his sword back in its scabbard the wrong way around.[6] But, *Musical America* ventured, sticking more to the point, "A competent artistic rank and file" had given "unfailingly spirited" performances for sold-out houses, which included many who had never heard an opera before.[7]

Encouraged, the company scheduled two weeks for the coming May. Giannini again opened the season, this time as Carmen, a role for which she was famous in Europe. But the big excitement would come eight days later, when *La Traviata* entered the repertoire. Not only was there interest in the Germont of Mack Harrell, who would be the first of many Met singers to try out a role at the Mecca he had never essayed at the bigger house, but everyone wanted to see Dorothy Kirsten. Indeed, word of this radio personality's successes in opera had been traveling the grapevine for some time; now, clearly poised on the threshold of a major career, the beautiful soprano embodied everything the fledgling company hoped to promote.

Born in Montclair, New Jersey, Kirsten was the granddaughter of a popular bandleader, and the great-niece, or so she believed, of Catherine Hayes, otherwise known as the Irish Jenny Lind.[8] Kirsten herself played the piano and vaguely dreamed of a Broadway career but, to ease the burden after her father, a building contractor, became ill, worked at a variety of jobs, including secretary to a voice teacher, who gave her lessons in return.

A daily fifteen-minute spot on radio had brought Kirsten her first fans, and one, a popular columnist, sang her praises not only in print but also in person to Grace Moore. "We'll make her a star. She has it," the diva, having long dreamed of having a protégée, had exclaimed after hearing the young soprano.[9] And then, after announcing her discovery to the world at a specially called press conference, Moore arranged for Kirsten to study for a year—all expenses paid by Moore herself—in Italy.

Kirsten had savored her time abroad, but with the declaration of war in 1939 she was grateful to escape with a deck chair for accommodations on a ship hastily painted white with red crosses. Back in the United States, she had made her operatic debut with the Chicago Opera in the tiny role of Poussette in Massenet's *Manon,* and the following season moved up to Musetta (to her mentor's Mimì) and Micaela. She also revived her radio career and performed a great deal of operetta. But it was her debut with Gallo's San Carlo in New York in May of 1942 that set the stage for the ultimate launching. "The exact moment a star is born is rarely a matter of record," *Newsweek* had written, "but last week the audience that heard Dorothy Kirsten sing [Mimì and Micaela] . . . was pretty close to being in at the birth of a new prima donna."[10]

Now in 1944, *Musical America* wrote: "It is no longer news that her voice is one of exceptional beauty and freshness. . . . [Miss Kirsten] sings without strain, labor or physical interference. The scale is unusually even, the organ flexible and responsive, the tones pure and unfailingly true to pitch."[11] In his office Edward Johnson heard the buzz and that same fall attended a performance himself. Though Moore had once advised her protégée to try the Auditions of the Air because she had a good chance of winning, Kirsten had been emphatic that she would wait to enter the Metropolitan Opera "through the 'front door' as a star."[12] Now, her contract virtually in hand, the company's chief executive was in her dressing room.

Indeed, attractive and gifted young American singers were thriving under Halasz. That fall, when the company opened with Kirsten as Puccini's Manon Lescaut, William Horne, a Curtis graduate who had won a Naumburg award and would soon create Peter Grimes in the American premiere of the Britten opera at Tanglewood, made a promising debut as Des Grieux. The next night, the Indiana-born bass Carlton Gauld, who would contribute many outstanding portrayals of roles large and small before becoming a stage director for the company in the late 1950s, bowed as Colline in *La Bohème.* And a few days later, fresh from entertaining the troops in the Pacific and on her way to Broadway and the Met, Polyna Stoska arrived as Saffi in Johann Strauss's *The Gypsy Baron.*

"Italy is a good example of a country which was built and continues to exist on 'sand lot opera,'" Edward Johnson had told an interviewer in 1941. "In the same respect, as young and inexperienced baseball players receive their start in the smallest minor leagues, and work upwards to the big leagues with scouts continually watching their progress and choosing the best for the better teams, young singers also graduate from the small stock companies to the larger opera houses. Italy has made itself the mecca of opera by following this principle, and with sufficient backing we can do the same here."[13]

Now, in the fall of 1944, with just such a sandlot company in his own backyard, the Met manager would show how the game was played as just sixteen blocks to the south his company prepared to welcome several of Halasz's singers. What is more, with thirteen new natives and virtually no new foreigners,[14] the season's roster boasted fifty-one Americans—more than half of the one hundred under contract (if only by one)—a milestone.

Amazingly, amid the somber headlines and numbing reports of battles in progress around the world, the *New York Times* still found space on its front page to report on the company's November 27th opening night. Though Johnson again eschewed his preferred white tie and tails for black tie and dinner jacket, the paper said, the audience was dressier than in previous wartime openings. And it thought *Faust,* which had not opened a season since it opened the house some sixty years prior, a timely choice, since Paris, liberated in October, had also opened its season with the Gounod work, touting it as "a symbol of the return of artistic, as well as political, freedom."[15]

But if foreigners took the principal roles, the growing Americanization—seven new natives in the first week alone—had not escaped the notice of the press, and there was exceptional interest in the mezzo making her debut in the secondary role of Siebel. Indeed, the daughter of the concert soprano Estelle Lakin, with whom she studied before winning a scholarship to Juilliard, Martha Lipton had been a singer to watch ever since 1939, when she took first place in the biennial Young Artists Auditions sponsored by the National Federation of Music Clubs. Since then, the native New Yorker had sung with the New Opera and the New York City Opera, and though she had failed in her bid to win the 1943 Auditions of the Air, a private audition had produced the contract. As it turned out, in her seventeen seasons at the Met Lipton would sing only an occasional leading role, but her many portrayals of secondary roles, notably her beauteous Maddalena, sympathetic Emilia in *Otello,* and vivid Annina in *Rosenkavalier,* stay in the memory.

On the other hand, the mezzo-soprano Blanche Thebom, who bowed the next night as Brangäne, would make an equally stalwart contribution in leading roles. When early in 1944 the great Karin Branzell, unhappy about her diminishing status (many of her roles having gone to her Swedish col-

Martha Lipton, whose debut as Siebel in the Metropolitan's first postwar opening night inaugurated a milestone season for natives

league Kerstin Thorborg), announced her impending retirement, her husband had told the press, "She hopes she is making a place for some gifted young American singer."[16] And that, as it happened, is just what she did; though, coincidentally, the gifted, young American from Ohio was of Swedish descent herself.

It was Marian Anderson's pianist, Kosti Vehanen, who, having heard the business school graduate sing in the ship's traditional last-night concert on a trip to her parents' homeland, first urged Blanche Thebom to pursue a singing career. Her only experience had been in church choirs and glee clubs. But with the financial help of her employer, for whom she worked as a secretary, Thebom had gone to New York for an intensive program that included everything from ballet to voice lessons, and then, on signing with Sol Hurok, got her feet wet singing recitals in small towns. Thereafter she had appeared with the Philadelphia and Minneapolis orchestras, and in 1943 she had made an attention-getting Town Hall recital debut. At her audition for the Metropolitan, management said they thought she was a dramatic soprano, but at her insistence they accepted her as a mezzo.

Thebom received accolades and unheard-of column inches of copy for her New York debut as Fricka in *Die Walküre* two weeks after her actual debut with the company as Brangäne in Philadelphia.[17] Jerome D. Bohm of the *Herald Tribune* raved, "This writer in sixteen years of reviewing musical events has never never encountered so remarkable a first appearance on the Metropolitan stage."[18] But if Noel Strauss of the *Times* thought her "poise" that "of a veteran artist of the lyric stage,"[19] in fact, Thebom had never been on an operatic stage and had never received any stage, orchestral, or ensemble rehearsal—she had never "even seen the stage set except as an auditor in the auditorium."[20] Management, it seems, had stayed with its rehearsal policy even in this extreme instance. Because Thorborg, who had been singing the role steadily with the company since 1936, was in the first cast, she received all the rehearsal; Thebom, as a member of the second cast, simply had to learn by watching.

As the American lineup continued apace, two Auditions winners, the baritones Hugh Thompson and William Hargrave, settled into small and secondary roles. "A fresh, manly voice, a fine vocal style and evident musicianship," Olin Downes wrote of Thompson, the new Schaunard,[21] while Oscar Thompson of the *New York Sun* discreetly called his son's voice just "a good one."[22] And in the first *Don Giovanni* of the season, Florence Kirk bowed as Donna Anna.

Since creating such a stir as Lady Macbeth with the New Opera, Kirk had sung under Toscanini and with the Chicago Opera. But now at the Met, her performance brought a mixed reaction. Virgil Thomson praised her acting and called hers "a handsome soprano voice of dramatic amplitude,"[23] while Downes protested her acting and her "forced, spread tones."[24] Kirk hung around for four seasons, covering often—at one time coming out of the audience mid-performance to take over for a failing Aida—but appearing seldom, though she was not the only one of the new Americans to have an uncertain relationship with the company. For from the season's newsworthy milestone crop, the bass Philip Whitfield and the tenor Morton Bowe, a cowinner in the previous season's Auditions of the Air, would survive only a handful of performances in small roles, while, after their debuts in *Die Walküre,* Beal Hober and Jeanne Palmer would enjoy spotty Met careers at best.

That Hober had gotten there at all is impressive, given that her parents had opposed any kind of career for their daughter, who had therefore married Mr. Hober at the age of sixteen, produced two children, and forgotten about music. But after being widowed at twenty-three, the soprano had begun to study again, and a critic attending her Town Hall recital in 1940 thought her "an interesting singer, [who] might even become a still more interesting one."[25] Johnson had listened to Hober sing segments of Isolde and given her a contract, but cast her only as Helmwige.

A native New Yorker, married to the Russian painter Serge Soudeikine, Palmer had been one of the few Americans to sing leading roles with Merö-Irion's first company, the Art of Musical Russia. Now for the Met she sang a chain of Waltrautes and Third Norns, broken by a single performance each of Isolde (replacing an indisposed Traubel, Varnay being unavailable) and Brünnhilde in *Die Walküre,* but, despite promising reviews, nothing else. Of Palmer's recording of arias, probably made in the 1950s, Philip Miller would write, "Hers is a big, vibrant voice which should have won her a larger reputation."[26]

On December 6, 1944, three years to the day after Varnay's stunning, unexpected bow, yet another young American stepped to the plate to pinch-hit yet another grand slam in yet another difficult role she had never performed before. The primary difference was that, though a year younger than Varnay had been, twenty-two-year-old Regina Resnik was considerably more experienced.

Of Ukrainian descent, born and raised in the Bronx, Resnik has said, "I owe my awareness of having a voice to the New York school system."[27] She was referring to the glee club that had been compulsory, the musical play in which she had had the lead, and the teacher who, noting her talent, had offered extra musical instruction. Indeed, the precocious Resnik, after skipping several grades, had sung ("yelled bloody murder," she would say)[28] Wagner's "Dich, teure Halle" at her high school graduation, and at the age of fifteen she had both won the Major Bowes Amateur Hour singing "Voi lo sapete" from *Cavalleria Rusticana* and entered Hunter College. Throughout, she had studied with Rosalie Miller, who, ambitious for her unusually talented student, had been the one to suggest she learn the formidable Lady Macbeth aria—the very one that had led to Resnik's professional debut substituting for Florence Kirk as Lady Macbeth at the New Opera at the age of twenty.

Following that success, Resnik had sung leading roles in Mexico City and roles both small and large with the New York City Opera, and then in 1944 she had won the Metropolitan Auditions of the Air. Her debut at the Met was to have been as Santuzza, a role she had sung the previous spring for the City Opera with such success that one critic had declared "her future . . . assured."[29] But when Milanov became ill and there were no other Leonoras available, Resnik, who knew *Trovatore* but had never performed it, agreed to step in on twenty-four hours' notice. The *New York Times* called the unexpected debut "auspicious," and noted that "one remarkable feature . . . was the fact that despite the impromptu character of her appearance, she handled herself with confidence and authority."[30] Two days later Resnik sang her originally scheduled Santuzza, a week after that Aida for a student benefit, and before the season was out, Leonore in *Fidelio*. Though in retrospect Resnik would say, "Once they saw I could do it, could hold up, they began to push, and I pushed myself," she would also insist that the same "they"—above all Johnson and the great conductors she sang under—protected her by virtue of their knowledge of singing.[31]

With Lily Pons away, management hoped to find reinforcement for its depleted coloratura wing—sustained at the time by Munsel and Antoine—in the person of a tiny coloratura of Russian descent from Connecticut, Mimi

Benzell, who, though only twenty-two, was not without experience. For after making her operatic debut as Hänsel at the Brooklyn Academy of Music, Benzell had portrayed Adele for the New Opera's long-running *Rosalinda,* and then sung Mozart roles with Sir Thomas Beecham in Mexico City, which is where she was when the Met, having heard her in audition, signed her.

If Benzell's ultralight voice was clearly not the dramatic coloratura required for the Queen of the Night, the role of her Met debut, her agility, pinpoint accuracy, and easy high notes sustained her vocalizing of it nicely enough. And, in fact, because the role was in neither the Munsel nor the Pons repertoire, she would sing it more often than the Gildas, Philines, and Musettas, which she also essayed regularly and suited her far better. But when on Pons's return the Met began assigning her smaller and smaller roles, and the downward slide finally reached Yniold in *Pelléas et Mélisande,* Benzell, with experience already in the best supper clubs, would turn opera in for a more lucrative life in show business.

On January 25, 1945, the Metropolitan introduced its last big winner in the American wartime sweepstakes, and the timing was good. For, whereas the war had opened a place for thirty-two-year-old Richard Tucker, the anticipated peace and return of the Europeans allowed management to let the tenor, whose only experience in opera had been two performances of Alfredo for Salmaggi, progress slowly. "'You're going to study two operas for us every year," Frank St. Leger (Johnson's second in command since Ziegler's retirement) told him before his introduction as Enzo Grimaldo in *La Gioconda.* "And you're going to sit on your fanny until we tell you that you're ready to perform them. You're not going to let yourself be used up."[32]

Born Reuben Ticker in the Williamsburg section of Brooklyn, Tucker was the son of Romanian Jews for whom the music of their faith and the hope that one day their son might become a cantor were everything. Tucker, whose regular job was selling dyed silk lining to the fur trade, was himself, however, ambitious to sing opera, and when his marriage to Sara Perelmuth made Jan Peerce his brother-in-law, he looked to the radio star, nine years older, to help him. In time the two tenors would develop a mutual dislike, but in Tucker's formative years Peerce's advice had been automatically sought and sometimes taken, as was his advice to study with the man who would be his only teacher, Paul Althouse.

Though, like Lipton, Tucker had entered but not won the 1944 Auditions of the Air, Pelletier had not forgotten him; as the need for a tenor grew, the conductor had urged Johnson to hear him at the Brooklyn Jewish Center, where Tucker was making a reputation as a cantor. Impressed, Johnson had asked for a formal audition, but he offered the tenor only the brief role of the Italian tenor in *Rosenkavalier* and a great deal of covering. Tucker had refused; he would wait the Met out. Indeed, when Johnson called again there was no further discussion of either secondary roles or covers.

There had not been many Jews on Metropolitan rosters in the company's early history. Undoubtedly, some on its board would have preferred there had been none, and the ethnicity of those already there was generally kept quiet. But the engagement of Tucker, whose reputation had been made in the synagogue, now brought out in the open the fact that in recent years the company had become awash with excellent Jewish singers—who moreover were not necessarily émigrés in flight from Hitler but were born in America, primarily New York. Most had Anglicized names: Warren, Stevens, Weede, Peerce, Lipton, Resnik, Tucker; soon to come were Robert Merrill and Roberta Peters. But now, though he too had changed his name, Tucker openly manifested his Jewishness more than any of these colleagues and, in bringing the same fervent religiosity and Hebraic pathos to his art that he brought to his faith, came to personify the Jewish-American opera singer at his most elemental.

Chapter Ten

1945

DESPITE THE DANK FOG and periods of pouring rain, despite, moreover, Hitler's New Year's declaration only hours earlier that the war would not end until 1946 unless by a German victory, the nearly 750,000 revelers in Times Square waiting to see the year in were optimistic. There were reports that General Patton was beginning a full-scale offensive, that Berlin and Tokyo were under heavy air attack, that the Russians were closing in on Budapest. And for the first time since 1941 the golden globe atop the Times building was lit. As it dropped, "huge Roman numerals were seen flashing 1945." Surely the final "V" stood for Allied victory. Though amplified one hundred times, Lucy Monroe's "Star-Spangled Banner" could hardly be heard for all the cheering.[1]

Operagoers almost certainly joined in, having wandered up from the Met three blocks to the south after the evening's performance of *La Bohème*. The wintry scenes and festive second act made the Puccini a nice choice for New Year's Eve, and war had not diminished the American love affair with Italian opera, or, for that matter, with opera in general. Tickets were still at the reduced wartime prices of two to six dollars, and the Met regularly sold out, even if casts were no longer as studded with European stars as with their homegrown replacements. Indeed, with Lily Pons now devoting herself to war work and thus unavailable, Patrice Munsel had recently essayed her first Lucia and her first Rosina; Josephine Antoine, herself busy singing at rallies for the War Finance Program, had helped out with Gildas; and there were high hopes that the pert and pretty Mimi Benzell would be able to handle other of the coloratura heroines so dear to Met audiences. After all, according to articles in *Newsweek* and *Life*—"The Met Grows Younger" and "The Met Has Big Crop of Opera Glamour Girls," respectively—to be young and good-looking was in fashion for opera singers.

But if anyone was worried about the old values, there was no reason to be. For in 1945, as in every year, opera was still all about great singing, a fact that couldn't have been clearer than on New Year's Day, when, as Aida, Zinka Milanov "demonstrated the newly acquired deft control of her higher voice with deeply gratifying results."[2] It was still about sentiment, as on February 23, when Lotte Lehmann returned for a single performance as the Marschallin and received one of the biggest ovations of the season. It was still about individual drama and achievement, as on February 3, when Traubel fell ill and "almost at the twelfth hour" Astrid Varnay stepped in and "without the benefit of so much as a solitary orchestra or stage rehearsal . . . [was] sensational" essaying her first Isolde.[3] And it was still about history and tradition, as on March 14, when for the first time at the Met, a mezzo, Jennie Tourel, instead of the usual coloratura soprano, sang the role of Rosina in *Barbiere di Siviglia* as it had originally been written.

Because there was no money, there were no new productions in 1945. But there were revivals; and four days into the new year, amid reports of Americans storming German outposts in ice and fog in the Battle of the Bulge, the return of *Pelléas et Mélisande* moved Olin Downes to write, "The opera falls on the ears in these days of turmoil and catastrophe like a blessed benediction from another world."[4] No matter that he barely mentioned Lawrence Tibbett as Golaud, a role well suited to a singer trying to avoid exposing his vocal problems: the great baritone, now celebrating twenty years since his landmark performance as Ford, was about to get plenty of press for his performance in another medium.

Indeed, Tibbett, who for some time had been looking to radio to revive his faltering career, was about to replace none other than Frank Sinatra as the star of the top-rated popular music program *Your Hit Parade*. It was a gutsy move for both Tibbett and the show's sponsors, Lucky Strike cigarettes—a move that had, in fact, sent shock waves through both the popular and the classical music worlds. The screaming "bobby-soxers" who every Saturday swarmed the CBS Radio Theatre on Broadway and Fifty-third Street to swoon over "the Voice," as Sinatra was known, would certainly not accept an aging opera singer in his stead. But on January 6, with Tibbett beside him, the crooner told his fans, "Now listen, this man is a friend of mine. You be very nice and sweet to him."[5] And they were, as every week for the next six months (for a weekly paycheck of forty-five hundred dollars and all the cartons of Luckies he wanted), Tibbett sang popular songs, ballads, and the number-one hit of the week—almost invariably Cole Porter's "Don't Fence Me In"—without incident and with enough success to inexplicably send the ratings up seven points.

In March, as though anticipating events, the Met returned *Fidelio* to the repertoire. "No other work of the operatic stage is more timely, and at present more symbolic than this high song of freedom and dignity," *Musical Courier* wrote. "Pizzaro [sic] seems to be the incarnation of all the dictators who are now doomed, and *Fidelio* stands for all the forces at work to seal the fate of those oppressors of mankind."[6] The opera had served to introduce Bruno Walter to Metropolitan audiences in 1941, when the allies were suffering defeat after defeat; now its revival for the eminent conductor's return to the company after a year's sabbatical found the Nazis in retreat and the end of their tyranny in sight.

This time, however, it was being performed in an English translation, and, presumably to better enunciate the words, the natives were assuming several of the challenging roles in lieu of such legendary European veterans as Kirsten Flagstad and Herbert Janssen. Resnik was Leonore, Greer was Marzelline, Hugh Thompson was Fernando, and in the role of Don Pizarro was Kenneth Schon. Schon, of German and Scandinavian descent, had tried out for and failed to win the Auditions of the Air. But after working with him privately, Walter had apparently found reason to recommend the big baritone.

Was casting a masterpiece of such singular profundity with so many young Americans going too far? Most critics thought so. "The real flaws of the performance lay in the immaturity of the principals, the inadequacy of their technical and stylistic accomplishments, their generally limited emotional resources and capacities of expression," Herbert Peyser wrote. He could applaud Resnik's "sincerity" and the "evident earnestness and study with which she had striven to master [Leonore's] difficulties," he said; but he regretted that the Met had cast one so young in a role of such "unmerciful exactions."[7] Indeed, following on the heels of disastrous performances of Rimsky-Korsakov's *Zolotoy Pyetushok* (*The Golden Cockerel*), also sung in English by virtually all-American casts, for a brief time in the spring of 1945 some questioned if the Americanization of the Met—at its peak now as far as numbers were concerned—was justifiable.

In 1945 radio, celebrating its silver anniversary and dispensing war news as fast as possible, put its best foot forward as it observed an uncustomary number of historical events, some calling for music. The death of Franklin Delano Roosevelt in April, in particular, "precipitated . . . an unprecedented emergency . . . with more [music] on the air at this time than ever before in radio's history."[8] Music editors would pronounce four days of music in tribute to Roosevelt on all networks, the outstanding musical event of the year.

Otherwise, radio and singers continued with their love fest. In 1945 Robert Merrill, who in March became the newest Metropolitan Auditions of the Air winner, got his own show, as did John Baker, a comprimario at the Met. If you were not well known, it was good to have a gimmick for your show; Baker's was that every week an unknown but promising female singer would be selected from a different state to be his guest. Another new show, *Harvest of Stars,* hosted by James Melton, tried spotlighting a different geographical section of the United States each week. But no one was more excited than Eleanor Steber, who would not only earn two hundred thousand dollars singing 208 performances around the country in 1945 but also sign a five-year contract with *Voice of Firestone* to appear on every other one of its prestigious broadcasts (or twenty-six annually). "An utterly fantastic development," she would say.[9]

Recording, banned since the summer of 1942, resumed in 1945. Everyone was enthusiastic about RCA Victor's plastic records, which sold for a hefty two dollars each—twice the price of shellac recordings, but unbreakable. And though there could be no regular production until wartime restrictions on certain materials were lifted, television, expected to be a natural for opera, was becoming a household word if not yet a household appliance.

Though Hollywood had also cut back during the war, in 1945 Lauritz Melchior won new fans by showing just how folksy an opera singer could be in *The Thrill of Romance,* while the movie star Jeanette MacDonald chose this year to try her hand at opera. Broadway, whether dimmed or burning brightly, as it would soon again, boomed. Musicals were as popular as ever; Rodgers and Hammerstein's *Oklahoma!* was still selling out and the team's latest, *Carousel,* which had Christine Johnson of the Met as Nettie Fowler, was the hit of the season. Other Met singers on the Great White Way included Irra Petina in *Song of Norway,* Lansing Hatfield in *Sadie Thompson,* and Annamary Dickey and George Rasely in *Hollywood Pinafore.* Bonelli toured with *The Great Waltz,* the story of Johann Strauss, and Jan Kiepura with the New Opera's *Merry Widow.*

"1945 is a year of unparalleled opportunity for young singers. New trends, new conditions and new musical consciousness are in the air . . .[though] underlying all, there is a feeling of uncertainty, a mingling of alertness, expectation and anxiety, doubtless due to the unusual conditions of the war period," the erstwhile soprano Mary Craig began her first column of the year for *Musical Courier.*[10] Indeed, as world events moved exponentially faster, Margaret Truman would remember the year as one of "multiplied crises."[11] The deaths of Roosevelt, Mussolini, and Hitler in just eighteen days; the succession to the presidency of Harry Truman; the meetings at Yalta and Potsdam; the Battle of the Bulge; the Allied advance into Germany and the Russian advance from the east; the surrender at Rheims; the firebombing of Japan; MacArthur's return to the Philippines; Iwo Jima, Corregidor, Okinawa, Hiroshima, Nagasaki, and the Japanese surrender—all created a chain of banner headlines.

Not fit for a headline, certainly, but to be applauded was the news that allied troops were showing impressive sensibility in recognizing the importance of restoring culture in the defeated regions of central Europe they now occupied. Finding Salzburg's Festspielhaus unscathed, for example, Americans helped get the great festival back on its feet by that very summer, and using costumes, scores, and other regalia the troops had found hidden in the salt tunnels at Heimboldhafen, they would join with the Russians to get the Berlin Opera back in operation as well.

More complicated was the problem of doing the right thing by those artists suspected of either collaborating with or performing for the enemy. Rumors abounded. "Artists who felt they had been unjustly neglected during the previous years now moved into the operatic scene with the determination to oust, if possible, those who had been more successful. It was easy to say, or to hint strongly, that success in their rivals had been due to political rather than to artistic reasons," the baritone Tito Gobbi, who had lain low and suffered hugely, recalled.[12] "I am no Communist! I am no Fascist! I sing good and Mussolini give me a medal! So what!" Tito Schipa answered reporters who questioned his wartime activity on the eve of his return to America.[13] And while some, like Flagstad, stood up to their accusers, others, like the French soprano Germaine Lubin, who was imprisoned for three years as a result of her Nazi friendships, saw their careers collapse.

With much of Milan's renowned opera house destroyed during a bombing attack in 1943, First Lieutenant Clement C. Petrillo, a concert pianist from Philadelphia, took charge of the reconstruction. But if the Milanese thought three years a long time to wait, the Viennese would have to wait a decade for their beloved opera house to reopen after the direct hit it received from American bombers in the last days of the European war. On the other hand, Parisians didn't have to wait a minute to reclaim their opera house, which had hosted German companies during the occupation. And Londoners, waiting for Covent Garden to reconvert from its wartime service as a dance hall, celebrated the return of the Sadler's Wells Company to its North London home with the world premiere of Benjamin Britten's *Peter Grimes* that very June.

That summer, as the war in the Pacific intensified, American singers again kept their international appearances restricted to the American continents. With Europeans as unavailable in South America as in the United States, and with too few singers of their own to satisfy the Latin appetite for opera, impresarios, mainly in Rio de Janeiro and Buenos Aires, had been forced "to gamble on U.S. imports" for their wartime seasons. But if initially they were "surprised that Americans could sing opera at all,"[14] South Americans had ended up liking the Yankees, who in turn were glad for such an important outlet during their summers—so glad, in fact, that they would continue to make the trek long after the war was over.

Meanwhile, at home the artists made the usual rounds. At New York's Lewisohn Stadium Swarthout and Kullman starred in *Carmen;* Melton, MacWatters, Merrill, and Pons were soloists with the orchestra; and on the night of August 6, back from a tour of eleven Latin American countries where he had inaugurated a Community Concert series, Todd Duncan sang spirituals for a hushed crowd of five thousand, who only that day had heard about a new kind of bomb their country had dropped in Japan.

Since V-E Day, the indefatigable Grace Moore had been singing almost nonstop for American troops abroad, giving daily concerts in the Sportsplatz in Nuremberg, where the Nazis had held conventions and rallies, and even at the Festspielhaus in Bayreuth, where the GIs presented her with a copy of the guest book from Wahnfried signed by all the Nazi leaders. But the climax of her tour had unquestionably been her appearance on the balcony of the Opéra in Paris following her sold-out concert on July 24. "Our Grace," and "Vive l'Amérique," the estimated half-million Parisians shouted from below, while the diva, thrilled to be back in the land where she had spent such a happy time before the war, celebrated their liberation by singing the two national anthems. Now back at Lewisohn Stadium, "bedecked in plumes and spangles" on the night of August 14, "only a few hours after the Japanese acceptance of the peace ultimatum," Moore added Albert Malotte's popular setting of "The Lord's Prayer" to her scheduled numbers, then joined the audience in a final "Auld Lang Syne."[15]

September found Todd Duncan back in the news with the announcement that the New York City Opera had engaged the baritone for the roles of Tonio in *Pagliacci* and Escamillo in *Carmen*. The Porgy creator was "one of the finest artists ever developed by his race," Halasz said, and the company was simply fulfilling its promise to present the best of American talent.[16]

It had been more than a decade since the Italian Salmaggi had hired blacks for his all-white company, thereby desegregating opera in America. But Jarboro as Aida and Bledsoe as Amonasro had sung only characters designated as black—characters that whites traditionally blackened themselves to play. Now in 1945, by assigning a black man to portray characters clearly intended as white, the Hungarian Halasz was lowering the racial barriers yet further. In two months time the Brooklyn Dodgers would sign the first black to play for organized baseball, but it would be two years before Jackie Robinson made the major leagues. Duncan was already there. "Mr. Halasz liked my singing, but I also knew that because I was an oddity, I was box-office," the baritone would say decades later. "A lot of the board members told him, 'You can't have a Negro.' But Mr. Halasz said 'We're going to have him' and that was it."[17]

And so on the second night of the young company's second fall season, September 28, Duncan made his bid. Opinions varied: *Musical America* found the baritone "somewhat self-conscious and unduly careful";[18] *Musical Courier* thought he "won an unqualified success, with singing as finished as it was expressive . . . and acting of resource and vividness."[19] As to the significance of the event: most of the press said nothing; but *Newsweek* headlined the story "Porgy to Pagli" and nailed it as the milestone it was. "This Tonio," said the popular weekly, "told a special story of his own . . . for he

Todd Duncan, about 1945, when he integrated
the New York City Opera

was Todd Duncan, famous as Porgy in Gershwin's *Porgy and Bess*. And, as far as American major-opera-company records reveal, he is the first Negro ever to have sung an operatic role not written with his race in mind."[20]

But if Duncan was having a big year, so was Doris Doree, courtesy as well of the New York City Opera. Doree's story was unusual. Born in Newark, New Jersey, the petite soprano had acted, sung in nightclubs, danced ballet at Radio City, managed a ballet school, and directed her own traveling vaudeville company; only when she suddenly had to fill in for an indisposed singer in one of these productions had she discovered she had an important voice. When a series of recommendations landed her at the Met for a season, the company had barely used her. But City Opera had been only too glad to engage such talent. "Miss Doree's singing . . . was so clear and vital in tonal quality, so forceful in its dramatic impact and so unremittingly true to pitch that one marveled that she had not been entrusted with more important duties while she was a member of the Metropolitan Opera," *Musical America* wrote of her debut as Senta in the *Der Fliegende Holländer*, which opened the spring season.[21] And now in the fall, adding Santuzza and Tosca to her credits, she again tore up the stage of the Mecca Temple with her fine voice and vivid dramatics.

Others new to the roster included a patrolman, Ian Cosman, who sang Turiddu, the radio singers Rosemarie Brancato and Lucille Manners, Violetta and Mimì respectively, and the mezzo Winifred Heidt as a Carmen "that would have done honor to any opera house."[22]

In 1945 Eileen Farrell married a cop, Christina Carroll a violinist, Licia Albanese a stockbroker, and the sopranos Hilda Reggiani and Serafina Bellantoni the tenors Bruno Landi and Anthony Amato, respectively. The Homers, the renowned contralto Louise and the song composer Sidney, celebrated their fiftieth wedding anniversary.

To be sure, the war was over and family was on everyone's mind. As servicemen returned to their jobs, the women who had filled them in their absence turned their attention back to full-time homemaking. After all, family was what every woman, including sopranos and mezzos, was supposed to want. In an article in the *Ladies' Home Journal* called "I Thought My Life Was Over," Lois White Eck, a former soprano who had sacrificed her career for her growing family, wrote, "There is more than one way to have a career, and old Mother Nature seems to have forced me to find the better way."[23] Happily for the soprano Jessye Norman and the mezzo Frederica von Stade, born that year, the choice would not be quite so drastic when their turn came.

Three noted writers on vocal matters died in 1945: Leonard Liebling, editor-in-chief of *Musical America,* Oscar Thompson, critic for the *New York Sun* and author of *The American Singer,* and Pierre Key, founder of *Musical Digest,* editor of an annual musical yearbook, and author of a book on Caruso. The Irish tenor John McCormack's passing drew two thousand mourners to New York's St. Patrick's Cathedral for a requiem mass. The composers Jerome Kern and Béla Bartók died in America; Mascagni, whose son had been killed in Ethiopia in 1936, died in Italy. The baritone Armando Borgioli was killed there as well when Allied bombers hit the train he was traveling on. And Anton von Webern, leaving tiny songs—atonal, minimal, exquisite—was accidentally shot and killed by an American soldier during the occupation of Austria.

With the war on both fronts truly over, opera first-nighters around the country could again flaunt their jewels and furs without embarrassment. San

Francisco opened its season on September 25 with Risë Stevens, fresh from her success in the movie *Going My Way*, taking on Carmen "with a vengeance à la Hollywood" opposite the Canadian Raoul Jobin. Escamillo was deemed a "poor choice" for Mack Harrell's debut with the company, but, as Micaela, Eleanor Steber, the other newcomer, won plaudits for the "best singing and most credible acting of the evening."[24] Steber joined Lehmann and Stevens in *Rosenkavalier;* Traubel, Melchior, and Janssen led *Tristan* and *Die Walküre;* and Pinza was Boris Godunov. Merola's new local singers included Evelynn Corvello as Olympia in *The Tales of Hoffmann,* and Robert Mills, a bus driver, as the Commendatore in *Don Giovanni* and Monterone in *Rigoletto.* Claramae Turner, a former chorister, continued in choice small roles, while the chorus welcomed Lucy Armaganian, an Armenian American who as Lucine Amara would soon sing solo at the Met. A Greek American who had changed her name from Maria Kaloyeropoulou auditioned. Denied a contract, Maria Callas vowed never to sing for Merola's company—and kept her word.

The glitter and glamour of prewar times also returned to the Chicago Civic, at this time managed by Fausto Cleva, for its opening *Manon* on October 8. With the exception of Bidù Sayão in the title role, however, the singing was less than glittering. "One of two courses is possible: let us have great opera or let us not have it at all," Chicago's *Musical Leader* concluded.[25] One more season, and it would be the latter.

By contrast, Pelosi's Philadelphia La Scala was in high gear, as was the overly ambitious, short-lived (as it turned out) Boston Grand Opera, which opened its second season on October 1 with a tour that included two weeks in New York City, followed by three at home in the old Boston Opera House.

On November 26, 1945, the Metropolitan Opera opened its first postwar season with a revival of Wagner's *Lohengrin* and "a flash of diamonds and a show of ermine and top hats unequaled at 39th and Broadway in more than a decade."[26] The conductor Fritz Busch in his Met debut generated the most interest; the Swedish tenor Torsten Ralf, also bowing with the company, was Lohengrin; and Traubel was Elsa. The Truman women, first lady and first daughter, attended. Backstage after the performance, Margaret, who herself harbored ambitions to be an opera singer, asked her fellow Missourian Traubel for her autograph—the first of many such encounters in what would soon become a thorny student-teacher relationship.

Because there were still so many shortages, plans for mounting Verdi's *Don Carlos,* Strauss's *Elektra,* and Prokofiev's *War and Peace* were scratched, which left Puccini's *Il Tabarro* as the company's only new production. And for the first time since World War I, there would be no complete *Ring.* Johnson depended too much on the increasingly undependable Melchior (Ralf notwithstanding) and simply could not take the risk. But *Madama Butterfly* was back, the Connecticut Opera Association having hazarded the Puccini favorite (dropped by all American companies after Pearl Harbor) the previous April with nary a complaint.

Instead of the expected flood of European artists, only three would make debuts in the Met's first post–World War II season: the Italian basso Giacomo Vaghi, and two Swedes, the tenor Ralf and the baritone Joel Berglund. But the return of Jussi Björling, yet another Swede, was also anticipated. During the war Swedish artists, though forced to restrict their careers to Scandinavia, had been fortunate that their country's neutrality permitted not only a full schedule of operatic activity but also one without competition from visiting artists. With commercial transatlantic travel reestablished, it was to be expected they would be first out of the gate. The Canadian soprano Pierette Alarie, a runner-up in the Auditions, and the Chilean tenor Ramon Vinay were also slated to make debuts. As for the natives: Kirsten and the two Auditions winners, Thomas Hayward and Robert Merrill, would commence long careers with the company; the sopranos Florence Quartararo and Mary Henderson would bow later in the season. More refugees, Leo Mueller and Max Rudolf, joined the musical staff. And Lily Pons was back in the saddle.

Meanwhile, Johnson's kids were in fine fettle. Munsel sang her first Juliette, Thebom her first Venus; and, just a week after taking on her first Laura in *Gioconda,* Stevens sang her first Met Carmen. In addition, Resnik anticipated her first Tosca in January and Leonard Warren his first Iago in February. Tucker replaced his ailing brother-in-law, Peerce, to try out his first Met Alfredo in a performance particularly memorable for the debut of their mutual friend, Bob Merrill. But as the same influenza that felled Peerce grew to epidemic proportions, by the end of the season's fourth week some twenty-four singers, including four leads and a substitute for one of the leads in a single performance of *Tannhäuser,* had canceled.

As the holidays approached, shortages of virtually everything remained acute. But the singing telegram was back; better yet, nylon stockings; and, best of all, the feeling that it was all right to be festive.

Chapter Eleven

Mushrooms and Lemonade

L IKE MUSHROOMS," Mary Craig wrote in *Musical Courier.* "Opera houses and operatic performances are springing up like mushrooms."[1] It was 1945, and, in fact, the annual survey by *Opera News* reported some 113 companies in the United States, up 25 in that one year alone.[2] None, of course, offered seasons remotely comparable in length to those of the provincial companies in Europe. Nevertheless, if a singer was clever, he might soon be able to string enough of them together to fashion a viable career without Europe, without the Met, without even the help of radio or concert.

Richard Torigi did. The Brooklyn baritone neither was comfortable with microphones nor "even knew there was such a thing as song."[3] But he had taken some voice lessons, memorized some roles, and set his sights on a career in opera. The war had gotten in the way, but the timing at least was good, for the mushrooms had barely begun to show; and by the time he returned from the Pacific, a first lieutenant in the Air Corps, they were sprouting nicely.

And so he began by enrolling in a new school in Manhattan. Founded to help GIs like himself, whose careers or studies in the performing arts had been interrupted by service to their country, the American Theater Wing boasted superb teachers of all kinds. Torigi took free lessons in voice, acting, fencing, and languages, and he learned standard stagings for the standard roles appropriate for his voice. And when the school deemed him salable—the point of it all—and the local opera in Rochester, New York, called needing an Escamillo, it recommended him. From there, it was on to sundry performances for Salmaggi and Gallo, and finally extended employment with Charles L. Wagner.

One of the country's most successful concert managers of the old school, Wagner had added single-production opera companies to his touring attractions in 1940. And though he had initially cast mostly second-string singers from the Metropolitan, on noting that—thanks to movies—audiences outside the big cities were as interested in a singer's looks as in his credentials, in recent years he had begun hiring attractive young freelancers like Torigi who, hungry for work, came cheaper. A Wagner tour was a "valuable try-out ground and experience-giver,"[4] he liked to say, citing Frances Greer, who trod his boards some twenty-seven times as Musetta before making her Met debut in the role. But like Gallo (though without the Italian's swagger, passion, or mustache), Wagner, of German descent, made a profit and ran a smooth operation. And even during the war, with only a rickety old bus with the scenery strapped to its roof for transportation, his troupe had traveled more than five thousand miles.

Indeed, the additional complications of wartime performance had not deterred what were lovingly dubbed the truck and bus companies. The Columbia Opera Company, for example, "carried a repertory of sixteen to eighteen operas and gave ten performances a week under all sorts of conditions," its conductor, Emerson Buckley, remembered. "We were always getting shifted out of the way so that a troop train could get through. Sometimes our costumes went to another city; sometimes half our cast was pared away."[5] Giorgio D'Andria's National Grand Opera and the Philadelphia La Scala went on the road. And the Columbia Concerts Opera Company, not to be confused with the Columbia Opera, went out with a highly successful *Carmen* with Resnik, Heidt, and the Canadian Mona Paulee, all on the brink of big careers, alternating in the title role, and Frances Yeend, just starting out, as a Micaela. Salvatore Baccaloni, the Met's great buffo basso, formed a troupe that presented scenes from opera featuring himself surrounded by young Americans. And, as we shall see, the Nine O'Clock Opera turned not only touring but opera production on its head with its smart, sprightly, streamlined shows.

But whereas conditions for touring naturally improved after the war, making a profit grew increasingly difficult for even the savviest companies. Travel was far more expensive; a plethora of new unions incurred all sorts of new costs; but, most significantly, there were fewer calls for their product. For apparently the communities they had once served now wanted to produce their own.

Dayton, Ohio, for example, had gone into the business virtually overnight after popular Robert Weede, in town for a recital, casually remarked to the woman in charge of the concert series that someday he would like to return to sing opera there. Excited by the idea, Miss Rosenthal had asked what she could do to make that happen; Weede had told her about Michael De Pace, a well-known casting representative in New York; and with De Pace on board, she had set the date for an inaugural *Faust* just five weeks thence, planned a series of additional operatic chestnuts to follow, and then set about rallying the astonished citizenry. Back in New York De Pace had arranged for the hall, rented the sets and costumes, and hired the orchestra, chorus, conductor, stage director, and artists—Weede among them, of course. For America's primo freelance baritone needed the annual Dayton Grand Opera Festival as much as it needed him. Indeed, unable to count on employment by the Metropolitan, Weede was just one of many native singers growing dependent on the new regional circuit, as it was called, to feed his family.

Yet another Roxy discovery, Weede (changed from Wiedefeld by the entrepreneur with an impulse for name changing) had been a leading baritone at Radio City Music Hall, singing four shows a day seven days a week, when the Met first hired him. His debut as Tonio in its 1937 Spring Season had received enthusiastic notices and he had followed it up with engagements in Philadelphia, San Francisco, St. Louis, and even Rio de Janeiro. But the Met, though keeping him on its roster for an occasional concert, curiously had not cast Weede in a role again until 1941. And though his vocally smooth, if dramatically rudimentary, portrayal of Rigoletto earned Weede a huge ovation and reviews that (as they had after his debut) again called him "a valuable acquisition,"[6] the company had dropped him altogether from the roster after just six performances. True, it would bring him back periodically over the years, but over ten intermittent seasons Weede would sing a total of only thirty-three performances with the company.

"Why the Met keeps this baritone hidden away is a mystery only management can unravel,"[7] Jay Harrison would write after hearing him as Scarpia in 1952—Weede's last season with the company. "I can't answer for the management," the baritone, at the time starring in the Broadway hit *Most Happy Fella,* would say in 1956, "but I didn't like the idea of sitting around, waiting, on call. I preferred to work. I had a family to look out for."[8] And indeed, Robert Weede, unquestionably one of the most successful and well-liked artists in the country, was always sure of work—as long as he kept on the move.

The soprano Vivian Della Chiesa, another favorite on the circuit (including Dayton), never did sing at the Metropolitan, but, even without its

Robert Weede (left) and Jan Peerce, on their way to Cincinnati, about 1938. Photo by Ralph Morgan, courtesy of Musical America *archives*

prestigious name, she still fashioned one of the busiest careers of the period. Of Italian descent, the daughter of a pianist and granddaughter of a conductor, Della Chiesa had studied music from an early age and in 1935, just twenty years old—but with "a voice that could ride the needle,"[9] she would say—won a radio contest for "Unknown Singers" from a field of thirty-seven hundred entrants. The prize, thirteen hundred dollars and a thirteen-week radio contract, had proved to be all her career needed. Launched on radio,

Vivian Della Chiesa. Courtesy of Vivian Della Chiesa

Della Chiesa the following year had made her operatic debut as Mimì with the Chicago Opera, at the time smarting from the criticism that its chief, Longone, cast young locals to save money. But the tall, patrician-looking blond with the ravishing lyric spinto—Chicago-born though she was—was clearly not of that ilk. Her success was authentic; Tito Schipa requested her as his Adina in *L'Elisir d'Amore;* and Della Chiesa was soon in demand for radio and opera around the country.

Winifred Heidt as Carmen

Winifred Heidt and Eugene Conley freelanced among the mushrooms to such a degree that their frequent meetings on the circuit may well have prompted their 1948 marriage. Born and raised in Detroit, Heidt had come to singing late. Though as a runner-up in the 1939 Metropolitan Auditions of the Air she had sung three concerts and two Grimgerdes in *Die Walküre* for the Met, the company had dropped her when her first husband, an attorney, accused her of neglecting her family and named the Met corespondent in their divorce proceedings.[10]

Losing not only her contract but also custody of her three children, the plucky mezzo had nevertheless persevered and, while still finding time to entertain the troops for the USO, performed with several of the companies springing up around the country. But it was her Carmen that arguably secured her reputation, especially after her 1945 debut in the role with the New York City Opera. For like Glade's exotic gypsy, Heidt's earthy, intuitive portrayal, sung in a big, sensuous voice that "rang with . . . freedom,"[11] was to become legend and keep her busy on the regional circuit thereafter. "The finest Carmen now to be found in this country," said Noel Strauss.[12] "One of the best post-war interpreters of the role," said Harold Rosenthal after her 1949 Covent Garden debut.[13]

From Lynn, Massachusetts, Conley had gotten his first break when NBC heard him in radio broadcasts from Boston and brought him to New York for a variety of programs, including his own *NBC Presents Eugene Conley.* Surviving a fly-by-the-seat-of-your-pants unrehearsed operatic debut as the Duke in *Rigoletto* for Salmaggi, which had his teacher shouting directions from the wings, the handsome tenor had sung with the San Carlo, Cincinnati, and Chicago opera companies before enlisting in the Army Air Corps in 1942, only to spend most of the war performing in its musical, *Winged Victory.* In the spring of 1945 Conley made his New York City Opera debut as Rodolfo, then took to the circuit. The Met appeared uninterested but, as we shall see, would change its mind.

Unlike the community groups, which were usually run by civic organizations, the opera companies that cropped up in larger cities in the 1940s were often (as was the case already in San Francisco, Chicago, and Philadelphia) the inspirations of immigrants. Miami, for instance, found its way onto the operatic map courtesy of a flamboyant Italian-born tenor by the name of Arturo di Filippi. Doctor Di, as he was affectionately called, had come to America as a child, studied at Juilliard, and enjoyed a modest career in opera abroad before returning to sing radio and concert, including three Town Hall recitals. But on becoming seriously ill, he had gone to Miami to recuperate, joined the faculty at the university there, and in 1942 presented (à la Salmaggi) a *Pagliacci* with himself in the role of Canio and locals and students filling out the cast. The principals sang in Italian and the chorus in English; women filled in for the male chorus members who had gone to war, but no one cared. For though the city would not see another performance by its new "company" until 1943 and not more than one annually until 1947, when two became average, the Miami Opera had been born.

Hartford, Connecticut, also owed its first permanent company to an Italian-born tenor-turned-teacher. Unlike di Filippi, Frank Pandolfi, or the "little Caruso," as Sigmund Romberg called the pint-sized tenor with Broadway experience, did not himself perform with the Connecticut Opera, which he officially launched in 1942 with a *Carmen* headed by Heidt and Conley. But, like the Floridian, he founded the company after the productions he mounted for his students revealed just how much the community wanted one. Indeed, the big Horace Bushnell Auditorium saw eight separate productions in the company's first season alone. But if the number of presentations would decrease almost immediately to an average of four or five, the Connecticut Opera (as would happen a little later in Miami) would boast some of the starriest casts on the circuit—partially because of its proximity to New York, partially because of the affection Metropolitan artists had for its genial director.

And in New Orleans, where the genre had thrived in the late 1800s, opera returned after outdoor performances of operatic chestnuts in the summer found such favor that in 1943 the city decided to engage the German-born conductor Walter Herbert to run a permanent company. More imaginative in matters of repertoire and production and generally more ambitious than his Italian counterparts, Herbert mounted as many as eight, often rarely heard, operas in a season, and engaged many of the best singers in the country, ranging from Met stars, such as Kirsten and Warren, and circuit regulars, such as Della Chiesa and Torigi, to unknown locals, such as the young Norman Treigle. Treigle, who for two decades would provide the New York City Opera with some of the most vivid portrayals in the bass-baritone repertoire and become one of America's greatest singer-actors, would, in fact, make his New Orleans Opera debut as Duke of Verona in *Roméo et Juliette* in 1947; from there he would work his way up the ladder, portraying some thirty-six roles with the company by the time of his last performance in 1968.

As the circuit grew, however, so too did the conventionality of many of its offerings. Because most companies had neither the audience for nor the financial resources to give more than a handful of performances at a time, it simply made good economic sense to stick to standard repertoire and use the same singers over and over, despite the system's eventual stultifying effect. After all, each city had a different audience, so it hardly mattered that the productions were so similar; who would care that the *Traviata* that played Dayton one week, for example, was almost indistinguishable from the one seen in Newark the following month? And so, virtually everyone and everything came from the same "official pools" in New York.

The Stivanello name, for example, loomed large in most productions, with Manhattan's Stivanello Company invariably supplying the costumes and, Anthony, the popular Venetian-born son of the founder, invariably directing. As one who sometimes went onstage in costume himself to keep things moving, Stivanello was "the perfect traffic cop."[14] Moreover, he was Mr. Instant Opera, able to put a performance together with almost no rehearsal, thereby saving his clients a great deal of money. After all, why spend time (and money) rehearsing a new opera or a new interpretation of an opera when, as Torigi (who believed he owed his own position on the circuit to his affiliation with the New York City Opera) pointed out, "Everyone knew the old ones. We'd get there on Sunday night; rehearse Monday, Tuesday, Wednesday; perform Thursday; day off Friday; perform Saturday, and go—about a week's work. I was never rich, but I could make it."[15]

If, however, by virtue of their predictability the regional companies were mushrooms of the hothouse kind, wild varieties were popping up as well. Short on money but strong on ideas and offering a wide-ranging experience for the aspirant looking to bridge the gap between studio and stage, this other type was also more often than not spawned by émigrés who saw in their adopted country a need they could fill.

Foremost among these companies were those founded by Vladimir Rosing, a Russian tenor who on first coming to the United States in the 1920s had been horrified to learn there was no national opera company that performed in the vernacular, as was customary abroad. Backed by the camera titan George Eastman, Rosing's first American Opera Company performed only in English and stressed total dramatic intelligibility. No singer was allowed to acknowledge applause or take center stage for an aria unless the action called for it. And even the best of the approximately ninety Americans who partook at one time or another, including future Met singers Kullman, Votipka, Olheim, and John Gurney, were expected to sing small as well as large parts.

Though eminently successful, the American Opera survived only about six years, ultimately felled by the Great Depression. But in 1939, after a period living in England, Rosing resurfaced in fast-growing Los Angeles, where performances of opera were spotty at best. The San Francisco Opera paid occasional visits; the Riverside Opera, founded by the soprano Marcella Craft, produced standard works in English using California singers whenever possible; and the Euterpe Opera Reading Club, which for several years had consisted of singers reading through scores for the founder and her friends in her living room, now presented fully staged productions for some one thousand members.

Rosing offered the city a variety of new ventures, and finally in 1941 one appeared to take hold. "Last night . . . Mr. Rosing again picked up the strands at just about the point he left off a generation ago," Albert Goldberg of the *Los Angeles Times* wrote of the first performance by the American Opera Company of Los Angeles—a *Faust* with a young bass, Jerome Hines, as Méphisto.[16] Two months later, the country went to war and Rosing was distracted. But the seed was planted, and when the company reopened in 1947—again with *Faust,* again with Hines (now of the Metropolitan)—Goldberg again praised Rosing's "individualistic method," in which "a work was periodically restudied and restaged, old and meaningless traditions discarded, and the opera approached as if it were a first performance with a new and fresh emphasis upon all its points."[17]

Incorporating many of the same principles, a different American Opera Company was launched in Philadelphia in 1946 under the direction of Vernon Hammond with an English language production of *Abduction from the Seraglio* with a cast that included James Pease, David Lloyd, Adelaide Bishop, and the fine Canadian tenor Leopold Simoneau. But nowhere did small companies proliferate as fast as in Manhattan, where undoubtedly one of the earliest and most innovative had to be the aforementioned Nine O'Clock Opera.

Comprising eight young Americans who had met at the Juilliard, the scrappy company had, in fact, been startling press and public alike with its elegant, fast-paced renditions of the classics since 1940. Inspired by Thornton Wilder's *Our Town,* which had won the Pulitzer Prize in 1938, the singers performed in modern evening dress with no scenery and only a suitcase-full of props. They sang in idiomatic English to piano accompaniment with a narrator filling in for whatever they had to leave out. "Never have I seen an audience enjoy, never have I myself enjoyed, 'Figaro' with such wholehearted gusto," wrote Virgil Thomson.[18] Signed by Columbia Concerts, the perky gang, which appeared at Town Hall at least once a season but spent most of its time on the road, was the talk of the business.

But rare as such enterprises were at the beginning of the decade, by the end any number had announced themselves. And if such mundane but upbeat names as Shoestring, Punch, Nine O'Clock, After Dinner, and Lemonade were calculated to disarm, they were also aimed at convincing the wary that opera without the high hat—lemonade, not champagne, to sip at intermission—could be fun, even if the companies themselves were sustained by little other than ingenuity and old-fashioned pluck.

To be sure, the way Anthony Amato, a tenor who had enjoyed a modest career primarily as a comprimario,[19] and Serafina (Sally) Bellantoni, his soprano wife, managed to keep the Amato Opera afloat remains an inspiration to this day. An offshoot of the opera workshop at the American Theater Wing, where Tony taught, the company was founded in 1948 with the couple's earnings from teaching. The primary aim was to give young singers, such as Torigi, who was one of the first to benefit, a chance to perform the standard repertoire in a way that might be expected of them in any traditional house. Amato auditioned the singers, prepared them musically, selected the repertoire, and staged and conducted the operas. Sally saw to everything from costumes to publicity. To meet union regulations but at the same time avoid having to hire professionals as stagehands and house staff, they passed a hat in lieu of selling tickets. For a long time singers sang without recompense; but this was no school. The company presented an average of four performances a week, and fifty years later and still going strong, the Amatos could claim that as many as ten thousand singers—all roles were double, triple, or even quadruple cast—had trod at least one of its several stages.

But if its lifetime was only a fraction of that of the Amato, no small company of the period caught the imagination of both public and press quite like the Lemonade. Bursting forth in the summer of 1947, it was gone by the summer of 1950; yet in that brief time magazines from *Time* to *Opera News* delighted in reporting its every escapade, and anyone lucky enough to have attended a performance probably remembers it to this day.

The Lemonade Opera Company performed at the Greenwich Mews Playhouse: in actuality, the dreary, dark-gray basement of the old Presbyterian Church on West Thirteenth Street in the area of Manhattan known as Greenwich Village. The church had permitted the actor José Ferrer, who was at the time playing Cyrano de Bergerac on Broadway, to use its 290-seat auditorium to present Chekhov plays as a showcase for young, deserving actors. Lemonade was born, or so the most likely story goes, when Nancy Kendall, its soprano soloist, and Max Leavitt, a former Broadway actor and future Met stage director, succeeded in persuading the minister (whom Nancy later married) to do the same for opera singers.

The company began as a cooperative. Singers paid twenty-five dollars to participate and shared equally in whatever profits there might be. (At the end of the first season, the eighteen hard-working guarantors took away $205 each and left $500 in the kitty for the next season.) In addition to performing, they did their own publicity, painted scenery, sewed costumes, even ushered. In other words, the young man who sold the tickets for a *Don Giovanni* might well be the Masetto after the lights went down.

Keeping in mind the minimal budget, the minuscule and wingless stage, the intention to perform everything in English, and the general lack of important voices, the members wisely avoided grand opera and, hoping to arouse curiosity, concentrated on novelties. Among their productions were the American premieres of Haydn's *The Man and the Moon*, Mendelssohn's *The Stranger*, Prokofiev's *The Duenna*, and the rarely heard *La Serva Padrona* of Pergolesi. The only standard repertoire was *Hansel and Gretel*, which they mounted every Christmas, and *Don Giovanni*. To avoid competition they generally performed in the summer, when they could sell their namesake lemonade—two and a half lemons with a cherry for twenty cents—between the acts in a little alley beside the church.

Two pianos served as orchestra and the scenery was minimal; in fact, *Down in the Valley* had virtually none, the production depending instead on some "unique lighting effects . . . achieved by a three-way floor-plug that was purchased at the ten-cent store."[20] Men dressed in the Sunday school room, women in the kitchen. All productions received repeated hearings. The last summer, 1950, in fact, saw three receive some 135 performances. From the beginning, performances regularly sold out, the result of a provocative repertoire and the company's wit, creativity, and high spirits.

Though the Lemonade boasted such directors and conductors as Herbert Grossman, Sam Morgenstern, John Gutman, Sheldon Soffer, the brilliant Max Leavitt, and a very young Thomas Schippers, all of whom would go on to bigger things, of the singers who participated only Ruth Kobart and Robert Goss appear to have had careers in the business. Kobart had come to New York from her native Iowa in 1945 with no idea of what she was going

Ruth Kobart as La Duenna in the Lemonade production of Prokofiev's
La Duenna. *Courtesy of the late Ruth Kobart*

to do. But rounded up as a charter member, the dynamic actress with the big mezzo who doubled—"because I knew how to type"[21]—as publicity director became probably the company's one star. After Lemonade disbanded, Kobart would cover for Helen Traubel (and appear some twenty times) in Rodger and Hammerstein's *Pipe Dream* on Broadway and sing leading roles with both the New York City Opera and the NBC Opera Theater. But she made her biggest reputation as a character actress on Broadway and in Hollywood.

With apparently little more than a "serviceable" voice, but with great intelligence and musicality, the baritone Robert Goss also fashioned a career beyond the Lemonade in a variety of mediums, even singing small roles in the touring Met production of *Die Fledermaus*. And when he sang a recital devoted to American song in 1950, the *Times* wrote, "Every word was understandable, every phrase was in context—a legacy of his Lemonade Opera . . . background."[22]

Chapter Twelve

"Thanks to Hitler"

IF PROSPECTS FOR PERFORMING were looking up, options for study and training were now the best in the world, in large part because of the input and influence of the political and Jewish refugee musicians who had escaped to America and, in search of work, fanned out across the country, enriching and stimulating every facet of its musical life. Indeed, the country was all but overwhelmed with good teachers—"thanks to Hitler,"[1] Mattiwilda Dobbs would say—and the education that once had been the privilege of only those who could afford a trip to Europe was now available to everyone.

"I benefited from the war," Bethany Beardslee recalled of her studies at Michigan State University in the mid-1940s; "I benefited from all the Jewish intellectuals who came over from Europe and created this fantastic music department. So when I came to New York I had a marvelous background."[2] "Our good fortune came from the appalling things going on with Hitler and the Jews," Blanche Thebom would agree. "It was possible to have the most wonderful private coachings, because every corner of Fifty-seventh Street was flooded with these incredibly trained, experienced people."[3]

At the Met the singers worked with them daily. Eleanor Steber studied stagecraft, acting, and the dramatic interpretation of her roles with Lothar Wallerstein, the former director from the Vienna State Opera. She coached the Italian repertoire with the "brilliant" Renato Bellini, the French with the "sensitive, articulate" Jean Paul Morel, and the German with the "superb" Felix Wolfes and the "very erudite, cerebral and impersonal" Hermann Weigert. She worked as well with the principal conductors: Erich Leinsdorf, for example, who "believed I could sing Sophie and . . . stuck with me," and Bruno Walter, who "set me on the path which led me to become the first American acknowledged as a premier interpreter of Mozart."[4]

151

Working one-on-one with the great conductors from abroad was not entirely new for Americans. Though in 1934 Tullio Serafin had returned to Italy to take charge of the Rome Opera and on Mussolini's orders remained there throughout the war, in his decade at the Metropolitan the gentle Venetian, finding American singers to be extremely gifted—just in need of extra help, he said—had been particularly instrumental in the development of many. He had stood by the young Tibbett in his bid as Ford, coached and conducted him in his triumphs in four American operas, and overseen his evolution into a great Verdi baritone. He had helped Bampton mold her voice to the tessitura of her new soprano roles and virtually empowered Ponselle to render some of her greatest portrayals. To be sure, Serafin, Gladys Swarthout believed, "did more for the American singer than any other single person."[5]

Fortunately, Mussolini had thought better of dallying too much with Arturo Toscanini, another of the great mentoring maestros, who after loudly voicing his dislike of the dictator and his politics, had settled in America for the duration. Toscanini's concert performances of opera with the NBC Symphony created many opportunities for singers, and a chance to perform with the much-loved, much-feared perfectionist was coveted almost as much for the learning experience as for the prestige. "In studying a score with Maestro seasoned artists became students again," Jan Peerce said. "With him I acquired study habits that I have utilized in all my work."[6] Always insistent on the most thorough preparation, even at the age of eighty-three Toscanini rehearsed the cast of *Falstaff* six hours at a time daily for weeks. Nan Merriman, who sang almost as often under him as Peerce did, remembered that for a performance of Gluck's *Orfeo* they worked together over a nine-month period.

"[Toscanini] brought me from obscurity to musical prominence," Merriman, who would go on to a notable career primarily abroad, would recall. "His love for music, his example of selfless musicianship, the unceasing efforts to achieve musical perfection, inspired me all my working life."[7] Toscanini had first heard the lovely Merriman's light mezzo with its distinguishing delicate vibrato in 1942 on a fifteen-minute broadcast on NBC (part of her award for winning a Federation of Music Clubs contest) and, after a private audition, engaged her to sing Verdi excerpts on a Treasury Department broadcast from Madison Square Garden. Merriman had extra reason to remember their first collaboration, for the date was July 25, 1943. During the intermission a special news flash reported that Mussolini had resigned, and when they returned to the stage for the final act of *Rigoletto*,[8] "the Maestro was so excited he simply set us on fire."[9]

Responding to the question as to why he remained in America when he had been offered prestigious positions in Europe, the Greek-born conductor Dimitri Mitropoulos probably spoke for many of these selfless foreigners when he wrote: "The Europeans don't need me as much. They are self-assured in matters of art; theirs is a long history and the riches of their culture are even greater than they realize. It is always gratifying for an artist to meet people who are willing to learn. That is why I believe I can be of much greater influence in America than in Europe. It is therefore a question of morality, not art, which causes me to stay in America."[10]

Even so, in certain areas of their vocal education Americans had already made real strides. And when in 1933 it was reported that Mussolini, an opera buff, had considered "curbing incompetent vocal teachers by statute, in order that the fair name of Italy, as applied to vocal art, not be sullied,"[11] American voice teachers could proudly say they had been "curbing" themselves for some time. Certainly, the problem of incompetence and even charlatanism in teaching voice was as old as singing itself. After all, anyone could hang up a shingle. But the establishment of the New York Singing Teachers Association[12] in 1906 had been an important first step in safeguarding vocal pedagogy in the young country. Moreover, it had given rise to such other organizations as the American Academy of Teachers of Singing, the Chicago Singing Teachers Guild, the New York Teachers of Singing, and, in 1944, during the darkest days of the war, the National Association of Teachers of Singing (NATS). These organizations had no real power, of course, but their influence was considerable, and their lofty goals of establishing and maintaining the highest standards when it came to the principles, practice, and competence of their teachers, of conducting research and disseminating the results, and of encouraging cooperation within the profession, as stated by NATS at its first meeting,[13] arguably served for any of them.

To be sure, there was a great deal for these groups to oversee. The émigré musicians had brought with them an assortment of vocal techniques, and though, because so many were Jewish, the German school in the country was gaining on the Italian, at the same time independent-thinking Americans were developing their own way of doing things. Essentially hybrids, the new American methods tended to combine the Old World schools, the individual teacher's own discoveries and personal ideas, and the latest research, which NATS published in its popular journal. One has only to peruse an *Etude* magazine or *Training the Singing Voice,* a 1947 study of methods by Alexander Fields, to realize how diverse private teaching had become. And if there was every reason to charge (as some did) that America lacked a single method of building a voice, Gladys Swarthout, for one, was proud to have "witnessed an entirely American school of singing in its development." For in her mind, as she told readers of *Etude* as early as 1934, "this school is the selecting of the best points of all the others and building them into a new and distinctive whole which is eminently our own. . . . [It] produces tones as the Italian does, projects them as cleverly as the Frenchman, and acquires the precision of the German, without flabbiness, without nasal quality, and without taut, harsh effort."[14] Years later, after hanging out her own shingle, Steber would write, "Today I am part of a great new family—one that didn't exist in my youth—the American school of teaching."[15]

Furthermore, though it was also charged that American singers were in too much of a hurry, the studio preparation they received was often exhaustive (if brief), which at least partially explains how so many from this period survived debuts in leading roles when they had never been on a stage before. Private voice teachers routinely assigned their students to outside teachers for drama, dance, theory, fencing, and languages, as well as to various coaches for the various repertoires. Even without a contract in hand, the serious student studied and memorized operatic roles in their entirety, fine-tuned them with a musical coach, and learned the scenetics of the roles with a dramatic coach. Indeed, as the soprano Mary Henderson would say, it was only because she had prepared some ten operatic roles in this way that she was ready when the San Carlo Opera suddenly needed her.

Certainly, the crack coloraturas Patrice Munsel, Roberta Peters, and Dolores Wilson received that kind of preparation from William Herman, who oversaw one of the strictest regimens in town. In addition to sometimes two voice lessons a day, in which they might not only intone the exercises of Garcia, Duprez, Damoreau, Bordogni, and (in some cases) even the great masters of flute and clarinet, but also work out with a punching bag, Herman's students coached with the appropriate expert for whatever repertoire they were learning and took lessons in piano, harmony, theory, French, Italian, fencing, and ballet. "They were all private teachers which was quite wonderful," Munsel remembered." In those days a French lesson was three dollars, and a voice lesson was five or ten at the most; so it was feasible to have a big program of study without going to a school. With eight hours a day I could cram an awful lot in."[16]

In her book, *A Debut at the Met,* Peters, who began with Herman when she was just fourteen and learned twenty operas "cold" in seven years under him, gives a pretty good idea just how intensive the teaching could be when she describes her Italian and drama lessons with Antonietta Stabile. In addition to conversing in Italian and reading Dante's *La Divina Commedia* and other Italian classics with the former diseuse, Peters studied the period and historic background of whatever operatic role she was studying with Herman at the time; examined the libretto word by word; studied how the character would move, stand, and use her eyes; and spoke—not sang—the lines as she acted them out.

Such private preparation was hardly available to everyone, however, and singers more than ever were heading to music schools, either of the conservatory type or—the new thing—as part of a college or university. The United States had seen an increase in music schools in the post–World War I years, at which time such notable examples as the Juilliard (then the Institute of Art), Eastman, and Curtis joined the existing New England and Peabody conservatories. Now "in large part the result of the opportunity and the need for training at home created by World War II," Herbert Graf observed in his 1951 study of the American opera scene, *Opera for the People,* their numbers soared. By the end of the war "the number of music schools in the United States had risen from fewer than twenty-five to some three hundred. About eighty of these schools give opera performances every year," the Austrian-born director wrote, "and some sixty have regular opera departments."[17]

Calling it a "little experimental opera theater, designed to fill the gap that exists in America between school training and engagements with major professional companies," Graf declared the opera "workshop," as found in America's educational institutions, an American invention that functioned as a kind of substitute for the Central European "Stadttheater."[18] Indeed, as that keen observer of American musical culture Hans Heinsheimer noted, "One can almost say that the American University is now taking the place of the archbishops and princes that supported opera in Europe in its beginnings."[19]

By the end of the 1940s opera departments could be found in academic institutions as widespread and various as Alabama's Polytech Institute, Bob Jones University in South Carolina, and the University of California at Berkeley, the last making news in 1946 when it presented Purcell's *Dido and Aeneas* with a Chinese soprano and a Negro mezzo. For that matter, California led the movement not only because it still lacked important private music schools but because it was a popular destination for the émigrés. Stanford University, where Dr. Jan Popper, who had fled Prague just before the German invasion, fired up a department that would count among its many triumphs the West Coast premiere of *Peter Grimes,* was typical.

But for sheer size and ambitiousness of its productions the opera department at Indiana University in Bloomington would come to reign supreme beginning in 1948, the year its music school's energetic and visionary director, Dr. William Blain, took two important steps toward establishing its ascendancy.

The first was the securing of Josephine Antoine of the Metropolitan for its voice department. Indeed, the option of teaching in academia, instead of privately or on the faculty of a music school or conservatory, was a new one for retiring professional singers. "If anyone had predicted a decade ago that at least six state universities and three junior colleges would bring Metropolitan Opera experience to their music departments," F. J. Freeman wrote in 1950, "that person would have been quickly reminded that since large cities usually remain distant from state universities, so would professional artists."[20] Yet, spurred by the rise of good music departments across the land, retiring Metropolitan artists were taking positions in colleges and universities and generally professing great satisfaction in the talent they found. Antoine, in fact, would be but the first of an unending stream of prestigious singers who would build Indiana University's voice department into one of the most illustrious in the world.

The second important step was for the music school first to establish an opera theater and then to have it present in its first year (1948) the world premiere of a new work by the popular émigré composer Kurt Weill, an event that drew a national press and generated enormous publicity for the university. Though Weill had been asked to write an opera appropriate for schools and small companies, Indiana launched the simple folklike work with a fifty-piece orchestra and an eighty-voice chorus; in the leading role was a very professional Marion Bell, fresh from starring in the Broadway musical *Brigadoon.* No matter; both opera department and opera enjoyed a veritable triumph; Weill wrote to his parents that "the newspapers praised my opera as the greatest event in America's musical life."[21] It wasn't long before *Down in the Valley* had "made its way . . . onto hundreds of stages, played by school workshops, amateur groups, and professional companies—testifying to the progress the new operatic movement had made."[22]

Meanwhile, Indiana's ambitious opera department continued in high gear, the very next year marshaling its students for nothing less than Wagner's mammoth *Parsifal* and mounting such a successful production that the school would repeat it virtually every Easter thereafter. By the 1950s Indiana University had become as popular a destination for operatic aspirants as the established music institutions in the East, even as the 1940s saw such veterans as Manhattan and Mannes in New York, Julius Hartt in Hartford, and the New England Conservatory in Boston add opera to their curriculums.

For, despite the fact that New England, the nation's oldest music school, had historically given opera only nodding attention, all that had changed in 1942 when, noting the trend, it engaged Boris Goldovsky to oversee its first department devoted to the genre. The Russian-born former pianist, who had come to the United States in the early 1930s and studied conducting with Fritz Reiner at the Curtis Institute, admitted to initially hating opera. But he had changed his mind when, invited to set up an opera department at the Cleveland Institute of Music in 1936, he had taken a crash course in opera with the great Viennese director Ernst Lert, who had shown him how different it could be if presented in a way that made theatrical sense.

And so, first in Cleveland, then at the New England Conservatory and Tanglewood, where an extraordinary cross section of American singers would receive training, Goldovsky began to teach his singers such specific— albeit often controversial—ideas about opera stagecraft as never looking at the conductor and moving according to the dictates of the music. And, in 1947, because "I felt I had no right to train exceptionally gifted people to become outstanding artists unless I could provide them with a professional outlet for their talents," he founded the New England Opera Theater.[23] Essentially an ensemble of singer-actors who looked their parts, enunciated clearly, and knew the music so well they could have performed without a conductor, among them could be found the likes of Adele Addison, Phyllis Curtin, Eunice Alberts, Mildred Miller, John McCollum, David Lloyd, and Sherill Milnes—his "kiddos," Goldovsky was heard to call them.

But perhaps the most innovative opera department of all was to be found at, of all unlikely places, Columbia University in New York and run not by foreign conductors, coaches, or former singers but, remarkably, by American composers. The composer Douglas Moore, who headed the university's music department, had organized a workshop in 1940, and in 1944 had expanded it when he hired Otto Luening, another composer, to head up what they called "Opera Projects," which were operas to be performed in conjunction with the theater department. Because the operas were almost invariably either first performances of American works or revivals of neglected classics, and because each year the Alice M. Ditson Fund commissioned a new American work for the project, the program received a great deal of attention from the music world. As the composer Jack Beeson, who assisted Luening, recalled, "At the time, the major companies and conservatories were reticent about doing new opera, particularly by Americans. We pointed the way."[24]

Though the preference was to use students from the workshop, professionals were occasionally brought in, glad for the attention and experience, though they were not paid. For example, the 1947 premiere of Virgil Thomson's *The Mother of Us All,* which had twenty-one roles to be filled, brought in (on the recommendation of the Metropolitan, where she had just unsuccessfully auditioned) Dorothy Dow, a soprano with considerable experience, to create the title role of Susan B. Anthony, and William Horne and Alice Howland, who had performed at the New York City Opera and elsewhere, in other leading roles. Teresa Stich, a student in the workshop, had a small role and understudied Dow. In 1948 Stich would create the title role in Luening's own *Evangeline* for Columbia. In 1949, under the name Stich-Randall, she would sing the High Priestess in *Aida* and Nannetta in *Falstaff* under Toscanini, and in 1950 she would commence a brilliant career in Europe.

In its seventeen years, Columbia's department presented some forty operas, including the premieres of Menotti's *The Medium,* Benjamin Britten's *Paul Bunyan,* and Moore's 1951 Pulitzer Prize–winning *Giants in the Earth.* Whether it set the example or simply reflected the times is hard to say, but there is no question that the innovative combination of training ground for singers and launching pad for contemporary indigenous opera spread like wildfire in the university system.[25]

If, however, the university's championing of the new repertoire did much to vitalize opera as an art form in America, it did little to produce singers for the real world of traditional opera performance. And in the spirit of Gallo, Salmaggi, and Merola, it was again primarily the Italian immigrants who saw to it that there were singers to keep the bread-and-butter operas on the table—Josephine La Puma, for example.

Arriving in New York in 1933, La Puma had immediately noticed the lack of any place for a young singer to get training and early experience in opera. The daughter of the famous buffo basso Giuseppe La Puma and the mother of Alberta Masiello, for two seasons a contralto with the City Opera and for years an esteemed coach at the Metropolitan, Josephine herself had performed in Italy and South America. Later naming her workshop, which was independent of any institution, the Mascagni Opera Guild in honor of the composer under whom she and her father had sung, the former soprano mounted two full operas a week using the most primitive of sets and tiniest of orchestras. Performances may not always have been very good, but for those in search of hands-on experience it was enough that they mimicked the real thing. Julius Rudel, under the name Rudolfo di Giulio, got early experience conducting for La Puma. The soprano Josephine Guido, who later made a nice career on both sides of the Atlantic before becoming a stage director, painted scenery, sang in the chorus, made her debut as Flora in *Traviata,* and finally sang leading roles for La Puma. And when Salmaggi called La Puma, needing someone to sing the role of Gretel on short notice and without rehearsal, Guido was ready.[26]

Similarly appalled by what they saw on their arrival in America, Luigi Rossini, a great-grandnephew of the composer and himself a tenor, and his wife, a vocal coach, founded the Rossini Opera Workshop in 1938. Operating out of the West Side YMCA, Rossini prepared and presented about twenty-five singers in seven or eight productions of standard repertoire a year. Here, emphasis was on acting, and graduates such as Jess Walters, Adelaide Bishop, and Elaine Malbin were superb examples of his training.

But independent ventures were popping up outside New York as well, mostly workshops like those headed by Rosa Raisa and her husband, Giacomo Rimini, in Chicago, Oscar Seagle at Schroon Lake in upstate New York, and Victor Fuchs in Hollywood. "I guess we have at least 100 opera schools for one opera company," Fuchs told the *New York Times* in 1951. "I think one opera school for 100 opera companies would be the right ratio."[27] True: opportunity for education was far outstripping opportunity for professional experience, which the émigré musicians without the kind of government subsidy they had experienced in their own countries were helpless to effect. Nevertheless, American singers were getting some of the best training in the world and, as a result, were now, if not better (as some would argue), at least as well prepared for the postwar vocal world as any of their foreign counterparts.

Chapter Thirteen

Transatlantic Turnabout

L ATE IN THE SUMMER OF 1947 the tenors Ramon Vinay and Eugene Conley and the soprano Christina Carroll were relaxing in a
small al fresco restaurant in Florence. As singers with Giorgio D'Andria's
National Grand Opera Company, they had come from America to join Tito
Gobbi, Mafalda Favero, and other Italians whose careers had survived the
war for a tour of Italy in several operas. But on this evening they were celebrating Vinay's birthday, and Conley had just finished offering up the usual
birthday song for his Chilean colleague and, at the request of a band of street
musicians who had joined in, "Torna a Sorrento" and "O Sole Mio," when
suddenly they saw an elderly man hurrying to them from across the square.

"Pardon my friends," the man said in English, "but I heard just now
from my window a great trained voice; I must meet the young singer to con-
gratulate him. You are so welcome, you and your fellow American operatic
singers, we need you. . . . Time was, not so long ago, when the United States
sent to Italy for my country's greatest artists, and they went. . . . In those
days, Italy had voices to give—but alas, now, her new crop of voices is too
small to fill the wants of the opera-lovers of my country. Too many young
dead; too many who lack the money, even the teachers or the places in
which to sing—in Italy, the home of grand opera, we need the strong, young
American voices to bring us once again the music we will sacrifice even food
to hear."[1] Introducing himself, he was—they were astonished to learn—the
great baritone Titta Ruffo. But how could it have come to this?

It had been a century since reports of Jenny Lind's exorbitant concert earnings in America first lured Europe's greatest singers to serve the culturally
impoverished New World with their art, and almost that long since young

Americans eager to imbibe that art at its source had begun making the voyage in reverse. Over the years, the exchange had not always been a happy one. But if Europeans deplored the invasion of privacy and circuslike promotional tactics they found in America, Americans deplored even more the way they were treated in Europe.

In 1928 Dorothy Speare had even written a series of articles for *Cosmopolitan* magazine—luridly titled "My Adventures with the Opera Pirates," "The Gallery of Blasted Reputations," and "Mouth of the Wolf"—in which she spelled out the abuses in no uncertain terms. For not only were Americans in Italy generally treated like "laughing-stocks," the erstwhile soprano claimed, they were expected to remake their voices for Italian ears and, worse, expected to pay to perform. There were, she estimated, some four thousand Americans studying opera in Milan, and almost that many being robbed of their money by Italian agents and producers, who either promised them performances that never happened or took their money and disappeared. She herself had paid, but when they demanded she pay more to ensure good reviews, she had refused and consequently been abandoned.[2]

What is more, immigration laws were unfair. If an American wanted to sing in Italy, he had to establish residence; in England and, to some degree, France, he had to prove himself better qualified for a job than a native; and in Germany, Russia, and Poland he was not allowed to take his earnings out of the country.[3] But for an alien to sing in America and make money to take home, he needed only a contract. Why should America be so nice?

Said to have taken offense at Salmaggi's remark that "like spaghetti, grand opera comes from Italy and belongs to the Italians," Representative Samuel Dickstein of New York, who headed the House Immigration Committee, in 1937 drew up a bill to counteract the injustice. "No manager could bring a musician in to this country unless he could prove to the satisfaction of the Secretary of Labor that there was no American of similar ability; alien artists would be admitted on the basis of one for each American accepted by the corresponding foreign government; no prominent musician could even visit America unprofessionally without special permission from the Secretary of Labor."[4]

The stunning measures set off a vigorous debate. Lawrence Tibbett, who supported the bill, explained that it applied only to countries where reciprocity was in order; Mrs. Belmont, speaking for the Metropolitan Opera Guild, said the country was still in a period of cultural transition and could not afford to exclude foreigners; the Concerts Association of America announced it would be out of business if it could not offer the public foreign artists. But the bigger problem, as anyone could see, was that the bill violated the very freedoms America stood for. And so Congress rejected Dickstein's bill, leaving European artists in America to breathe a sigh of relief even as their own governments remained implacable toward Americans.

But now war appeared to have changed everything. Though America too had suffered great losses on the battlefield, there had been no fighting on its shores. And though the country had endured shortages and inconveniences, after years of economic depression the war had actually done much to restore its spirit as well as its wealth. America was now the leader of the free world; New York was the capital of the music world; and the American singer, well fed, well educated, and finally proven, was ready to work.

The European experience, however, could not have been more different, and as the first scouts set out for the Continent, everyone wondered what they would find. Who was still alive, still active, still in good voice? Which opera houses and concert halls were still functioning? Was anybody performing; if so, under what circumstances? Were there any new singers? Did they need Americans? Did they want Americans?

There was some good news to report. A considerable amount of music making had taken place even as the bombs rained, and a considerable amount was already under way. Of Europe's twenty-six major opera houses, most, in fact, were operating in some makeshift fashion. Where theaters were in ruins, the companies were finding such alternative sites as a beer hall in Frankfurt and the stock exchange in Dresden. But the bad news was that a whole generation of artists—many of whom should have been in their prime—was weary, distracted, undernourished, and out of practice. Opera rosters were badly depleted, their gaping holes crying out for healthy voices.

That America could easily supply them created an interesting and delicate state of affairs. American singers no longer needed the European training—nor, sadly, was Europe able to offer it anymore—but they did still need places to perform. Europe had the places, but Europeans, debilitated and knowing little of the progress the Americans had made during the war, were wary. The Americans would have to prove themselves at every turn; they would have to tread lightly, be humble, and show great respect.

For Dorothy Dow the going was initially difficult and even unpleasant. However, as the first American to be signed by the Zurich Staatsoper after the war, she would stick it out and in time make herself indispensable, not only in Zurich but also in houses across the continent—an achievement all the more impressive in that Dow had grown up in Galveston, Texas, where, she would say, there was "no cultural life of any kind." To be sure, in an early

Dorothy Dow as Norma

demonstration of her grit, the very grit she would need to survive in postwar Europe, she had won a scholarship to Juilliard and, by the time the director from Zurich arrived to audition singers, already pieced together the beginnings of a freelance career.

"It was a long time before they accepted me," Dow would recall, speaking of the predominantly German staff that saw all Americans as arrogant in their victory. "But I was greedy, I wanted to sing everything, and I was a fast learner. If anyone got sick, I was there."[5] And so she had sung leading roles from Bellini's Norma to Strauss's Salome; and she had sung a great deal of modern music. For with her particular facility for learning complex, often unorthodox scores, Dow clearly had a decided advantage when it came to the contemporary repertoire—as did many Americans. Composition would fairly explode in Europe after the war. But, although in America, for lack of money, new works sat unperformed on composers' shelves, in Europe, thanks to subsidies, the problem was only one of finding capable performers, and Americans—versatile, quick to learn, well educated, free of the constraints of traditions, and eager to get ahead—were often the solution.

In 1951 the conductor Herbert von Karajan engaged Dow to sing Venus in *Tannhäuser* at La Scala; over the next decade she would not only secure her reputation at that most prestigious of theaters essaying such heroines as Walton's Cressida, Bartók's Judith, Berg's Marie, and, as a change of pace, Ponchielli's Gioconda, but also perform throughout Italy, at Glyndebourne, Covent Garden, and the Teatro Colón in Buenos Aires. Occasionally she would even try the waters at home—for example, when she sang Schoenberg's *Erwartung* under Mitropoulos, a performance the *New York Times* called "astonishing."[6] And when in the mid-1960s, worn-out from the grueling schedule and difficult roles, she returned to Texas to teach, she had no regrets about where she had spent the better part of her career. "Europe was my place; I could not have had a career in America,"[7] she said. And she was probably right. Europe better suited Dow's artistic sensibilities—a reality that held true for other Americans as well.

If in the decade following the war Germany could be said to have at best tolerated Americans, clearly no other country offered them more or better opportunities that they in turn were only too glad to snatch up. "There's an opera house in every middle village, but they don't have the singers to fill them," the black soprano Gloria Davy said. "If you look on the list of every

Ellabelle Davis, about 1951. Photo by Yvonne

German opera house, three-quarters of the people are American."[8] And indeed, for black singers especially, Europe in general was a haven.

Ellabelle Davis, for example, was an early and grateful recipient of Europe's balm. The former seamstress from New York—discovered as she sang "Depuis le jour" to herself while pinning a dress on a wealthy white customer who then financed voice lessons—would never live there, as so many of her colleagues did. However, staggered by the reception accorded her first

European tour in 1948, she would return repeatedly throughout the late 1940s and 1950s to enjoy the unconditional acceptance that eluded her at home. During her third tour, *Musical Courier* reported Davis had become "such a personage in the music world of Europe that at her appearance on stage the assemblage often rises and in some instances the applause lasts for five or more minutes."[9] And though she had to refuse because of other commitments, even La Scala was said to have wanted her for Aida,[10] a role that she had sung with great success in Mexico City, though never in her own country, where she only concertized.

But no matter how accustomed to the trek Americans became, singing in Germany and elsewhere in Central Europe was unlike anything they had experienced in the United States and, especially in the first postwar years, fraught with uncertainty. One problem was that the singer had to know German. If he didn't, he aroused further anti-American feeling and put himself at a serious business and artistic disadvantage. All operas were performed in the vernacular; one had to be able to follow staging and musical instruction; and one had to be able to negotiate a contract and discuss scheduling in houses that were on the whole well organized and tightly run. Another was that because many of the intendants, conductors, and directors came to their positions after the war and were not as knowledgeable about singing as their predecessors, they often cast singers inappropriately and overworked them.

Yet few complained. A position in an opera house in Germany, Austria, or Switzerland assured solid, virtually year-round employment with health-care benefits and a pension. And because the repertoire was broader, the ensemble and theatrical values higher, and the time for rehearsal more extensive than anywhere at home, the experience offered a superb chance to grow as an artist.

As the "trek" from America grew apace, reaching floodlike proportions by the mid 1950s, an epochal and ironic moment occurred in 1949 when anti-Semitic Austria found itself a new star in an American Jewish baritone, the power of whose artistry triggered almost overnight a fundamental shift in the way Europeans viewed American singers. For not only did George London have every qualification required of a great singer-actor but, even more unusual to their way of thinking, he had the soul Europeans liked to claim Americans lacked. "George forced the chauvinistic European music world to acknowledge that an American-trained singer could cut it in Mozart, Wagner or Verdi," the baritone Thomas Stewart recalled. He was a "a pioneer, a pathfinder . . . the epitome of the American who conquered the Continent."[11]

The son of Russian émigrés who had become American citizens before moving to Canada, London, though born in Montreal, had begun his singing career in Hollywood, where the family moved because of his father's health when he was fifteen. Stirred by the Metropolitan Opera broadcasts and encouraged by compliments about his voice, London studied opera with Dr. Hugo Strelitzer, yet another Jewish refugee and the founder of one of the earliest workshops. Still, in the real world of Southern California, there were few jobs for opera singers. So London had done everything from singing in synagogues and churches to touring with an Ice Follies quartet and singing "La Marseillaise" for the movie *Casablanca.* But in 1941 he had made his operatic debut as the doctor in *Traviata* at the Hollywood Bowl, and in 1943, after changing his last name from the original Burnstein to Burnson (he would change it a final time in 1949), bowed with the San Francisco Opera as Monterone in *Rigoletto.*

Arthur Judson heard the baritone in a touring production of *Desert Song* in 1946 and, after signing him for Columbia, assigned him to its newest touring attraction, the Bel Canto Trio. The huge success of the trio, which also featured the soprano Frances Yeend and the tenor Mario Lanza, added significantly to the recognition factor of each of the singers, as for two seasons it toured the country, with appearances in Mexico and Canada as well. But time was passing, and "to avoid the inevitable fate of young American singers who wait hat in hand at the Metropolitan," London concluded in 1949 that he too must go abroad.[12] For, as he wrote to his parents on the eve of his departure, "The opera experience I receive over the next couple of years in Europe will (I hope) lay the foundation for a spectacular success here when I finally make my debut on this side."[13]

London arrived in Paris in June 1949, and as a result of a specially arranged audition for the Austrian conductor Karl Böhm, that September—a decade to the day since the outbreak of war—made his debut as Amonasro with the Vienna State Opera. A few nights later, opposite the Carmen of Dusolina Giannini, he appeared as Escamillo (ideal, one hesitates to add, for showing off his exotic, dark good looks and shapely legs). The reserved Viennese went into a frenzy, the critics raved, and by the end of the year London had given Vienna as well Méphistophélès, all four villains in *Les Contes d'Hoffmann,* Prince Galitzky in *Prince Igor,* and Boris Godunov. "He is not yet Chaliapin," wrote Vienna's esteemed Heinrich Kralik of the last, "but he's very remarkable"[14]

And so, over the next two years Vienna's new heartthrob juggled his obligations to its opera with an annual American concert tour for Columbia Artists and guest appearances with top European houses. In 1951 London and Astrid Varnay became the first Americans in over a generation to sing at Bayreuth, paving the way for countless others of their compatriots at the great Wagnerian festival. And that fall he made his Metropolitan Opera debut. But in dividing his singing time almost equally between Europe and America, London, who was to all intents and purposes America's first international star of the postwar generation, was an exception. There was as yet no jet airplane to speed the trip, and most careers were still weighted on one side of the ocean or the other.

Outside Central Europe there were far fewer opportunities for Americans, however, and, Ruffo's heartfelt welcome notwithstanding, no country was more wary of them, more nationalistic, or, as one American manager noted, more "proud and tenacious of its lyric theater" than Italy.[15]

It was, for instance, big news in 1947 when the Rome Opera awarded a resident contract to Lilly Windsor of upstate New York, because, management said, the soprano had been so thoroughly prepared and needed so little rehearsal for her guest appearance as Marguerite that she had actually saved the company money. Some twenty-five years had passed since an American had been so honored—the last none other than Edward Johnson—and Windsor's good fortune set off a wave of requests for auditions from American hopefuls, who, however, made no further inroads.

La Scala was equally resistant. It always had been. Amazingly, not one of America's greatest singers had ever sung at that most prestigious of theaters—not Nordica, Eames, Farrar, Homer, or even Ponselle—and the lesser-known Johnson, Valentino, Somigli, Pagliughi, Dow, and Cecil were essentially anomalies. So when in January 1950 the company engaged Eugene Conley, who, since impressing Ruffo in Florence, had been touring Europe with notable success while anticipating a Metropolitan debut later in the month, *Time* offered that La Scala simply needed a tenor with high notes for the treacherous role of Arturo in Bellini's *I Puritani* and all the Italian tenors were in the United States. But as it was, Conley's assured delivery of

Eugene Conley, about 1950, the year of his La Scala
and Metropolitan debuts. Photo by Bruno

the notorious arias, replete with the original high Cs and D flats, sent the Milanese into such ecstasy that one old-timer was heard to grumble, "It takes an American to come here and show us how a tenor should sing."[16]

Outside the big houses, however, as they had in the days when Hackett, Jagel, Johnson, and Bentonelli played them, the rest of Italy's approximately four hundred operational houses needed singers so badly that they had fewer qualms about engaging Americans. Lucy Kelston would say that even had she not married her Italian coach, she probably would have stayed in Italy: "I was able to sing constantly and gain the kind of experience I could never have found at home." It was a perfect time, although a time, she would admit, that lasted only a few years.[17]

After reportedly turning down a Met contract to sing comprimario roles, the soprano Dolores Wilson built her reputation on the Italian circuit. A typical product of the William Herman studio, the pretty, curvaceous blonde had several languages and some twenty roles ready at her command when she first went to Italy in 1948. Taking the name Dolores Vilsoni, she had studied with Toti Dal Monte, made her Italian debut as Rosina *(Barbiere di Siviglia)* in Brescia, then worked her way up the hierarchy of theaters (somewhere along the way reclaiming her rightful name) to make a triumphant debut as Gilda at La Fenice in Venice in 1951. The Metropolitan's new manager, Rudolf Bing, heard her there in a private audition, and when the Philadelphia native made her Met debut in 1954, an enthusiastic Max de Schauensee was glad to report back to her hometown that "without doubt, her several seasons in Italy stood her in good stead."[18]

Under the name Anna de Cavalieri, Anne McKnight also made an excellent career in Italy, despite little training and but one performance in America, a *Bohème* broadcast under Toscanini. Curiously, the maestro had selected the twenty-year-old soprano from Aurora, Illinois, to sing his Musetta from some thirty prospects, despite the fact her only experience was as a church soloist and her Italian pronunciation was, he acknowledged, "very funny."[19] But in Italy Serafin apparently also saw something in the sizable, warm voice and commanding presence, and he took over the mentoring. De Cavalieri soon had leading roles at La Scala, Rome, and throughout Italy. And when she returned to the United States in 1952 to open the New York City Opera season as Tosca, Serafin, back in the country for the first time since 1935, was in the pit.

But largely thanks to her teacher and future husband, Ettore Verna, arguably few owed more to postwar Italian experience than Mary Curtis of Salem, Massachusetts. It had been standard practice before the war for American teachers familiar with the Italian situation to arrange performances for their American students in one or another of Italy's houses. Now, with the war over, Verna, who had once been a teaching assistant to Tetrazzini in Milan, resumed the practice, arranging for his most advanced

*Mary Curtis-Verna, when she was still Maria Curtis
in Italy. Photo by Bruno*

New York students to perform at the Teatro Lirico in Milan, sometimes even alongside established Italian artists. And though he doubted his New Englander's temperament for Italian opera, in the summer of 1949 Verna had included Mary Curtis, thinking to "get it out of her system"; as it happened, it would do anything but. Of her debut as Desdemona opposite the Iago of the great Stabile, the press would declare Maria Curtis "a fine and sensitive artist [who] was equal to her co-stars and shared with them a well-earned success."[20]

Thus launched, Curtis set out to build her career like an Italian, patiently working her way up from the small theaters in the provinces to the topmost rung of the Italian opera hierarchy. It was "difficult, heavy, heavy work," she would remember. Hired by an impresario for a season of one or two months at some small theater, "you would have a week or more of rehearsal . . . and then maybe three performances in a row."[21] The value of such experience was incalculable, however, especially for an American, and by the time a scout for Bing arrived bearing a contract for the Met, Mary Curtis-Verna (for she would marry her teacher in 1954) had sung leading roles from Naples to San Francisco.

With even fewer opera companies than the United States, historically England rarely gave foreign singers resident contracts. In the decade preceding the war, a handful of Americans—notably Giannini, Kullman, Thomas, Ponselle, Moore, Bampton, Pagliughi, and Tibbett—appeared at Covent Garden, but only as guests. The Colorado-born, part–Cherokee Indian soprano Ina Souez gave up her Italian career to marry an Englishman and stay on in the country. But aside from her two Covent Garden appearances (a debut as a last-minute replacement as Liù and one Micaela) and her much-admired performances of Donna Anna and Fiordiligi for the fledgling Glyndebourne Festival, the soprano had found it almost impossible to sustain a career in England other than in concert and oratorio. And, in fact, after one of the first bombing raids of the war destroyed her London home, Souez had returned to the United States, made her American debut as Fiordiligi for the New Opera, then joined the Woman's Army Corp for the duration.

But after the war, with the new Covent Garden Opera Company[22] finally opening its doors to all nationalities, the Americans found themselves not only with a place of entry but, because the productions were to be in English, with an advantage as well. England was still struggling with severe shortages of food and fuel when, in the winter of 1947, Jess Walters, Virginia MacWatters, Doris Doree, and Hubert Norville arrived for the new company's inaugural season. But the Yankees piled on extra sweaters, lit candles when necessary, and lived on tea and fish and chips. And when MacWatters mentioned in a radio interview that she missed swallowing a raw egg before going on stage, English fans lucky enough to have some sent her theirs.

The coloratura, in fact, after a hefty handful of such leading roles as Manon, would stay only a season before returning to her flourishing career at the New York City Opera. But Norville, in roles that included Tamino in *The Magic Flute* and Walther in *Meistersinger,* and Doree, who essayed everything from Aida and Butterfly to Sieglinde and the Marschallin, would stay several seasons. And, though acceptance would come slowly for Jess Walters, the baritone who had so impressed as Macbeth with the New Opera, would ultimately remain for twelve seasons, singing almost seven hundred performances of roles ranging from Mozart's comic Papageno to Verdi's dramatic Amonasro, which he sings opposite Maria Callas on a performance recording.

Meanwhile, Americans also arrived for guest appearances, even as the casts boasted more and more international stars, despite the requirement of singing in English. Varnay alternated with Flagstad as Brünnhilde and Isolde. Conley sang Rodolfo and the Duke opposite Elisabeth Schwarzkopf, while his wife, Winifred Heidt, triumphed in a *Carmen* that also featured Willa Stewart, an American on her way to Vienna. Anthony Marlowe, a Philadelphia-born tenor with a career that included films in Hollywood and six seasons as a comprimario at the Met, substituted as Cavaradossi and the Duke. And Theodor Uppman sang Marcello and Papageno and won international recognition for his creation of Britten's Billy Budd.

Glyndebourne reopened in 1946 and resumed engaging Americans. And under the direction of Rudolf Bing, Glyndebourne's general manager, in 1947 the Edinburgh Festival opened and also welcomed Yankees. Todd Duncan, making his European debut, shared vocal recital honors with Elisabeth Schumann; Frank Valentino was Verdi's Macbeth; and Eleanor Steber, also making her first appearance outside the United States, portrayed the Countess Almaviva in *Le Nozze di Figaro.*

On her return home, Steber "waxed . . . enthusiastic" about America's new stature on the international stage, telling *Opera News:* "We American singers who have come along in the past seven years at the Metropolitan, where we have had a magnificent training with all our great conductors, have a very real place in the world at large. I have personally felt a real responsibility to show our European lovers of music that we also can produce and develop fine talent and so with all my heart I have tried to sing and play to them all with the accumulated knowledge and experience our own beloved country has given me."[23]

Chapter Fourteen

Purple Pins and Pioneers

E ARLY IN JANUARY 1946 "one of the greatest gatherings of nationally and internationally celebrated concert artists New York has ever
seen" turned out for a Silver Jubilee Dinner-Dance at the Plaza Hotel in
honor of Civic Concerts and its "organized audience plan." With the nation's triumph over tyranny still resonating, O. O. Bottorff, one of its Chicago founders, was proud to be showing off the plan's democratic principles
at such a moment in history. "Low membership dues that can include all
peoples, no reserved seats so that all may share alike, and the presentation of
only the finest in concert entertainment without guarantors or deficits are
the factors that are responsible for the permanency of the Civic Music institution," he told the guests.[1] It was, said *Musical America,* "perhaps the most
revolutionary idea ever introduced in the realm of concert-giving in this
country."[2] What is more, it had been so successful that in 1927 the powerful
Columbia Artists Organization, promising "A Carnegie Hall in Every
Town," had followed suit with its own Community Concerts.

Happily, the nation had room for both. With good music now accessible
to everyone, thanks to the radio and phonograph, the demand to hear it live
had not declined, as originally feared, but actually grown. By the early 1940s
Civic and Columbia together were serving almost two thousand communities, and in 1945 Ward French, Columbia's director, explained how that was
possible:

> In matters of taste, compare the musical excellence of programs,
> which an artist brings to the public of all communities today, with
> the "Old Black Joe" repertoire of the Chautauqua singers of 30 years
> ago. In terms of stability, compare the chagrin of a town which man-
> aged to raise only $600 instead of the $1,500 promised an artist for a

concert with the present assurance of the artist's fee a year in advance. In terms of the spread of music and opportunity for the artist, compare the ten or fifteen concerts sung by the average artist in 1915 with the 40 to 50 today, and the opportunities provided by this vast new audience to young or unknown artists of great merit who have yet to attain box-office name-value. Finally, compare the musical maps of the two periods. Twenty-five years ago, a few large population centers dotted the maps; today the same map is black with dots representing groups of some 600 to 4,000 people devoted to the best in music and able to bring it into their own auditoriums through the Organized Audience Plan.[3]

According to *Variety,* the plan (in this case, Civic's) worked like this:

The executives . . . decide on a certain town that apparently can support concerts. This town, through some civic body, perhaps, is approached and a committee formed for a one-week drive for membership to the subscription plan. Memberships can be secured for $5.00, with $2.50 for children charged. At the close of the week no one else can purchase a membership. After the money is counted, the town is allotted as many concerts as it can pay for.[4]

Four to nine concerts per year were average for a community. Because celebrities were limited in number and cost a great deal more, the number usually depended on how many lesser-known artists it was willing to accept. "Of about $5,500,000 grossed by thousands of concert performers in the United States annually, about 80 performers snare approximately half of that amount," *Variety* reported. "The smaller singers and instrumentalists are thus cut to a bare living and it is doubtful if more than 10% of those actually trying to make a living in concert earn as much as $30 weekly."[5] With a wife and baby to care for, young Frank Guarrera, after a grueling six-week winter stint in Minnesota, despaired when he realized how little he had brought home. Compared to the $125 a week he was earning in his first season with the Met, he had thought the $500 he would earn for an average of four concerts a week wonderful. But he had failed to factor in such extra expenses as hotels, food, and transportation for his accompanist as well as himself, and, for that matter, his accompanist's fee.

And a concert tour was more than just traveling and singing. "Although it was not specifically in the contract, it was understood that all artists were expected to be entertained by local sponsors for whom, particularly in the war years, concerts were the highlight of the social season," Eleanor Steber recalled.[6] Thus, a reception after the concert was all but obligatory, and no matter how tired the artist might be, how desperate to sit down, how early he had to get up the next morning to catch the next train, he smiled—even if they forgot to feed him. Some minded; others, like the gregarious Steber, thrived on the sociability and made lifelong friends around the country.

Meanwhile, from their offices managers kept track of their artists by sticking pins into the towns where they were performing on large maps of the United States—each artist represented by a different color. "When my concert entourage went on the road," recalled the soprano Margaret Truman, the president's daughter, under contract to the independent manager Jim Davidson, "we were referred to as 'The Purple Pins.'"[7]

Back in New York, the concert business boomed as well. Carnegie and Town Halls even added 5:30 time slots to their popular weekend schedules to help meet the demand. But unlike going on the road as a pin, giving a concert in a Manhattan hall was not about making money, rather about spending it in the hopes of being repaid by the prestige and reviews that could then sell the artist outside the city. In 1942 *Time* reported that to give a recital in New York cost between seven hundred and twelve hundred dollars. This included the hall (Carnegie Hall at four hundred dollars was the top), piano, publicity, ticket printing, an accompanist, and a manager to oversee it all. If the artist was lucky, ticket sales might offset the anticipated loss by a few hundred dollars.[8]

One exception was to perform for a music club, which, though critics rarely attended, could in fact be lucrative and even prestigious. Albert Morris Bagby, a former piano student of and whist partner to Franz Liszt, had died in 1941, but an invitation to sing for the subscription audience of society ladies at one of the Musical Mornings that still bore his name in the grand ballroom of the old Waldorf Astoria (later at the Plaza) was—even after a half century of its existence—still coveted. "At that hour of the morning I can't even spit," Nellie Melba had reportedly snapped when told about the unheard-of 11 A.M. performance time, but for the whopping fee she somehow found her voice.[9] "Only in America,"[10] exclaimed Frieda Hempel, herself a regular guest.

"Only in America" as well at the Verdi Club, where Florence Foster

Jenkins, its founder and president, held court, and where anyone wanting to be invited back to one of the soprano's incomparable recitals—and everyone did—kept his reactions in check. Indeed, while one man unable to control his laughing was seen stuffing a handkerchief in his mouth, critics fortunate enough to attend fine-tuned the art of double entendre. "A large and appreciative audience heard the soprano in a program which showed her remarkable versatility and aptitude for intensive study, her individual voice of light texture and penchant for florid vocalization," was a typical review from *Musical Courier.*[11]

But when in October 1944, at the age of seventy-something, Lady Florence (as she liked to be called) decided to try her art before a paying public and rented Carnegie Hall for what would be, as one critic wrote, "one of the weirdest mass jokes New York has ever seen,"[12] the gloves came off. For, as *Newsweek* reported, "Where stifled chuckles and occasional outbursts had once sufficed at the Ritz, unabashed roars were the order of the evening at Carnegie."

"Her notes range from the impossible to the fantastic and bear no relation to any known score or scale. . . . [She] changed costume three times [including one with wings, which she called the "Angel of Inspiration"], and roamed her range from Mozart's 'Queen of the Night' to a Russian item with words by Pushkin, melody by Pavlovich, and accompaniment by Johannes Sebastian Bach." During Valverde's "Clavelitos" she tossed tiny flowers "jerkily hither and yon," and when the audience demanded an encore, she made her accompanist retrieve every one so she could toss them all again.[13]

But if "howls of laughter drowned her celestial efforts," the magazine added, the house was sold out, two thousand fans were turned away, and the concert grossed an astronomical six thousand dollars. Indeed, though some believe the singer took herself so absolutely seriously that her death a month after the Carnegie Hall concert was the result of a broken heart, others maintain Florence Foster Jenkins was a keen businesswoman who knew exactly what she was doing. Whichever the case, fortunately she left recordings, or no one would have believed it.

New York's "recital mill" offered more than "divas and dowagers," however. There were as well, said *Time,* "prodigies and spaghetti tenors . . . European celebrities and art-conscious radio crooners—all intent on their big moment before the nation's most exacting (and jaded) high-brow musical audience."[14] Even folksingers were checking out Town Hall: John Jacob Niles, Burl Ives, and, in white tie and tails, Richard Dyer. In truth, as the clock ticked toward the mid-century mark, the city's halls were awash with an uncanny variety of music makers, including, of course, many the press once called "colored" and now called "Negro." For even though times were changing so fast critics were poised to drop mention of their color altogether and several were on the roster at the New York City Opera, virtually all black singers still looked to the concert stage as the best hope for a career. And, though none would achieve the same stature or fame, an exciting new generation was springing up in the wake of Roland Hayes, Paul Robeson, Marian Anderson, and Dorothy Maynor, all of whom were themselves still active.

To be sure, the tenor's pace may have slowed, but a Hayes concert tour or New York recital was still an eagerly anticipated annual event and his influence still considerable. Marian Anderson had ducked the spotlight long enough to marry and establish a semblance of home life on a large farm in Connecticut, but her whirlwind concert career had barely slowed. And when in 1946 her portrait graced the cover of *Time*'s Christmas issue, inside her story appeared not under Music, but under Religion. Where better to explore the almost palpable religiosity black singers brought to their singing, most potently in the songs of their common bondage—the spirituals.

"The black race is very good at interpretation, I think," the black mezzo Inez Matthews would muse. "I think it's really from the plantation days of suffering. I really feel this was a special gift God gave to us—to interpret. It came out of the suffering of our forefathers."[15] With the shrinking of the globe in the jet age, singers would unwittingly begin to lose the expressive characteristics that once identified their race or nationality. But halfway through the twentieth century, with the inherent sorrow and dignity of their legacy still intact and with their spirituality still firmly imbedded in the church, black artists still expressed what the great French tenor Jean de Reszke once regretted his American students mostly lacked: the "deep, tragic note."[16]

Paul Robeson too continued in concert, though his political views, including an intractable admiration for the Soviet Union, where he had lived for two years, were beginning to affect his career negatively. Even after spending the greater part of the 1930s abroad, his popularity had surged on his return to America in 1939. His impassioned delivery of John Latouche's patriotic text celebrating the equality and freedoms that were America's destiny had fairly electrified listeners across the land in the world premiere broadcast of Earl Robinson's "Ballad for Americans," a cantata for baritone and chorus. But as he toured the nation, no longer just singing but railing against racism and voicing his communist sympathies, the public began to recoil. And with the country in the grip of a terrible Red scare, the government began to tap his phone and follow him; then, in 1950, it effectively ended his career for good by taking away his passport because he refused to sign a statement that he was not a member of the Communist party.[17]

Meanwhile, the soft-spoken Dorothy Maynor, whom Koussevitzky had launched with such fanfare in 1939, continued her solid career with little mishap. And in 1946 the conductor took it upon himself to further the career of a second black artist when he told a specially invited audience at Symphony Hall in Boston, "Today we discover another great singer—Carol Brice." Never mind that the contralto had already performed and recorded with Fritz Reiner, who himself had predicted she would become "one of the outstanding singers of our generation."[18] Never mind that the previous year the Juilliard graduate had been the first black to win the Naumburg Award and consequently already given an acclaimed Town Hall recital. As was his wont, Koussevitzky backed his enthusiasm with action and over the years engaged the tall, handsome Indiana native multiple times—with good reason. Brice had, said Virgil Thomson, "a rich and round mezzo voice of wide range, accurate pitch and perfect production."[19]

Thomson, for that matter, also liked Helen Thigpen, "mistress of the finest spun, the most penetrating true pianissimo now available, to my knowledge, on the American concert stage . . . an artist and a musician through and through . . . [with] a voice of great natural beauty."[20] But while the soprano continued to concertize, often programming the art songs of such upcoming black composers as Howard Swanson, she is probably best remembered for her Serena in the 1950s revival of *Porgy and Bess.*

Whereas European singers rarely ventured outside their own language and often even their own nationality in their recitals, Americans offered most repertoire in its original language and (following the programming format introduced by Marcella Sembrich in the early 1900s as an alternative to the customary potpourris of arias and ballads) presented groupings of songs of various nationalities in approximate chronological order of composition. A typical program progressed from the classics (early Italian, Bach, Handel,

Haydn, or Mozart) to romantic German lieder to impressionist French mélodies and finally to contemporary English or American art song with possibly a familiar aria or something light to close.

There were exceptions to this model, of course. Sembrich herself had given a groundbreaking recital devoted to folk song, and Europeans, especially those considered specialists in the idiom, were surprisingly successful in America with all-lieder programs. Conversely, artists such as Eva Gauthier and Povla Frijsh, whose native Canada and Netherlands, like America, had not provided significant repertoires of their own for their singers, attracted a kind of fringe audience with their fearless juxtaposition of styles and languages and spirit of anything goes. Gauthier's programming of Bartók, Schoenberg, Hindemith, Milhaud, Arthur Bliss, William Byrd, Purcell, Irving Berlin, Kern, and Gershwin in a single program had, in fact, shaken the music world to its core in 1923. But now a small coterie of Americans (some compensating with imagination, intelligence, and intellectual curiosity for what they lacked in voice) thrived in the wake of such newfound freedom.

It was, therefore, no longer unusual to find, amid the glut of New York recitals, singers taking real chances with their offerings. In the fall of 1948, for instance, we find the radio star Margaret Speaks programming Britten, Honegger, and Chausson; the Broadway star Marion Bell singing in six languages; and in a series of three recitals the Met baritone Mack Harrell offering Mussorgsky's rarely heard *Songs and Dances of Death,* Schumann's *Dichterliebe,* Brahms's *Schöne Magelone,* Schubert's *Die Schöne Müllerin,* and a world premiere by Victor Babin. "It is doubtful whether any American artist has ever gained command of the refined art of lieder singing as satisfyingly as Mr. Harrell now has," Cecil Smith wrote during the marathon. "Indeed, few singers of foreign origin are his equal in this field today."[21] "Harrell, the Versatile,"[22] *Newsweek* would declare the baritone, whose limp from childhood polio and less than large voice limited his roles at the Met, but whose superlative contributions to oratorio and concert and notable facility for contemporary music kept him one of the busiest artists in the country.

And if, in an article assessing the postwar "Music Mart" that same fall, *Newsweek* reported a "slackening off" in the quantity of recitals, it also noted that the quality was "higher than usual." The Danish tenor Aksel Schiøtz, visiting the United States for the first time, had given three recitals; the French baritone Pierre Bernac had made his long-awaited debut singing the

Alice Howland, about 1950. Courtesy of Alice Howland's family

songs of Francis Poulenc with the composer himself at the piano; and then there were the American mezzos Nell Tangeman and Alice Howland. "'Almost everything one could wish for in a singer—an artist right off the top shelf,'" the magazine quoted Virgil Thomson on Tangeman, and "'just plain perfect,'" the usually crusty critic broke down to describe Howland.[23]

Born of an American father and German mother in Berlin, where her father was in business, Alice Howland had not made the United States home until 1934. But in the early 1940s, after studies at Juilliard, she had performed opera, including Carmen, across the country, chalked up many hours of radio work, and in 1946 given a highly acclaimed New York recital. And now, partly on the strength of this recital, she would see her reputation for contemporary music grow apace. For while still continuing in the classical repertoire, Howland would not only sing many first performances of native composers, including, as a notable example, Aaron Copland's "Twelve Poems by Emily Dickinson," but also become the first American to record Schoenberg's *Pierrot Lunaire,* before closing out her brief career as Mozart's Dorabella at Glyndebourne in 1951. Married since 1945 and frustrated by the lack of opportunity for her singing, like so many women of her generation, in the end she chose family over career.

Nell Tangeman, on the other hand, managed to give her career more years but, sadly, no such happy ending. Like Howland and Harrell, the Ohio-born former violin student was a musicianly singer who distinguished herself in everything from Bach to Mahler and Stravinsky. A favorite of conductors and composers, she sang important premieres and in the early 1950s created several roles, including Mother Goose in *The Rake's Progress.* Ned Rorem, to whom Tangeman was close for many years and whose songs she often sang, has described her voice as a "lush contralto."[24] Nadia Boulanger, he said, called her the "American Kathleen Ferrier."[25] Her career, however, was constantly getting off track, primarily the result of a dissolute life, which probably contributed as well to her unexplained early death.

But if their artistic proclivities were not typical, Howland and Tangeman were by no means alone in their willingness to tackle different and often challenging repertoire. The number of intelligent young Americans looking beyond the mainstream was growing fast, as was a lively new interest in early and contemporary music by a certain segment of the musical population. Small groups such as the Society for Forgotten Music, the American Society of Ancient Instruments, the Composers Forum, and New Friends of Music had been quietly cropping up since the 1920s. And the émigré musicians, including important composers, who brought with them not only a heightened consciousness for this music but also the latest research and techniques needed to develop it, had fueled their fires. Born into the melting pot that was America, Americans traditionally opened themselves to the new. Now with so much exciting uncharted territory to explore, some of the more enterprising singers elected to forfeit the life of the purple pins for that of the pioneer.

Helen Boatwright. Photo by J. Abresch, courtesy of Helen Boatwright

To be sure, Helen Boatwright worked both the old and new so success-
fully, few realized she could also sing all the music in between; for though
the voice was of a breathtaking purity, private recordings show Boatwright
also had the temperament and range of expression for Verdi. Nevertheless,
though she had a handful of credits in the idiom, including singing opposite
Mario Lanza in *The Merry Wives of Windsor* at Tanglewood, opera's accou-

trements were not for this sylphlike soprano, who needed but a simple evening gown and a plain concert platform to work her magic in a repertoire that was apt to leapfrog the nineteenth century.

Born in Wisconsin of German descent, Boatwright (née Strassburger) had first learned the exactitudes of music making at home when every night her father led the family in the singing of chorales a cappella in full harmony. She had then built on that strong foundation at Oberlin College, where she learned about the new American song literature from the composer Norman Lockwood and earned her Master's with a thesis on the soprano arias in Bach's church cantatas. Even with such unorthodox preparation, a traditional singing career would still have been the obvious route for the young soprano, but marriage to the violinist and composer Howard Boatwright, whom she met while competing as a regional winner in the National Federation of Music Clubs, would lure her off course for good.

Following her husband to Yale in 1945, where Paul Hindemith was introducing studies in early music, Boatwright became the principal soloist for the German-born composer's Collegium Musicum and soon found herself in demand for oratorio and Elizabethan and baroque music. "That Helen Boatwright is a nearly perfect singer of baroque music will surprise no one who has heard her in person," one critic wrote of her recording of Buxtehude.[26] At the same time, surrounded by living composers, she became ever more involved with contemporary music: singing with the Composer's Society; performing and recording the songs of Ernst Bacon and Charles Ives; introducing new works by such composers as Jack Beeson, Louise Talma, and Elliott Carter at the summer festival at Yaddo in Saratoga Springs, New York. Over the years, her reputation as a specialist in both contemporary and early music, her strong associations with academia, and her responsibilities as a mother living, moreover, some distance from New York would keep Boatwright from achieving a place in mainstream music. But if her place on the periphery prohibited mainstream recognition, like others of her sensibility she gladly exchanged it for the excitement and satisfaction that came with charting new ground.

Bethany Beardslee would sing a hefty share of early music herself, as well as the standard song and orchestral literature from Mozart to Debussy. But it was the "despised" modern music she would serve. For to this soprano's way of thinking, "The big interest in early music was the concert audience's validation for hating modern music; their way of showing they were chic and interested in an undiscovered field of music; their way of not having to go to all those awful contemporary music concerts."[27]

Bethany Beardslee and Jacques Monod. Courtesy of Bethany Beardslee

Like Boatwright, Beardslee had grown up in the upper Midwest, but in her case it was the refugee Jewish intellectuals she studied with at Michigan State University who both grounded and inspired her music making. For in high school she had sung in the glee club and starred in musicals, and she might well have gone into musical comedy had the war not driven those musicians to her doorstep. Instead, with an allowance of twenty-five dollars a week and a scholarship to Juilliard, she had headed for New York, where, though she sang Susanna in the opera department's production of *Le Nozze di Figaro,* she soon realized she had neither the voice (too small) nor the passion for opera. It was song and chamber music she prized. And with her "crystalline focus and clarity, keen musicality, and almost hypnotic ability to draw a listener's attention,"[28] her path became clearer still one day when a young French conductor, steeped in twentieth-century music, heard her. Beardslee would marry Jacques Monod; and then, either under his baton or with him at the piano, she would set off to champion (often on the fast-growing college circuit) the contemporary vocal idiom—above all, the atonal and serial music of the Viennese school of Berg, Webern, and Schoenberg and, later, the Princeton school of Milton Babbitt and her second husband, Godfrey Winham.

In the summer of 1948 the Newberry Library in Chicago received for its collection a bequest of some fifteen hundred songs from a native of the city who had died of Hodgkins lymphoma the previous September. As most of the songs were from the twentieth century, many were manuscripts in the composers' hands, while many others—civilization still wanting for copy machines—the donor had laboriously copied out herself. Of the twenty-five boxes, eight were devoted to American composers.

The library paid the collection little mind. It was insignificant compared to its other vast and distinguished holdings. No one had much interest in contemporary song, especially American; and outside a certain small circle, few had ever heard of Janet Fairbank in spite of the fact that *Time* magazine had thought to cover her last recital. To be sure, no one knew it would be her last—few, in fact, knew she was already very ill—but somehow the magazine had seen a story in a singer whose service to song was so much appreciated that critics "never give her a bad review." And so under the headline "Song Plugger," the reporter for *Time* began:

> The song recital was like a new Schiaperelli showing. The people who filled Manhattan's Carnegie Chamber Hall were largely buyers of music: singers, teachers and publishers. On stage like a mannequin modeling a new plunging neckline, brown-haired, willowy Janet Fairbank paraded the latest creations in art songs. . . .
>
> Most singers consider the program foolhardy that has more than two songs by living composers—but not 44-year-old Janet Fairbank. In eight New York concerts she has given more than 100 songs by

some two dozen composers their first performance. . . . A year ago every song Janet Fairbank sang was purchased by publishers the morning after the recital. This year the publishers didn't wait. They bought almost her entire program before the recital.[29]

Certainly Janet Fairbank was not the first to champion America's art song composers. Early in the century, Mina Hager, for example, had introduced many John Alden Carpenter songs and even some Charles Ives; Gauthier regularly programmed Charles Griffes, Wintter Watts, Bainbridge Crist; occasionally, too, a famous singer such as John McCormack or Alma Gluck included a more serious effort. But generally the better-known singers, who by their very celebrity might have inspired others to look beyond, had been loath to give up the big, commercially oriented, easily digested concert ballads, which showed off their operatic voices; with such competition, the tiny art song genre seemed to lose even its small momentum. And then at some point in the mid-1930s a new generation of Americans began to give it a second look. More secure in revealing their personal voices, this new generation of composers (among them Bacon, Copland, Paul Bowles, Chanler, David Diamond, John Edmunds, Paul Nordoff, Thomson, and soon William Flanagan, Rorem, and Barber) sought out quality poetry and, with a fresh sensibility, produced a treasure trove of songs—songs needing only a voice to give them life.

It should be said that Fairbank did not commission the songs she introduced; such a notion was still uncommon. What she did—at least initially, for later they would seek her out—was find the composers and ask to see any songs they might have. And because they rarely got to hear their songs performed, for the most part the composers—after wiping off the dust—had been glad to ply her with anything they had. After all, whoever she was, she might give them life, however briefly.

Fairbank then took her treasures back to her tiny walk-up apartment on East Fifty-fifth Street in Manhattan, paid a pianist to help her study them (the library reported evidence that she had reviewed more than three thousand compositions), made her selections, and rented a hall. All this she could afford because (despite the way she chose to live) she came from a wealthy as well as socially and artistically prominent family. Her grandfather N. K. Fairbank, who had helped found the Chicago Symphony, had made the family fortune in Gold Dust Twins washing powder. Janet had grown up in mansions in Chicago and on Wisconsin's Lake Geneva, where her father, a lawyer, and her mother, a novelist and political activist,[30] regularly enter-tained celebrities. "Everyone who came to Chicago went through our house," she told *Time*. "I always knew a lot of composers. Prokofiev and John Alden Carpenter were in & out of the house."

After graduating from Radcliffe College, Fairbank had studied music in Germany, then made her professional bow in a joint recital with John Charles Thomas in Chicago. She appeared with the Chicago Symphony, sang small roles with the Chicago Opera and secondary roles with Gallo's San Carlo Opera, and in 1941 programmed assorted European composers in her first New York recital. Receiving only a nod from the critics, she tried again in 1943 but this time, in part to better get their attention, programmed solely new American songs, including first performances of what would be-come classics by Virgil Thomson, Ernst Bacon, Paul Bowles, Theodore Chanler, and John Cage. "People thought it was going to be a nut stunt," she said. "When I started, the American songs that were sung were mostly the 'I Love Life' type. I think I made people realize that there were good American songs."

Now, those who heard her generally agree that Janet Fairbank did not have much voice. But she knew her limitations and, as one critic said, used what she had "with discretion . . . her performances . . . so carefully con-trived that the music becomes the focal point for the audience's attention, rather than the interpreter."[31] "Her success in showing the values of a skillful integration of poetry and music to both composers and the public has had a beneficial effect upon the quality of songwriting," Cecil Smith wrote in 1947. "From the point of view of the American composer she is our most im-portant singer today."[32]

Ned Rorem, who as a young man spent a year as her rehearsal pianist, has often told of the day he both learned of Janet Fairbank's death on the phone and received in the mail his first complimentary copies of his first published song, the prizewinning "The Lordly Hudson," which he had dedi-cated to her. Indeed, in that golden age of American song one finds many dedications "To Janet" atop the sheet music—a symbol, in some ways, of a crucial relationship finally being formed between native composer and native singer.

Chapter Fifteen

Broadway Opera and the Halasz Gang

ON JANUARY 9, 1947, a new musical by Kurt Weill opened at the Adelphi Theater on Broadway, and the next morning Brooks Atkinson of the *New York Times* praised the "superb singers who . . . helped make [it] one of the memorable nights in theater going." In recent years it had been difficult to find actors who could sing, the paper's famous drama critic said, but the producers of *Street Scene* had solved that problem by finding singers who could act—opera singers no less.[1]

Not that there was anything new about opera singers on Broadway. Primarily because only a classically trained voice could properly render the aria-like proportions of Nettie's "When You Walk through a Storm" or Billy's "Soliloquy," Christine Johnson, a contralto who had sung with the Met, and John Raitt, a baritone experienced in light opera and concert, were even then starring in the new Rodgers and Hammerstein musical *Carousel.* But in *Street Scene* all the principals were opera singers. If the producers called it a musical drama it was only because they did not want to frighten potential customers. "Call it lyric drama, lyric theater, musical drama, musical theater, Broadway opera: call it what you will," the composer Marc Blitzstein would sound off in 1950, referring to the works like it that followed. "It is a form, this new thing, something like opera (don't say the naughty word)."[2] But Weill said it, even proclaimed it on the published score: "*Street Scene*—an American opera."

Since taking refuge in the United States in 1935, the German Jewish composer, whose own *Mahagonny* and *Die Dreigroschenoper* had electrified his native Berlin, had always dreamed of seeing opera—native opera—on Broadway. "Broadway represents the living theater in this country, and an

American opera . . . should be part of the living theater," he said.[3] He had looked to *Porgy and Bess* to point the way. But Americans, worn down by the Depression, still preferred escape in mindless extravaganzas and revues; the Gershwin work had not proved commercially viable; and since then only a few serious musical plays (notably Vernon Duke's *Cabin in the Sky* and Weill's own *Lady in the Dark*) had sought to advance the cause.

But then in March 1943 a new show opened at the St. James that suddenly made everything seem possible. It was no mere evening's diversion; its songs and dances propelled and defined an emotional, meaningful story. Its every aspect—theatrical, dramatic, musical—was fully integrated: *Oklahoma!* was potent lyric theater that broke the conventional mold. And because it was an unexpected and instantaneous box-office hit, "librettists, lyricists and composers," Richard Rodgers, its composer, would write, "now had a new incentive to explore a multitude of themes and techniques within the framework of the commercial musical theater."[4]

That the first out of the gate was the show's own librettist, Oscar Hammerstein II, was almost to be expected. For it had been a particular and long-held dream of the grandson of the great opera impresario, whose name he bore, to help make opera, specifically Bizet's *Carmen,* more accessible to the public by adapting it for Broadway. The idea was not to change the music, but to write new words and modernize the story. No cigarette factory and gypsies in nineteenth-century Spain, this Carmen was a Negro who worked in a parachute factory in South Carolina in World War II and sang "Dat's love," not "L'amour," to her Negro friends.

From its first performance in December 1943, *Carmen Jones* realized Hammerstein's every hope. And with the Bizet arias transformed into popular hit songs, fourteen classically trained black singers had their best chance since *Porgy and Bess* to show white audiences what they could do, with none benefiting more than the three who alternated in the title role, Muriel Smith, Muriel Rahn, and Inez Matthews.

"A born actress of the histrionic mold" with a voice as "rich and slick as peanut butter"[5] was the composer Ned Rorem's description of the role's creator, Muriel Smith, whom he knew from Curtis, where she had been studying with Elisabeth Schumann when she got the call to audition. The mezzo would, in fact, manage to graduate from Curtis, even while delivering her "torridly realistic"[6] portrayal of Carmen Jones in New York. Later, she would reprise the show in London, sing the original Bizet at the Royal Opera, and perform musical theater at home and abroad into the 1950s.

The petite soprano Muriel Rahn would also enjoy a solid post–Carmen Jones career, singing Aida for Salmaggi and Gallo as well as Cora in Jan Meyerowitz's musical play *The Barrier* at Columbia University and again on Broadway, before moving on to Europe to both sing in and direct opera. And the mezzo Inez Matthews, a later alternate, would costar with Todd Duncan in Weill's next quasi-operatic musical, *Lost in the Stars,* sing leading roles in revivals of *Four Saints in Three Acts,* and, above all, distinguish herself in concert. Decades later Matthews, who came from a musical family, would recount how Billy Rose had selected her from a big group of singers hoping for a chance to audition for the show because he recognized her as the sister of Edward Matthews, the star of the original *Four Saints in Three Acts.* She had sung Mozart's "Voi che sapete" for the colorful producer—a curious choice for someone hoping to sing Carmen—but Rose had hired her for the chorus, quickly moved her up to general understudy, and finally chosen her for the title role.[7]

But if *Carmen Jones* proved opera could be made fun enough to play the Great White Way, *Street Scene* was out to prove that opera as serious musical theater belonged there as well, even if its success depended on a bunch of heavy-hitting opera singers to make the point. And indeed, among the names in the original cast could be found Norman Cordon, who had just completed the last of many seasons with the Met; Polyna Stoska and Brian Sullivan, both on the verge of Met careers; Sidney Rayner, winding up a long operatic career that included the Met; Randolph Symonette,[8] who would find his way there in time, and Anne Jeffreys, a former movie star who had recently essayed Tosca for Salmaggi. Jeffreys, who remained in the theater, would later criticize her colleagues' acting,[9] but the fact remains that their performances, as Atkinson said from the top, had much to do with the success of *Street Scene* and, as a result, with the coming of opera to Broadway. That the next effort would come so soon, succeed as authentic opera (regardless of being called otherwise), and accelerate the trend to such a degree was more than anyone could imagine.

Years later, the soprano Brenda Lewis would credit the courage and vision of certain "culturally advanced" producers with putting opera on Broadway, among them Chandler Cowles and Efrem Zimbalist Jr.[10] For Gian Carlo Menotti had not written *The Medium* for Broadway, nor, for that matter, for the Metropolitan, which, despite the honor accorded the composer, had already sorely disappointed him with its poor productions of two of his operas.[11] But after Columbia University premiered the little melodrama in 1946, Menotti had composed *The Telephone,* a one-act comedy to fill out the evening; he had then, under the auspices of the Ballet Theater, taken the double bill to the uptown Heckscher Theater, and it was only there that Cowles and Zimbalist picked it up for Broadway. With a contract for the Met in her pocket, Claramae Turner, who had created the title role at Columbia, had left the show by then. But to replace her Menotti had found a Madame Flora whose acting and singing was about to prove the best possible validation for opera singers on Broadway.

When Menotti first heard about her, Marie Powers was performing with the San Carlo in Seattle. But in fact the Pennsylvania-born contralto had once enjoyed a significant career in Europe, where she had been launched when Toscanini engaged her for small Wagnerian roles at La Scala. Marriage to an Italian count had given her entrée into court circles, and she had sung leading roles, including Dalila and Orfeo, in Paris and Monte Carlo. But when, shortly after her husband died, the war broke out, Powers had returned home. Inexplicably penniless, she had sung for Salmaggi, given a joint recital at Town Hall, auditioned for the Met, and, when nothing materialized, signed with Gallo.

Taken to meet the composer, Powers questioned the wisdom of opera on Broadway, insisted on being called Countess, bragged about her career, vacillated about taking the role, then flung herself on the couch, saying, "Oh, for God's sake, let's cut this out. I've got exactly forty cents in my pocket and I may as well say yes. Of course I'll do it."[12] Despite her eccentricities—for example, Powers, a Roman Catholic, took a cold shower and roller-skated to mass every morning—Menotti knew immediately that "she was the Madame Flora I was looking for. It wasn't just her voice or her acting. It was her electrifying vitality."[13] "Miss Powers will not long be an unknown quantity to our public," Olin Downes predicted.[14] And indeed, once word got out, *The Medium* was a triumph, as was Powers. Her career thus resurrected, Powers would virtually own the role for much of the next decade,[15] singing it some 2,341 times (by her count) on three continents and appearing in a film version.

In light of the recent failures of Menotti's operas at the Met, the success of *The Medium* and *The Telephone* was as well a resurrection for the Italian composer. Though he never became an American citizen, he now showed himself ever more adept at pinpointing exactly what Americans wanted and, to ensure they got it, wrote not only the music but the book and libretto for his operas, directed their first productions, and chose their first casts. At its best a Menotti opera was a seamless blending of music, word, and theater, built on Italian opera traditions but wholly relevant to America and the times. His characters were believable, and the English they sang was clear, idiomatic, and eminently well set for the voice. All added up to both artistic and commercial success, which in turn inspired the single greatest period of native opera the country had ever known. "Whether you like his music or not," Rorem explained, "the fact exists that due to Menotti, and only Menotti, the whole point of view of contemporary opera in America . . . is different from what it would have been had he not existed. . . . After the success of *The Medium* every composer in America said, 'If Menotti can hit the jackpot, so can I.'"[16]

The phenomenon of opera on Broadway lasted only a few years, and (not forgetting such quasi-operatic shows as *My Darlin' Aida* and *Most Happy Fella'* and the many that depended on opera singers for specific roles) it included *Street Scene* (1947), *The Telephone,* and *The Medium* (1947), Britten's *The Rape of Lucretia* (1948), Weill's *Lost in the Stars* (1949), Blitzstein's *Regina* (1949), Meyerowitz's *The Barrier* (1950), Menotti's *The Consul* (1950) and *The Saint of Bleeker Street* (1954), as well as important revivals of *Porgy and Bess, Four Saints in Three Acts,* and *The Threepenny Opera.* Though with the exception of *Porgy* decades later, none would ever be produced by the Metropolitan; with the exception of *The Barrier,* all would be picked up by the New York City Opera.

Indeed, since its cut-and-paste first seasons, Laszlo Halasz's fledgling company had been growing apace not only in size (as the fast-growing numbers of performances, productions, and singers suggest), but also in spirit, sophistication, and sense of purpose. New York delighted in its new company, and as the ink turned black, its dynamic director grew ever more daring in his leadership. Expanding on the original purpose of giving New Yorkers opera they could afford to include opera to which they could relate, Halasz began to explore the contemporary repertoire, emphasize dramatic credibility, and hire more young natives, who, unencumbered by European traditions, were more inclined to render opera as the living lyric theater one found on Broadway.

The addition to the roster of one James Pease, a former law student from Indiana, certainly boded well for his vision. A runner-up in the 1943 Auditions of the Air, the handsome bass-baritone had been poised to accept a

Met contract but instead enlisted in the Air Force. Now in the spring of 1946, after years of transporting bombers to Europe, he made his City Opera debut as Sparafucile and in no time was lending his considerable talents as a singer-actor to roles as diverse as Don Giovanni, Méphistophélès, Baron Ochs, and Hans Sachs.

Camilla Williams also made her debut that first postwar spring. The former schoolteacher from Virginia who liked to call herself a "democratic enterprise, because so many people have contributed,"[17] had sung for Halasz after the great American soprano Geraldine Farrar wrote her manager, Arthur Judson, insisting Williams "be given every chance in opera."[18] After hearing her "Un bel dì," Halasz had written on her audition card, "When we can do 'Butterfly' again, call this girl."[19] That "this girl" had never been in an opera, knew nothing but the aria, and was black were not concerns. He would personally teach her the role and see that the production was staged in a way that allowed for prevailing sensibilities. For her part, Williams, after spending the better part of her $150 salary to be transformed into a Japanese geisha by the great makeup artist Eddie Senz, would achieve "an instant and pronounced success"[20] as, said Farrar, North America's first to sing the Puccini, "one of the great Butterflies of our day."[21]

Theatrically sound performance was also reinforced that spring with the arrival of pretty Virginia MacWatters, who, though making only a slight impression in her bow as Mabel in *The Pirates of Penzance,* brought down the house the following fall singing the formidable role of Zerbinetta "with an ease which would have astonished all the European canaries who have long strained their vocal cords over its demands."[22]

Richard Strauss's *Ariadne auf Naxos* had received its American premiere in Philadelphia in 1928, but, except for a Juilliard production in 1934, had never been heard in New York. Of the City Opera's 1946 production Virgil Thomson complained that the Hungarian Ella Flesch, as Ariadne, "mostly stood around looking like the Statue of Liberty and sang flat,"[23] but otherwise Halasz's gang, especially Stoska, as the Composer, and MacWatters, was stellar. The English-language production was a triumph, and over the next few seasons it would serve to introduce other important natives, among them Wilma Spence, a spinto soprano, as the Composer; Virginia Haskins, an excellent soubrette, if over her head as Zerbinetta; Ann Ayars, a former actress and soon-to-be leading lyric with the company, in a small role; and Suzy Morris, new to opera but an authentic dramatic soprano, as Ariadne.

"Voices of this caliber are said to be almost non-existent in this country,"

Camilla Williams as Madama Butterfly in Vienna.
Courtesy of Camilla Williams

Howard Taubman wrote after Morris's debut, "but here was a singer who produced tones of opulence, power, wide range and who used them with mature, musical effect. . . . She could be a prima donna worthy of any opera house."[24] "A singer who cannot lose her way to the top of her profession,"[25] said *Musical America* of her Tosca the following spring.

But Suzy Morris would neither lose her way nor go to the top as a singer. From the culturally and socially prominent Frelinghuysen family of New Jersey, the handsome soprano, who had grown up a student of painting as well as music, had auditioned for the New York City Opera primarily at the urging of her voice teacher; she had been uncomfortable with the prospect because Newbold Morris, the City Center founder, was her brother-in-law. Now, stressed further by both the performing experience and her sudden celebrity, and plagued by bronchitis as well, she would sing only an occasional Tosca, Ariadne, Santuzza, and Amneris for Halasz, and an Amelia in *Ballo in Maschera* in New Orleans, before retiring to her studio in Massachusetts to reemerge Suzy Frelinghuysen, abstract painter.

In retrospect Halasz pointed to *Ariadne* as a turning point. In its first venture into twentieth-century repertoire, the company had proven not only that it was capable of new and difficult repertoire but also that it could make a commercial success of it. And when to follow up he mounted *Salome,* "by daring to choose a work which never receives an entirely satisfactory representation even under the most experienced auspices," *Theater Arts* wrote, "Laszlo Halasz demonstrated the completeness of his confidence in the intrepid young operatic organization he had built up in the last three years."[26] In two years' time the Metropolitan's production of *Salome* with the conductor Fritz Reiner and the Bulgarian soprano Ljuba Welitsch would stand the opera world on its head. But in the spring of 1947 Halasz wisely used Strauss's reduced orchestration, engaged Frederick Jagel to portray a "superlative" Herod, and cast, as his depraved daughter, Brenda Lewis, who "sang the music so well you forgot it was difficult, and . . . acted Salome so beautifully that singing and acting merged into a characterization that had passion and even a touch of pity."[27]

The versatile Lewis was on hand the following fall for the company's first Mozart, an all-American *Don Giovanni,* which also featured Pease, Conley, Haskins, Cordon (over from *Street Scene*) as Leporello, and Ellen Faull, a "green" soprano, she herself would say, making her debut as Donna Anna. Though Faull had studied at the Curtis Institute and appeared in opera scenes, she had never performed a complete role. But overheard singing

Brenda Lewis as Salome. Courtesy of Brenda Lewis

"Non mi dir" at another audition, she had been taken to sing for Halasz, engaged, told to cover Donna Anna, and, at the last possible moment, assigned the first performance. With a "soprano of unlimited range," which, as Rorem said, "flowed with unflawed naturalness from her larynx like a cloud of peridot chiffon,"[28] Faull would develop into not only a great Mozartian but an all-round artist of exceptional versatility. She was, said Julius Rudel, "the epitome of [the] new kind of opera singer . . . a good colleague, a good musician, believable looking, willing to take direction, cooperative and American."[29]

She might well have been, in fact, the singer Cecil Smith was referring to when that spring he wrote that the company had "a way of bringing forward extraordinarily gifted young artists noncommittally and without advance fanfare, leaving the excitement of discovery to the audience." But in this case, the young artist was the lovely titian-haired Adelaide Bishop, "a lyric-coloratura . . . so gleaming of voice that there is obviously room for her in any opera house where the management has an ear for lovely tone, and so honest and true in her deportment and expression of feeling that the legitimate theater might do well to pay attention to her."[30]

Though only nineteen years old at the time of her debut as Gilda, Bishop, a Manhattan native, came experienced in opera and operetta. Menotti had recommended her after seeing her as Laetitia in a performance of his *Old Maid and the Thief* in Philadelphia, an opera Halasz had presented earlier in the season with MacWatters in the role. Coupled with his *Amelia Goes to the Ball*, the Menotti double bill had been City Opera's first venture into both contemporary and American opera. As Miss Todd, Marie Powers in her company debut had proven as brilliant in comedy as in the high drama of *The Medium*, while the well-seasoned soprano Frances Yeend, whose robust looks had not detracted from her highly acclaimed debut earlier as the consumptive Violetta, had fairly dazzled as Amelia.

Since arriving in New York from Oregon shortly after the war and getting a job as the anonymous hymn singer with Phil Spitalny and his all girl orchestra on radio, Yeend in fact had been making quite a name for herself. In opera she had portrayed not only Ellen in the American premiere of Britten's *Peter Grimes* at Tanglewood but all four heroines in *Tales of Hoffmann* in New Orleans, a feat all the more amazing because the strapping soprano and former student of ballet performed the coloratura role of the doll Olympia on pointe. Under contract to Columbia Artists, Yeend was the soprano in the popular Bel Canto Trio, and with a clarion voice, capable of riding any orchestra, she was as well rapidly becoming the nation's busiest symphonic soloist.

To be sure, the year 1948 was turning into a banner one for natives at the New York City Opera, a banner one that could be said, in fact, to have peaked that fall with the arrival of a tall, trim former medical student from Massachusetts by the name of Robert Rounseville. For, despite the yeoman service of Conley and William Horne, Halasz had relied heavily on imports—namely the estimable Ramon Vinay, Giulio Gari, and Rudolf Petrak—to fill the tenor slot. Rounseville was not only another American but, as Bishop would describe the new tenor who so perfectly represented the ideals of the company, "the whole package."[31]

Relatively new to opera, having made his reputation in radio, musicals, and nightclubs as a baritone who went by the name Robert Field, Rounseville had only in the past year retaken his birth name and retrained his robust, wide-ranging voice as a tenor in the hopes of achieving his original ambition of opera. And when that summer at Tanglewood his performance in a single scene from *Pelléas et Mélisande* created a stir, Halasz had engaged him for the same role that fall. Indeed, Rounseville was admirable in his debut as Pelléas, opposite Maggie Teyte, the legendary Scottish soprano who at sixty was attempting a return to the stage.[32] But it was the following spring when he rendered Offenbach's Hoffmann "a figure of distinction and romantic bearing, who sang brilliantly and warmly and pathetically by turns,"[33] then almost topped himself in the comic role of the witless Prince in Prokofiev's *Love for Three Oranges,* that the depth and extent of this superb singer-actor's contribution began to be realized.

The year also heard a stronger American accent in the bass and baritone department. Here, too, with the exception of Pease and Weede (the latter, ever on the move to eke out a living, would sing just two seasons for the company), Halasz had looked to foreigners—above all, George Czaplicki, Ralph Herbert, Giuseppe Valdengo, and Oscar Natzka—to keep the wing afloat. But now, boasting many of the same attributes as the new tenor, the baritones Walter Cassel and Lawrence Winters weighed anchor.

Indeed, the hugely versatile Cassel arrived already well known in many areas of entertainment, his reputation having grown steadily since the day in 1934 when he left his native Iowa and, with a family to provide for and just forty dollars stuffed in a shoe, rode a cattle train for five cold days and nights to New York. For success in radio, operetta, and musicals had come quickly for the handsome singer-actor with the rich, virile baritone. And in 1942 he had even added Metropolitan Opera to his résumé. But, after three seasons of mostly secondary roles, Cassel had left the company and, ambitious to be singing leads, made his way onto the circuit and eventually to the New York City Opera. Of his debut as Escamillo one critic would say, "His stage demeanor had too much the empty confidence of an operetta singer."[34] But the

Walter Cassel, about 1945. Photo by De Bellis

depth and effectiveness of Cassel's portrayals would grow notably with the seasons, and by the time he returned to the Met in 1955, he had become an important and valuable leading singer—willing and able even to sing Scarpia, Jochanaan, and Kurwenal in one twenty-hour period for the company if it would solve an emergency, as it did in 1958.

The son of a South Carolina cotton picker, Winters had studied with Todd Duncan while working his way through Howard University. He had made his New York debut in the title role of Clarence Cameron White's opera *Ouanga* and then alternated with his teacher in the first revival of *Porgy and Bess*. After service in the army, he had starred in the Broadway revue *Call Me Mister* and, with the money he saved from the show, made a Town Hall debut recital. Now of his debut as Amonasro at City Opera opposite Camilla Williams, under the headline "Black and White Aida," *Time* wrote, "His voice was fine, strong and ringing on the top; and what he lacked in power, polish and poise should come with time."[35] This, in fact, is just what happened, as over the next eight seasons Winters lent his authoritative singing and acting to such exacting and diverse roles (some of which were new for black singers) as Rigoletto, Scarpia, Bartók's Bluebeard, and the four villains in *The Tales of Hoffmann*.

Curiously, when the company presented William Grant Still's *Troubled Island* in 1949, neither Winters nor Williams was in the cast. Given his record and the fact that almost all the characters are black, one would certainly have thought that Halasz would have cast the opera, the first by a black composer to be produced by a white company, with as many blacks as possible. But the Hungarian may have been as color-blind as Williams once said, for with the sole exception of the yet unknown Robert McFerrin making his debut in a small role, in "a reverse twist," *Time* reported, "the company performed the world premiere of a Negro opera . . . [without] a single Negro in a major role."[36] The large cast of white singers simply did what they always did and put on blackface—among them a mezzo from the shores of Lake Ontario doing double duty in the roles of Second Servant and Mango Vendor.

Fresh from eight years at Juilliard (five in graduate school), Frances Bible had made her debut the previous fall. Her teacher, Queena Mario, had arranged the audition, recognizing that the city's new company probably better suited her habitually self-effacing student than the high-powered Met, and Halasz had hired Bible on the spot. Though barely noticed in her debut in the tiny, unseen role of the Shepherd in the opening-night *Tosca*, Bible

Frances Bible. Courtesy of Francis Bible

had filled in for the stalwart Rosalind Nadell (with whom she would share many a role over the years) as Cherubino in the company's first ever *Nozze di Figaro* the following week and drawn raves.

Indeed, the disparity in her roles and the absence of a star system appealed to the hardworking mezzo, whose velvet vocalism and unforgettable portrayals of such roles as Octavian, Cenerentola, and Augusta Tabor in *The Ballad of Baby Doe* would be acclaimed around the world, but whose name would always be associated first and foremost with the New York City Opera and all it represented.[37] "We did all the parts, big and little—a real repertoire family and it was fun," she happily reminisced, adding, "We could rehearse from ten in the morning till practically midnight and do performances too—sometimes seven a week, and we didn't get much pay."[38] As it was, Bible's salary would be raised in only her second season as she quickly and unavoidably became a star. Yet she would continue to sing the Priestess in *Aida* one day and Amneris the next, for that's the way she liked it and that's the way it was supposed to be in an ensemble company.

And so in just five years Halasz had built a significant resident roster. Indeed, some of the casts were truly remarkable. Consider, for instance, an *Aida* with Williams, Vinay, Morris (as Amneris), Winters, Natzka, Pease, and Bible (as the Priestess). Moreover, as Bishop explained it, "The spirit in the company was marvelous. It really was a family and we supported and liked each other. When things were new and we were all in the same leaky boat, we knew it was to our benefit to stick together. It was a kind of new era and we all believed in it. We inspired each other, held each other to high standards, and were so grateful to have a venue in which we could do what we would have done for nothing anyway. There were many times I'd bring my check home from the opera and pay the babysitter a little more than I made."[39]

When the final curtain fell on the 1948 season, *Musical America* paused to review the company's first five years. It called the musical standards "not always first rate" and the stage direction old-fashioned, and recommended more English-language productions. (Listening to the singers attempt *Eugene Onegin* in Russian, it said, was a painful experience.) But it praised the company's solvency, adventurous repertoire, fresh spirit, and, above all, willingness to give such a large number of young Americans a chance to both display their wares and "gain their stage legs as they develop into seasoned performers."[40]

In 1949 *Life* magazine celebrated the New York City Opera's new season, which—spring and fall combined—now lasted some seventeen weeks, with a cover that showed Halasz standing on some steps surrounded by a selection of his most attractive leading ladies. Inside there was a photographic spread of some four pages, a headline proclaiming, "Handsome young troupe brightens U.S. music scene," and a paragraph describing the company's productions as "closer in approach to Broadway than to orthodox grand opera," and its singers as "almost all native-born Americans."[41]

Chapter Sixteen

Final Kids and Farewell

T HE CAPTION READ, "Opera: A New Era for Americans." The picture showed two sopranos, each with a champagne glass in hand, bejeweled and costumed (one in black, the other in white) as Violetta in *La Traviata*. Inside, the two-page cover story began, "Dorothy Kirsten and Eleanor Steber have good cause to drink the toast they offer on this week's cover of NEWSWEEK. With their American brothers and sisters in the operatic world, they have proved in the first full postwar year of music that they have come of age. The challenge—and the opportunity—that the war offered, they accepted. With a plus in youth and ambition they faced a minus in tradition and experience. Like Minerva they sprang full-grown from their Jupiter, the Metropolitan Opera."[1]

Case closed. Whether achieved as part of a master plan in which management developed native singers in anticipation of the war, as Johnson liked to imply, or simply higgledy-piggledy, as his critics said, the Americanization of the Met appeared to be not only a fait accompli but one that—as the February 24, 1947, cover demonstrated—warranted a toast. Americans now constituted as much as half the roster, Emily Coleman, the article's unnamed reporter, said. Moreover, with their youth and good looks, they were helping the Met meet the demands of a new audience who, raised on a more sophisticated Broadway and Hollywood culture, now expected "credibility with its arias."

Indeed, for Louis Biancolli, writing of the beauteous Kirsten's debut in that first peacetime December, "Voice and drama blended as one thing, and you felt Mimi's pathos as a rich compound of tone and acting."[2] And if two weeks later Robert Merrill, cashing in his prize for winning the Auditions of the Air, was dramatically only a routine Germont, vocally the good-looking Jewish kid from the Brooklyn tenements had "brought down the house."[3]

It was a long way for the baritone to have come, to be sure, but to his mother, "flushed and triumphant . . . *kvelling*," it was meant to be. Married by arrangement in a Warsaw ghetto, the gifted soprano had long before decided her son would realize her own thwarted dreams of a career in opera. "Singer mine," she called him, and Merrill, in turn, had given up a chance to pitch semipro baseball to fulfill them. He had studied with a top New York teacher and plied his craft from mountain resorts to cruise ships. He had entered the Metropolitan Auditions of the Air, and, though his slapstick, arrogant (by his own admission) delivery of the "Largo al factotum" had fallen flat, he had taken it to the Major Bowes Amateur Hour and won. During the war, 4-F because of allergies, he had made a recording of the national anthem, which played in every movie house in the land, and he had earned ninety dollars a week singing three fifteen-minute broadcasts for Phil Spitalny. Moving up the ladder, he had signed with management, made a concert tour, performed his first operatic role—Amonasro in Newark—and, in the spring of 1945, summoned the courage to reenter the Met Auditions. This time, firing off Iago's "Credo," he had taken the big prize, and at the award ceremonies his mother had applauded "with her hands over her head like a boxer."[4]

But when the season opened, and he watched his Auditions' cowinner, Thomas Hayward, make his debut in the secondary role of Tybalt in *Roméo and Juliette,* Merrill, who had been assigned nothing but small roles to prepare, had grown nervous. Only about two dozen of the Americans on Johnson's rosters sang leads on any consistent basis, and it was generally acknowledged that it was in the area of secondary roles that Americans had, in fact, made their biggest advances in opera. Indeed, the Metropolitan pointed with pride to the American women, led by Thelma Votipka, Lucielle Browning, Thelma Altman, and Maxine Stellman, who, as the inevitable maid or confidante to the leading lady of the evening, now represented virtually the entire roster of its female secondary singers or comprimarios, as such minor parts are often called. And if the Italian Alessio de Paolis and the Russian George Cehanovsky continued to dominate the male comprimarios, when it came to portraying such potent cameo characters as Sciarrone, Schlemil, and Shouisky, the Americans George Rasely, Donald Dame, John Gurney, Lansing Hatfield, Arthur Kent, Clifford Harvuot, Hugh Thompson, William Hargrave, and Osie Hawkins now did yeoman service in more pedestrian fare, and sometimes—albeit usually in an emergency—even sang a leading role. Hawkins, for example, had essayed Kurwenal, Amfortas, Telramund, and even Wotan.

But, as a rule, if a secondary singer wanted to sing leads, he found his opportunities outside the house and out of season. In fact the attractive Hayward, an excellent actor possessed of a lovely lyric tenor, would regularly sing leading roles on the circuit but at the Met remain for the most part a comprimario.[5]

In any case, after initially tormenting Merrill with the prospect of small roles (perhaps only to cool off the cocky baritone with the show-biz background), management had finally assigned him the big one, ideal to show off his ravishing instrument. If his acting had proved rudimentary in the role of Alfredo's stern father, artistic growth would come with maturity, Johnson and the assistant manager, Frank St. Leger, allowed. And so they eased their young charge into other of the lyric roles vacated by the just-retired Bonelli—Valentin, Figaro, Di Luna—until three seasons later he surprised them with a maturity of another kind. "The gentleman couldn't believe his ears,"[6] Merrill would later describe St. Leger's reaction to his refusal to sing the formidable role of Rigoletto. But, steeling himself for the inevitable pressure that followed, he held his ground, refusing to sing the role for several more seasons and, even then, not before he had tried it out first in Cincinnati, where the stress was far less.

Certainly, pressure to take on roles that were too demanding and to perform without proper preparation, too often, or under particularly stressful conditions, could be a problem for neophyte Americans desperate to be heard. A career could turn on how one dealt with it, as even some of the greatest among them discovered. For whereas years later Merrill would ascribe his vocal longevity in large part to his good judgment in such matters, his colleague Jerome Hines would never forget how his own singing career almost came to an early end because of the brief period when he lacked it.

Born and raised in Hollywood, California, kicked out of his school's glee club because he couldn't carry a tune, the man many consider to be America's first great bass might never have become a singer at all, in fact, had his mother not thought singing lessons good therapy for his introspective personality. For that matter, Hines's intention was to have a career in chemistry or mathematics, which were his majors at the University of California. But under the superb tutelage of Gennaro Curci, who quickly discovered the towering sixteen-year-old could indeed carry a tune, small singing jobs locally had turned into big ones across the country, and the ensuing recognition had grown too great to ignore.

In any case, only twenty-four years old when he auditioned for and signed on with the Met—a fact that inspired Johnson to call the six-foot-seven bass his baby—Hines, harboring many of the same concerns as Merrill, had been relieved to be cast as Gounod's Méphistophélès just three weeks after his debut in the small role of a frontier guard in *Boris Godunov.* But Méphisto was only one of two dozen major roles he had been assigned to cover. As a result, required to rehearse as much as six hours almost every day—foolishly singing full voice because he did not know how to mark—by the end of the season, Hines had found himself in such vocal distress that it had taken him many months of careful study to repair the damage and, above all, regain his confidence.[7]

But if Hines would catch the problem before it was too late and go on to ultimately sustain the longest career of any leading singer at the Met in the twentieth century, not every story of a young singer's compliance with management had such a happy ending.

It is, for instance, often asked whatever happened to the lovely Florence Quartararo, whose radiant lyric spinto, movie-star beauty, and innate theatricality briefly stole so many hearts. And the answer appears to be that the San Francisco soprano, despite having grown up in an Italian home filled with opera, where Merola was a family friend, embarked on a major career before she had sufficiently secured a technique that could cope with such rigors as a Metropolitan on the loose with its casting. When Earle Lewis heard her at the Hollywood Bowl (replacing Traubel) and took her to Bruno Walter and then the Met, she was simply not ready—despite her superb natural gifts. Howard Taubman seems to have suspected it right from the start, writing of her debut at the age of twenty-three early in 1946, "The young lady sang [Micaela] with astonishing assurance, she may be the find of the season. She has a voice of size, range and true lyric quality. It is produced with a smoothness and accuracy that makes you wonder how it happened that the voice has been so well placed. One gathered that she had not had much formal schooling."[8] And a few weeks later, "This girl will go places . . . if she is allowed time—and that means several seasons—to develop naturally."[9]

But evidently management, having on her arrival plied Quartararo with leading roles to prepare (much as it had Hines), did not have the time. In the

Florence Quartararo

1940s, with no absolute system of covering roles in place and no nearby opera house to borrow from as was customary in Europe, if an artist was indisposed, the Met had no choice but to cast about within its own ranks for a replacement. And, unfortunately, it allowed the hook to land repeatedly on the very vulnerable soprano. For as time and time again Quartararo was sent onstage to sing a leading role, often for the first time, usually with little or no rehearsal, always (or so it seemed) at the last minute, the cracks in her uncertain technique widened under the stress. And though Taubman continued to hear "enchantment in her throat" (reminiscent even of Ponselle, he ventured), he now raised the red flag. "Florence Quartararo seems destined to make her way through the Metropolitan Opera repertory the hard way. She sang Violetta here for the first time last night as a replacement for Bidù Sayão. . . . Some weeks ago she pinch-hit as Desdemona. If there is a more exacting way to face an audience in a prima donna role, it will probably turn up for this young American soprano."[10]

Quartararo hobbled out of the Metropolitan in the spring of 1949. In 1951 Max de Schauensee wrote of her Thaïs in Philadelphia, "The young soprano has a very pretty voice, which she could produce far better than she does. Her highest notes are spread and hard driven, and there were moments when she was not strictly on pitch."[11] Quartararo sang a while longer in Italy, then settled down to domestic life with her new husband, the basso Italo Tajo, to whose Gianni Schicchi she had once played Lauretta at the Met. "Had I remained in my career I would have paced myself differently," she would say years later. "Youth wants to give, give. Maturity knows restraint, holds back so the climax takes shape."[12]

Marilyn Cotlow and Frank Guarrera, receiving Metropolitan Opera Auditions of the Air awards from Edward Johnson (left) and George Sloane, the chairman of the board (right). Courtesy of Marilyn Cotlow

Marilyn Cotlow, a winner of the 1948 Auditions of the Air, also fell by the wayside, owing to management's mismanagement of its young charges—but in a reverse of the scenario. For, unlike Quartararo, Cotlow not only knew her limits and was willing (naively she would say) to state them, she arrived armed with technique, experience, and even name recognition. Indeed, the pixie coloratura had spent some seven years polishing her gleaming instrument with Hans Clemens in Los Angeles, and she had amassed credits from symphonic appearances under Dimitri Mitropoulos to creating the lead, Lucy, in Menotti's *The Telephone* on Broadway. Of her debut as Philine in a broadcast *Mignon,* the *Times,* though it questioned the size of her voice, appreciated that "she made no attempt to push on her tones," and said that "her singing was accurate and clean, and all florid passages . . . delivered with admirable flexibility and freedom of emission."[13]

But if Cotlow felt momentarily on top of the world, she was dismayed to find a management unwilling to listen to her protests that she did not feel ready for the Lucias and other demanding roles they were scheduling for her. As a result, though the company had her finish out the season with more Philines and one Adina and told her to be available for the next season, for which she had already been contracted, when it came, she was neither cast nor permitted to sing anywhere else. Finally free, Cotlow headed overseas, where she triumphed on the rosters of Basel and Bremen and in concerts and operatic guest appearances across the Continent—"a star that shone in all colors with the brilliance of diamonds," one critic said.[14] But when her husband, whose own career as a violinist was not going well, wanted to go home, Cotlow, feeling it her duty, followed him and withdrew from the professional scene altogether. "I could have been a great singer," she would say.[15] And reviews and private recordings bear her out.

In October 1945, anticipating the company's first postwar season, the Metropolitan Opera's war-weary manager told readers of *Opera News* not to expect any immediate return to prewar normalcy. "Most European artists are still unavailable," he said. "The governments of Europe are anxious to keep their own artists for their own cultural rehabilitation until such time as there can be an exchange between nations. Until the Consular Service is thoroughly organized again . . . the artists will have difficulty in obtaining visas."[16]

And so, as the world reacquainted itself with peace, Metropolitan audiences welcomed not the great flood of European singers many had expected but at most a small stream. And a variable lot they were. For while Set Svanholm, Ferruccio Tagliavini, Giuseppe di Stefano, Italo Tajo, Giuseppe Valdengo, Dezsö Ernster, Paul Schöffler, Ljuba Welitsch, Erna Berger, Cloe Elmo and, to some degree, Pia Tassinari and Daniza Ilitsch greatly enhanced the company's image in Johnson's last seasons with the company, the brief stays of Jacques Jansen, Elisabetta Barbato, Elen Dosia, Renée Mazella, Hjördis Schymberg, Erna Schlüchter, and Claudia Pinza notably tarnished it.

As for natives, Johnson engaged but a couple dozen in his final trimester—only a fraction of his tenure's total. In addition to those already mentioned, in 1946 Mario Berini arrived for a few performances of dramatic roles; the popular radio tenor Felix Knight took on the lyric repertoire; Claramae Turner traded in starring on Broadway in *The Medium* for secondary roles; and the lovely Alabama-born Irene Jordan quit her weekly radio program on NBC, *Songs by Irene,* to placate Lily Pons, who wanted a lighter mezzo than was being offered for the role of her confidante, Mallika, with whom she sings a duet in *Lakmé.*

But if Jordan succeeded so admirably that she finished the season holding the record for most performances by a secondary singer, between seasons she made two decisions that gravely affected her future with the company. First, despite Johnson's warning to her not to get involved with a member of the orchestra, Jordan infuriated the manager by marrying one of its violinists. Second, with the encouragement of her new husband, who noticed her exceptional facility in a very high range, she began to retrain as a dramatic coloratura. Neither of these decisions was well received at the Met. But, after finishing her second season, Jordan would go on to sing everything from the Queen of the Night at Covent Garden (and once in 1957 at the Met) to Leonore in *Fidelio* on television. To be sure, some of the recordings of her live performances from this period are quite remarkable and leave one to think her career should have been bigger.

After four seasons with the company, Claramae Turner would also move on, though in her case to thrive as a symphonic soloist and in leading roles on the regional circuit. Of her single performance of a leading role at the Met—an Amneris on short notice—Kolodin said the full-figured California native, who had once sung in the chorus of the San Francisco Opera, had "a truly magnificent voice, full of richness and plangence," adding that the King of Egypt was "a good provider."[17] But despite losing some forty pounds, Turner had remained mired in character roles.

Irene Jordan as Lola in Cavalleria Rusticana,
1948. Courtesy of Irene Jordan

In 1947 Paula Lenchner, Evelyn Sachs, and Lawrence Davidson arrived for secondary roles, and Polyna Stoska and Brian Sullivan, colleagues from *Street Scene,* for leads. In addition to her recent Donaldson Award for "best musical supporting actress on Broadway," Stoska boasted sturdy credentials. Of Lithuanian descent, the handsome soprano, who had worked as a model while attending Juilliard, had spent four years with the Deutsche Oper in Berlin, having been triumphantly launched when the soprano she was covering in *Euryanthe*—"a typical Nazi and very jealous"—suddenly bowed out hoping, or so Stoska believed, to make a fool of the American who would have to perform without rehearsal.[18] She had also performed with great success with the New York City Opera. Now she made her Met debut as Donna Elvira in *Don Giovanni;* three months later she was already on her sixth role for Johnson when, as Ellen Orford in *Peter Grimes,* she reunited with Sullivan, making his debut in the demanding title role.

And "an uncommonly auspicious" debut it was, said Cecil Smith. "The voice is one of unusual and sympathetic beauty, technically schooled to a high degree. . . . Moreover, the newcomer has personality, bearing, presence and not a little dramatic resource."[19] Indeed, the newcomer, a strapping six-footer who had studied voice at the University of Southern California on a football scholarship, had enjoyed considerable experience in opera and musical theater in roles ranging from Sam the Jew in *Street Scene* and Ravenal in *Show Boat* to Almaviva in *Il Barbiere di Siviglia* and Florestan in *Fidelio.* Brian Sullivan would give the Met a dozen solid seasons, lending his fine lyric spinto and handsome figure to some twenty roles, notably Tamino and Lohengrin, before leaving in 1961. But his plans to build a career as a Heldentenor would end tragically in 1969 with his drowning in Lake Geneva, where he had gone to essay Siegfried in *Götterdämmerung.*

With nine of the twelve new singers American-born, the 1948–49 season resembled the good old war days. The resumption of the Auditions of the Air, suspended for two seasons for want of sponsorship, was in large part responsible. And if the story of one of the year's winners, Cotlow, would end badly, that of the other, Frank Guarrera, could hardly have been happier. In a house replete with those who sang his repertoire, Guarrera might well have been dispensable; but his solid singing, swarthy good looks, energetic stage presence, and all-American reliability in fact rendered him just the opposite. For three decades Guarrera played second fiddle to the likes of Merrill, Warren, and Bastianini; yet for three decades he sang only leading roles and hardly knew a day when he was not either performing or on call.

Born to Sicilian immigrants in the Italian neighborhood of South Philadelphia, Guarrera had been studying at Curtis when the Met and Toscanini discovered him at almost the same moment in 1948. For the maestro first heard Guarrera on one of the Auditions of the Air broadcasts, and, needing a baritone for a tribute to Boito he was to conduct at La Scala that summer, he requested a private hearing. It would be quite a year for Guarrera. Not only would he win the Auditions and sing the Boito, but when a strike delayed the opening of the Met he was able to remain in Italy long enough to sing leading roles in *Les Pêcheurs de Perles* and *L'Amore dei Tre Re* at La Scala and still make it home in time for a Met debut as Escamillo before the new year rang in.

The Auditions runners-up, Anne Bollinger, a lyric soprano from Idaho, and Gertrude Ribla, a dramatic soprano from Brooklyn, also made debuts that season. Bollinger, who had essayed Fiordiligi in Central City the previous summer, would sing mostly small or secondary roles at the Met, but in the early 1950s she would move on to a major career in Hamburg. Ribla, already known from a Toscanini broadcast[20] and appearances with regional companies and the New York City Opera, would now fairly suck the air right out of the auditorium in her Met debut as Aida. Cecil Smith, for one, described himself as being altogether "spellbound" by the soprano, who, though by no means "letter-perfect," was "alive every instant of the time, and genuinely thrilling."[21] Exasperatingly inconsistent, Ribla would sing infrequently for Johnson, however, and then be dropped altogether by his successor.

The season, too, saw the Boston-born tenor Paul Franke commence thirty-nine years as one of the company's greatest character comprimarios, and a mezzo from Centralia, Illinois, Jean Browning Madeira, bow in the small role of the First Norn in *Götterdämmerung* to begin a Met career that would lead to international stardom. A piano prodigy, Madeira had entered Juilliard as a student of Olga Samaroff and transferred to the voice department after the great teacher heard her sing. (Coincidentally, Samaroff would recommend another of her students, Francis Madeira, pursue conducting.) As Jean Browning (for she had yet to marry the conductor), she had barnstormed for two seasons with the San Carlo and replaced Marie Powers in a run of *The Medium* in Paris. Now at the Met she worked her way up through some seventeen secondary roles until, in the last days of his tenure, Johnson gave her a chance to show herself as Carmen and Amneris, roles that perfectly suited her rich contralto, innate theatricality, and feline, dark looks, presumably inherited from her part-Cherokee father.

Most people had thought the next manager of the Metropolitan Opera would come from within the ranks. Names such as Tibbett, Brownlee, St. Leger, even Melchior, had been on wagging tongues ever since the announcement early in 1949 of Johnson's retirement. Hardly anyone had even heard of Rudolf Bing. But in town on business, the Vienna-born director of the new Edinburgh Festival and former manager of the Glyndebourne Festival, where he had worked after Hitler came to power, had stopped by Johnson's office to pay a courtesy call and answered in the affirmative when the worn-out Met leader half jokingly asked if he would like to be his successor—or so the favorite story goes. In any case, following a flurry of activity behind the scenes, on June 2, 1949, the board announced the appointment of the sleeper manager and, to ensure a smooth transition, it explained, announced as well that he would spend the next season at the house as an observer.

And so in the fall of 1949, with Rudolf Bing staring over his shoulder, Edward Johnson struggled to bring his fifteen-year tenure to a happy conclusion. *Der Rosenkavalier,* televised, as *Otello* had been the previous year, opened the season. Stevens, as usual, sang the title role, and Steber her first Marschallin. No native had ever portrayed the Princess—a role Bing thought "unsuitable for an American girl," Steber would say.[22] But the role befit the now thirty-five-year-old soprano's artistic maturity, even if it meant leaving the ingénue Sophie, which she had sung some thirty-six times since her bow in the role, to the legendary German Erna Berger, making her own Met debut at forty-eight. The veteran Emanuel List was, as always, the Baron Ochs; Giuseppe di Stefano, now in his second season, the Italian Singer; Thompson, Lipton, and Votipka performed their accustomed character roles, and Lois Hunt, a cowinner (with the Canadian Dennis Harbour) of the 1949 Auditions of the Air, bowed in the tiny role of the Milliner. Happy to be moved up to Musetta two weeks later, Hunt would remember that, though it was the first *Bohème* of the season, there had been so little rehearsal that she never saw the sets. As a result, she could not find the door in the last act and, while a stage manager crawled on his hands and knees to her rescue, she had sung her first line through the window. "Johnson was winding down," she said. "The budget was winding down. It was kind of sad."[23]

As the first week progressed, Johnson continued to show off his Americans. Stevens was Dalila to Vinay's Samson; Dorothy Kirsten, showing "no evidence that her current radio stint with Frank Sinatra had impaired her powers as a diva,"[24] contributed "the outstanding performance of her career thus far" as Puccini's Manon;[25] and Tucker, Varnay (in her first Italian assignment), and Leonard Warren, now elevated from his debut role of Paoli to the Doge himself, led the *Simon Boccanegra* cast. In January Johnson introduced his last native, Eugene Conley, who, back from his triumphs at La Scala, did not disappoint as Faust. In February he mounted his last novelty, an English-language production of Mussorgsky's *Khovanshchina* with a virtually all-American cast. Generally, though, it was a lackluster season.

Historians have not been especially kind to Johnson. In his "candid history" of the company, Kolodin, who began reviewing for the *Saturday Review* toward the end of the Johnson regime, criticized his "laissez faire" approach, which reached an inexcusable level with blonde Toscas and the like. The "guiding principle," he complained, was one of "improvisation—let's try this, him, her, or it."[26] Martin Mayer in his history of the company, which is blatantly critical of Johnson, calls it "catch as catch can."[27] But one can argue that if indeed management was often as unable to discipline itself as its artists, with some poor decisions regarding them being the result, the times almost insisted on an improvisatorial style.

For in all fairness, "the era from 1935 to 1950 had more complexities and perplexities than any preceding one,"[28] as even Kolodin acknowledged. Unlike any of his predecessors, Johnson never had a clean slate on which to write a season, for never had the history being written outside the opera house so affected that being made inside for such an extended period of time, and even the surliest of critics and historians applaud Johnson for pulling the organization through under the difficult conditions. For that matter, even the surliest applaud him for signing such world-class conductors as Bruno Walter, Sir Thomas Beecham, George Szell, Fritz Busch, and Fritz Reiner; for restoring Mozart and such overlooked masterpieces as *Fidelio, Otello, Falstaff, Simon Boccanegra,* and *Un Ballo in Maschera* to their rightful places, thereby greatly improving the quality of the repertoire and in turn the public's taste; indeed, for making opera more accessible to the general public generally through such innovations as the Metropolitan Opera Guild, the student matinees, the public drive that brought in one million dollars for the company to buy the theater from the stockholders, and, of course, the Metropolitan Auditions of the Air. For, while making no excuses for the way he handled certain individuals, it may well be that the critics applaud him over all else for taking advantage of the history being written around him to finally open the door of the nation's most important opera company all the way to the native artist.

Looking ahead: soon after the curtain fell in Rochester, New York, signaling the end of the opera, the tour, the season, and his tenure, Edward Johnson, about to turn sixty-five, packed up his antiques and rare books and moved back home to Guelph to busy himself as chairman of the boards of the Toronto Opera Festival and the Royal Conservatory of Music (of the University of Toronto), for whom he organized an opera school. But on April 20, 1959, while attending the ballet at Guelph Memorial Gardens, he collapsed from a heart attack and died later that night in the hospital. On April 24, after a funeral service in the same church he had sung in as choir-boy and soloist, Johnson was buried in his native city. And on the first of May an overflow crowd gathered at St. Bartholomew's Episcopal Church in Manhattan to pay tribute to the much-loved tenor and manager.

Chapter Seventeen

1950

I T BEING A SUNDAY, and Sunday night concerts having been discontinued in 1946, the first day of the second half of the twentieth century found the Metropolitan Opera House dark. For that matter, the *Times* listed no opera performances in New York City theaters that day. But if one owned a television set, from 5:00 to 6:20 that evening CBS had scheduled a live performance of *Carmen*. Lawrence Tibbett, the artistic director, was to narrate the abridged version and Boris Goldovsky, who had staged it, would conduct. The starry cast boasted Gladys Swarthout, Robert Rounseville, Robert Merrill, and from *Regina,* the Marc Blitzstein opera that had just closed after seven weeks on Broadway, Priscilla Gillette. Among those in smaller roles were the up-and-coming Phyllis Curtin, Evelyn Sachs, and Norman Scott.

Rehearsals for the eagerly awaited performance had been going on for weeks, for there was a great deal to be worked out. Though there had been experimental telecasts of small operas and operatic scenes as well as two telecasts of Metropolitan opening nights in the past, this *Carmen* was thought to be the first-ever performance of grand opera to emanate from a studio. Because it would be seen as far away as Chicago and shown to the rest of the country at a later date, and because it was widely believed that television could help build an audience for opera, much was riding on its success.

Happily, everything went off without a hitch. Reviewing both the *Carmen* and NBC's telecast of Kurt Weill's *Down in the Valley* just two weeks later, Quaintance Eaton said the performances achieved "a measure of success."[1] The Weill lacked big-name singers but had the advantage of being shorter, more intimate, and in English; the *Carmen* had the names but was less accessible because it was sung in French and, being grand opera, suffered

*Lawrence Tibbett congratulates Robert Merrill, Gladys Swarthout,
and Robert Rounseville after the January 1, 1950, telecast
of* Carmen. Courtesy of Musical America *archives*

from the cutting and visual restrictions. Nevertheless, each in its own way
succeeded well enough, and the consensus was that the networks should
keep trying.

Certainly CBS's next telecast, a *Traviata* sung in English, "marked a notable stride forward in operatic video," Eaton reported in March. In addition
to improvements in staging, sets, and camera work, though the baritone was
"not in good voice," there were "excellent visual performances" by Tibbett as
the elder Germont and Brooks McCormack as his son, and "Elaine Malbin,
a nineteen-year-old soprano with a vivid personality and a brilliant voice,
made a touching and believable Violetta."[2]

Despite her youth, the new Violetta, however, was by no means inexperienced. As a fourteen-year-old, Malbin had sung lieder and operatic arias to
the accompaniment of the legendary Conrad von Bos in a Town Hall debut
recital. She had appeared on radio and with the Carnegie Hall Pops, and she
had sung leading roles in operetta as well as Musetta with Gallo's San Carlo.

And now, only nineteen, she was about to become a television star. For when the CBS venture folded shortly after the *Traviata*, NBC swept Malbin up. She was, after all, pretty and petite; she had an appealing lyric voice that she readily stretched into a more dramatic repertoire; she was a superb musician who had no problem with the contemporary scores that would come to play an important part in NBC's programming; and her acting, Louis Biancolli said, was "of such caliber as to be worthy of an operatic Academy Award."[3] Indeed, it is safe to say no one would sing more leading roles with the new television company than Eileen Malbin.

Essentially the brainchild of the conductor Peter Herman Adler and the producer Samuel Chotzinoff, the NBC Opera Theater had been born in 1949 with a live telecast of excerpts from the last act of *La Bohème* privately presented for David Sarnoff to convince the network's president that opera and television were compatible. To make the added point that the network could save money by not using expensive stars, lesser-known singers had been cast in leading as well as minor roles. Never mind that George London, the Marcello, was clearly poised for a major career. Never mind that Mario Lanza, the Rodolfo, born in Philadelphia the same year the great Caruso died in Naples, would in a few months' time star in a movie portraying his idol to become an idol himself—but allow his undisciplined body not only to get the upper hand on his God-given voice but to precipitate his death before the decade was out. As Chotzinoff would remember, for this all-important demonstration Mario Lanza did "the best singing of his life" and left "his auditors weeping."[4] Sarnoff gave the go-ahead, and NBC went into the opera business.

Though happily there was no shortage of authentic singer-actors grateful for the wonderful dramatic training, the national recognition, and the excellent pay, the work was nonetheless demanding and time-consuming. A job with the new opera theater typically involved weeks of musical and staging rehearsals and days of mapping out positions on the stage with cameras before the dress rehearsal on the morning of the performance. Moreover, because the orchestra was on a different floor, the singers—each followed by his own pickup boom with its own technician—took their cues from assistant conductors, who themselves watched the conductor on a monitor as they moved around the set, hiding under tables and behind screens so as not to be caught on camera. But if with so many complications singers might well have pined for the days of radio, radio, pushed to the wall by television and even more seriously by the new long-playing record, could no longer be depended on for income.

Indeed, with its ability to produce uninterrupted and extraneous noise–free sound for approximately twenty-three minutes, the new microgroove disc of unbreakable vinalyte plastic, which played at 33⅓ revolutions per minute, as opposed to the customary 78, had turned not only music on radio but the entire recording industry upside down. No more hissing sound of the needle on the shellac and, of particular interest to the classical music lover, no more cutting up of operas and symphonies into segments of five minutes at most. The new technology had been officially introduced by Columbia in 1948. And within a year so many companies were on board that William Joseph Schwann, the owner of a record store in Cambridge, Massachusetts, had begun a list to keep track of all the new releases. Typed by hand and then mimeographed, the first Schwann catalog appeared in October 1949, sold eleven thousand copies, and listed 674 long-playing records—LPs—on eleven labels. The original becoming obsolete in a matter of weeks, by 1950 Schwann was publishing a new issue every month.

With the new year under way at the Met, the mood backstage was tense as the general manager–designate roamed the corridors, sat in on rehearsals, auditioned singers, and reviewed contracts. Feeling second-guessed at every turn, the outgoing Johnson grew testy; his singers and staff, their futures on the line, became anxious. And when Bing let it be known that Flagstad would return the following season, Traubel and Melchior exploded. Where, they demanded to know in separate statements to the press, were their own contracts?

At his first press conference on February 1, Bing had no comment on Melchior's threat to quit, but said he had reached an agreement with Traubel. The great Wagnerian sopranos would divide Ring cycles and Isoldes equally, and to balance Flagstad's Leonore in *Fidelio,* Traubel would get a chance at the Marschallin, a role she had long coveted. He then announced his plans and policies for the Metropolitan, including a threat of his own that if singers did not allow enough time in their busy schedules for rehearsal and repeat performances, changes would be made. He said he understood the uneasiness some artists were feeling—a reference to the weeding out process under way—and wanted "the company to feel secure and happy." But, he warned, "I must expect from our artists that they will put the Metropolitan's interests first and not only use it as a label to improve their market value for concerts. We want an ensemble, an ensemble of stars—not comets. I will go out to find more American singers and to further them, but this is the largest and leading opera of the world; in the last resort quality and only quality must decide."[5] On February 2, Melchior, who had managed to keep his dispute with Bing on the front page of the *Times* for four days running, sang Lohengrin and announced it was his "swan song."

On February 28 the company honored Johnson with a performance of *Tosca* (Welitsch, Tagliavini, and Tibbett), followed by a pageant of sixty singers costumed as characters in the operas presented during his tenure. There were as well testimonial speeches, gifts, rounds of "Hail, Hail, the Gang's All Here" and "He's a Jolly Good Fellow," and heartfelt words of thanks and farewell from the man of the hour. On March 25 the season's final broadcast, a *Bohème*, devoted its three intermissions to Johnson, with a synopsis of his career, a quiz with questions relating to his management, and an address from the outgoing chief himself. Included in his remarks was the statistic that 115 American singers had appeared at the Metropolitan while he was its general manager. On April 8 two of them, Warren and Munsel, starred in *Rigoletto*. The performance marked the 1,809th performance of Johnson's tenure, and his last in the house. A final tour, and his work would be done.

As the Met season concluded, the New York City Opera opened with *The Love for Three Oranges*. The Prokofiev spoof had been the previous season's surprise box-office hit. New to the repertoire was Puccini's *Turandot* with the Yugoslav soprano Dragica (Carla) Martinis winning kudos in her debut as the Princess. At Town Hall Thomas Scherman led the Little Orchestra Society in concert versions of *Orfeo ed Euridice* with the British contralto Kathleen Ferrier and *The Abduction from the Seraglio* with Rounseville, Hines, Erna Berger, and a lovely new soubrette from Amsterdam, New York, Genevieve Warner.

But the biggest excitement was Gian Carlo Menotti's new opera, *The Consul,* which, after its premiere in Philadelphia on March 1, began an eight-month run on Broadway, followed by a national tour. Though still euphemistically labeled a "musical drama," the opera, with a timely plot that dealt with humanitarian issues in an unnamed police state, would win not only that year's Pulitzer Prize in music but also the New York Drama Critics Circle Award. And just two short years since giving up her job as a secretary, the mezzo Gloria Lane would take home two Tony awards—best debut of the season and best supporting actress—for her onstage portrayal of the consul's mistress of red tape. In addition to Lane, the cast comprised "a remarkable group of young American singers,"[6] including Marie Powers from *The Medium*, Cornell MacNeil, a new baritone from Minneapolis, and, in the leading role of Magda Sorel, Patricia Neway, a young soprano from Staten Island. Tall, dark-haired, pale, and boney, Neway not only looked the incarnation of the beleaguered wife of a resistance fighter but portrayed her battle to obtain a visa for her husband with shattering intensity. If her voice was "somewhat metallic in timbre and not always perfectly produced," she was, everyone agreed, "born for the role."[7]

Tucked into a season rife with big names on the concert stage, including first New York recitals by Victoria de los Angeles, Eileen Farrell, and Jeannette MacDonald, the debut recital of the unknown black baritone William Warfield on March 19, 1950, caught the critics off guard. Since serving in the war, the sharecropper's son from Arkansas, who had grown up in Rochester, New York, and graduated from Eastman, had been studying at the American Theater Wing, courtesy of the G.I. Bill, and singing to his own piano accompaniments in nightclubs to make a living.

Of a Town Hall recital, therefore, William Warfield could only dream. But one night in Toronto, wowed by the burly entertainer's rendering of everything from scat to operatic arias, a stockbroker in the audience had offered to pay for one. The critics were unanimous: "A truly extraordinary singer, endowed with a phenomenal voice which he projected with complete artistry."[8] The offers poured in. Warfield toured Australia and, on his return, like Bledsoe and Robeson before him, went to Hollywood to play Joe in yet a third remake of *Show Boat*. Indeed, Warfield would recall, "At the end of that pivotal year 1950—midway through the 'American Century,' the year I turned thirty, the year I started off counting my pocket change and ended up with more money than I knew what to do with—I found that I had enough in the bank to buy my parents' home for them."[9]

Eleanor Steber gave her first New York recital that spring as well, but with less happy results. Wanting to make a strong impression by performing works off the beaten path, the soprano, with the esteemed conductor Dimitri Mitropoulos as her pianist, was instead lambasted for her programming of Hugo Wolf, Marc Delmas, and Ernst Krenek. "I am convinced that one of the reasons the program was received as it was, was because I was an American," she would say in retrospect. "If a European had done that concert, critics would have been hypnotized by the continental mystique and there would have been gasps of wonder all over the place."[10]

On May 17 Bing, his wife, Nina, and their dachshund, Pip, sailed on the *Queen Mary* for three months in Europe. In June, with his daughter and two grandchildren, Johnson left to spend the summer in a villa he rented in Florence—his first vacation abroad since 1935.

Back home, summer offered the usual festivals. At Lewisohn Stadium and the Robin Hood Dell, the thirteen-year-old Italian soprano Anna Maria Alberghetti, who with her mother at the piano had made her American debut at Carnegie Hall in April, now coolly wowed audiences singing Lucia's Mad Scene in a short, pink party dress. Hines, Tucker, and Conner opened the Hollywood Bowl with *Faust*. The Opera Theater at Tanglewood put on *La Finta Giardiniera*, a Mozart rarity that the Amato Opera had exhumed earlier in the season. A festival in Aspen, Colorado, enjoyed its second year. And at the Zoo Opera in Cincinnati, John Alexander, a graduate of the local conservatory, went from a debut as the Second Philistine in the opening *Samson et Dalila* to a triumph as Gounod's Faust in under a month.

Though the Lemonade Opera, brought down by rifts within the managerial ranks, would evaporate into opera lore after the summer of 1950, leaving Arthur Jacobs, a visiting English critic, to lament, "The gap left by Lemonade Opera cries out to be filled,"[11] in fact, innovative little companies were still popping up all over. The latest entrant, the After Dinner Opera Company, which, under Richard Flusser, its founder and its director for the next fifty years, had introduced itself in the last days of 1949 with a triple bill of contemporary operas and lost twenty-five dollars in the venture, decided to give it another try in June. And when this time, thanks in part to the addition of Lucas Foss's winning new opera, *The Jumping Frog of Calaveras County*, the debt was only two and a half dollars, the tiny company with a predilection for farce, fantasy, and tomfoolery was off and romping.

In September the San Francisco Opera set the bar high for the coming opera season. Flying out to hear the rising Italian stars Mario Del Monaco and

Renata Tebaldi shortly after their debuts in the opening *Aida,* the new man-ager of the Metropolitan told reporters, "We shall have to pull up our socks to do better than that, or even match it."[12] Since Chicago was still without opera, Merola's company remained the most prestigious in the country after the Met, and the jaunty impresario was as determined as ever that his adopted city hear the best singers in the world. Europeans dominated most Merola productions, but many of America's best (and not only from the Metropolitan) also performed. In 1950 they included Weede as Amonasro and Gérard (to Del Monaco's Chénier); Lewis as Salome; and Conley in *Barbiere.* Charles Kullman and the lovely Dorothy Warenskjold, a native Californian who would sing seven seasons with the San Franciscans and alto-gether make a strong career in radio and television nationwide, were the lovers in *The Magic Flute.* And San Francisco's own Frances Quartararo replaced Tebaldi when the Italian, scheduled to sing not only Aida and Desdemona but also, curiously, the Countess Almaviva in *Le Nozze di Figaro,* withdrew from the Mozart at the last minute, saying she was not prepared.

Meanwhile, Halasz's company was enjoying its longest season ever: al-most seven weeks. Newcomers included Bampton, no longer of the Met, who essayed the Marschallin; Elaine Malbin, over from television, who sang both small roles and Liù in the new *Turandot;* and the versatile David Lloyd, who bowed as David in *Die Meistersinger.* The lyric tenor from Minneapolis, whose studies at Curtis had been interrupted to fly bombers in the Pacific, was well known in oratorio and on the Community Concert trail. He had, moreover, created the title role in the American premiere of Britten's *Albert Herring* at Tanglewood, and performed such leading roles as Don José and Rodolfo for the New England Opera Theater. But now at City Opera, he settled for "soubrette tenor" par excellence, for, after all, as he would say, "the wonderful spirit made it a joy to sing for a few dollars."[13]

In addition to *Meistersinger,* the company mounted its first *Faust,* casting two tenors (Giulio Gari and Rudolf Petrak) to better depict the philoso-pher's different ages, said Vladimir Rosing, who since his arrival the previous fall had been rapidly improving the quality of the stage direction. Frances Yeend, recently named one of the ten best-chapeaued women in America, was leading lady in both productions. Rounseville took advantage of the new commercial transatlantic air service to commute from England, where he and Ann Ayars were shooting a film version of *The Tales of Hoffmann,* for performances of *Carmen* and, Rosing's first hit, *The Love for Three Oranges.*

Having agreed to honor the union contract that "required [him] to hire American soloists in a ratio of at least two to one as against foreign soloists,"[14] Bing engaged six new natives (all women) for the upcoming Metropolitan season. Five were sopranos: Roberta Peters, a New Yorker who had never sung professionally; Marguerite Piazza, whose considerable experience ranged from the New York City Opera to a weekly television show; Barbara Troxell, who had recently sung Mozart under Thomas Beecham in Mexico City; Genevieve Warner, whose operatic debut in the Opera's Society's *Abduction* earlier that year had caught the Met's attention; and Lucine Amara, a young San Franciscan of Armenian descent who, since her early years in the chorus of the San Francisco Opera, had gone on to win the two-thousand-dollar Atwater Kent Award and to appear in opera and concert on the West Coast. The one mezzo, Margaret Roggero, was a veteran of Charles Wagner tours and had performed on Broadway in *The Consul.*

Meanwhile, getting Verdi's *Don Carlos* ready in time to open his regime was proving to be a baptism by fire for the new manager. The McCarran Internal Security Act, which Congress had just passed over Truman's veto in response to the Red scare gripping the country, denied visas to anyone believed to have Fascist, Nazi, or Communist ties. As a result, the Italian mezzo Fedora Barbieri, detained on Ellis Island, was late for rehearsals, and the Bulgarian bass Boris Christoff had to cancel altogether, and Bing had to scurry to secure Cesare Siepi, a young Italian bass who by virtue of having spent the war in Switzerland was above reproach. And because both the Hungarian Mihaly Szekely and the German Gottlob Frick, either of whom would have sung the Grand Inquisitor, were also detained, Bing's only option was to check out the stable of young Americans his predecessor left him and finger its only bass, Jerome Hines. For the role of Rodrigo he had wanted Warren, but because the baritone had limited time to give, owing to other obligations (it would take a while to get over that bad beginning), he had given the job to Merrill, who was delighted by the honor and delighted as well to see his salary rise from four hundred dollars a week to five hundred per performance and escalate steadily thereafter. Other Americans in the cast were Emery Darcy and Anne Bollinger, who had minor roles, and Amara, who made her debut singing briefly, invisibly, but unforgettably the Celestial Voice.

Margaret Webster, the great Shakespearian whom Bing had persuaded to direct, despaired of the mayhem and several of the singers' histrionics. Nevertheless, on November 6, 1950, the opera went on as scheduled. And if at one point, it being the night before midterm elections, a plea for votes from a passing sound truck filtered into the maroon and gilt auditorium, it hardly mattered: so entranced was the audience, few heard it. Indeed, in the days that followed, Bing received high marks for his inaugural performance, which took in "the biggest opening night gross (after taxes) in Met history: more than $50,000."[15]

With the season properly launched, the next night saw a new production of *Der Fliegender Holländer* with Hans Hotter making his debut, Varnay as Senta (filling in for Welitsch, who was also delayed), Set Svanholm, and in the smaller role of Mary, Margaret Harshaw, who in eleven days' time would herself essay Senta for her first soprano role with the company and the beginning of a whole new career. In fact, things were looking good for the natives, who would not stand aside for an all-European night until almost a month into the season. Kirsten was Violetta and Manon Lescaut; Conley, Ottavio and Alfredo; Tucker, Des Grieux; and Traubel, Isolde and soon (as promised) the Marschallin. Steber, Thebom, and Tucker, moreover, replaced the imports in some *Don Carlos* performances, and with Hans Hotter taking on the Inquisitor, Hines got to try on the King's robes. *Die Zauberflöte* was virtually all-American, and *Don Giovanni* also saw a fair share of natives. And just ten days into the season it was a *Giovanni* that gave Bing his first good look at American spunk in the person of a twenty-year-old Dresden doll from the Bronx, who, despite never having set foot on a professional stage in her life, essayed Zerlina on the grandest of them all with only a few hours' notice.

Bing had heard Roberta Peters in a private audition the previous winter and, after having her sing the second Queen of the Night aria from *Die Zauberflöte* (infamous for its many high Fs) not just once but some four times, so that others of his staff could confirm his amazement, awarded her a contract. But aware that she had no experience, he had also enrolled her in the new Kathryn Turney Long courses. Set up by Johnson, shortly before he left office, with funds left in trust by Mrs. Long, an original board member, these intensive twelve-week fall and spring training sessions were to provide young singers in whom the company was interested with lessons in everything from stage deportment to French diction and with thorough preparation of specific roles. Moreover, because Max Rudolf, the director of the mini-school, and virtually all the teachers were from the Metropolitan's own staff, management was easily able to keep track of its young charges.

And so on the afternoon of November 17, when Nadine Conner, scheduled to sing Zerlina in that evening's *Don Giovanni,* called in sick with food poisoning, Bing and Rudolf with no time to spare had looked to the school and called in Peters. They had every confidence that she was ready, they told the stunned soprano, who was to have made her debut as the Queen of the Night in January and, in fact, had tickets to attend the *Giovanni* with her mother. And, as it turned out, supremely talented and superbly trained she was.

Elsewhere, the month saw the New York Philharmonic under Dimitri Mitropoulos perform concert versions of Darius Milhaud's *Les Choéphores* and Maurice Ravel's *L'Heure Espagnole* with Eileen Farrell, Mack Harrell, David Lloyd, and Frances Greer as soloists. After reminding readers of Greer's much-loved Musetta at the Met, Cecil Smith said her well-nigh perfect performance of Concepcion in the Ravel added "a new dimension to her already outstanding artistic record."[16] But Greer was no more of the Met. Incensed to have to audition like a beginner for the new manager, she had quit on her own accord, she would say, and her brief but brilliant career was almost over.

On December 5, Margaret Truman sang at Constitution Hall in Washington, D.C. Though one of his dearest friends had died that day, the president, so as not to worry his daughter, attended as planned with Great Britain's prime minister, Clement Atlee, as his guest, and all went well. But early the next morning on opening the *Washington Post* and reading a "savage review of my performance," Margaret would remember, the president "saw red. . . . His best friend had just died, the world situation was going from bad to awful, and now a critic was attacking his daughter with what seemed to be more malice than judgment. Dad sat down and wrote Mr. [Paul] Hume a very angry, longhand letter . . . [calling him] 'an eight-ulcer man on a four-ulcer job and all four ulcers working.' Mr. Hume published the letter and the uproar was vast."[17]

On December 22 Walter Damrosch died at his home at the age of eighty-eight. The year had already seen the deaths of the singers Edyth Walker, Giuseppe de Luca, and Gemma Bellincioni; the critic and playwright George Bernard Shaw; the dancer Nijinsky; and the composers Francesco Cilea and Kurt Weill. Only fifty years old at the time of his death, Weill had been working on a new American musical based on *Huckleberry Finn.*

On Christmas Day the NBC Opera Theater offered *Hansel and Gretel* with Virginia Haskins and, instead of the usual mezzo dressed as a boy,

David Lloyd as Hansel. On New Year's Eve the Met mounted Johann Strauss's *Die Fledermaus*. The operetta, which had not been heard at the Met since 1905, was Bing's third new production, and it had roared into the opera house on December 20 just in time for the holidays. Though the Viennese manager, wary that despite the English translation American singers would not understand the style, had initially cast Welitsch and Svanholm as Rosalinde and Eisenstein, it had been the Americans—Tucker, Stevens and, above all, Munsel—who, with their instincts for the show-biz staging of the Broadway director Garson Kanin, in fact walked off with the kudos.

In the seven seasons since her debut, Munsel, now all of twenty-five, had tried on virtually every coloratura role in the company's repertoire, but it was in the soubrette roles, which she had only recently begun to essay, that many thought she found her best place. Now critics were unanimous that, as Adele the maid, she stole the show. One even suggested she might move up Broadway and into musical theater.

In any case, the Viennese operetta became even more like American musical theater on New Year's Eve 1950, when Charles Kullman took over for Svanholm, who one critic said had seemed "a fish out of water"[18] in the production, and a few days later, when Marguerite Piazza replaced Welitsch.

The following March Bing announced a touring company of the surprise hit, saying that "he hoped to give the United States a 'mixture of a first-class Broadway musical with Metropolitan Opera House musical standards.'"[19] And that same week, the cover of jaunty little *Quick* magazine showed the beauteous Piazza in a low-cut strapless evening dress; the caption asked, "New Life for a Dying Opera?"[20]

Chapter Eighteen

Fifties Fallout

THE 1950s WERE UNDER WAY. On both sides of the Atlantic and in large numbers American singers thrived. Finally relieved of the inferiority complex that had done so much to stint their progress over their brief history and fairly unfazed by the lingering traces of the European bias that had spawned it, they had only to ride the wave of their breakthroughs. A munificent mid-century waited. Notwithstanding communism, inflation, bomb shelters, and its dark-skinned citizens' growing demand for equal rights, America was the leader of the free world—economically prosperous, brimming with vitality, and culturally on top of the world.

"Once in a great while a society explodes in a flood of new ideas, new tastes, new standards," *Reader's Digest* said. "A fresh and exciting age emerges, alive with expanding opportunities. Today's Americans are living in one of those extraordinary periods."[1] It was, William Warfield remembered, the "sense that opportunity was all around you, that anything could happen."[2] And at least for the baritone and his wife, it did. Catching the wave early in the decade, by its end Warfield and Leontyne Price were international stars. For, as Todd Duncan said, "If the modern singer is truly ambitious—and versatile—he can travel just about anywhere he wants to . . . from grand opera to the musical comedy stage and back again, with the pleasant likelihood of a highly profitable stopover in Hollywood."[3]

Signing on for a new production of *Porgy and Bess* in 1952, Warfield had, in fact, already made that trip (with the exception of opera), and was moreover already a star. And if his Bess (and soon-to-be wife) was unknown, Mary, as they called the soprano Leontyne Price at Juilliard, where producers found her singing Alice Ford in *Falstaff*, would soon be an even bigger one. For now, though, the team of Warfield and Price—her name on the program in small letters and well below his—would lead a cast of extraordinary black

232

*Leontyne Price and William Warfield arriving in Vienna in 1952
to sing* Porgy and Bess. *Urylee Leonardos, who alternated with
Price, is in the rear. The goat was part of the performance.
Courtesy of United Press*

talent across America and on to Europe.[4] What better way to repair hard feelings and warm some of the cold winds blowing in from the Soviet bloc than a State Department–sponsored tour of *Porgy and Bess,* "America's Greatest Musical,"[5] as performed by its misunderstood blacks.

As it was, conservative Vienna lavished some twenty-five minutes of applause on what it called "the dark ladies and gentlemen";[6] Berlin demanded twenty-one curtain calls; London and Paris held them over for additional weeks of performance. And everywhere they went, from Milan, where they played a week at La Scala, to Tel Aviv and Cairo, to Zagreb, Leningrad, and Moscow behind the Iron Curtain, the performers were—the press reported and Maya Angelou (who joined the show as a dancer) wrote in her memoirs—stared at, mobbed, and lionized, until finally, in June 1956, some four years later, they came to rest in Amsterdam.

That by then Leontyne Price was long gone from the show was to be expected. Her smoldering portrayal of Bess had brought her major recognition; her recitals in 1954 in New York and Washington, D.C., where she premiered Samuel Barber's *Hermit Songs,* had shown her to be an artist of the first order; and her portrayal of Tosca on television in January 1955 had alerted the opera world. Indeed, the first black to appear on an opera telecast at a time when many programs still refrained from showing black performers of any kind (eleven cities, in fact, refused to broadcast the live *Tosca*), the twenty-six-year-old soprano, performing "without special makeup," had sung "with a flair worthy of the Met," *Time* said.[7] And though there would be more roles for Price on the NBC Opera Theater, as well as six seasons of triumphs on both sides of the Atlantic, before they saw her particular "flair" at 1417 Broadway, one could make such allusions now, for only two weeks before her historic performance on television another black singer had made history at the Metropolitan itself.

Two decades had passed since Jarboro sang Aida for Salmaggi, thereby integrating a white American company for the first time, and one since Duncan integrated the all-white New York City Opera, portraying Tonio, a character clearly intended to be white. Halasz had continued to employ blacks, not only Williams and Winters but also Lucretia West and Margaret Tynes. And Adele Addison, with experience in opera under Goldovsky— though her clear, ineffably sweet soprano and rare artistic sensibilities would prove best in recital and oratorio—would be well received in her debut as Mimì that March; in April Everett Lee would make his debut leading

Traviata to become the company's first black conductor. That the Metropolitan, which in 1951 had engaged its first black, the dancer Janet Collins, had hired Lee's wife, Sylvia, as a coach in 1954, thereby breaking its offstage color barrier, suggested things were moving.

Nevertheless, in the matter of singers, the nation's most important company had still not taken the ultimate step, and with civil rights burning a hole in the national conscience, the Metropolitan Opera's engagement of Marian Anderson to sing the role of the sorceress Ulrica in Verdi's *Un Ballo in Maschera* had been headline news. And so it was that on that seventh day of 1955, when the curtain went up to reveal the legendary contralto center stage, the fire over which she stirred her cauldron illuminating her beloved face, before she could sing even one note the audience had "applauded and applauded." She "trembled," she would recall,[8] and with the weight of the world on her and her voice no longer in its prime, her voice trembled as well. But no one cared. Marian Anderson was singing at the Metropolitan Opera, and, as one reporter noted, "Men as well as women in the audience were dabbing at their eyes."[9]

The door thus swung wide, just twenty days later Robert McFerrin bowed in *Aida*—without makeup. Though not the first black singer to place—that honor having gone to the baritone Fred Thomas of Norristown, Pennsylvania, in 1951—the Arkansas baritone had been a runner-up in the 1953 Metropolitan Opera Auditions. Now, successful as Amonasro, McFerrin lightened his skin to portray Valentin and Rigoletto, paving the way for Mattiwilda Dobbs—her star having risen so fast on both sides of the Atlantic that many thought she might have been the first even over Anderson—to bow as Gilda in the fall of 1956. And by the end of the decade Gloria Davy in leading roles and Martina Arroyo initially in small roles were also on the roster—the two sopranos, like Dobbs, having already enjoyed major experience in Europe, where American singers of both races were currently found in profusion.

Indeed, since the late 1940s, when "an American singer was still apt to arouse the kind of incredulous wonderment we would reserve for, say, a violin-playing Eskimo,"[10] the natives had significantly picked up the pace to Europe. Often with the help of grants from such foundations as the Fulbright and Guggenheim—the postwar solution, one could say, to the absent prewar patrons—many, in fact, would proceed to make the better part of their careers on the Continent. Claire Watson and her husband, David

Thaw, for example, were stars in Munich, as were Pease and Bollinger in Hamburg, Lucille Udovick in Italy, Gladys Kuchta in Berlin, Sylvia Stahlman in Brussels, and Teresa Stich-Randall in Vienna.

To be sure, the former Teresa Stich, after quite literally making a splash in her European debut when, as the Mermaid in Weber's *Oberon* in the Boboli Gardens in Florence, she swam across a one-hundred-foot lagoon, emerged to sing an aria, then submerged again to swim off into darkness—a tour de force said to have stolen the show—had become an important artist in Europe, renowned, above all, for her Mozart. Later she would contribute a handful of Donna Annas and Fiordiligis for the Met; but Europe, and especially Vienna, where her repertoire of roles was vast and varied, and where, like Watson in Munich, she had been honored with the title Kammersängerin, would remain her professional home.

Mildred Miller, Nell Rankin, Irene Dalis, and Giorgio Tozzi were all singing in Europe when Bing snapped them up in the 1950s. Others, such as the married couples Evelyn Lear and Thomas Stewart and James McCracken and Sandra Warfield, gave up uncertain careers in America to find recognition abroad and ultimately international stature. For whereas to the casual observer America was enjoying something like an operatic boom, in truth it continued to offer its singers nothing resembling what they could find abroad, especially in the state theaters of Central Europe, where the seasons were long enough to make a living. As one foreign critic observed, "The lot of the free-lance opera singer in the United States is a rat race business of skipping from pick-up performance to pick-up performance, from short season to short season, scrounging for engagements, and hoping that the next three months will bring in enough to pay the rent."[11]

The nation's campuses offered experience but not a livelihood, and for all the appearance of activity the regional companies gave, including important new ones in Houston and Dallas, their sporadic offerings of at most a dozen performances annually provided no real solutions either. Only Chicago, where opera returned in 1954 after a seven-year hiatus, enjoyed a season of any real length (about six weeks)—a season at times so spectacular, for that matter, it could only have fueled the notion that opera in America flourished. For Carol Fox, the new company's director,[12] stopped at nothing to get the best. A typical star-studded season, like that of 1955, boasted Rosanna Carteri, Ebe Stignani, Giulietta Simionato, Anita Cerquetti, Giuseppe di Stefano, Jussi Björling, Carlo Bergonzi, Ettore Bastianini, Tito Gobbi, Nicola Rossi-Lemeni, Renata Tebaldi, and her rival, the Greek-

American Maria Callas (the last two alternating, incredibly, for nine consecutive performances), in addition to natives Stich-Randall, appearing in her first opera in America since achieving stardom abroad, Ribla, Varnay, Kirsten, Weede, and, in secondary roles, Mignon Dunn, William Wildermann, Richard Torigi, Eunice Alberts, and Claramae Turner.

Opera in concert form, however, was a somewhat new option to help fill out a schedule. Toscanini, of course, had been performing the standard operatic repertoire in concert for some time, giving breaks to many Americans along the way. But the new interest in seldom-heard repertoire meant that lesser-known singers, grateful for a chance in the spotlight and therefore willing to give the time to a score they might never sing again, often got the call.

In addition to several presentations of twentieth-century opera by the New York Philharmonic under Mitropoulos, in response to the growing interest in bel canto, which was inspired largely by the rise of the sensational Maria Callas, Thomas Scherman's Little Orchestra Society presented several rarely heard works by Bellini and Donizetti with such excellent young natives as the soprano Laurel Hurley, a Pennsylvania-born Naumburg winner and City Opera favorite, even before she lit up the Met. And Allen Sven Oxenburg's American Opera Society, which in the 1950s moved from the living rooms of Westchester, New York, where it had originated, to Town Hall and then again to Carnegie, presented any number of fascinating offerings and singers. It was, in fact, with both these groups that Eileen Farrell first wet her operatic toes.

The radio singer's career had been skyrocketing in concert. Recently she had supplied the voice of Marjorie Lawrence in *Interrupted Melody*, a movie adaptation of the great Australian Wagnerian's autobiography, and she had spread her wings yet further by becoming a regular soloist with the estimable Bach Aria Group, which had already hired the opera singer Jan Peerce as tenor soloist—both unorthodox choices surprising the concert world. Now she triumphed in her operatic debut as Medea in the American premiere of the Cherubini opera for Oxenburg and as Strauss's Ariadne for Scherman.

But it was in the offerings of the myriad amateur or semiprofessional groups, primarily educational, that America's operatic coming of age was arguably most clearly manifest. Not only were the grass-roots groups and university opera departments taking the genre to out-of-the-way places and giving young singers badly needed experience, they were revitalizing the repertory with either unfamiliar or contemporary works as well. "If the composers keep on writing operas and the workshops go on producing them,"

Taubman wrote after attending an evening of three new operas by the con-temporary composers Martinů, Tcherepnin, and Meyrowitz at Hunter College, "we may discover one fine day that we have a contemporary repertory."[13]

Southern institutions were especially active. In 1955, for example, Tulane University gave the world premiere of Rafaello de Banfield's *Lord Byron's Love Letter*, which the Chicago Lyric then mounted as part of its regular sea-son; and, importing Phyllis Curtin and Mack Harrell to bolster the other-wise student cast, Florida State introduced Carlisle Floyd's *Susannah*, even before it went to the New York City Opera and thereafter to every school and small company in the country. The New Orleans Opera launched the Experimental Opera Theater of America, which for a few heady years pro-vided, usually via a competition, such up-and-coming talent as Josephine Guido, Mignon Dunn, Eddy Ruhl, Maria di Gerlando, and John Reardon with a place to try out roles in the standard repertoire for base union pay. North Carolina's National Grass Roots Opera Company toured below the Mason-Dixon line. And when at the end of the decade the company re-named itself simply the National Opera Company, *Opera News* thought the move implied "the spadework in making the United States opera-conscious has been completed."[14]

In its 1960 annual survey, *Opera News* would cite as many as 754 opera-producing organizations nationwide, certainly impressive compared to the 124 listed in its first survey in 1941. "Mortality was high, but it was matched by the rate of replacement," one chronicler noted[15]—good reason to found the Central Opera Service (1954) and National Opera Association (1955).

Television was also living up to expectations. *Omnibus*, a CBS program devoted to the arts, included a variety of opera presentations in its series, ranging from a highly successful performance of the Metropolitan's *Fleder-maus* to a disastrous American premiere of Respighi's *La bella Addormentata nel Bosco*. *Opera Cameos*, hosted by Giovanni Martinelli, presented operatic highlights as performed by a mix of celebrities and unknowns. Still in her twenties, Beverly Sills sang not only the title roles of *Thaïs* and *Traviata* (op-posite Martial Singher and Bastianini, respectively) for the show but also commercials for its sponsors, Gallo wines and Progresso foods.

But no program generated more interest in opera than the NBC Opera Theater, which in several live telecasts a year throughout the decade pre-sented first-rate singer-actors in a breathtaking range of repertoire. Indeed, the television company mounted everything from the tried-and-true to the

American premieres of Prokofiev's *War and Peace*, with David Lloyd as Pierre, and *Billy Budd* with Theodor Uppman, fresh from creating the title role at Covent Garden. And it even presented six operas it commissioned itself, among them Lucas Foss's *Griffelkin*, with Adelaide Bishop in the title role, Norman Dello Joio's *The Trial of Rouen*, with Malbin as Joan of Arc, and Menotti's *Amahl and the Night Visitors*, with Rosemary Kuhlman as the Mother and a series of boy sopranos beginning with Chet Allen as Amahl. *Amahl*, which was immediately adopted by thousands of schools, churches, and community groups across the nation for their own Christmas observances, would become a perennial favorite on the NBC theater.

"Gradually, thanks to TV, Americans are beginning to appreciate that Rhinegold isn't necessarily Ballantine's big competition, that Parsifal isn't a vegetable, that Mignon doesn't have to be eaten with onions," Malbin said in 1956.[16] A television set, which had cost seven hundred dollars in 1947, in the mid-1950s cost two hundred. No longer a toy for the affluent, the magic box was going democratic, and that meant programming would have to have broader appeal. As the NBC Opera Theater watched its audience dwindle to minority status, it took on its first sponsors, to survive. And when it ended with the death of Chotzinoff in 1964, it left the field to the NET Opera Theater, which, founded in 1957, would keep televised opera alive for another twenty years, but only on an educational network.

With audiences wanting more and more entertainment with their edification, group attractions, which presumably offered more variety than soloists, were the trend in concerts across the country. But in sophisticated urban centers, where audiences were more concerned with novelty than numbers, recitalists scrambled to find new repertoire, and performances of early and modern music proliferated. Russell Oberlin, who had studied at Juilliard as a high tenor, burst on the scene as America's first recognized countertenor, opening up all sorts of possibilities for the early music movement. Cathy Berberian, known for her multicolored, three-octave mezzo and vivid personality, arrived to champion aleatoric and other perceived outrages of the avant-garde. And with the death of her husband, who had forbidden her to sing in public, fifty-three-year-old Alice Esty began a series of annual concerts at Carnegie Recital Hall comprising primarily songs she had commissioned for the occasion. Like Janet Fairbank's, Esty's soprano was little more than serviceable, but her good taste and enthusiasm more than made up.

Poulenc, Milhaud, Rorem, Thomson, and countless lesser-known composers gladly responded to her requests for new pieces, and, again as with Fairbank, many are the dedications "To Alice" found on the sheet music of the period.

This, though, was singing for love; money was best found in show business, albeit still a thorny issue between opera singers and their managements. "Opera Dismisses Baritone Merrill 'A.W.O.L' for Hollywood Movie," the *Times* headline read in 1951. It seems Robert Merrill had been too busy making a film called, incredibly, *Aaron Slick from Punkin Crick,* to show up for the Metropolitan's spring tour. Reinstating the contrite baritone eighteen months and a public apology later, Rudolf Bing would say simply that the company had "sustained a principle without which there could be no hope of first-class opera productions ever."[17] But two years later, when the manager found himself trying to uphold a similar, but less clear-cut, principle in the face of a not-so-contrite Wagnerian diva, the outcome was quite different.

Never comfortable with the pomp of opera and shameless in her penchant for lowbrow, Helen Traubel had gotten away with whooping it up with Jimmy Durante on television. But when he found her performing in a nightclub in Chicago shortly before the season, Bing had had enough. In a letter to the soprano regarding her upcoming contract, he asked that, in deference to the image of the august opera company, she not appear in a nightclub in the New York area before her appearances at the Metropolitan and for at least one month afterward; he further suggested she might want to "miss" a season and return when she was ready "to change back to the more serious aspects of [her] art."[18] "Artistic dignity is not a matter of where one sings," retorted the diva to end the matter.[19]

"America is a country in which social categories shift and change with cloudlike rapidity and the same phenomenon applies to the professional field," Vincent Sheean would offer by way of explanation for Traubel, who of course never sang at the Met again. "In music we have seen persons of talent move from one category to another with an ease almost unknown in Europe."[20] And, certainly, in light of the fact that most American singers thought it perfectly natural to do it all, the Traubel-Bing incident looked a little silly. Attractive singer-actors such as Brenda Lewis and Robert Rounseville thought nothing of mixing opera with musicals, or, in the tenor's case, movies as well.

Still, show business was seductive. And if it was one thing for Pinza, Tibbett, Weede, Peerce, and Merrill to extend their careers on Broadway after retiring from opera, it was another for Piazza, Munsel, Mimi Benzell, and Dolores Wilson to leave opera in the prime of their careers for television, musicals, and, yes, nightclubs. Though she would lose in her legal showdown with Bing over her right to bill herself a star of the Metropolitan, Benzell, who later costarred with Robert Weede in the musical *Milk and Honey,* even gave Las Vegas a whirl—as did Munsel. In fact, the girl who in *Fledermaus* showed the Met the power of show business at the box office would, as some had predicted, enter it herself full-time in the late 1950s, at one point even hosting her own television show, like her *Fledermaus* colleague Piazza, another "thrush-of-all-trades."[21]

And it was not long after Lois Hunt sang Adele in the Met's *Omnibus* telecast of *Fledermaus* in 1953 that she too would leave the company for show business and a concert career of a new kind with the rich-voiced Earl Wrightson. The baritone from Baltimore and former student of Robert Weede had done it all as well. But in recent years, he had been especially successful on fast-growing television, where he was able to make the most of his extreme good looks and engaging personality, and where Hunt first met him. Since both had done musical theater as well as classical music, they had initially thought to sing both but soon abandoned the idea in favor of a program devoted to American theater music. It was a new concept and Hunt and Wrightson—"classical music's answer to Steve [Lawrence] and Eydie [Gormé],"[22] Beverly Sills said—were soon being engaged by full symphony orchestras to sing programs that opened with early American operetta and closed with songs from the latest Broadway shows. But while one critic in 1963 described the team as "popular entertainers," who "came to Carnegie Hall in the full regalia of concert artists" and "sang everything straight up with no attempt to jazz up or modernize anything," he also noted, when his eyes were not "riveted on the ravishing brunette in her . . . sequin gown," that "about 8/10ths of those present were between 45 and 60."[23]

The reality was that after some two decades of steady progress, John Q. Public's acceptance of classical singing probably had reached its high with the movies of Mario Lanza of the mid-1950s, overlapping as they did with the first appearances of a baritone by the name of Elvis Presley, who sang neither classical nor popular, but something called rock and roll. For if the teenage idol and symbol of their liberation was not "the greatest cultural

Lois Hunt and Earl Wrightson. Courtesy of Lois Hunt

force in the twentieth century,"[24] as Leonard Bernstein once remarked, certainly his coming marked the end of a time when young and old shared the same music and popular and classical a common ground.

Johnson was gone; his kids were grown. Opera everywhere was striving to regain its prewar status, and Bing, intent that the Met should lead the way, repeatedly warned that his first responsibility was to quality, no matter where he found his singers. And yet, whether for reasons of practicality, AGMA quotas, or authentic respect for the natives, Americans easily constituted about 55 percent of the new manager's first rosters—a majority, which was, Bing said, "entirely as it should be" and due to his predecessor's efforts.[25]

Still, for Thomas Hayward and other Johnson's kids, the change in personality was "as though a great iron curtain had been lowered."[26] Jan Peerce, for example, thought Bing the most unpleasant of men and worked around him; Kirsten found him cold, and so out-iced him; Varnay, Resnik, and Madeira, sure that Europe understood them better, took off; Steber hung around but found herself looking increasingly for outside work. Indeed, as the unhappy soprano would lament, "When Mr. Bing took over . . . the 'happy family' broke up in a battle of wills between the new manager and his new company. Dozens of artists simply vanished, and those who remained became preoccupied with the task of simple survival. . . . Losing Mr. Johnson . . . was a terrible wrench, especially for me as one of 'Johnson's Kids,' who had grown up under his guidance in an American-oriented Met."[27]

And yet, for all the wringing of hands, the coupling of Bing and the Americans was in many ways serendipity—for everyone. Bing's early experience with opera had come at a time and place (1920s and 1930s in Central Europe) when it was being performed with optimum seriousness and the latest in production techniques and theatrical design. Horrified at the shoddy and old-fashioned productions he had seen in his year of observing the Met, the new manager had made theatrical and visual viability for his productions a first goal. And who better to achieve it than the stage directors and designers of Broadway he engaged and the attractive young American singers raised on that very culture he cast?

What was obvious to all from the box-office response to the new *Fledermaus* was stunningly confirmed the following season when the Met mounted a new Broadway-inspired, Alfred Lunt–directed production of Mozart's *Così Fan Tutte* and once again found itself with a hit. Singing the vernacular English translation, Munsel, Guarrera, and Thebom all turned in performances worthy of any legitimate stage, and Steber and Tucker not only showed unexpected gifts for comedy but ravished the ear. ("For fear some one in Europe would hear this remarkably beautiful voice and steal the man away," Tucker had been one of the first Americans Bing signed.[28])

But if the first cast, with the exception of John Brownlee as Alfonso, was all-American, it was also all-Johnson, and it would, in fact, be some time before the Johnson legacy of Americans no longer dominated the house. For—not forgetting that it takes time to build a roster and that Irene Dalis, Cornell MacNeil, Mildred Miller, Nell Rankin, Giorgio Tozzi, Amara, Curtis-Verna, Peters, and Uppman were all estimable artists in whom he could take pride—the Americans Bing engaged in his first decade, with the notable exception of George London, could not compete with such formidable Johnson recruits as Steber, Stevens, Kirsten, Warren, Merrill, Traubel, Varnay, Resnik, Peerce, Tucker, and Hines. And yet, it is important to remember that it was under Bing that many of them became world-class. And this was not only because they had matured or were responding to the challenge of the superlative European talent with whom they now shared the stage—good enough reasons as they were—but because from *Fledermaus* and *Così* to such other fully realized new productions as the *Rigoletto* he mounted for Warren and the *Carmen* for Stevens, Bing provided the vehicles for these now-veteran Americans to realize their full potential.

And if such an artist as Steber had reason to resent Bing for favoring the Europeans when it came to salary and the casting of such bread-and-butter plums as Tosca, which she ached to sing, it was "indicative of her approach to opera and Bing's regard for her that . . . she created at the Metropolitan the roles of Arabella, Vanessa, and Marie, while turning in incomparable performances of Mozart." In any case, as George Martin happily concluded his survey of the decade's last season, perhaps to end the subject once and for all, "American singers are sprinkled liberally through every cast, and that battle should be regarded as won."[29]

Whereas the Metropolitan steered a relatively steady course under its new leader in the 1950s, the New York City Opera, which had enjoyed several years of steady, solid growth, saw four leaders and nearly folded after the tenure of Laszlo Halasz came to an ugly end in 1951. That situation was ostensibly the result of a conflict with the board over his insistence on mounting David Tamkin's *Dybbuk;* but a growing number of complaints about the fiery Hungarian, some even from his performers, ranging from small matters of salaries and contracts to big ones of personality and policy, had clearly aggravated the situation.

And yet, even as the situation grew rockier still with his replacements—Joseph Rosenstock, then, briefly, Erich Leinsdorf—the confidence and enterprising spirit not only prevailed but was reinforced by the gifted native artists who continued to seek out the old Mecca Temple, among them Patricia Neway, Gloria Lane, Phyllis Curtin, David Poleri, Cornell MacNeil, Barry Morrell, Walter Fredericks, John Reardon, Donald Gramm, Norman Treigle, and, after auditioning some nine times for her chance, Beverly Sills. "We were young Americans who didn't feel opera belonged to the Europeans," Sills recalled. "We didn't feel we were better than other singers. But we knew we were just as good."[30]

And about their company they were passionate—a truth that became abundantly clear in the winter of 1957, when the company, seeing itself threatened with extinction by recent mismanagement, sent out a petition to save the New York City Opera by naming one of their own as its director. To be sure, Julius Rudel was not a singer, but he had been with the company since its inception. A refugee from Vienna, fresh out of Mannes, he had played piano for the first singers to audition for Halasz, filled in wherever else was needed, and slowly worked his way up to conductor and assistant administrator. Now named its new director, with his work to save the company cut out for him, Rudel canceled the spring season and mounted a modest fall season. Then, accompanied by Morton Baum, City Opera's popular cofounder, he went to visit the director of the Ford Foundation's new Program in the Humanities and the Arts in search of money. And when the foundation said it gave money only for special projects, Rudel said: then how about a season of nothing but contemporary American opera?

Certainly, contemporary American opera was not new to the company. From Still's *Troubled Island* under Halasz to Floyd's *Susannah* under Leinsdorf, as many as eleven had been introduced by one or another of its directors. But now with a whole season to be devoted to it, from two hundred submissions Rudel chose ten new American operas, though only one would be a world premiere. For, as the Austrian-born director wisely contended, only by giving operas second hearings could a native canon ever develop.

The "Panorama of Opera—USA," as it was officially called, opened on April 3, 1958, with Douglas Moore's *Ballad of Baby Doe* and closed five weeks later with Floyd's *Susannah*. A sixth week of Weill's popular *Lost in the Stars* was tacked on to make up for some of the losses incurred by the less accessible choices. The auditorium was rarely more than half full and the season showed a deficit of $139,234, but since Ford covered $100,000 of it, the experiment, a critical and public relations success, seemed to bear repeating, and the following spring the company presented twelve American operas, four carried over from the previous festival.

For the virtually 100 percent American casts, the seasons of American opera at the New York City Opera were very exciting. Among the proven champions of the new, the native, and the vernacular already on the roster, Curtin, Lewis, Neway, Bishop, Bible, Lawrence Kelley, Treigle, Gramm, Cassel, and Chester Ludgin made notable contributions, as did others brought in for the event, including Carol Brice, Chester Watson, Beverly Wolf, Lee Venora, McHenry Boatwright, and, from the old Lemonade troupe, Ruth Kobart. Shirley Carter—who would soon find fame as Shirley Verrett-Carter and ultimately just Shirley Verrett—shone in her debut in *Lost in the Stars* (her first opera anywhere), and after a diet of Rosalindes and Violettas, Beverly Sills found her first taste of true stardom as Baby Doe. "[Young American] artists take to localized opera as professionally as ducks take to the village creek," a voice teacher once said.[31] And, indeed, these gifted young Americans relished the opportunity to sing without a filter; to wrap their tongues around their own distinctive speech patterns; to fashion their own technique for best rendering their own distinctive feelings, thoughts, experiences.

In retrospect, it is ironic that just as the once-distinctive vocal styles of other nations were beginning to meld into a sorry uniformity of sound, victims of a shrinking world, the American singer, who for so long had sought to imitate them, should find his own indigenous voice. If some among them would reject it, preferring the prescribed European traditions, and others, energized by the new repertoire, would embrace it, most would continue to make the most of their polyglot heritage and—chameleon-like—do it all. But there it finally was, for the taking, just as Lawrence Tibbett had predicted. For as the great American baritone had said in 1934, "The losing of our sense of inferiority is making possible the development of real American artists. . . . We no longer shy away from an expression of ourselves. . . . The birth of an American school of performers is inevitable."[32] Tibbett would die in 1960, but not before seeing the American singer find a tradition, style, and voice to finally call his own and, with those crucial missing pieces of his identity in place, give birth to just that—an American school.

So much had happened in such a short period of time. True, not all the handicaps that had confronted the American singer in the 1930s had gone away, or, for that matter, ever would. But the whirlwind ride was over, the hard work as far as it could be done had been done, the breakthroughs that could be made had been made. There would be no more American singer as

Adelaide Bishop in the NBC Television Opera Theater
production of Lukas Foss's Griffelkin, 1955.
Courtesy of National Broadcasting Company, Inc.

pioneer battling to be "received in his own country like the European,"[33] as Jerome Hines once described Richard Tucker; no more American singer as hero stepping into the breach; and no more American singer as isolated star. The American singer "as a general category, not as a particular instance,"[34] as Bing correctly pointed out the difference, was now welcomed around the world.

So pause now and remember some of the young Americans—both ordinary and extraordinary—who made so much of the unprecedented opportunity this breathtaking period of technological advances, global war, and civil and social unrest afforded them. Remember the lovely Jessica Dragonette, whose conscious decision to woo that cold, steely microphone gave rise to a whole new breed called the radio singer; the resolute Janet Fairbank, whose annual plugging of her native songs inspired their begetters to keep begetting because one day there would be more like her; the dark-skinned Todd Duncan, whose willingness to lighten his face to portray Tonio in *Pagliacci* at the New York City Opera opened the doors for those of his color not only to sing with white companies but, just as important, to sing roles designated as white. Remember, too, the singer-actors who put opera on Broadway, the indefatigable San Carloans, who took it to the people, and the intrepid individuals who were the first to offer their services to a continent devastated by war and wary of what they had to offer. Remember the spirited Halasz gang and the spunky Lemonaders. And remember Johnson's kids, who braved that mammoth and prestigious stage of the Metropolitan Opera and amazed even their own countrymen with their mettle, ability, and dedication.

Appendix

The following provides select curricula vitae, bibliography, and discography for almost all the American singers whose careers began or ended in the period 1935–1950 and who are referred to in the text. Personal details such as marriages, children, or causes of death are noted only when of particular interest. A bibliography is included only if there exist articles or books devoted to or giving notable attention to a singer; with the exception of *Current Biography Yearbook,* it does not include any reference works. Unless identified as available only on LP, recordings either are now or have been at one time available on CD. Specifics are not provided for a singer's recordings that are numerous and readily available.

Abbreviations

b.	born	MA	*Musical America*
CBY	*Current Biography Year-book*	MC	*Musical Courier*
		Met	Metropolitan
Cons.	Conservatory	NYCO	New York City Opera
CUNY	City University of New York	NYT	*New York Times*
		obit.	obituary
d.	died	ON	*Opera News*
esp.	especially	OQ	*Opera Quarterly*
int.	intermittent (refers to seasons at opera companies, as opposed to consecutive)	RC	*Record Collector*
		Univ.	University

Addison, Adele—soprano; b. New York, July 24, 1925; grew up in Springfield, Mass.; studied with Ruth Eckberg and at Westminster Choir College; opera: New England Opera Theater, NYCO (1955–61, int.), Opera Society of Washington, D.C.; roles: Mimì, Liù, Mélisande; best known for concert and recital; N.Y. debut recital (1952); toured Russia in 1962; dubbed Bess for Dandridge in film of *Porgy and Bess;* taught at Aspen and Manhattan School; recordings: *Time Cycle* (Foss), "Emily Dickinson Songs" (Copland), much Bach and Handel.

Alexander, John—tenor; b. Meridian, Miss., Oct. 21, 1923; d. Meridian, Miss., Dec. 8, 1990; studied at Cincinnati Cons. and with Robert Weede; opera: Cincinnati, NYCO (1957–77, int.), Charles Wagner, NBC Opera Theater, Met (1961–87), San Francisco, Boston, Vienna, Covent Garden; roles: Alfredo, Ferrando, Pollione; much oratorio; taught at Cincinnati Cons.; bibliography: ON (2/15/64, 4/12/80); recording: *Norma.*

Althouse, Paul—tenor; b. Reading, Pa., Dec. 2, 1889; d. New York, Feb. 6, 1954; studied with Percy Rector Stevens and Oscar Saenger; opera: Met (1912–40, int.), San Francisco, Chicago, Berlin, Stuttgart, Stockholm, Salzburg; roles: Grigory in American premiere of *Boris Godunov,* Tristan, Siegfried; sang American premieres of Schoenberg's *Gurrelieder* and Stravinsky's *Oedipus Rex* under Stokowski; taught privately in N.Y.; recordings: *Gurrelieder,* compilations.

Altman, Thelma—mezzo soprano; b. Buffalo, N.Y., Sept. 17, 1919; studied with Nicholas Konraty at Eastman; opera: Met (1943–50), Cincinnati, Miami, San Antonio; roles: Annina (*Traviata*), Giovanna; bibliography: ON (11/29/43).

Amara (Armaganian), Lucine—soprano; b. Hartford, Conn., March 1, 1925; grew up in San Francisco; in San Francisco Opera chorus; studied with Stella Eisner-Eyn and at Univ. of Southern Calif.; winner of 1948 Atwater Kent competition; opera: Met (1950–91, int.), San Francisco, Cincinnati, Glyndebourne, Vienna, Stuttgart, Russia; roles: Micaela, Nedda, Aida, Tatiana, Ellen Orford; film: appears in *The Great Caruso;* bibliography: ON (11/13/50, 2/16/74), OQ (Autumn 1992), *Classical Singer* (10/98); recordings: albums and many Met Club (LPs), *Pagliacci, La Bohème,* Verdi Requiem, *Lohengrin.*

Anderson, Marian—contralto; b. Philadelphia, Feb. 17, 1897; d. Portland, Ore., April 8, 1993; studied with Agnes Reifsnyder, Joseph Borghetti, Frank La Forge; won competition sponsored by N.Y. Philharmonic (1925); opera: Met (1955–56); role: Ulrica; best known as recitalist; N.Y. debut recital (1929); London debut recital (1930); bibliography: *My Lord, What a Morning* (autobiography), *Marian Anderson* (Keiler), *Marian Anderson* (Kosti Vehanen), *Time* (1/13/36, 12/30/46), *NATS Bulletin* (Nov./Dec. 1985); recordings: many albums, *Alto Rhapsody, Ballo in Maschera.*

Antoine, Josephine—soprano; b. Colorado, Oct. 27, 1908; d. Jamestown, N.Y., Oct. 30, 1971; grew up in Boulder, Colo.; studied at Univ. of Colorado and with Marcella Sembrich at Curtis and Juilliard; winner of 1929 Atwater Kent competition; opera: Met (1936–48), San Francisco, Chicago, Cincinnati; roles: Philine, Gilda, Queen of the Night; radio: *Contented Hour;* taught at Univ. of Colorado, Indiana Univ., Univ. of Texas, Eastman, Chautauqua; bibliography: ON (2/23/42), CBY 1944; recording: selections on *American Prima Donna* (Eklipse).

Ayars, Ann—soprano; b. Los Angeles, 1919; d. Hemet, Calif., Feb. 27,

1995; studied with Qurino Pelliciotti; began as a movie actress; opera: NYCO (1947–53), Philadelphia La Scala, Glyndebourne, Edinburgh; roles: Violetta, Manon, Antonia, Euridice; toured in the musical *Rio Rita;* film: *Tales of Hoffmann;* recording: *Tales of Hoffmann* (LP).

Baker, John—baritone; b. Passaic, N.J., ?; studied with Percy Rector Stephens, Bernard Taylor at Juilliard, and Queena Mario, who used him to demonstrate exercises on the Columbia recording *The Queena Mario School of Singing;* opera: New Opera, Met (1943–51); *Lady in the Dark* on Broadway; roles: Morales, Fiorello; bibliography: ON (3/15/43, 12/27/43).

Baker, Kenny—tenor; b. Monrovia, Calif., Sept. 30 1912; d. 1985; won competition sponsored by Texaco (1935); radio: *Texaco Star Theater, Pabst Blue Ribbon,* Fred Allen and Jack Benny shows; many films: *Goldwyn Follies, 52nd Street, Mikado; One Touch of Venus* on Broadway; bibliography: MC (5/20/44); recordings: *One Touch of Venus, Babes in Toyland.*

Bampton, Rose—soprano (began career as a mezzo-soprano); b. Lakewood, Ohio, Nov. 28, 1907; studied with Horatio Connell and Queena Mario at Curtis, later briefly with Frances Alda in New York; opera: Philadelphia Grand, Met (1932–50), NYCO (1950), Covent Garden, Buenos Aires, San Francisco, Chicago; roles: Sieglinde, Donna Anna, Kundry, Aida, Amneris; much concert and recital; radio: *Smith Brothers; Yerma* (Paul Bowles); taught at Juilliard, Manhattan School, North Carolina School of the Arts; married the conductor Wilfrid Pelletier; bibliography: CBY 1940, ON (1/15/40, 3/30/42, 3/18/89), RC (11/88); recordings: aria album (LP), Wagner and Verdi selections (VAI), various broadcasts, including *Fidelio* under Toscanini, *Daphne* from Buenos Aires, and *Gurrelieder* with Philadelphia Orchestra.

Baromeo, Chase (Chase Baromeo Sikes)—bass; b. Augusta, Ga., Aug. 19, 1892 (1893?); d. Birmingham, Mich., Aug. 7, 1973; grew up in Detroit; studied at Univ. of Michigan and in Italy with Giuseppe Campanari; opera: La Scala, Chicago, Cosmopolitan (N.Y.), Met. (1935–38); world premiere *Merry Mount* in Ann Arbor; roles: Sparafucile, Ramfis, Méphistophélès; taught at Univ. of Texas and Univ. of Michigan (Ann Arbor).

Beardslee, Bethany—soprano; b. Lansing, Mich., Dec. 25, 1925; studied with Fred Patton, J. Herbert Swanson, Kathryn Aspinall, and at Michigan State Univ. and Juilliard; best known as a concert singer and specialist in 20th-century music; sang numerous premieres; married the conductor Jacques Monod and later the composer Godfrey Winham; taught at Westminster Choir College, Univ. of Texas (Austin), Brooklyn College, CUNY; recordings: many of such contemporary composers as Babbitt, Schoenberg, Webern, Stravinsky, also Bach, Pergolesi, Debussy, Ravel, and American art song.

Bentonelli (Benton), Joseph—tenor; b. Sayre, Okla., Sept. 10, 1898; d. Oklahoma City, April 4, 1975; studied at Univ. of Oklahoma, Chicago Musical

College with Oscar Saenger, in France with Jean de Reszke, and in Italy with Vittorio Vanzo; opera: Rome, Verona, Belgium, Netherlands, No. Africa, Chicago, Met (1936–37); roles: Des Grieux (*Manon*), Alfredo, Faust; sang in the American premieres of Respighi's *La Fiamma* and Gluck's *Iphigénie en Aulide;* taught at Univ. of Oklahoma; bibliography: *Oklahoma Tenor* (Benton); recording: excerpt from *Manon* on *Lucrezia Bori in Concert* (Eklipse).

Benzell, Mimi—soprano; b. Bridgeport, Conn., April 6, 1922; d. Manhasset, N.Y., Dec. 23, 1970, of cancer; attended Hunter College and Mannes; studied with Olga Eisner; opera: New Opera, Mexico City, Met (1944–49); roles: Queen of the Night, Musetta, Philine, Gilda; much summer stock, operetta, nightclubs; *Milk and Honey* on Broadway; bibliography: ON (1/1/45); recordings: album, operettas (LPs), *Milk and Honey.*

Berberian, Cathy—mezzo-soprano: b. Attleboro, Mass., July 4, 1925; d. Rome, Italy, March 6, 1983; studied at Columbia Univ., New York Univ., and with Giorgina del Vigo in Italy; known throughout Europe and America as a specialist of the avant-garde but also sang early music and some standard repertoire; also composed; married the composer Luciano Berio; bibliography: *High Fidelity/MA* (7/70), NYT (obit. 3/8/83); recordings: much Berio and John Cage, Monteverdi's *L'Incoronazione di Poppea.*

Berini, Mario—tenor, b. Russia, May 27, 1910 (?); d. New York, March 3, 1993; grew up in Los Angeles; attended Curtis; studied with Charles Dalmorès in Los Angeles and Bernado de Muro in N.Y.; film: dubbed singing in *Damsel in Distress;* Radio City Music Hall; opera: San Carlo, NYCO (1944), Met (1946–48), Mexico City, Chicago, San Francisco; roles: Don José, Turridu, Faust; world premiere broadcast of Montemezzi's *L'Incantesimo; A Flag Is Born* on Broadway; replaced Mario Lanza in Bel Canto Trio; stopped singing in early 1950s when his vocal cord was severed during surgery; taught privately; bibliography: MC (2/15/47).

Bible, Frances—mezzo-soprano; b. Sacketts Harbor, N.Y., Jan. 26, 1919; d. Hemet, Calif., Jan. 29, 2001; studied with Belle Julie Soudant and Queena Mario at Juilliard; opera: NYCO (1948–77), San Francisco, Glyndebourne, Dublin, NBC Opera Theater; roles: Angelina (*Cenerentola*), Octavian, Augusta Tabor (*Ballad of Baby Doe*); created Elizabeth Proctor in Ward's *The Crucible* and Frade in Tamkin's *The Dybbuk;* taught at Rice Univ. before settling in California in 1991; bibliography: MC (10/58), ON (2/3/68); recordings: *Ballad of Baby Doe, The Crucible, L'Incoronazione di Poppea.*

Bishop, Adelaide—b. New York, June 23, 1928; studied with Louis Polanski and at the Rossini Workshop; opera: American Opera Company (Philadelphia), NYCO (1948–60), NBC Opera Theater; roles: Gilda, Sophie; created title role of *Griffelkin* (Foss); became a stage director after automobile accident ended singing career; taught at Mannes, Hartt College of Music, and Boston Univ.; recording: *The Stronger* (Weisgall) (LP).

Bledsoe, Jules (Julius)—baritone; b. Waco, Tex., Dec. 29, 1898; d. Hollywood, July 14, 1943; studied at Central Texas College, Bishop College, Virginia Union, Columbia Univ. Medical School, and with Claude Warford, Lazar Samoiloff, Luigi Parisolti in New York; opera: Salmaggi (N.Y.), Aeolian (N.Y.), Netherlands, Cleveland; roles: Emperor Jones, Amonasro, Boris Godunov; created Tizan (*Deep River*) and Joe (*Show Boat*) on Broadway; films: *Show Boat, Drums of the Congo;* N.Y. debut recital (1924), recital and concert in Europe and United States; also composed; died of a heart attack, having just completed an army camp tour; bibliography: MC (4/1/38), NYT (obit. 7/16/43); recording: selections on *Brother, Can You Spare a Dime?* (Pearl).

Boatwright, Helen Strassburger—soprano; b. Sheboygan, Wis., Nov. 17, 1916; studied with Anna Shram Irving, at Oberlin with Marion Sims, and in Texas with Chase Baromeo; opera: Berkshire Music Center, Austin, San Antonio; roles: Anna (*Merry Wives of Windsor*), Countess Almaviva; best known for concert and recital throughout Europe and the U.S.; N.Y. debut recital (1967); married the composer Howard Boatwright (1943); taught at Syracuse and Cornell; recordings: Buxtehude, Handel, Johann Rosenmüller (LPs), Ives and Bacon (CRI).

Bodanya (Bodanskaya), Natalie—soprano; b. New York, 1914 (?); studied with Marcella Sembrich and Queena Mario at Curtis; opera: Philadelphia Orchestra, Met (1936–42); NYCO (1944–45); roles: Micaela, Musetta; Radio City Music Hall; N.Y. debut recital (1934); taught at Manhattan School, and privately in Santa Barbara, Calif.; bibliography: *Newsweek* (7/26/43).

Bollinger, Anne—soprano; b. Lewiston, Idaho, Dec. 22, 1922 (?); d. Zurich, July 11, 1962, of cancer; studied at Universities of Idaho and Southern California, and with Rosalie Miller and Lotte Lehmann; winner in 1943 of a competition sponsored by the Hollywood Bowl; opera: Central City, Met (1949–53), NYCO (1952), Dublin, Berlin, Paris, Zurich, and Hamburg State Opera (1953–59), where she sang leading roles and opened its new house as Pamina in 1955; roles: Micaela, Zdenka, Fiordiligi; bibliography: ON (1/3/49).

Bonelli (Bunn), Richard—baritone; b. Fort Byron, N.Y., Feb. 6, 1887; d. Los Angeles, June 7, 1980; grew up in Syracuse, N.Y.; studied at Syracuse Univ. and with Arthur Alexander, William Vilonat, and Jean de Reszke; opera: Aborn, San Carlo (Gallo), Monte Carlo, La Scala, Paris, Chicago (1925–31), San Francisco, Met (1932–1945, int.), NYCO (1948–52, int.), Los Angeles; roles: Valentin, Amonasro, Germont, Sharpless; taught at Curtis, Music Academy of the West; sang Valentin (*Faust*) in the first opera broadcast nationally from an opera house (Chicago) (1927); films: early Fox Movietone shorts, *Enter Madam, Hard-boiled Canary;* settled in Los Angeles with second wife, the poet Mona Modini Wood; bibliography: NYT (obit. 6/11/80); recordings: recital albums (Delos), opera broadcasts.

Brancato, Rosemarie—soprano; b. Kansas City, Mo., 1911; d. New York,

June 18, 1994; studied with Thomas Austin-Ball, Estelle Liebling, and at Eastman; opera: Chicago, Detroit, Cincinnati, NYCO (1945–46); roles: Gilda, Violetta; much radio.

Brice, Carol—contralto; b. Indianapolis, April 16, 1918; d. Norman, Okla., Feb. 15, 1985; grew up in Sedalia, N.C.; studied at Palmer Memorial Institute, Talladega College, and with Francis Rogers at Juilliard; first black musician to win Naumburg (1944); N.Y. debut recital (1945); recital and concert throughout U.S., South America, and Europe; opera: NYCO (1958–65, int.); musicals, including *Show Boat, Finnian's Rainbow, Porgy and Bess, Carousel;* married to the baritone Thomas Carey; taught at Univ. of Oklahoma; founded the Cimarron Circuit Opera Co. with her husband; recordings: albums of Bach and de Falla (LPs), also Mahler, *Regina* (Blitzstein) and *Porgy and Bess.*

Brown, Anne—soprano; b. Baltimore, 1912; studied with Lucia Dunham at Juilliard and with Lotte Lehmann; opera: Oslo; roles: Bess, Belinda (*Dido and Aeneas*), Magda (*The Consul*); created Bess in *Porgy and Bess;* recital and concert throughout U.S. and Europe; settled in Norway in late 1940s; retired from singing as a result of respiratory problems; became a teacher and stage director; bibliography: *Newsweek* (10/12/42), NYT (3/29/98), an autobiography in Norwegian to be translated into *Songs from a Frozen Branch;* recording: *Porgy and Bess.*

Browning, Lucielle—mezzo-soprano; b. Jacksonville, N.C., Feb. 19, 1913; grew up in Durham, N.C.; studied at North Carolina College and with Marcella Sembrich and Florence Page Kimball at Juilliard; opera: Philadelphia Orchestra, Charles Wagner, Met (1936–51); roles: Suzuki, Mercedes; bibliography: ON 1/1/1951; recordings: *Madama Butterfly* highlights (LP), opera broadcasts.

Burke, Hilda—soprano; b. Baltimore, 1904; Burke is her first husband's name; studied in Baltimore with George Castelle and in Dresden on a Juilliard scholarship; two-time winner of Civic Opera Contest in Baltimore; opera: De Feo, San Carlo (Gallo), Chicago (1928–38, int.), Met (1935–42); roles: Micaela, Aida, Marguerite; married the baritone and stage director Désiré Defrère, divorced; bibliography: MA (1/10/36), MC (8/41); recordings: broadcasts of *Carmen* with Ponselle.

Carroll, Christina—soprano; b. Tinca, Romania, Dec. 9, 1920; d. Tempe, Ariz., ?; grew up in Cleveland; studied at the Univ. of Southern California and with Estelle Heilborn and Hans Clemens; opera: St. Louis, San Francisco, Cincinnati, Philadelphia La Scala, National Opera (D'Andria), Met (1943–46), NYCO (1949), Mexico City, Italy, Glyndebourne; roles: Musetta, Micaela, Donna Elvira; much operetta; taught in Arizona; bibliography: ON (1/3/44); recordings: albums (LPs).

Cassel, Walter—baritone; b. Council Bluffs, Iowa, May 15, 1910; d. Bloomington, Ind., July 3, 2000; studied with Harry Cooper, Frank La Forge; opera: NYCO (1948–69 int.), Met (1942–74, int.), Cincinnati, Chicago, Barcelona, Vienna; roles: Scarpia, Flying Dutchman, Jochanaan; created Horace Tabor in *Ballad of Baby Doe;* much radio and light opera; taught at Indiana Univ.; married the soprano Gail Manners; bibliography: ON (1/25/43, 3/18/61, 1/22/66), MC (1/15/55), MA (11/15/59); recordings: Met Club LPs, *Ballad of Baby Doe.*

Cecil, Winifred—soprano; b. Staten Island, August 31, 1907; d. New York, Sept. 13, 1985; studied with Marcella Sembrich, Elena Gerhardt; opera: San Carlo (Naples), Vienna, La Scala, Prague; roles: Aida, Elisabeth (*Tannhäuser*); much radio early; much recital; N.Y. debut recital (1935); married to president of Turin Opera, lived in Italy; returned to U.S. in 1949; taught at Juilliard, Univ. of Buffalo; founded Joy of Singing; bibliography: ON (1/15/72); recordings: albums (Town Hall LPs).

Chamlee, Mario (Archer Cholmondelay)—tenor; b. Los Angeles, May 29, 1892; d. Los Angeles, Nov. 13, 1966; studied with Achille Alberti in L.A. and with Sibella in N.Y.; early career sang under the name Mario Rodolfi; opera: Aborn, Antonio Scotti touring, Met (1920–39, int.), Chicago, San Francisco, London, Paris, Brussels; roles: Cavaradossi, Faust, Marouf; married the soprano Ruth Miller; taught privately in Los Angeles; recordings: albums and compilations.

Conley, Eugene—b. Lynn, Mass., March 12, 1908; d. Denton, Tex., Dec. 18, 1981; studied with Harriet Barrows and Ettore Verna; much radio, including *NBC Presents Eugene Conley* and *Magic Key;* opera: Salmaggi (N.Y.), San Carlo (Naples and Gallo), National Opera (D'Andria), Cincinnati, Mexico City, Covent Garden, Stockholm, Turin, Florence, La Scala, NYCO (1945–50, int.), Met (1950–56); roles: Faust, Arturo (*Puritani*), Don Ottavio, Tom in Met premiere of Stravinsky's *Rake's Progress;* married the mezzo-soprano Winifred Heidt, divorced; taught at North Texas State Univ.; bibliography: CBY 1954, ON (2/27/50), *Etude* (3/50); recordings: aria album, *Rigoletto, The Rake's Progress.*

Conner, Nadine (Evelyn Nadine Henderson)—soprano; b. Compton, Calif., Feb. 20, 1907; d. Los Alamitos, Calif., March 1, 2003; Conner was her first husband's name; studied at Univ. of Southern California and with Horatio Cogswell, Florence Easton, Frantz Proschowski, and esp. Amador Fernandez; much early radio, including *Vicks Open House, Coca Cola Hour;* opera: Met (1941–60, int.), Los Angeles, San Francisco, Amsterdam; roles: Micaela, Zerlina, Pamina; Mimì, Marguerite, Mélisande, Sophie; soloist with N.Y. Philharmonic; films: *Of Men and Music;* Mimì on *Omnibus Bohème;* bibliography: ON (12/22/41), *Etude* (5/45), MA (12/15/53), CBY 1955, NYT (obit.

3/10/03); recordings: *Hänsel und Gretel* (LP), *Carmen* highlights, *St. Matthew Passion* under Walter, broadcast of *Nozze di Figaro* (Legend).

Cordon, Norman—bass; b. Washington, N.C., Jan. 20, 1904; d. Chapel Hill, N.C., March 1, 1964; studied at Nashville Cons. and with Gaetano de Luca and Hadley Outland; opera: Chicago (1933–35), San Francisco, San Carlo (Gallo), Met (1936–46), NYCO (1947–49); roles: Colline, Basilio, Oroveso, Sparafucile, Méphistophélès; created Mr. Maurant (*Street Scene*) on Broadway; taught at Univ. of North Carolina; bibliography: ON (4/13/42, 2/18/57); recordings: albums (LPs), opera broadcasts, *Street Scene, Norma.*

Cotlow, Marilyn—soprano; b. Minneapolis, Jan. 10, 1924; grew up in Los Angeles; studied with Hans Clemens; cowinner of 1948 Met Auditions of the Air, opera: American Opera Co. (Rosing), Central City, Met (1948–49), Germany, England; roles: Philine, Adina, Violetta, Rosina; created Lucy in *The Telephone;* taught at Peabody, Univ. of Michigan, and Catholic Univ. of America; bibliography: ON (11/29/48), *Etude* (4/49); recording: *The Telephone.*

Cravi, Mina—soprano; b. Bari, Italy, Aug. 24, 1918; d. New York, Feb. 10, 1983; grew up in New Haven, Conn.; studied in N.Y.; opera: Cosmopolitan (San Francisco), Cincinnati, San Carlo (Gallo); roles: Mimì, Violetta, Cio-Cio-San; founded Richmond Opera on Staten Island (1958); toured Europe and South America; married the Italian bass Fausta Bozza.

Crooks, Richard (Alexander Richard Crooks)—tenor; b. Trenton, N.J., June 26, 1900; d. Portola Valley, Calif., Sept. 29, 1972; studied with Frank La Forge, Sydney Bourne, Léon Rothier; opera: Hamburg (1927), Berlin, Chicago, San Francisco, Philadelphia, Met (1933–42); roles: Des Grieux (*Manon*), Alfredo, Lohengrin; much radio, including *Voice of Firestone;* concert and recital around the world; bibliography: ON (4/9/66), RC (12/72, 11/86), *NATS Bulletin* (1/85); recordings: many albums.

Curtin, Phyllis Smith—soprano; b. Clarksburg, W.V., Dec. 3, 1922; graduated from Wellesley; studied with Olga Averino and Joseph Regneas; opera: New England Opera Theater; NYCO (1953–64, int.), Met (1961–73, int.), Chicago, Vienna, Buenos Aires, La Scala; roles: Salome, Fiordiligi, Violetta; created Floyd's Susannah and Cathy (*Wuthering Heights*); much recital and concert; N.Y. recital debut (1950); bibliography: NYT (3/21/54, 5/14/72, 7/5/98), MC (10/57), *Time* (12/1/61), CBY 1964, ON (1/14/67, 11/90); recordings: Chanler's *Eight Epitaphs,* Purcell's *The Fairy Queen, Songs of Latin America* (LPs), recital and aria albums.

Curtis-Verna (Curtis), Mary—soprano; b. Salem, Mass., May 9, 1921; studied at Hollins College and with Ettore Verna, whom she later married; opera: Italy, Monte Carlo, Lisbon, Barcelona, London, Buenos Aires, San Francisco, Cincinnati, NYCO (1957), Met (1957–66); roles: Aida, Leonora

(*Trovatore* and *Forza del Destino*), Donna Anna, Tosca: bibliography: ON (2/ 17/58); recordings: *Aida, Don Giovanni, Ballo in Maschera,* opera broadcasts.

Dame, Donald—tenor; b. Cleveland, June 1, 1917; d. Lincoln, Neb., Jan. 21, 1952; studied with Vera Schwartz and at Juilliard; opera: New Opera, Met (1943–45); roles: Laërte (*Mignon*), Gabriel in *Fledermaus;* died of a heart attack while on Met tour of *Fledermaus;* several N.Y. Town Hall recitals, Worcester Festival, Chautauqua, much radio; bibliography: ON (12/20/43), *Etude* (8/46); recordings: *Music Master* and *New Moon* (LPs).

Darcy, Emery—tenor (early career as a baritone); b. Chicago, Dec. 9, 1908; studied with Lucie Lenox, Hermann Weigert, Walter Taussig; opera: Chicago English Opera, Hollywood Bowl, Met (1940–53); roles: mostly comprimario, but also Siegmund, Parsifal, Melot (*Tristan*); bibliography: ON (12/ 23/40), *Newsweek* (4/10/44), *Time* (4/10/44), MC (5/5/44), recording: excerpts from *Die Walküre* (LP).

Davis, Agnes—soprano; b. Colorado Springs, Colo., May 11, 1905; d. Bloomington, Ind., Oct. 10, 1967; studied at Colorado State Teachers College and with Emilio de Gorgorza at Curtis; first winner of the Atwater Kent competition; opera: Philadelphia Grand, Philadelphia Orchestra, Met Spring Season (1937); roles: Elsa, Alice Ford; Lulu in concert under Otto Klemperer in N.Y. and Roxane in Damrosch's *Cyrano de Bergerac;* primarily an orchestral soloist; taught at Philadelphia Cons., Indiana Univ.; married the baritone Benjamin de Loache, divorced; recording: Immolation Scene from *Götterdämmerung* with Philadelphia Orchestra.

Davis, Ellabelle—soprano; b. New Rochelle, N.Y., 1907; d. New Rochelle, N.Y., Nov. 15, 1960, of cancer; studied with Idelle Patterson and Reina le Zaro; appeared in revival of William Boyce's *The Chaplet* at the Museum of Modern Art (1941); opera: Mexico City, Buenos Aires; role: Aida; N.Y. recital debut (1942); best known for recital and concert in Europe, South America, and U.S.; named American Singer of the Year by League of Composers (1947); premiered *Song of Songs* by Lukas Foss with Boston Symphony; bibliography: MC (2/1/46, 7/48, 6/50), *Time* (7/29/46), *Newsweek* (3/17/47); recording: aria album (LP).

De Cavalieri, Anna; see McKnight, Anne.

Della Chiesa, Vivian—soprano: b. Chicago, Oct. 9, 1914; studied with Gabriel Czarnowski, Forrest Lamont; winner of "Unknown Singers" radio competition (1935); opera: Chicago, Cincinnati, San Francisco, Havana, St. Louis, NYCO (1947), New Orleans; roles: Mimì, Alice Ford, Nedda, Desdemona, Marguerite; world premiere broadcast of Montemezzi's *L'Incantesimo;* soloist under Toscanini; toured Australia and New Zealand; much radio, including *American Melody Hour;* later TV; supper clubs, including the

Empire Room and Coconut Grove, also Las Vegas; taught privately; bibliography: *Etude* (9/42, 9/48), CBY 1943; recordings: albums of popular music (LPs), Brahms *Deutsches Requiem* and trio from *I Lombardi* with Toscanini, *Falstaff* (VAI), compilations.

Dickenson, Jean—soprano; b. Montreal, 1909; d. ?, 1989; because of father's career in mine engineering, grew up in India, South Africa, New York, San Francisco, and Denver; studied with Cesare Sturani; opera: Denver Grand, Met (1940–41); role: Philine; much radio, including *Album of Familiar Music;* bibliography: ON (1/22/40), *Etude* (3/44), MC (6/45); recording: radio compilation (IRCC).

Dickey, Annamary—soprano; b. Decatur, Ill., April 11, 1911; d. Tampa, June 1, 1999; studied with Marcella Sembrich at Juilliard; winner of 1939 Met Auditions of the Air; opera: Cincinnati, St. Louis, Met (1939–44); roles: Musetta; created Marjorie Taylor in *Allegro* (Rodgers and Hammerstein); replaced Gertrude Lawrence in *The King and I;* bibliography: MC (2/15/46); recordings: *Bohème* broadcast (1940), *Allegro.*

Dickson, Donald—baritone (tenor after 1956); b. Cleveland, Nov. 13, 1915; d. ?, 1972; protégé of Artur Rodzinski in Cleveland; studied with Warren Whitney, Ellen Toedt, Paul Althouse, and at Juilliard, where he created the title role in Albert Stoessel's *Garrick;* opera: Cleveland, Chautauqua, Columbia Opera, Philadelphia La Scala, Chicago, Met (1937–38); roles: Valentin, Ford; much radio, including *Chase and Sanborne Hour;* much recital; N.Y. debut recital (1941); debut as tenor in the role of Canio (1956); bibliography: MC (3/1/45); recordings: some compilations.

Doe, Doris—mezzo-soprano; b. Bar Harbor, Maine, 1905; d. Chattanooga, Dec. 26, 1985; studied with Louise Homer, Sybil McDemid; opera: Dresden, Met (1932–47); roles: Annina (*Rosenkavalier*), Waltraute; much concert and recital; N.Y. debut recital (1925); taught at Univ. of Tennessee; bibliography: ON (2/14/38); recordings: opera broadcasts.

Doree, Doris—soprano; b. Newark, Dec. 29, 1911; d. New York, Oct. 14, 1971; studied at the Settlement School of Music (Philadelphia) and with Eufemia Gregory and Adele Newfield; taught and performed dance; opera: Met (1942–44), Charles Wagner, NYCO (1945–50, int.), Covent Garden, Stockholm, Copenhagen; roles: Senta, Santuzza, Ellen Orford (*Peter Grimes*), Marschallin, Sieglinde; bibliography: ON (3/1/43), MC (1/15/49).

Dow, Dorothy—soprano; b. Houston, Tex., Oct. 8, 1920; grew up in Galveston; studied with Edward Bing in Texas and at Juilliard; opera: Zurich, La Scala, Covent Garden, Buenos Aires; roles: Salome, Norma, Lady Macbeth, and Marie (*Wozzeck*) in La Scala premiere; created many roles, including Renata in Prokofiev's *Flaming Angel* in Venice and Susan B. Anthony in Virgil Thomson's *Mother of Us All;* taught in Texas; recording: *Erwartung.*

Dragonette, Jessica—soprano; b. Calcutta, India, February 14, 1901, 1904, or 1910 (?); d. New York, March 18, 1980; grew up in Lansdowne, Pa.; studied with Estelle Liebling; radio debut (1926), first commercial artist to sign exclusive contract with NBC; much radio, including *Coca-Cola Hour, Philco Theater Memories, Cities Service Hour* (1930–37), *Saturday Night Serenade;* concert tours of U.S. and Canada; bibliography: *Faith Is a Song* (autobiography), *Musical Digest* (8/38), many radio magazines; recording: *Five Ladies of Song* (LP).

Duncan, Todd—baritone; b. Danville, Ky., Feb. 12, 1903; d. Washington, D.C., Feb. 28, 1998; grew up in Indianapolis; studied at Butler College and Columbia Univ.; opera: Aeolian, NYCO (1945); roles: Alfio, Tonio, Escamillo; created Porgy in *Porgy and Bess,* Lord's General in *Cabin in the Sky,* and Stephen Kumalo in *Lost in the Stars* on Broadway; some legitimate theater; film: *Syncopation, Unchained;* N.Y. debut recital (1944); concert and recital around the world; taught at Howard Univ. (1931–45), Curtis Institute, and privately in Washington, D.C.; bibliography: CBY 1942, *Newsweek* (10/8/45), MC (5/15/48), MA (2/1/55); *NATS Bulletin* (5/81), ON (3/16/85); recordings: spirituals (LP), *Porgy and Bess, Lost in the Stars.*

Eddy, Nelson—baritone; b. Providence, R.I., June 29, 1901; d. Miami Beach, March 6, 1967; studied with many teachers, including William Vilonat and David Bispham; opera: Philadelphia Civic, Philadelphia Grand, San Francisco; roles: Tonio, Wolfram, Drum Major (*Wozzeck*); much concert and recital; N.Y. debut recital (1934); many films, including *Naughty Marietta, Rose Marie, Phantom of the Opera;* bibliography: *Sweethearts* (Sharon Rich), *Nelson Eddy: The Opera Years* (Sharon Rich), MA (1/15/51), OQ (Spring 1997), radio magazines; recordings: many albums.

Elzy, Ruby—soprano; b. Pontotoc, Miss., 1908; d. Detroit, June 27, 1943, following routine surgery; attended Ohio State, Juilliard; opera: created the role of Serena in *Porgy and Bess;* films: *Emperor Jones, Birth of the Blues;* N.Y. debut recital (1937); bibliography: *Black Diva of the Thirties: The Life of Ruby Elzy* (David G. Weaver), *Etude* (8/43); recordings: though Anne Brown sings Serena on the original cast *Porgy and Bess,* Elzy can be heard in a rehearsal recording under Gershwin (*Gershwin Performs Gershwin*) and in a 1937 Hollywood Bowl memorial concert to Gershwin.

Fairbank, Janet—soprano; b. Chicago, 1903; d. Chicago, Sept. 6, 1947, of Hodgkin's disease; attended Univ. of Chicago, Radcliffe College; studied in Germany; opera: Chicago, Cincinnati, San Carlo (Gallo); roles: Siebel, Micaela; N.Y. debut recital (1941); devoted eight N.Y. recitals to contemporary songs; bibliography: *Time* (12/16/46).

Farrell, Eileen—soprano; b. Willamantic, Conn., Feb. 13, 1920; d. Park Ridge, N.J., March 23, 2002; grew up in Woonsocket, R.I.; studied with Merle Alcock and Eleanor McClellan; much radio, including *Eileen Farrell*

Sings; opera: San Francisco, Chicago, Met (1960–66, int.), concert opera; roles: Gioconda, Alceste; stage debut in Tampa as Santuzza (1956); N.Y. recital debut (1950); Bach Aria Group; much recital and concert; dubbed the voice of Marjorie Lawrence in *Interrupted Melody;* TV, including *The Carol Burnett Show;* taught at Indiana Univ. and Univ. of Maine; video: *Eileen Farrell—An American Prima Donna* (VAI); bibliography: *Can't Help Singing* (autobiography); *Etude* (7/52), *Time* (1/2/56), *High Fidelity* (1/60), CBY 1961, ON (2/11/61, 7/92, 6/02), NYT (2/8/70, 6/6/92), *NATS Bulletin* (9/02); recordings: albums, including many of pop standards, Wagner selections (Stokowski), *Wozzeck* (Mitropoulos), *Maria Stuarda.*

Faull, Ellen—soprano: b. Pittsburgh, Oct. 14, 1918; studied with Mildred Lissfelt in Pittsburgh, with Eufemia Gregory at Curtis, and with Joseph Regneas in N.Y.; opera: After Dinner Opera, New England Opera, NYCO (1947–79, int.), San Francisco, Chicago, Yugoslavia; roles: Donna Anna, Countess Almaviva; created roles in *Lizzie Borden, Carrie Nation,* and *Regina;* sang Lady Billows in American premiere of *Albert Herring;* much oratorio and concert; taught at Manhattan School, Juilliard, and privately in Washington state, where she settled; bibliography: ON (2/99), OQ (Summer 2000); recordings: *Lizzie Borden,* album (VAI).

Fisher, Susanne—soprano: b. Sutton, W.V., ?; d. Panama City, Feb. 15, 1990; studied piano at Cincinnati Cons., and voice at Juilliard and with Oscar Daniel in Paris; opera: Berlin Staatsoper, Paris Opéra-Comique, Met (1935–40, int.); roles: Cio-Cio-San, Marguerite, Nedda; N.Y. debut recital (1943); bibliography: *Time* (1/6/36).

Franke, Paul—tenor; b. Boston, Dec. 23, 1920; studied with William Whitney at New England Cons., and with Fritz Kitzinger; Berkshire Music Center; opera: Boston Grand, Santa Fe, Met (1948–87); roles: Goro, Remendado, Spalanzani; bibliography: ON (1/10/49, 4/18/64).

Galli-Campi, Amri (Irmemgard Gallenkamp)—soprano; b. Honesdale, Pa., 1899; d. New York, May 9, 1997; studied with her mother, the soprano Christine Volker, and Herbert Braham; opera: Italy, London, Cincinnati, Met (1938, one performance on tour); roles: Gilda, Queen of the Night, Lucia; much radio, esp. *Evening in Paris Hour,* a program built around her; Carnegie Hall recital (1945); taught privately; bibliography: MC (3/30/35).

Gauld, Carlton—bass; b. Bedford, Ind., 1901; d. London, March 2, 1975; studied at Wabash College and in France with Jean de Reszke; sang Leporello in de Reszke production of *Don Giovanni;* opera: Buenos Aires, Paris Opéra-Comique (1932–37), San Francisco, Met (1931–38, int.), NYCO (1944–58); roles: Méphistophélès, Golaud, Lothario (*Mignon*); remained at NYCO as a stage director (1957–61).

Giannini, Dusolina—soprano; b. Philadelphia, Dec. 19, 1902; d. Zurich, June 29, 1986; studied with her father, Ferruccio Giannini, and Marcella

Sembrich; opera: Hamburg, Berlin, Covent Garden, Vienna, Salzburg, San Francisco, Chicago, Met (1936–41), NYCO (1944–51, int.); roles: Aida, Tosca, Carmen, Santuzza; much recital; taught at Zurich International Opera Center; her brother was the composer Vittorio Giannini and her sister, Eufemia Gregory, taught voice at Curtis; bibliography: *Time* (2/24/36), MA (11/25/46), RC (2/54), ON (4/11/64, 12/15/79, 12/6/86); recordings: albums, *Aida*.

Glade, Coe—mezzo-soprano; b. Chicago, Aug. 12, 1900; d. New York, Sept. 23, 1985; studied with Homer Moore in Tampa; opera: San Carlo (Gallo), Cincinnati, Chicago; roles: Carmen, Amneris, Mignon, Dalila, Adalgisa (*Norma*); sang *Carmen* excerpts at opening of Radio City Music Hall in 1932; taught privately; bibliography: MA (3/10/31), ON (1/12/74); recording: *Carmen* Act 3 (Unique LP).

Greco, Norina—soprano; b. Campobasso, Italy, ?; came to U.S. when she was eight and grew up in Brooklyn; brother was the famous dancer José Greco; studied with Antonio Moratto and Maria Gay; opera: Salmaggi, San Carlo (Gallo), Cincinnati, Rio de Janeiro, Met (1940–42); roles: Aida, Nedda, Leonora (*Trovatore*), Violetta; reportedly settled in Brazil; bibliography: ON (12/16/40); recordings: some compilations, broadcast *Trovatore*.

Greer, Frances—lyric soprano; b. Piggott, Ark., Jan. 12, 1917; studied at Louisiana State Univ. and with Nina Heden and Maria Gay; winner of Philadelphia Orchestra Youth Award, cowinner of 1942 Met Auditions of the Air; opera: Philadelphia Opera Company, Charles Wagner, St. Louis, Met (1942–50); roles: Musetta, Oscar, Susanna; much radio; taught at Univ. of Michigan at Ann Arbor; marriages include Robert Gay, baritone, and Victor Trucco, an assistant conductor at the Met; bibliography: ON (12/7/42); recordings: *The Music Master, New Moon* (LPs), broadcasts of *Ballo in Maschera* and *Fidelio*.

Guarrera, Frank—baritone; b. Philadelphia, Dec. 3, 1923; studied with Richard Bonelli and Eufemia Gregory at Curtis; cowinner of 1948 Met Auditions of the Air; opera: NYCO (1947), La Scala, Met (1948–76), San Francisco, Cincinnati, Chicago; roles: Escamillo, Valentin, Gugliemo, Ford, Simon Boccanegra; taught at Univ. of Washington, Seattle; bibliography: ON (2/14/49, 4/3/50, 12/24/60); recordings: aria album (LP), broadcasts, *Falstaff* under Toscanini.

Guido, Josephine—soprano; b. Youngstown, Ohio, July 24, 1924; grew up in N.Y.; studied with Giuseppina La Puma, Luigi Ricci, Thelma Votipka; opera: Mascagni Opera Guild, Charles Wagner, Italy, New Orleans Experimental Theater; roles: Musetta, Gilda, Cio-Cio-San; became a stage director; recordings: *Ballo in Maschera, Don Pasquale* (Remington LPs).

Gurney, John—bass; b. Jamestown, N.Y., June 13, 1902; d. Aug. 6, 1997; studied at Oberlin and Harvard, and with Jean Mauran in Paris; much early experience in vaudeville, musical comedy, Ziegfield Follies; opera: American Opera Co. (Rosing), Charles Wagner, San Carlo (Gallo), Buenos Aires,

Cincinnati, Met (1935–45); roles: Sparafucile, Ferrando (*Trovatore*); later much concert and recital.

Hackett, Charles—tenor; b. Worcester, Mass., Nov. 4, 1889; d. New York, Jan. 1, 1942; brother, Arthur, was a concert and oratorio tenor; studied with Arthur Hubbard in Boston and Vincenzo Lombardi in Italy; sang Rossini's *Stabat Mater* with Lillian Nordica in Providence, R.I. (1911); opera: La Scala, Rome, South America, Chicago, Met (1919–39, int.); roles: Des Grieux (*Manon*), Roméo, Faust, Don Ottavio, much recital and concert; married the prima ballerina at La Scala, Virginia Zucchi; bibliography: *Harper's Bazaar* (2/20), RC (2/75); recordings: several albums.

Hargrave, William—bass; b. Philadelphia, ?; grew up in Culver City, Calif.; studied with James Spencer Kelley; cowinner of 1944 Met Auditions of the Air; opera: Hollywood Grand, Met (1944–47), role: Monterone; bibliography: ON (4/17/44).

Harrell, Mack—baritone; b. Celeste, Tex., Oct. 8, 1909; d. Dallas, Jan. 29, 1960; began as a violinist; studied with Robert Lawrence Wier and with Anna Schoen-René at Juilliard; cowinner of 1939 Met Auditions of the Air; opera: Met (1939–58, int.), NYCO (1944–59, int.), San Francisco, Chicago; roles: Kothner, Papageno, Masetto, Nick Shadow in Met premiere of *Rake's Progress;* N.Y. debut recital (1938); much concert and recital; European tours; taught at Juilliard, Southern Methodist Univ., and Aspen; married to the violinist Marjorie Fulton; father of the cellist Lynn Harrell; bibliography: ON (12/11/39), *Opera and Concert* (3/49), *Etude* (8/49), *Time* (8/18/52), *Newsweek* (11/17/52); recordings: albums (LPs), *Rake's Progress, Wozzeck* (Mitropoulos), *St. Matthew Passion* (Walter), opera broadcasts.

Harshaw, Margaret—soprano (mezzo-soprano until approx. 1950); b. Philadelphia, May 12, 1909; d. Lake Forest, Ill., Nov. 7, 1997; studied with Anna Schoen-René at Juilliard; winner of Eisteddford and National Federation of Music Clubs competitions, cowinner of 1942 Met Auditions of the Air; opera: Steel Pier, Met (1942–64, int.), Cincinnati, Philadelphia, San Francisco, Covent Garden, Glyndebourne; roles: Amneris, Ortrud, Donna Anna, Kundry, Isolde; taught at Curtis, Indiana Univ.; bibliography: ON (3/1/43, 3/20/44, 3/14/55, 3/2/96), *Time* (2/11/52, 2/22/54); recordings: "Liebestod" under Walter, *Cavalleria Rusticana* (LP), *Parsifal* broadcast.

Harvuot, Clifford—baritone: b. Norwood, Ohio, Sept. 10, 1912; d. Suffern, Long Island, N.Y., July 22, 1990; studied at Cincinnati Cons. and with Laura May Wright, Dan Beddoe, and Mme. William Neidlinger, and with Anna Schoen-René at Juilliard; opera: Chautauqua, Met (1942–75, int); roles: Schaunard, Zuniga, Sharpless, the Bonze, Grenvil; bibliography: ON (1/5/48); recordings: various Met Club LPs.

Haskins, Virginia—soprano; b. Centralia, Ill., Oct. 17, 1916; studied with Bernard Ferguson, Rosa Raisa; opera: Europe, including Verona, where she sang Gilda in 1938, Chicago Civic, NYCO (1947–57, int.), NBC Opera Theater; roles: Oscar, Zerlina, Susanna; recordings: *Ballo in Maschera* (RCA), *Oklahoma!* (with Nelson Eddy), *Robin Hood, The Chocolate Soldier.*

Hatfield, Lansing—bass; b. Franklin, Va., 1910 (?), d. Asheville, N.C., Aug. 24, 1954; grew up in N.C.; studied at Peabody Cons. and with Frank Bibb; cowinner of 1941 Met Auditions of the Air; opera: St. Louis, Met (1941–44); roles: King (*Aida*); much Broadway and radio; bibliography: *Musician* (6/38), MC (1/1/45), *Etude* (5/46).

Hawkins, Osie—baritone; b. Phenix City, Ala., Aug. 16, 1913; d. Phenix City, Ala., July 13, 1993; studied with Margaret Hecht, Friedrich Schorr; opera: Central City, Cincinnati, Met (1942–63); roles: primarily comprimario and secondary, but also Amfortas, Telramund, Wotan, Kurvenal; on retiring from singing became executive stage director at the Met; bibliography: ON (4/21/58, 1/16/71); recordings: broadcasts.

Hayes, Roland—tenor; b. Curryville, Ga., June 3, 1887; d. Boston, Jan. 1, 1977; studied at Fisk Univ. and with Arthur Hubbard in Boston; recital and concert throughout Europe and America; N.Y. debut recital (1923); documentary film: *The Musical Legacy of Roland Hayes;* bibliography: *Angel Mo' and Her Son, Roland Hayes* (Helm), CBY 1942, MC (12/15/54); recordings: albums (Vanguard LPs), album (Smithsonian).

Hayward, Thomas (Thomas Albert Tibbet)—tenor; b. Kansas City, Kans., Dec. 1, 1920; d. Las Vegas, Feb. 2 (?), 1995; Lawrence Tibbett was his father's cousin; studied with Renato Bellini; cowinner of 1945 Met Auditions of the Air; opera: NYCO (1945), Met (1945–57), Cincinnati; roles: Beppe, Italian Singer (*Rosenkavalier*), Rinuccio; Alfred in *Omnibus Fledermaus* on TV; taught at Southern Methodist Univ; bibliography: ON (11/19/45); recordings: albums (LPs), *Traviata* (VAI), opera broadcasts.

Heidt, Winifred Huntoon—mezzo-soprano; b. Grand Rapids, Mich., between 1899 and 1906; d. Boynton Beach, Fla., 1986; grew up in Detroit; Heidt was her first husband's name; studied with Harriet Ingersoll and Riccardo Dellera; opera: San Carlo (Gallo), Met (1939–40), New Opera, NYCO (1945–50), Cincinnati, San Francisco, Mexico City, Covent Garden, San Carlo (Italy), NBC Opera Theater; roles: Carmen, Amneris, Azucena; married the tenor Eugene Conley, divorced; grandmother of dancer Karen Ziemba; bibliography: ON (1/8/40), *Musician* (6/40), *Etude* (1/53); recording: *Carmen* live from Hollywood Bowl (Eklipse).

Henders, Harriet—soprano; b. Marengo, Iowa, 1904; d. Carmel, N.Y., May 8, 1972; grew up in California; studied at Simpson College in Iowa and with Gutheil-Schoder in Vienna; opera: Graz, Prague, Leipzig, Hamburg, Budapest, Salzburg, Met (1939); roles: Sophie, Arabella, Mimì, Desdemona; taught privately; bibliography: ON (12/25/39), MA (12/25/39).

Henderson, Mary Friedman—soprano; b. Longueuil, Quebec, Dec. 17,

1912; studied at McGill Univ. and with Henri Pontbriand, Pauline Donalda, C. Waldemar Alves, Paul Althouse; opera: New Opera, San Carlo, Cincinnati, Met (1946–47); roles: Mimì, Cio-Cio-San, Marguerite; much radio; taught at Manhattan School and privately; married the conductor Emerson Buckley; recording: aria album (LP)

Hines (Heinz), Jerome—bass; b. Hollywood, Nov. 8, 1921; d. New York, Feb. 4, 2003; studied at Univ. of California and with Gennaro Curci and Samuel Margolis; opera: San Francisco, Cincinnati, Met (1946–87), Munich, Berlin, Glyndebourne, Bayreuth, La Scala, Bolshoi; roles: Don Giovanni, Méphistophélès, Boris Godunov, Basilio, Sarastro, Ramfis; married to the soprano Lucia Evangelista; founded Opera Music Theater International and Opera Link for training young singers; wrote books, including *This Is My Story, This Is My Song, Great Singers on Great Singing, The Four Voices of Man;* video: *Voice of Firestone* (VAI); bibliography: ON (12/2/46, 4/6/68, 11/1/80, 12/21/91), *Time* (3/1/54), MA (11/15/55), CBY 1963, *NATS Bulletin* (1/95); recordings: albums (LPs), opera broadcasts, *Macbeth,* Brahms *Deutsches Requiem.*

Hober, Beal—soprano; b. ?; studied with Franz Proschowski; opera: Met (1944–46); role: Helmwige (*Walküre*); symphonic soloist; bibliography: ON (11/27/44).

Horne, William—tenor; b. New York, Aug. 10, 1913; d. New York, April 19, 1983; studied at Curtis; winner of Naumburg Award (1939); opera: NYCO (1944–48, int.); Cincinnati; roles: Des Grieux (*Manon Lescaut*); created title role in American premiere of *Peter Grimes;* appeared in *This Is the Army* on Broadway (1942); much recital; recording: lieder album (LP).

Howland, Alice—mezzo-soprano; b. Berlin, Germany, May 15, 1914; d. New York, July 8, 1998; returned to U.S. in 1934; studied with Anna Schoen-René at Juilliard; opera: Philadelphia, Montreal, New Opera, NYCO (1944–45); roles: Carmen, Dorabella; created Constance Fletcher in *Mother of Us All* and Bianca in the American premiere of *Rape of Lucretia;* much recital and contemporary music, including first performance of Copland's "Emily Dickinson Songs"; recordings: *Pierrot Lunaire* (first recording by an American), Brahms lieder (LPs).

Huehn, Julius—baritone; b. Revere, Mass., Jan. 12, 1909 (?); d. Rochester, N.Y., June 8, 1971; grew up in Pittsburgh; studied with Anna Schoen-René at Juilliard; opera: Philadelphia Orchestra, Chicago, Chautauqua, Met (1935–46, int.), San Francisco, roles: Escamillo, Friedrich (*Lohengrin*), Kurwenal, Gianni Schicchi; bibliography: *Musical Digest* (6/36), ON (2/1/43); recordings: broadcast operas.

Hunt, Lois Marcus—soprano; b. York, Pa., Nov. 26, 1924; grew up in Philadelphia; the publisher Morton Hunt was her first husband; studied with Marion Freschl, Frantz Proschowski, John Howell, Emile Renan; cowinner of

1949 Met Auditions of the Air: opera: Central City, American Opera (Philadelphia), Met (1949–53); roles: Musetta, Marzellina (*Fidelio*); Monica in the first televised *Medium* (1948); Adele in *Omnibus Fledermaus;* much operetta, radio, television, and concert, often with her companion, the baritone Earl Wrightson; bibliography: *Newsweek* (3/21/49), ON (4/11/49), MC (5/15/49); recordings: show tune albums with Wrightson, *The Faithful Shepherd* (LPs).

Jagel, Frederick—tenor; b. Brooklyn, June 10, 1897; d. San Francisco, July 5, 1982; studied with William Brady in N.Y. and with Corace Cataldi-Tassoni in Milan; sang under the name Federico Jeghelli in Italy; opera: Italy, Netherlands, Met (1927–50), San Francisco, Buenos Aires, Chicago, NYCO (1947–49, int.); roles: Radamès, Turridu, Pollione, Peter Grimes; performed Luka in Janáček's *From the House of the Dead* on television (1969); taught at New England Cons. and in San Francisco; married the Scottish soprano Nancy Weir; bibliography: MA (5/10/30, 6/31), *NY Post* (2/1/36), *Musician* (9/39), ON (2/16/42, 3/8/48), *Etude* (8/47); recordings: broadcast operas, *Wozzeck* (Mitropoulos).

Jarboro, Caterina (Catherine Yarborough)—soprano; b. Wilmington, N.C., July 24, 1903; d. New York, Aug. 13, 1986; grew up in Brooklyn; opera: Puccini Theater in Milan, Vichy, Brussels, Monte Carlo, Salmaggi; roles: Aida, Sélika (*L'Africaine*), Tosca, Gounod's Queen of Sheba; N.Y. debut recital (1942); *Shuffle Along* and *Running Wild* on Broadway; bibliography: *Time* (7/31/33).

Jaynes, Betty (Betty Jane Schultz)—soprano; b. Chicago, 1921; studied with Hermann Devries; opera: Chicago (1936); role: Mimì; some radio and concert; films: secondary roles in *Sweethearts* and *Babes in Arms;* married the baritone Douglas McPhail, who played her sweetheart in these films, divorced; stopped making films in the mid-1940s.

Jenkins, Florence Foster—soprano; b. Wilkes-Barre, Pa., 1868 (?); d. New York, Nov. 26, 1944; grew up in Philadelphia; divorced her husband, Jenkins, in 1902; studied with Carlo Edwards; founded the Verdi Club in 1912; Carnegie Hall recital (1944); bibliography: RC (9/53), ON (3/16/63, 6/01); recording: album (*The Glory??? of the Human Voice*).

Jepson, Helen—soprano; b. Titusville, Pa., Nov. 18, 1904; d. Bradenton, Fla., Sept. 16, 1997; grew up in Akron; studied with Horatio Cornell and Queena Mario at Curtis and Mary Garden in Chicago and New York; opera: Met (1935–44), Chicago, San Francisco; roles: Marguerite, Violetta, Thaïs; much radio, including *Kraft Cheese Show* with Paul Whiteman; film: *Goldwyn Follies* of 1938; after throat ailment caused early retirement, she became a speech therapist; bibliography: *Musician* (4/35), *Time* (11/25/35), MC (3/29/36, 10/15/45), ON (11/9/42, 12/30/57), radio magazines; recordings: some Met broadcasts; album (Parnassus LP), *Porgy and Bess* highlights.

Johnson, Christine—mezzo-soprano; b. Hopkinsville, Ky., 1911; studied with Gaetano de Luca at Nashville Cons.; began as a staff singer for NBC; cowinner of 1942 Met Auditions of the Air; opera: New Opera, San Francisco, Met (1943–44); roles: Erda (*Rheingold*), Lola, Maddalena; created Nettie Fowler in *Carousel;* bibliography: ON (3/15/43) recording: *Carousel.*

Jordan, Irene—mezzo-soprano (became a coloratura and dramatic soprano in the 1950s); b. Birmingham, Ala., April 25, 1919; studied with Ivan Rasmussan, Clytie Mundy, Marti Folgado; radio and theater; opera: Met (1946–57, int.), Chicago, NYCO (1957), NBC Opera Theater; roles: Mallika (*Lakmé*), Lola; later Queen of the Night, Gilda, Leonore (*Fidelio*); much concert, including Weber's *Euryanthe* with the Little Orchestra Society; married the violinist Arnold Caplan; taught at Northwestern Univ., Eastman, Manhattan School, Kennesaw College; bibliography: ON (11/18/46), MA (9/60); recording: album of songs and arias.

Kaskas, Anna—mezzo-soprano; b. Bridgeport, Conn., Jan. 4, 1907; d. Wellsboro, Pa., March 19, 1998; grew up in Hartford; studied at Hartford Cons. and with Enrico Rosati in N.Y. and Ferdinand Ferrara in Milan; first winner of Met Auditions of the Air (1936); opera: Lithuania, Italy, San Carlo (Gallo), Met (1936–46); roles: Lola, Maddalena, Schwertleite (*Walküre*), Third Lady (*Zauberflöte*); taught at Indiana Univ., Eastman; bibliography: *Musician* (4/37), *Etude* (2/44); recordings: opera broadcasts.

Kaye, Selma—b. Brooklyn, 1919 (?); daughter of a Russian-born soprano; Radio City Music Hall; opera: San Carlo (Gallo), New Opera; roles: Leonora (*Trovatore*), Lisa (*Pique Dame*), Santuzza; recording; Verdi Requiem (Urania LP).

Kelston, Lucy—soprano; b. New York, 1922; studied with Giuseppe de Luca, Samuel Margolis; opera: Charles Wagner, Italy; roles: Leonora (*Trovatore* and *Forza del Destino*), Lady Macbeth; married the conductor Franco Ferraris and settled in Italy; recording: *Luisa Miller* (Cetra Fonit LP).

Kent (Caputo), Arthur—baritone; b. New York, 1910; brother of the baritone Alfred Drake; studied with Eric Dudley at Cornell and with Pompilio Malatesta, Clytie Mundy; a winner of 1940 Met Auditions of the Air; opera: Steel Pier, St. Louis Municipal, Met (1940–46, int.); roles: Masetto, Angelotti; bibliography: ON (12/23/40, 12/10/45).

Kirk, Florence—soprano; b. Philadelphia, Dec. 28, 1908; d. Westminster, Md., June 6, 1999; studied at Univ. of Pennsylvania and with Emilio de Gogorza and Elisabeth Schumann at Curtis, and with Paul Althouse; opera: Buenos Aires, Rio de Janeiro, Mexico City, San Francisco, New Opera, Charles Wagner, St. Louis Grand, Met (1944–48); roles: Lady Macbeth, Aida, Donna Anna; married Paul Keppel, the Met's comptroller; sang Leonore (*Fidelio*) in Athens (1949), where the couple lived for a while; bibliography:

ON (12/4/44); recording: Mendelssohn's *Midsummer Night's Dream* with Toscanini (RCA).

Kirsten, Dorothy—soprano; b. Montclair, N.J., July 6, 1910; d. Los Angeles, Nov. 18, 1992; studied with Louis Dornay, Astolfo Pescia (in Italy), and Ludwig Fabri; opera: Chicago, Cincinnati, San Francisco, San Carlo (Gallo), NYCO (1944–46, int.), Met (1945–79, int.), Bolshoi; roles: Marguerite, Louise, Violetta, and most Puccini heroines; created Cressida and Blanche in American premieres of *Troilus and Cressida* and *Dialogues of the Carmelites;* much operetta; films: *Mr. Music, Great Caruso;* much radio, including *Keepsakes, Voice of Firestone,* and *Light Up Time* with Frank Sinatra; bibliography: *A Time To Sing* (autobiography), *The Last Prima Donnas* (Rasponi), *Newsweek* (5/25/42), *Time* (11/27/44), ON (12/17/45, 10/8/60, 3/6/71, 1/3/76, 1/30/93, 7/03); recordings: albums, opera broadcasts, esp. *Madama Butterfly* (VAI).

Knight, Felix—tenor; b. Macon, Ga., Nov. 1, 1908; d. New York, June 18, 1998; grew up in Florida; studied with William Stillman in California and Mehane Beasley in New York; opera: Hollywood Bowl, St. Louis Grand, Chicago, Cincinnati, Central City, Met (1946–50); roles: Almaviva (*Barbiere*), Gérald *(Lakmé)*, Alfredo; N.Y. debut recital (1939), NBC Opera Theater; much radio, including *Magic Key;* films include *Bohemian Girl, Babes in Toyland;* taught privately in NYC; bibliography: *Musical Digest* (2/39), ON (1/6/47), MC (2/1/47); recordings: operettas (LPs).

Kobart (Kohn), Ruth—mezzo-soprano; b. Des Moines, April 24, 1924; d. San Francisco, Dec. 14, 2002; studied at American Cons. (Chicago), Hunter College, and with Suzanne Sten; opera: Lemonade, NYCO (1958–66, int.), NBC Opera Theater; roles: Augusta Tabor (*The Ballad of Baby Doe*), the Witch (*Hansel and Gretel*), Miss Todd (*Old Maid and the Thief); Pipe Dream, How to Succeed in Business without Really Trying* (also the film), *A Funny Thing Happened on the Way to the Forum* on Broadway; N.Y. debut recital (1948); much theater, including Miss Hannigan in national tour of *Annie;* helped found American Conservatory Theater in San Francisco; bibliography: *Playbill* (obit. 12/18/02).

Kullman, Charles—tenor; b. New Haven, Conn., Jan. 13, 1903; d. New Haven, Conn., Feb. 8, 1983; studied at Yale Univ., at Juilliard with Anna Schoen-René, and at American Cons. (Fontainebleau); opera: American Opera (Rosing), Berlin, Salzburg, Vienna, Covent Garden, Met (1935–60, int.), Chicago, San Francisco, Cincinnati; roles: Eisenstein (*Fledermaus*), Don José, Tamino, Ottavio, Pinkerton; much concert, including Verdi Requiem under Toscanini; film: *Goldwyn Follies of 1938, Song of Scheherazade;* taught at Indiana Univ. (1956–71); bibliography: NYT (6/14/35), ON (3/16/42, 12/18/50), RC (12/72); recordings: albums, opera broadcasts, *Das Lied von der Erde.*

Laholm, Eyvind (Edwin Johnson)—tenor; b. Eau Clair, Wis., 1894; d.

New York, July 18, 1958; grew up in Boulder, Colo.; studied with William Brady; opera: Berlin, Munich, Vienna, Rome, Verona, London, Chicago, Met (1939), Mexico City, Cincinnati; roles: Tannhäuser, Tristan, Parsifal, Radamès, Canio; taught privately in N.Y.; bibliography: *Etude* (5/40), RC (3/97); recordings: *Tristan und Isolde,* act 2, with Flagstad (LP).

Lane, Gloria (Gussie Seit)—mezzo-soprano, later some soprano; b. Trenton, N.J., June 6, 1925; studied with Elizabeth Westmoreland at Curtis; won Philadelphia Inquirer's "Voice of Tomorrow" contest; Radio City Music Hall; opera: NYCO (1952–62, int.), Cincinnati, San Francisco, Spain, Australia, Covent Garden, Glyndebourne, Italy, including Rome and La Scala, where she was first American to sing Carmen; roles: Carmen, Amneris, Ariadne, Lady Macbeth; created the Secretary in *The Consul* and Desideria in *The Saint of Bleeker Street* on Broadway; married the conductor Samuel Krachmalnick; eventually settled in Calif., where she teaches; bibliography: *Time* (3/28/60); recordings: *The Consul, The Saint of Bleeker Street, El Amor Brujo,* various live opera performances.

Lanza, Mario (Alfred Arnold Cocozza)—tenor; b. Philadelphia, Jan. 31, 1921; d. Rome, Italy, Oct. 7, 1959, of heart attack; studied with Irene Williams and Enrico Rosati; opera: Nicolai's *Merry Wives of Windsor* at the Berkshire Music Center and Pinkerton in New Orleans; much radio; many films, including *The Great Caruso, Serenade;* video: *Mario Lanza: The American Caruso* (Kultur); bibliography: *Time* (cover story 8/6/51), *Mario Lanza* (Bessette), *Lanza* (Raymond Strait and Terry Robinson), *Be My Love* (Damon Lanza, Bob Dolfi, Mark Muller); recordings: many albums.

Lenchner, Paula—soprano; b. Vienna, Austria, 1920 (?); grew up in the Bronx; studied with Lotte Leonard at Cincinnati Cons.; in 1945 won both Naumburg and National Federation of Music Clubs competitions; opera: Met (1947–53), Bremen, Mainz, Bayreuth; roles: mostly comprimario at Met, but also Marguerite, Micaela; after marriage, sang under the name Paula Lenchner-Schmidt; bibliography: ON (1/5/48); recordings: Frasquita in *Carmen* (RCA), various Bayreuth releases.

Lewis, Brenda—soprano; b. Sunbury, Pa., March 2, 1921; studied with Marion Freschl in Philadelphia; opera: Philadelphia Opera, New Opera, Rio de Janeiro, Montreal, NYCO (1945–67, int.), Cincinnati, San Francisco, Chicago; roles: Salome, Donna Elvira, Marie (*Wozzeck*), Musetta; created Birdie in *Regina* on Broadway (later sang the title role) and Lizzie Borden; musical comedy: *Annie Get Your Gun* in Vienna, *Girl in Pink Tights* on Broadway, *Call Me Madam;* TV: Rosalinde in *Omnibus Fledermaus;* bibliography: ON (3/99); recordings: album (LP), *Lizzie Borden, Regina.*

Lipton, Martha—mezzo-soprano; b. New York, April 6, 1913; studied with her mother, the soprano Estelle Lakin, with Mme. Gutmann-Rice and

Paul Reimers at Juilliard, and with Ettore Verna; winner of National Federation of Music Clubs competition; opera: New Opera, NYCO (1944, 1958, 1961), Met (1944–61), Chicago, Amsterdam, Edinburgh, Rio de Janeiro, Vienna, Paris; roles: Emilia, Maddalena, Annina (*Rosenkavalier*); created Augusta Tabor (*Ballad of Baby Doe*) in Central City; N.Y. debut recital (1941); much oratorio and concert; taught at Indiana Univ.; bibliography: *Musician* (2/40), ON (11/20/44); recordings: *Messiah, Alto Rhapsody,* Copland's "Emily Dickinson Songs."

Lloyd, David (David Lloyd Jenkins)—tenor; b. Minneapolis, Feb. 29, 1920; studied at the Minneapolis College of Music, with Richard Bonelli and Eufemia Gregory at Curtis, and with Joseph Regneas and John Daggett Howell; opera: New England Opera Theater, American Opera (Philadelphia), NYCO (1950–76, int.), Glyndebourne, Athens, NBC Opera Theater; roles: Tamino, David (*Meistersinger*), Alfredo; sang the title role in American premiere of *Albert Herring;* much oratorio and concert; taught at Univ. of Illinois, Urbana, and privately in N.Y.; director of opera at Hunter College, director of Lake George Opera Festival; recordings: *Messiah, St. Matthew Passion, Wozzeck.*

London (Burnstein), George—baritone; b. Montreal, May 30, 1920; d. Armonk, N.Y., March 24, 1985; moved to California in 1935; studied at Los Angeles City College with Richard Lert and Hugo Strelitzer, also with Nathan Stewart, Enrico Rosati, and Paola Novikova; sang for a while under the name George Burnson; Bel Canto Trio; opera: Vienna, Bayreuth, Met (1951–66); roles: Boris Godunov, Eugene Onegin, Don Giovanni, Flying Dutchman; when throat problems ended his singing career, became director of National Opera Institute and Opera Society of Washington, D.C.; video: *Voice of Firestone, Tosca* (VAI); bibliography: *Aria for George* (Nora London), *Time* (1/9/50), CBY 1953, ON (1/19/53, 2/2/63, 4/10/76, 7/85, 11/01), MA (3/53), *Newsweek* (10/31/55), *New Yorker* (profile 10/26/57), OQ (Spring 1993); recordings: many albums and operas.

Lushanya, Mobley—soprano, b. Oklahoma (?), Dec. 4, 1906; d. Dec. 19, 1990; American Indian (Chickasaw); opera: Chicago, San Carlo (Gallo); roles: Leonora (*Trovatore*), Aida, Santuzza; N.Y. debut recital (1940); married the tenor Ramon Vinay.

MacDonald, Jeanette—soprano; b. Philadelphia, June 18, 1903; d. Houston, Jan. 14, 1965; studied with Ferdinand Torriani and Grace Adell Newell; early musicals in N.Y.; opera: Montreal, Chicago, Cincinnati; roles: Juliette, Marguerite; much concert; N.Y. debut recital (1950); 29 films, primarily operetta; bibliography: *Hollywood Diva* (Turk), *Sweethearts* (Sharon Rich), *Etude* (6/38, 11/53), ON (8/95), OQ (Spring 1999), movie magazines; recordings: many albums.

MacWatters, Virginia—soprano; b. Philadelphia, 1918 (?); studied with Zeckwer-Hahn at Philadelphia Music Academy, at Curtis, and with Greta Stauber; opera: New Opera, Philadelphia La Scala, San Francisco, Covent Garden, NYCO (1946–51), Met (1951–59, int., esp. *Fledermaus* on tour); roles: Adele, Susanna, Zerbinetta; taught at Indiana Univ.; bibliography: ON (1/18/54).

Madeira, Jean Browning—mezzo-soprano; b. Centralia, Ill., Nov. 14, 1918; d. Providence, R.I., July 10, 1972; serious pianist as a child; studied with Florence Page Kimball at Juilliard, Mrs. William Neidlinger, and Frau Köhler in Vienna; opera: Chautauqua, San Carlo (Gallo), Met (1948–71), Cincinnati, Vienna, Munich, Salzburg, Bayreuth, Covent Garden; roles: Carmen, Erda, Maddalena, Azucena, Ulrica, Klytämnestra; married the conductor Francis Madeira; sang American premiere of de Falla's *Atlántida* opening week of Avery Fisher Hall (1962); early death from cancer; bibliography: ON (11/29/48, 3/25/61), MA (12/1/59), CBY 1963; recordings: many broadcasts, *Carmen* (Vox LP), *Elektra* (DGG).

Malbin, Elaine—soprano; b. New York, May 24, 1930; grew up in Brooklyn; studied with William Herman; N.Y. recital debut (1945); opera: NYCO (1950–53, int.), San Francisco, Glyndebourne, Central City, NBC Opera Theater; roles: Violetta, Mimì, Manon, Salome; musicals: *My Darlin' Aida* and *Kismet;* much radio and TV; video: *Voice of Firestone: Verdi Festival* (VAI); bibliography: CBY 1959; recordings: many operettas (RCA LPs), duets with Mario Lanza, Busoni's *Arlecchino* (HMV).

Manners, Lucille—soprano; b. Newark, ?; studied with Louis Dornay, Betsy Culp; opera: NYCO (1945–49), New Orleans, St. Louis; roles: Mimì, Nedda, Marguerite; much radio; bibliography: *Etude* (3/38), MC (10/1/45), radio magazines.

Mario, Queena (Queena Marion Tillotson)—soprano; b. Akron, Ohio, Aug. 21, 1896; d. New York, May 28, 1951; grew up in N.J.; studied with Oscar Saenger, Marcella Sembrich; opera: San Carlo (Gallo), Scotti Grand Opera, Met (1922–38), Chicago, San Francisco, where she sang Mimì in its inaugural performance (1923) and the Child in the American premiere of Ravel's *L'Enfant et les Sortilèges* (1930); roles: Sophie, Gretel, Nedda, Micaela; wrote mystery novels under the name Tillotson and newspaper columns, which she signed Florence Bryan; married the conductor Wilfrid Pelletier (1925), divorced (1936); taught at Curtis and Juilliard; bibliography: MA (7/14/28), *Musical Digest* (1/38), *Musician* (1/42); recording: *American Singer,* vol. 2 (IRCC)

Marlowe, Anthony (Albert Mahler)—tenor; b. Philadelphia, Feb. 5, 1910 (?); d. Detroit, June 29, 1962; studied at Curtis; opera: Philadelphia Grand, Chicago, San Francisco, Met (1939–49, int.), Covent Garden; roles:

comprimario at Met, leading roles at Covent Garden (where he created Red Whiskers in world premiere of *Billy Budd*), Cavaradossi, the Duke (*Rigoletto*); bibliography: MC (11/1/52); recordings: opera broadcasts.

Matthews, Inez—mezzo-soprano; b. Ossining, N.Y., Aug. 23, 1917; sister of the baritone Edward Matthews (1904–54), who created the role of St. Ignatius in *Four Saints in Three Acts;* studied with Katherine Moran Douglas, Paula Novikova, Frederick Wilkerson; sang in original Broadway productions of *Carmen Jones* and *Lost in the Stars;* N.Y. recital debut (1947); recitals abroad; bibliography: MC (8/54), *NATS Bulletin* (May/June 1997); recordings: albums of spirituals and lieder (LPs), *Four Saints in Three Acts, Lost in the Stars, Porgy and Bess.*

Maynor (Mainor), Dorothy—soprano; b. Norfolk, Va., Sept. 3, 1910; d. West Chester, Pa., Feb. 19, 1996; studied at Hampton Institute with Nathaniel Dett, at Westminster Choir School, and with Wilfried Klamroth and John Alan Haughton in N.Y.; much concert and recital throughout U.S., Latin America, and Europe; N.Y. debut recital (1939); in 1952 became first black since the Anderson debacle to sing a commercial performance at Constitution Hall; founded Harlem School of the Arts (1963); bibliography: NYT (8/13/39, obit. 2/24/96), *Newsweek* (8/21/39), *Time* (8/21/39, 11/27/39, 11/4/40), *New Yorker* (11/18/39), CBY 1940, *Collier's* (3/2/40), MA (5/56), ON (2/27/93); recordings: albums (Library of Congress and RCA).

McFerrin, Robert—baritone: b. Marianna, Ark., March 19, 1921; grew up in St. Louis; studied at Fisk Univ. and with George Graham at the Chicago College of Music; winner of 1953 Met Auditions of the Air; opera: NYCO (1949), New England Opera; San Carlo (Naples), National (Washington, D.C.), Met (1955–57); appeared on Broadway in *Lost in the Stars* and a revival of *Green Pastures;* roles: Amonasro, Rigoletto; much concert in Europe, South America and U.S.; N.Y. Town Hall debut recital (1955); sings Porgy (for Sidney Poitier) in film of *Porgy and Bess;* taught at Nelson School of Fine Arts in British Columbia and at Roosevelt Univ.; father of the jazz vocalist and composer Bobby McFerrin; bibliography: ON (2/20/56); recordings: *Rigoletto* (Met Club LP), spirituals (Riverside LP).

McKnight, Anne—soprano; b. Aurora, Ill., 1926; sang throughout Italy under the name Anna de Cavalieri; opera: San Carlo (Naples), La Scala, Rome, Verona, Brussels, Toulouse, NYCO (1952–60, int.); roles: Aida, Tosca, Turandot, Fedora, Musetta; recordings: *La Bohème* under Toscanini, live broadcasts, including *Gli Ugonotti* and *Mefistofele.*

Meisle, Kathryn—mezzo-soprano; b. Philadelphia, Oct. 12, 1895 (1899?); d. New York, Jan. 17, 1970; studied at Philadelphia Cons. and with Ada Turner Kurtz and William Brady; winner of 1915 National Federation of

Women's Clubs competition; opera: San Francisco, Chicago, Met (1935–38); roles: Amneris, Azucena, Brangäne; N.Y. debut recital (1934); much oratorio and concert; married to the concert manager Calvin Franklin; bibliography: *Musical Digest* (7/37), ON (2/6/39), *Musician* (11/39).

Melton, James—tenor; b. Moultrie, Ga., Jan. 2, 1904; d. New York, April 21, 1961, of pneumonia; grew up in Florida; attended Univ. of Florida and Univ. of Georgia, studied with Gaetano de Luca at the Ward-Belmont Cons. in Nashville, Enrico Rosati in N.Y., Michael Raucheisen in Berlin; much radio, including *The Jack Benny Show* and *Harvest of Stars;* a member of the Revelers Quartet; N.Y. recital debut (1932); tour with Gershwin; opera: Cincinnati, San Carlo (Gallo), Chicago, Met (1942–50); roles: Pinkerton, Wilhelm Meister, Tamino, Alfredo; films include *Stars over Broadway;* bibliography: ON (12/7/42, 9/30/61), CBY 1945, MC (2/1/45), MA (2/51, 4/15/53); recordings: albums, *Die Fledermaus* and *Madama Butterfly* highlights (LPs).

Merrill, Robert (Moishe Miller)—baritone; b. Brooklyn, June 4, 1917; studied with Samuel Margolis; first sang as Morris Miller; much early radio; cowinner of 1945 Met Auditions of the Air; opera: Met (1945–76, int.), San Francisco, Cincinnati, Chicago, Covent Garden, Italy; roles: Germont, Rigoletto, Di Luna, Figaro, Escamillo; films: *Aaron Slick from Punkin Crick;* much TV; Broadway: *Fiddler on the Roof;* briefly married to the soprano Roberta Peters; married Marion Machno, a pianist; wrote a novel called *The Divas* (1978); video: *Voice of Firestone* (VAI); bibliography: *Once More from the Beginning* (Merrill), *Between the Acts* (Merrill), ON (1/10/45, 2/26/66, 1/9/71), MA (11/15/45), MC (8/46), *Etude* (6/47, 1/55), CBY 1952, NYT (8/17/75); recordings: many albums and operas.

Merriman, Nan (Katherine Ann)—mezzo-soprano; b. Pittsburgh, April 28, 1920; moved to Los Angeles in 1936; studied with Alexia Bassian; winner of Cincinnati Opera Contest (1942), Federation of Music Clubs competition (1943); opera: Cincinnati, Glyndebourne, Aix-en-Provence, San Francisco, Vienna, Piccola Scala; roles: Dorabella, Baba the Turk; much concert, esp. under Toscanini; bibliography: *Etude* (10/45), MC (5/15/46), MA (1/1/59); recordings: album of French and Spanish songs, Verdi Requiem under Ormandy, *Così Fan Tutte*, Toscanini broadcasts.

Monroe, Lucy—soprano; b. New York, 1906; d. 1987; a direct descendant of President James Monroe; daughter of the actress Anna Laughlin; studied with Estelle Liebling, Queena Mario; early revues and musicals; opera: Chicago (Salmaggi), St. Louis Grand, Met Spring Season (1937), Cincinnati; roles: Marguerite, Musetta, Juliette; much radio; known for her singing of "The Star-Spangled Banner"; became head of patriotic music at RCA Victor; bibliography: *Newsweek* (8/18/41, 9/28/42), CBY 1942; recording: compilation *America the Beautiful* (Romophone).

Moore, Grace (Mary Willie Grace)—soprano; b. Nough, Tenn., Dec. 5, 1898; d. airplane crash near Copenhagen, Jan. 26, 1947; studied with P. Mario Marafioti in N.Y., and Richard Bathelémy in France; early revues and musicals; opera: Met (1928–46, int.), Covent Garden, Paris Opéra-Comique, Chicago, San Francisco, Cincinnati; roles: Mimì, Tosca, Louise, Manon; films: *One Night of Love, Love Me Forever,* and *Louise;* much radio; married the Spanish movie actor Valentine Parera; bibliography: *You're Only Human Once* (Moore), ON (3/31/41, 3/18/57, 12/20/69, 9/98), *Newsweek* (4/28/41, 3/6/44, 3/3/47), CBY 1944, *Time* (3/13/44), MC (3/15/47), *Theater Arts* (1/57); recordings: many albums and opera broadcasts.

Morris, Suzy (Estelle Frelinghuysen)—soprano; b. Newark, May 7, 1911; d. Pittsfield, Mass., March 19, 1988; studied with Sidney Dietch; opera: NYCO (1947–50), New Orleans; roles: Ariadne, Tosca, Amneris, Amelia (*Ballo in Maschera*); married the abstract painter George L. K. Morris; retired from singing to paint under the name Suzy Frelinghuysen; recording: *Ballo in Maschera* from New Orleans (VAI).

Munsel (Munsil), Patrice—soprano; b. Spokane, May 14, 1925; studied with William Herman; cowinner of 1943 Met Auditions of the Air; opera: Met (1943–58), San Francisco; roles: Philine, Lucia, Rosina, Adele, Despina; European tours; film: *Melba;* much radio, TV, operetta, musicals, and other theater; video: *Voice of Firestone* (VAI); bibliography: *Time* (11/22/43, cover story 12/3/51), ON (12/20/43, 1/1/45), CBY 1945, NYT (1/14/51), MA (11/15/53); recordings: album of Strauss waltzes (LP), *Fledermaus* and *Lucia di Lammermoor* highlights (LPs), opera broadcasts, compilations.

Nadworney, Devora—mezzo-soprano; b. New York, 1902 (?); d. New York, Jan. 7, 1948; attended Hunter College; won National Federation of Music Clubs competition; opera: Chicago, San Carlo (Gallo), National (Washington, D.C.), Art of Musical Russia, Steel Pier; roles: Dalila, Azucena; much radio, including *The Voice of Gold,* a daily program in which she was featured; bibliography: *Musician* (9/34).

Neway, Patricia—soprano; b. Brooklyn, Sept. 30, 1919; grew up in Staten Island; studied at Mannes and with the tenor Morris Gesell, whom she married; opera: Chautauqua, NYCO (1951–66, int.), Paris Opéra-Comique, Aix-en-Provence; roles: Fiordiligi, Tosca, Female Chorus (*Rape of Lucretia*); created Magda (*The Consul*) and the Mother Abbess (*The Sound of Music*) on Broadway, the Mother (*Maria Golovin*) at the Brussel's World's Fair, and Leah in Tamkin's *The Dybbuk* at NYCO; opened her own opera workshop in 1956; video: *The Consul* (VAI); bibliography: NYT (5/22/50); recordings: *The Consul,* Pergolesi's *Salve Regina, Iphigénie en Tauride,* and album of James Joyce texts (LPs), also Barber's *Hand of Bridge* (Vanguard), Carlisle Floyd's *The Sojourner* and *Mollie Sinclair* (VAI).

Olheim (Oelheim), Helen—mezzo-soprano; b. Buffalo, N.Y., 1905 (?); d. Sarasota, Fla., June 29, 1992; studied at Eastman; opera: American Opera (Rosing), Met (1935–44); roles: Mercedes, Siebel, Maddalena; taught at Mt. Holyoke; bibliography: ON (2/20/39).

Pagliughi, Lina—soprano; b. Brooklyn, May 27, 1907; d. near Cesena, Italy, Oct. 1, 1980; grew up in San Francisco; lived in Italy from age 15; protégée of Luisa Tetrazzini; studied with Manlio Bavagnoli in Milan; opera: La Scala, San Carlo (Naples), Rome, Monte Carlo, Covent Garden; roles: Gilda, Lucia, Queen of the Night, Elvira (*Puritani*); N.Y. debut recital (1940); taught privately; married the Italian tenor Primo Montanari; bibliography: *Gramophone* (7/43), ON (1/19/80); recordings: album (Preiser), many compilations and operas.

Palmer, Jeanne—soprano; b. New York, 1914; studied with Maude Douglas Tweedy; opera: Art of Musical Russia, Met (1944–51); roles: primarily small at the Met, but also Isolde, Brünnhilde (*Walküre*); married to the Russian painter Sergei Soudeikine; bibliography: ON (11/27/44); recording: album (Coliseum LP).

Pease, James—bass-baritone; b. Franklin, Ind., Jan. 9, 1916; d. New York, April 26, 1967, of a heart attack; degree in law from Indiana Univ.; studied voice at Academy of Vocal Arts (Philadelphia); Balstrode in American premiere of *Peter Grimes;* runner-up in 1943 Met Auditions of the Air, Pease returned contract to enlist as a pilot; opera: Philadelphia Opera (Levin), NYCO (1946–67, int.), Hamburg, Zurich, Covent Garden, Paris, Glyndebourne, San Francisco, Chicago, Cincinnati, NBC Opera Theater; roles: Don Giovanni, Hans Sachs, Méphistophélès, Wozzeck; much concert; married to the British soprano Adele Leigh, divorced; bibliography: ON (3/15/43), NYT (obit. 4/28/67); recordings: Brahms *Deutsches Requiem* (RCA), *Peter Grimes* (Decca).

Peerce, Jan (Jacob Pincus Perelmuth)—tenor; b. New York, June 3, 1904; d. New York, Dec. 15, 1984; studied with Richard Boghetti; Radio City Music Hall; much early radio; opera: Philadelphia, San Francisco, Cincinnati, Met (1941–68, int.); roles: Alfredo, Edgardo, Rodolfo, Ottavio, Riccardo; N.Y. debut recital (1939); many appearances with Toscanini; Bach Aria Group; musicals: *Fiddler on the Roof;* film: *Of Men and Music, Tonight We Sing, Goodbye, Columbus;* video: *If I Were a Rich Man* (Proscenium), *Voice of Firestone* (VAI); bibliography: *Bluebird of Happiness* (autobiography), *Newsweek* (9/8/41, 9/6/48), ON (11/24/41, 1/29/66, 4/13/85, 2/29/92), *Etude* (4/44), MA (12/1/53), *High Fidelity* (11/56); recordings: many albums and operas, Toscanini broadcasts.

Peters (Petermann), Roberta—soprano; b. the Bronx, May 4, 1930; studied with William Herman; children's radio shows; opera: Met (1950–85, int.), Cincinnati, Chicago, Covent Garden, Salzburg, Vienna, Munich, Berlin, Russia; roles: Queen of the Night, Rosina, Gilda, Oscar, Zerlina; concert tour through Soviet Union; film: *Tonight We Sing;* TV: 65 appearances on *The Ed Sullivan Show;* much concertizing; briefly married to Robert Merrill; video: *Voice of Firestone* (VAI); bibliography: *Debut at the Met* (autobiography), CBY 1954, *Time* (2/8/54), MA (1/15/55), ON (3/23/59, 1/9/65, 12/6/75, 11/85), NYT (11/17/75, 11/16/00); recordings: many albums and operas.

Piazza (Luft), Marguerite—soprano; b. New Orleans, May 6, 1926; Piazza was her mother's maiden name; studied at Loyola Univ. with Ferdinand Dunkley and at Louisiana State Univ. with Pasquale Amato; winner of National Federation of Music Clubs competition; opera: NYCO (1944–49, int.), Met (1951), Cincinnati; roles: Rosalinde (*Fledermaus*), Nedda, Mimì; much television, esp. *Your Show of Shows;* nightclubs; bibliography: ON (1/15/51), MA (11/15/52); recordings: albums (LPs).

Ponselle (Ponzillo), Rosa Melba—soprano; b. Meriden, Conn., Jan. 22, 1897; d. Baltimore, May 25, 1981; vaudeville act with her sister, the mezzo-soprano Carmela; studied briefly with William Thorner; coached with Romano Romani; opera: Met (1918–37); Covent Garden, Maggio Musicale Fiorentino; roles: Violetta, Leonora (*Forza del Destino* and *Trovatore*), Gioconda, Carmen; radio and concert; settled in Baltimore area, where she did some teaching and helped found Baltimore Opera; bibliography: *Ponselle* (Ponselle and Drake), *Rosa Ponselle* (Drake), *Rosa Ponselle* (Phillips-Matz), ON (11/24/52, 3/12/77, 1/11/97), *NATS Bulletin* (Nov./Dec. 1984); recordings: many albums and compilations, broadcasts of *Traviata* and *Carmen.*

Powers, Marie—mezzo-soprano; b. Mount Carmel, Pa., 1900 (?); d. New York, Dec. 28, 1973; studied at Cornell Univ., with Giannina Russ in Florence, and with Schumann-Heink; sang in Europe, often under her husband's name of Crescentini; opera: Chicago (Salmaggi), La Scala, Paris, Rome, San Carlo (Gallo), NYCO (1948–49); roles: Orfeo, Dalila, Amneris, Azucena; created Madame Flora (*The Medium*) and the Mother (*The Consul*) on Broadway; some legitimate theater; film: *The Medium;* bibliography: *Time* (6/30/47), CBY 1951, ON (2/26/72), NYT (1/13/74); recordings: *The Consul* (LP), *The Medium.*

Price, Leontyne (Mary Violet)—soprano; b. Laurel, Miss., Feb. 10, 1927; studied with Catherine van Buren at Wilberforce College and Florence Kimball at Juilliard; opera: Chicago, Met (1963–85, int.), San Francisco, Vienna, Covent Garden, La Scala, NBC Opera Theater; roles: Aida, Leonora (*Trovatore* and *Forza del Destino*), Tosca, Pamina, Bess; created the role of Cleopatra in Barber's *Anthony and Cleopatra* to open the new Met in 1966; much concert and recital; N.Y. debut recital (1954); married to the baritone William Warfield, divorced; bibliography: *Time* (1/31/55, cover story 3/10/61), MC (12/

1/56), ON (2/4/61, 2/12/72, 3/6/76, 1/23/82, 7/85, 8/85, 10/96), MA (1/62); recordings: many albums and operas.

Quartararo, Florence (Fiorenza)—soprano; b. San Francisco, May 31, 1922; d. San Francisco, June 6, 1994; also sang as Florence Alba; graduated from San Francisco State College; studied voice with Elizabeth Wells in San Francisco and Pietro Cimini in Los Angeles; radio: *Kraft Music Hall* with Bing Crosby; Hollywood Bowl (1945); opera: Met (1946–49), Central City, San Francisco, Philadelphia, Cincinnati, Rome, Naples; roles: Countess Almaviva, Donna Elvira, Desdemona, Nedda, Violetta; married for a time to the bass Italo Tajo; bibliography: *Time* (1/28/46), ON (3/11/46); recordings: *Tosca* duet with Vinay (RCA LP); compilations.

Rahn, Muriel—soprano; b. Boston, 1911; d. New York, Aug. 8, 1961, of cancer; grew up in Alabama, where her parents were teachers at Tuskegee Institute; graduated from Univ. of Nebraska, studied at Columbia Univ. and with Gerhard Pechner; opera: Salmaggi, San Carlo (Gallo) Yugoslavia, Cairo, Genoa; roles: Aida, Salome; portrayed Carmen Jones and Cora in *The Barrier* on Broadway; Rahn and William Warfield were the first black concert artists to appear on television (*Ed Sullivan Show*, 1951); stage director for *Bells Are Ringing* in Frankfurt, Germany; bibliography: MC (2/15/43, 5/15/45), *Variety* (1/13/60).

Rasely, George—tenor; b. St. Louis, 1891; d. Lawrence, Kans., Jan. 4, 1965; church soloist; musicals and operetta; much radio; opera: Met (1936–44); roles: comprimario; bibliography: *Musician* (9/37), MA (8/54).

Raymondi (Ventimiglia), Lillian—soprano; b. Scranton, Pa., 1922 (1923?); studied with Frances Alda; opera: Met (1942–51); roles: Papagena, Micaela, Dew Fairy; bibliography: ON (11/23/42).

Rayner, Sidney—tenor; b. New Orleans, Dec. 12, 1895; d. New York, Sept. 14, 1981; studied in Milan; opera: Rome, Berlin, Paris Opéra-Comique (1930–35), Chicago, Met (1936–38), Salmaggi, San Carlo (Gallo); roles: Des Grieux (*Manon* and *Manon Lescaut*), Don José, Turridu; taught in N.Y.; bibliography: MA (12/10/30), MC (2/1/36), NYT (6/12/36), *Musician* (5/37); recordings: album (Rubini LP), broadcast *Cavalleria* (Walhall).

Rea, Virginia—soprano; b. Louisville, Ky., 1895; d. 1941; studied at Drake University, with Holmes Cowper, in France and with Sergei Klibansky and Blanche Marchesi; sometimes sang under the name Le Rae; opera: Hinshaw, Salmaggi; role: Gilda; much radio, esp. *The Palmolive Hour* (under the pseudonym Olive Palmer) and *American Album of Familiar Music;* N.Y. debut recital (1923); many believe her death was a suicide; bibliography: *Musician* (11/37), RC (11/87); recordings: many 78s.

Renan, Emile—bass-baritone; b. Brooklyn, June 18, 1913; d. Englewood, N.J., Dec. 8, 2001; studied with Eleanor McLellan and John Daggett Howell;

opera: Chicago, Philadelphia, NYCO (1944–59); debut as the Sacristan in NYCO's inaugural *Tosca* and thereafter sang 32 character roles with the company; later a stage director and voice teacher; bibliography: NYT (obit. 1/7/02); recording: compilation *America the Beautiful* (Romophone).

Resnik, Regina—soprano until the mid-1950s, then a mezzo-soprano; b. the Bronx, Aug. 30, 1922; studied at Hunter College, and privately with Rosalie Miller; winner of 1944 Met Auditions of the Air; opera: New Opera, NYCO (1944–58, int.), Mexico City, Met (1944–83, int.), San Francisco, Chicago, Cincinnati, Covent Garden, Bayreuth, Vienna; roles: Leonora (*Trovatore*), Santuzza, Rosalinde, Donna Elvira, Carmen, Klytämnestra; created the Baroness (*Vanessa*); N.Y. debut recital (1948); appeared in musicals, *A Little Night Music* and *Cabaret;* became teacher, stage director, producer; married the artist Arbit Blatas, who designed some sets for her productions; bibliography: MC (5/5/44), *Time* (8/25/47), *Etude* (5/48), CBY 1956, MA (5/58, 4/64), ON (1/23/60, 4/17/71, 12/8/84, 12/10/94), NYT (8/23/90), OQ (Spring 1993); recordings: many albums and operas.

Ribla (Ribler), Gertrude—soprano; b. Brooklyn, Sept. 11, 1918; d. Bloomington, Ind., March 20, 1980; studied with Frances Alda, Karl Kritz, Renato Bellini; opera: Salmaggi, San Carlo (Gallo), NYCO (1947–59, int.) Cincinnati, Met (1949–50), Germany, Italy, Cuba; roles: Leonora (*Trovatore*), Aida, Santuzza, Turandot; taught at Indiana Univ.; bibliography: *Newsweek* (8/2/43), NYT (obit. 3/24/80); recordings: Toscanini all-Verdi broadcast (RCA), *Wozzeck* selections (Columbia LP), *Lord Byron's Love Letter* (RCA LP).

Robeson, Paul—bass-baritone; b. Princeton, N.J., May 9, 1898; d. Philadelphia, Jan. 23, 1976; graduated from Rutgers and from Columbia with a law degree; some vocal study with Frantz Proschowskya, Teresa Armitage, Jerry Swinford; much concert; N.Y. debut recital (1925); *Show Boat* on Broadway (1927); legitimate theater includes *Emperor Jones, Othello;* films include *Show Boat* (1936); bibliography: *Here I Stand* (autobiography), *Paul Robeson: Artist and Citizen* (Jeffrey C. Stewart), *Paul Robeson* (Duberman), NYT (obit. 1/24/76, 3/29/98); recordings: many albums, *Show Boat, Ballad for Americans.*

Roggero, Margaret—mezzo-soprano: b. the Bronx, 1921 (?); studied with Belle Julie Soudant and Sergius Kagen at Juilliard; opera: Charles Wagner, Met (1950–63); roles: Mercedes, Suzuki, Siebel, Lola; Secretary (*The Consul*) on Broadway; bibliography: ON (11/13/50).

Ross, Lanny—tenor; b. Seattle, Jan. 19, 1906; d. 1988; graduated from Yale, studied law at Columbia, and voice with Anna Schoen-René at Juilliard; primarily radio, including *Maxwell House Showboat* and *Your Hit Parade;* N.Y. debut recital (1936); film: *Gulliver's Travels;* bibliography: *The Mighty Music Box* (De Long), radio magazines.

Rounseville, Robert—tenor; b. Attleboro, Mass., March 25, 1914; d. New

York, Aug. 6, 1974; great-nephew of Lillian Nordica; studied medicine at Tufts Univ. and voice with William Herman; sang as a baritone under the name Robert Fields in vaudeville, operetta, and night clubs, where he introduced the song "Praise the Lord and Pass the Ammunition"; opera: NYCO (1948–66, int.), NBC Opera Theater; roles: Hoffmann, Don José, Prince in *Love for Three Oranges;* created Tom Rakewell in *The Rake's Progress,* Channon in Tamkin's *Dybbuk,* and Bernstein's Candide; played Don José in first grand opera telecast from a studio, *Carmen* (1950); some legitimate theater; films: *Tales of Hoffmann, Carousel;* bibliography: *Time* (4/18/49), NYT (obit. 8/8/74); recordings: *Tales of Hoffmann, The Rake's Progress, Candide,* and various operettas.

Sachs, Evelyn—mezzo-soprano; b. Brooklyn, Aug. 10, 1924; studied at Cornell and Juilliard, and privately with Emma Zador and Ernesto Barbini; opera: Chicago, Montreal, Met (1947–48), later in Italy; roles: Meg, La Cieca, Suzuki; video: *The Consul* (VAI); bibliography: ON (1/5/48); recording: *Falstaff* from New Orleans (VAI).

Sarnoff, Dorothy—soprano (later mezzo); b. New York, May 25, 1917; studied voice in Paris with Mme. Renée Gilly and with Queena Mario, and with Florence Easton and Ettore Verna in N.Y.; created Miss Pinkerton in *Old Maid and the Thief* on NBC radio; opera: Philadelphia Opera, New Opera, NYCO (1945–47), New Orleans; roles: Rosalinde, Tosca, Mimì; created Amneris in *My Darlin' Aida* and Lady Thiang in *The King and I* on Broadway; recordings: *Old Maid and the Thief, The King and I.*

Schon, Kenneth—baritone; b. Esdale, Wis., 1910 (?); d. Lake Worth, Fla., Jan. 24, 1986; grew up in Minneapolis; studied with Gertrude Hull, Forrest Lamont, Luigi Giuffrida, later Estelle Liebling and Richard Lert; opera: Met (1945–52, int.), San Francisco, NYCO (1950); roles: Don Pizarro, Frank (*Fledermaus*), Monterone; bibliography: ON (3/12/45); recording: broadcast of *Fidelio.*

Sills, Beverly (Belle Silverman)—soprano; b. Brooklyn, May 25, 1929; studied with Estelle Liebling; coached with Roland Gagnon; won *Major Bowes Amateur Hour;* much early radio; opera debut as Frasquita in Philadelphia (1946); Charles Wagner, San Francisco, NYCO (1955–79, int.), Met (1966–79, int.), La Scala, Vienna, Covent Garden; roles: Baby Doe, Lucia, Violetta, Manon, Cleopatra (*Giulio Cesare*), Donizetti's Tudor queens; much TV, including *The Carol Burnett Show;* director of NYCO and executive positions at the Met and Lincoln Center for Performing Arts; bibliography: *Beverly* (autobiography), CBY 1969, 1982, ON (9/19/70, 10/80), *Time* (11/22/71), NYT (4/6/75, 9/23/79), *NATS Bulletin* (March/April 1982); recordings: many albums and operas.

Smith, Muriel—mezzo-soprano; b. New York, Feb. 23, 1923; d. Richmond, Va., Sept. 13, 1985; studied with Elisabeth Schumann at Curtis; created role of Carmen Jones on Broadway (1943); Carmen with Salmaggi (1948); went to London in 1950 for *Carmen Jones* and musicals, including *The King and I* (Lady Thiang) and *South Pacific* (Bloody Mary); Bizet's Carmen at Covent Garden (1956); appeared as Aicha in the film *Moulin Rouge;* joined Moral Rearmament, a fringe Fundamentalist sect, in 1957 and toured with them in *The Crowning Experience;* concert tour of Brazil; legitimate theater; recordings: Christmas album (LP), *Carmen Jones, The King and I.*

Somigli, Franca (Marion Bruce Clark)—soprano; b. Chicago, March 17, 1901 (1908?); d. Trieste, Italy, May 14, 1974; studied with Mario Malatesta, Antonio Votto, and Rosina Storchio in Italy; debut at Rovigo (1926) at which time she took the Italian name; opera: Salzburg, Chicago, Met (1937), La Scala (1933–44), Rome, Buenos Aires; roles: Cio-Cio-San, Mimì, Salome, Fedora; created Contarina in Pizzetti's *Orsèolo;* married Giuseppe Antonicelli, the conductor and director of the Teatro Verdi in Trieste; bibliography: ON (3/8/37); recording: Salzburg *Falstaff* under Toscanini.

Souez, Ina Rains—soprano; b. Windsor, Colo., June 3, 1903; d. Dec. 8 (9?), 1992, Santa Monica, Calif.; studied with Florence Lamont Hinman and Sofia del Campo in Milan; debut as Mimì at Ivrea (1928); opera: Palermo, Stockholm, Covent Garden, Glyndebourne, New Opera; roles: Liù, Micaela, Fiordiligi, Donna Anna; also the *Trovatore* Leonora for the BBC, and a tour of the Verdi Requiem in Scandinavia; returned to U.S. in 1939; served in WACS during the war; was the "prima donna absurda" with Spike Jones and his City Slickers; taught in California; bibliography: *Opera* (9/84, 2/93); recordings: album (LP), *Don Giovanni, Così Fan Tutte.*

Speaks, Margaret—soprano; b. Columbus, Ohio, 1906 (?); d. 1977; attended Ohio State Univ., studied with Helen Chase; much early radio, including *Voice of Firestone;* recital and concert in U.S. and Europe; taught at Ohio State Univ.; niece of the composer Oley Speaks; bibliography: radio magazines.

Steber, Eleanor—soprano; b. Wheeling, W.Va., July 17, 1914; d. Langhorne, Pa., Oct. 3, 1990; studied with William Whitney at New England Cons. and Paul Althouse in N.Y.; cowinner 1940 Met Auditions of the Air; opera: Met (1940–66, int.), Cincinnati, Chicago, San Francisco, Bayreuth, Vienna, Florence; roles: Countess Almaviva, Fiordiligi, Konstanze, Violetta; first Arabella (*Arabella*) and Marie (*Wozzeck*) at the Met; created Barber's Vanessa and introduced his "Knoxville, Summer of 1915"; much radio and television; video: *Voice of Firestone;* bibliography: *Eleanor Steber* (autobiography), *He Loves Me When I Sing* (Buffington), ON (12/23/40, 3/43, 12/15/80, 10/90, 12/8/90), CBY 1943, *Newsweek* (8/28/44), *Etude* (7/46), MA (12/1/52), MC (2/56), *NATS Bulletin* (May/June 1984); recordings: many albums and operas.

Stellman, Maxine—soprano; b. Brattleboro, Vt., May 13, 1906; d. June 25, 1972; studied with Marcella Sembrich at Juilliard; cowinner of 1937 Metropolitan Auditions of the Air; opera: Met (1936–50); roles: small, but in 1942 completed a performance of *Lohengrin* in Boston for Varnay, who became ill; taught privately.

Stevens (Steenberg), Risë—mezzo-soprano; b. the Bronx, June 11, 1913; studied with Anna Schoen-René at Juilliard; much early radio, including children's shows; opera: Prague, Buenos Aires, La Scala, Glyndebourne, Met (1938–61), San Francisco, Cincinnati; roles: Carmen, Mignon, Octavian, Orfeo, Cherubino; films: *The Chocolate Soldier, Going My Way;* video: *Voice of Firestone;* married the Hungarian actor Walter Surovy (1939); since retiring in 1965 has held many executive positions in music, including director of the Metropolitan Opera National Council auditions and president of Mannes College; bibliography: *Subway to the Met* (Crichton), ON (11/28/38, 12/8/41, 11/24/58, 3/7/64, 3/14/87, 12/24/88), CBY 1941, *Etude* (5/47), *Newsweek* (cover story 2/11/52), MA (2/15/55, 10/64), MC (6/55), NYT (2/9/64, 3/25/77); recordings: many albums and operas.

Stich-Randall (Stich), Teresa—soprano; b. West Hartford, Conn., Dec. 24, 1927; attended Hartford School of Music and Columbia Univ., where she created roles in *Evangeline* and *The Mother of Us All;* sang the Priestess (*Aida*) and Nannetta (*Falstaff*) under Toscanini; in 1951 went to Europe on a Fulbright and won Concours International in Lausanne, Switzerland; opera: Florence, Salzburg, Vienna, Chicago, Met (1961–66, int.), Aix-en-Provence; roles: Fiordiligi, Ariadne, Violetta, Gilda, Norma; bibliography: ON (4/14/62, 6/63), *High Fidelity* (4/62); recordings: many albums and operas.

Stoska, Polyna (Apolyna Stoskus)—soprano; b. Worcester, Mass., 1914; studied with Frank Doyle in Boston, at Juilliard, and with Gadski-Busch in Berlin; opera: Chautauqua, Berlin, NYCO (1944–46, int.), Met (1947–50), Barcelona, Vienna; roles: Donna Elvira, Ellen Orford, Eva (*Meistersinger*); created Mrs. Maurrant (*Street Scene*) on Broadway; N.Y. debut recital (1943); bibliography: ON (11/3/47), *Newsweek* (11/17/47), *Etude* (5/49); recording: *Street Scene.*

Sullivan, Brian (Harry Joseph)—tenor; b. Oakland, Calif., Aug. 9, 1917; d. Geneva, Switzerland, June 17, 1969; studied at Univ. of Southern California and with Lillian Backstrand-Wilson; early musicals and operetta; opera: California, Central City, Met (1948–61, int.), San Francisco, Chicago, Vienna; roles: Tamino, Lohengrin, Gabriel (*Fledermaus*); created Sam Kaplan (*Street Scene*) on Broadway; some believe his drowning death was a suicide; bibliography: *Newsweek* (3/8/48), ON (2/7/49, 1/26/59), MA (3/56), CBY 1957; recordings: album (Parnassus LP), *Street Scene.*

Swarthout, Gladys—mezzo-soprano; b. Deepwater, Mo., Dec. 25, 1900;

d. Florence, Italy, July 7, 1969; studied with Belle Vickers at the Bush Cons. in Chicago, and with Leopoldo Mugnone; opera: Chicago, Met (1929–45, int.), San Francisco, Cincinnati; roles: Adalgisa, Carmen, Mignon; films include *Rose of the Rancho, Champagne Waltz, Romance in the Dark;* much radio, concert, and recital; wrote *Come Soon, Tomorrow!,* a novel, based on her own career; married the baritone Frank Chapman; bibliography: *Last Prima Donnas* (Rasponi), *Etude* (12/34, 8/50), NYT (3/15/36, obit. 7/9/69), ON (11/16/42, 1/10/44, 11/19/60, 9/20/69), CBY 1944, MC (3/1/45, 2/15/52); recordings: albums, esp. French operatic arias and *Songs of Auvergne, Carmen* highlights (LPs), album (Preiser).

Symons, Charlotte—soprano; b. Battle Creek, Mich., ?; studied with Marcella Sembrich at Curtis, later Estelle Liebling; opera: San Carlo (Gallo), Philadelphia Grand, Met (1935–40, int.), Chicago Civic; roles: primarily comprimario; N.Y. debut recital (1936).

Tangeman, Nell Schelky—mezzo-soprano; b. Columbus, Ohio, Dec. 23, 1917; d. Washington, D.C., Feb. 15, 1965; began as a violinist; studied at the Cleveland Institute and in N.Y. with Fritz Lehmann, Friedrich Schorr, and Margarete Matzenauer; N.Y. debut recital (1948); much concert; New Friends of Music; created Mother Goose (*The Rake's Progress*) and Dinah (*Trouble in Tahiti*); many premieres, including Rorem and Honegger songs; recording: *Gurrelieder* (Vox LP).

Tennyson, Jean—soprano; b. Chicago, 1905 (?); d. La Tour de Peilz, Switzerland, 1991; studied with Cattone in Italy, Mary Garden and Madame Gilly in Paris; Earl Carroll's *Vanities;* musicals; opera: Italy, Chicago, San Francisco, San Carlo (Gallo); radio: star of *Great Moments of Music* (1942–46); married Camille Dreyfus, founder of Celanese Corp. and president of Camille and Henry Dreyfus Foundation; bibliography: *Musical Digest* (11/33), MC (10/15/45); recordings: radio compilations.

Tentoni, Rosa—soprano; b. Buhl, Minn.; studied with Enrico Rosati; second prize in Atwater Kent competition (1931); opera: Cincinnati, San Francisco, Philadelphia Orchestra, Met (1936–37, Spring Seasons only), Hollywood Bowl; roles include Cio-Cio-San, Aida, Mimì; title role in Gluck's *Iphigénie en Aulide* in first American performance in Philadelphia; married to the baritone Joseph Royer; recording: Beethoven Ninth Symphony under Toscanini (LP).

Thebom, Blanche—mezzo-soprano; b. Monessen, Pa., Sept. 19, 1918; grew up in Canton, Ohio; studied with Margarete Matzenauer and Edyth Walker; opera: Met (1944–67, int.), San Francisco, Glyndebourne, Soviet Union, La Scala, Covent Garden; roles: Brangäne, Amneris, Carmen, Dalila, Dido in first English production of *Les Troyens;* N.Y. debut recital (1943); film: brief appearances in *When Irish Eyes Are Smiling, The Great Caruso;* settled in

San Francisco, where she teaches and has directed various programs to help young singers; video: *Voice of Firestone* (VAI); bibliography: ON (12/11/44, 1/3/55, 4/3/65, 11/77, 12/24/83, 11/91); *Time* (2/12/45, 3/23/53), *Newsweek* (12/2/46), CBY 1948, *Etude* (7/48, 6/53); recordings: album (Preiser), *Così Fan Tutte*, *Tristan und Isolde* with Flagstad, compilations, opera broadcasts.

Thibault, Conrad—baritone; b. Northbridge, Mass., Nov. 1, 1908 (?); d. New York, Jan. 8, 1987; studied with Emilio de Gogorza at Curtis; opera: Philadelphia Grand; concert; N.Y. debut recital (1936); much radio; bibliography: MC (1/18/36).

Thigpen, Helen—soprano; b. Washington, D.C., ?; d. 1966; N.Y. debut recital (1949); played Serena on European tour of *Porgy and Bess* and the Strawberry Woman in the Preminger film of the same; married Earl Jackson, who played Sportin' Life; recording: Howard Swanson's *Seven Songs* (Decca LP).

Thomas, John Charles—baritone; b. Meyersdale, Pa., Sept. 6, 1891; d. Apple Valley, Calif., Dec. 13, 1960; studied with Adelin Fermin at Peabody Cons.; early musical comedy and vaudeville; opera: Washington, D.C., Brussels, Covent Garden, Berlin, Vienna, Chicago, Philadelphia, Met (1934–43, int.), San Francisco; roles: Germont, Figaro (*Barbiere*), Tonio; N.Y. debut recital (1918); much recital and radio; bibliography: *Etude* (1/41, 11/43), CBY 1943, ON (3/11/61), RC (3/79); recordings: many albums.

Thompson, Hugh—baritone; b. Tacoma, Wash., June 19, 1915; studied with Anna Schoen-René at Juilliard; cowinner of 1944 Met Auditions of the Air; opera: Chautauqua, Nine O'Clock, San Carlo (Gallo), San Francisco, Cincinnati, NYCO (1944, 1954), Met (1944–53, int.); roles: primarily secondary, esp. Faninal, Schaunard, Frank (*Fledermaus*); became a stage director; son of the critic and music editor Oscar Thompson; bibliography: ON (5/17/44).

Tibbett (Tibbet), Lawrence—baritone; b. Bakersfield, Calif., Nov. 16, 1896; d. New York, July 15, 1960; studied with Basil Ruysdael in Los Angeles and Frank La Forge in New York; opera: Met (1923–50), San Francisco, Cincinnati, Chicago, Covent Garden; roles: Simon Boccanegra, Rigoletto, Iago, Scarpia; created leading roles in *The King's Henchman, Peter Ibbetson, The Emperor Jones, Merry Mount, Don Juan de Mañara* (Goossens); films: *The Rogue Song, New Moon, Metropolitan;* much radio, including *Voice of Firestone* and *Your Hit Parade;* founder and first president of the American Guild of Musical Artists, a founder and later president of the American Federation of Radio Artists (AFRA); served on the Committee to Save Carnegie Hall and on the board of the New York City Center of Music and Drama; bibliography: *Lawrence Tibbett* (ed. Farkas), *Dear Rogue* (Weinstat and Wechsler), *Time* (cover story 1/16/33, 7/25/60), MA (2/10/38, 2/49), ON (10/29/60, 11/96), RC (8/77), *NATS Bulletin* (Sept./Oct. 85), NYT (12/15/96); recordings: many albums and opera broadcasts.

Torigi (Tortorigi), Richard (Santo)—baritone; b. Brooklyn, Oct. 30, 1917; studied with Eleanor McClellan, Dick Marzullo; attended the American Theater Wing; opera: Salmaggi, Charles Wagner, San Carlo, NYCO (1951–69, int.), Chicago, Cincinnati, NBC Opera Theater; roles: Marcello, Escamillo, Germont; musicals: covered, then replaced Weede in *Most Happy Fella;* film: Alfio in *Cavalleria Rusticana,* starring Mario del Monaco (Opera Cameos); recordings: *Falstaff* and *Madama Butterfly* from New Orleans (VAI), *Bomarzo* (Ginastera).

Traubel, Helen—soprano; b. St. Louis, June 20, 1899; d. Santa Monica, Calif., July 28, 1972; studied with Vetta Karst; opera: Met (1937–53, int.), Chicago, San Francisco; roles: Wagner heroines; much concert, radio, and TV; film: *Deep in My Heart;* starred in *Pipe Dream* on Broadway; wrote autobiography and *Murder at the Met;* video: *Voice of Firestone* (VAI); bibliography: *St Louis Woman* (autobiography), ON (12/25/39, 2/5/51, 4/03), CBY 1940, *Musical Digest* (1/40), *Newsweek* (4/21/41), *Etude* (1/43), *Time* (1/22/43, cover story 11/11/46), CBY 1952, *Musical Courier* (5/15/54); recordings: albums (LP), *Traubel in Concert* (1941–46), compilations, *Tristan und Isolde* (Buenos Aires), "Wesendonck Lieder" (Stokowski).

Treigle, Norman—bass-baritone; b. New Orleans, March 6, 1927; d. New Orleans, Feb. 16, 1975; studied with Elizabeth Wood and at Loyola University; opera: New Orleans, NYCO (1953–72, int.), Covent Garden, Hamburg, Milan; roles: Méphistophélès, Boris Godunov, Don Giovanni, Olin Blitch in *Susannah;* his early death was from an overdose of sleeping pills; video: *Susannah* (VAI); bibliography: NYT (obit. 2/18/75), ON 5/75; recordings: *Mefistofele* (Boito), *Susannah* (Floyd).

Troxell, Barbara—soprano; b. Easton, Pa., Sept. 10, 1916; d. Ithaca, N.Y., Sept. 23, 1984; studied with Elisabeth Schumann at Curtis; opera: Mexico City, Met (1950–51), and Europe; roles: comprimario at Met, but elsewhere Donna Anna, Countess Almaviva, Eva; taught at Cornell Univ.; director of Ithaca Opera Association; bibliography: ON (1/8/51); recordings: albums of Britten, Hindemith, Mozart, and sacred songs (LPs).

Truman, Margaret—soprano; b. Independence, Mo., Feb. 17, 1924; studied with Mrs. Thomas Strickler and Helen Traubel; concerts and radio; radio debut with Detroit Orchestra (1947), N.Y. debut in Carnegie Hall (1949); daughter of president Harry Truman; became a successful author; bibliography: *Souvenirs* (autobiography), NYT (8/8/46), *Newsweek* (9/1/47), CBY 1950, *Time* (cover story 2/26/51); recordings: albums (RCA LPs)

Tucker (Ticker), Richard (Reuben)—tenor; b. Brooklyn, Aug. 28, 1913; d. Kalamazoo, Mich., Jan. 8, 1975; studied with Paul Althouse; well known as a cantor; much radio; opera: Met (1945–74), European debut in Verona opposite Callas in *Gioconda* (1947), London, Vienna, Buenos Aires, Israel, Chicago, San Francisco, Cincinnati; roles: Duke (*Rigoletto*), Manrico, Canio, Rodolfo,

Andrea Chénier, Don José, Ferrando (*Così*); married to the sister of Jan Peerce; bibliography: *Richard Tucker* (Drake), MC (12/1/48), *Life* (11/3/52), *Etude* (11/54), ON (2/28/55, 11/11/57, 12/30/61, 6/4/66, 4/12/75, 1/21/95), CBY 1956, MA (11/61), NYT (1/7/73, obit. 1/9/75); recordings: many albums and operas.

Tully, Alice—soprano (began as a mezzo-soprano); b. Corning, N.Y., Sept. 11, 1902; d. New York, Dec. 10, 1993; studied with Jean Périer in Paris; debut with Pasdeloup Orchestra (1927); opera: Salmaggi, Manhattan Opera; roles: Santuzza, Carmen; N.Y. debut recital (1936); much recital in Europe and America; granddaughter of Amory Houghton, who founded Corning Glass; after retiring in 1950 Tully became a philanthropist; the recital hall at Lincoln Center in N.Y. is named for her; bibliography: *Alice Tully* (Fuller), ON (3/26/88), NYT (obit. 12/11/93).

Tuminia, Josephine—soprano; b. St. Louis, 1914 (?); grew up in San Francisco; sang with swing bands; studied with Alberto Terrasi and Nino Comel in San Francisco and Mario Cordona in Milan; opera: San Francisco, Palermo, Bologna, Belgrade, Chicago, Met (1941–42), Cincinnati; roles: Gilda, Rosina, Lucia; bibliography: ON (2/3/41); recording: songs with Tommy Dorsey (Decca LP).

Turner, Claramae Haas—mezzo-soprano; b. Dinuba, Calif., Oct. 28, 1920; studied with Nino Comel, Giacomo Spadoni, Dick Marzollo; early career in radio and Gilbert and Sullivan; opera: San Francisco (5 years in the chorus, 1 in comprimario roles), Met (1946–50), Cincinnati, Chicago, Venice, South America, NYCO (1953–69, int.); roles: Carmen, Azucena, Amneris; created Madame Flora in *The Medium* (1946); symphonic soloist; N.Y. debut recital (1965); film: Nettie in *Carousel;* introduced "I Left My Heart in San Francisco" (1954); bibliography: MA (11/1/53), MC (1/15/54), *Etude* (5/54), ON (4/7/62, 12/24/94); recordings: album (LP), *Ballo in Maschera* with Toscanini, Copland's *Tender Land, Carousel, La Gioconda* from New Orleans (Standing Room Only).

Uppman, Theodor—baritone; b. Santa Clara, Calif., Jan. 12, 1920; studied at Stanford Univ., at Curtis with Steuart Wilson, and with Herbert Janssen; winner of 1947 Atwater Kent Award; opera: NYCO (1948, 1962), Met (1953–78, int.); roles: Pelléas, Masetto, Papageno, Sharpless; created title roles in Britten's *Billy Budd* at Covent Garden (1951) and Floyd's *The Passion of Jonathan Wade* at City Opera (1962); N.Y. debut recital (1950); film: dubbing in *Morning Becomes Elektra* and *Toast of New Orleans;* brother John Uppman sang with Rosing's American Opera; taught at Mannes and Manhattan; bibliography: ON (12/28/53, 1/19/63, 3/28/92), MC (3/15/56); recordings: album (VAI), *Billy Budd.*

Valentino, Frank (Francis Valentine Dinhaupt)—baritone; b. the Bronx, Jan. 6, 1907; d. New York, June 14, 1991; grew up in Denver; studied at Denver

Cons. and with Emilio Piccoli in Milan; winner of Philadelphia Sesquicenten-
nial prize (1926); opera: Italy (including La Scala), Glyndebourne, Zurich,
Met (1940–61), Cincinnati, San Francisco; roles: Marcello, Enrico (*Lucia*),
Germont; taught at Peabody; bibliography: ON (12/16/40); recordings: album
(LP, Allegro-Royale), opera broadcasts, *Rigoletto* Act 4 and *Bohème* under
Toscanini (RCA).

Varnay, Astrid (Ibolyka Maria)—soprano (later mezzo); b. Stockholm,
Sweden, Apr. 25, 1918; grew up in New York and New Jersey; studied with her
mother, Maria Yavor, a coloratura soprano, and Paul Althouse; coached with
Hermann Weigert, whom she married in 1944; opera: Met (1941–79, int.),
Mexico, Chicago, San Francisco, Covent Garden, Bayreuth, Munich, Berlin,
Vienna; roles: Brünnhilde, Isolde, Elektra, Lady Macbeth; created Telea in
The Island God (Menotti); taught in Düsseldorf Musikhochschule; bibliography: *55 Years in Five Acts* (autobiography), ON (12/22/41, 3/16/42, 5/5/62, 12/
21/74, 6/97, 12/00), MA (12/25/41, 5/53), *Etude* (10/43), *Time* (6/14/48), CBY
1951, *Opera* (10/58), OQ (Autumn 1997); recordings: many albums and live
performances, esp. from Bayreuth.

Votipka, Thelma—soprano; b. Cleveland, Dec. 20, 1906; d. New York,
Oct. 24, 1972; studied at Oberlin; opera: American Opera (Rosing), Chicago,
Met (1935–66, int.); roles: comprimario, esp. Frasquita, Marthe (*Faust*), Flora
(*Traviata*), Witch (*Hänsel und Gretel*); bibliography: ON (4/8/40, 1/1/51, 4/16/
60, 12/23/72, 1/22/94), NYT (1/1/50, 12/6/59, 10/27/72); recordings: selections
and an interview on *American Singer* (Eklipse), *Hänsel und Gretel* (LP), opera
broadcasts.

Walters, Jess (Josuoh Wolk)—baritone; b. Brooklyn, Nov. 18, 1908; d.
Austin, Tex., Oct. 8, 2000; studied agriculture at the National Farm School in
Pa.; studied voice with Mario Pagano and Luigi Giuffridi, and at the Rossini
Opera Workshop; finalist in *Major Bowes Amateur Hour;* opera: Salmaggi,
New Opera, NYCO, Chicago, San Francisco, Covent Garden, Netherlands;
roles: Macbeth, Germont, Marcello, Papageno; returned to U.S. in 1965;
taught at Univ. of Texas; recording: *Aida* (with Callas) live from Covent Gar-
den.

Warenskjold, Dorothy—soprano; b. Piedmont, Calif., ?; studied at Mills
College and with Mabel Riegelman in San Francisco; much radio, including
Railroad Hour, Harvest of Stars, and *Standard Hour;* opera: San Francisco
(1948–55), Cincinnati, NBC Opera Theater; roles: Marguerite, Micaela,
Cherubino, Sophie, Pamina; video: *Voice of Firestone* with George London
(VAI); founded and directed her own touring musical theater; taught in Cali-
fornia; bibliography: MC (11/15/54), MA (7/56); recordings: albums (LP), al-
bum (Cambria);

Warfield, William—baritone; b. West Helena, Ark., Jan. 22, 1920; d. Chicago, Aug. 25, 2002; grew up in Rochester, N.Y.; studied at Eastman and with Yves Tinayre and Otto Herz at the American Theater Wing; much recital and concert; N.Y. debut recital (1950); played Joe in film of *Show Boat;* best known as Porgy; performed De Lawd in *Green Pastures* on TV; married the soprano Leontyne Price; taught at Univ. of Illinois at Champaign-Urbana and North-western Univ.; bibliography: *William Warfield* (autobiography), MC (4/1/54), *Etude* (2/55), MA (12/1/57); recordings: albums (LP), Copland's *Old American Songs, Porgy and Bess* excerpts, much oratorio, including *Messiah.*

Warner, Genevieve—soprano; b. Amsterdam, N.Y., 1925; studied at Juilliard with Francis Rogers, and privately with Franz and Stephanie Rupp; winner of Marian Anderson Award; opera: Met (1950–54), Glyndebourne, Ed-inburgh, Germany; roles: Gilda, Zerlina, Susanna; career faltered after being attacked and nearly strangled in Edinburgh; bibliography: ON (11/20/50); re-cordings: album of Mozart and Schubert, *Merry Widow,* and Handel's *The Faithful Shepherd* (LPs).

Warren (Warenoff), Leonard—baritone; b. the Bronx, April 21, 1911; d. New York, March 4, 1960; studied with Sidney Dietch and Giuseppe De Luca; Radio City Glee Club; cowinner of 1938 Met Auditions of the Air; op-era: Met (1938–60), La Scala, Soviet Union, South America, San Francisco, Chicago, Cincinnati; roles: Rigoletto, Iago, Simon Boccanegra, Scarpia, Tonio; film: *Irish Eyes Are Smiling;* died onstage, stricken by a cerebral vascular hemorrhage during performance of *Forza del Destino;* video: *Voice of Firestone* (VAI); bibliography: *Leonard Warren* (Phillips-Matz), ON (11/23/42, 3/22/75, 4/00), *Newsweek* (12/13/48), *Etude* (3/49), CBY 1953, NYT (2/9/59, 10/25/59, 3/5/60, 3/13/60, 4/2/60), *Opera* (6/60), *High Fidelity* (6/60); recordings: many albums and operas.

Weede (Wiedefeld), Robert—baritone; b. Baltimore, Feb. 11, 1903; d. Walnut Creek, Calif., July 9, 1972; studied with George Castelle in Baltimore, Adeline Fermin at Eastman, and Oscar Anselmi in Milan; winner of National Federation of Music Clubs competition and Caruso Memorial Foundation contest; soloist at Radio City; much radio, including premiere of *Old Maid and the Thief;* opera: Met (1937–53, int.), NYCO (1948–49), San Francisco, Chicago, Cincinnati, Mexico City, Rio de Janeiro; roles: Rigoletto, Tonio, Scarpia; *Most Happy Fella, Milk and Honey, Cry for Us All* on Broadway; two sons became singers; bibliography: *The Musician* (6/37), ON (1/26/42), *Etude* (12/47), *Saturday Review* (5/5/56), CBY 1957, NYT (obit. 7/11/72); recordings: album (Capitol LP), *Carmen* highlights, complete live *Aida* and *Tosca* with Callas from Mexico City, *Most Happy Fella.*

Wildermann, William—bass; b. Stuttgart, Germany, Dec. 2, 1919; d. Stamford, N.Y., May 17, 2004; grew up in America; studied with Carl Yost; opera: Chicago, Cincinnati, San Carlo (Gallo), NYCO (1953–81, int.), Met

(1958–84, int.), San Francisco, San Carlo (Naples), Stuttgart, Brussels, Munich; roles: Colline, Ferrando (*Trovatore*), Sparafucile; *Regina* and *My Darlin' Aida* on Broadway; recording: *Rigoletto* (VAI), *St. Matthew Passion,* opera broadcasts.

Wilkins, Marie—soprano; b. Cortland, N.Y.; studied with Malnory-Marseillac in Paris and with Cataldi in Italy, where she made her debut with her husband, Joseph Wilkins, in *Barbiere di Siviglia;* opera: some light opera in the U.S., Met (1942–43); roles: Lakmé, Queen of the Night; N.Y. debut recital (1939); bibliography: *Time* (12/14/42), *Newsweek* (12/14/42), ON (1/25/43).

Williams, Camilla—soprano; b. Danville, Va., Oct. 18, 1922; studied with Marion Freschl in Philadelphia; winner of 1943 and 1944 Marian Anderson Award; opera: NYCO (1946–54), Vienna, Berlin; roles: Cio-Cio-San, Aida, Saint of Bleeker Street; much concert and recital, including African and Far East tours; taught at Brooklyn College, Indiana Univ.; bibliography: *Newsweek* (5/27/46), *Time* (9/30/46), *NY Post* (10/3/46), CBY 1952, *Etude* (2/54), OQ (Spring 2002); recordings: album, *Aida* highlights from NYCO, and *Porgy and Bess* (all LPs).

Wilson, Dolores—soprano; b. Philadelphia, Aug. 9, 1929 (1926?); studied with William Herman in N.Y., Toti dal Monte in Italy; starred in a 1944 TV production of the musical *Boys from Boise;* opera: throughout Europe, esp. Italy, Met (1954–59); roles: Lucia, Gilda, Rosina; created Moore's Baby Doe at Central City; sang in and directed *Fiddler on the Roof;* bibliography: ON (2/1/54); recordings: *Lucia di Lammemoor* (Urania LP), *Don Pasquale* (Met Club LP).

Winters (Whisonant), Lawrence—baritone; b. King's Creek, S.C., Nov. 12, 1916 (1915?); d. Hamburg, Germany, Sept. 24, 1965; studied with Todd Duncan at Howard Univ; *Porgy and Bess* (1942 revival); opera: NYCO (1948–62, int.), Sweden, Finland, Norway, Hamburg, Berlin; roles: Amonasro, Scarpia, Rigoletto; N.Y. debut recital (1947); *Call Me Mister* and *My Darlin' Aida* on Broadway; bibliography: *Newsweek* (10/22/51); recordings: *Aida* highlights from NYCO (LP), *Devil and Daniel Webster* (Desto LP), *Porgy and Bess, Call Me Mister.*

Wrightson, Earl—baritone: b. Baltimore, Jan. 1, 1916; d. New York, March 7, 1993; studied with Robert Weede; opera: Charles Wagner, Trenton: roles: Silvio, Figaro (*Barbiere*); much radio, including *The Prudential Family Hour* and *The Coca-Cola Hour;* TV: hosted *The Earl Wrightson Show* (1948–52); starred in Kurt Weill's *Firebrand of Florence* on Broadway; many musicals; performed in concert as a duo with Lois Hunt, who was also his companion in private life; bibliography: NYT (obit. 3/9/93): recordings: various operettas (LP).

Yeend, Frances Lynch—soprano: b. Vancouver, Wash., Jan. 28, 1918; grew up in Portland, Ore.; Yeend was first husband's name; studied violin and ballet; various voice teachers include William Herman; much radio; Columbia Concerts Tour of *Carmen;* Bel Canto Trio; opera: NYCO (1948–59, int.), Met (1961–63), Verona, Covent Garden, Vienna, Munich; roles: Violetta, Turandot, Marguerite, Chrysothemis; created role of Ellen Orford in American premiere of *Peter Grimes;* renowned as a symphonic soloist; taught at West Virginia Univ.; married to the pianist James Benner; bibliography: MA (7/55), ON (2/23/63); recordings: Beethoven Ninth Symphony, Bruckner *Te Deum, Faust* highlights from NYCO (LP), scenes from *Elektra,* duets with Mario Lanza live from the Hollywood Bowl.

Notes

Note to Preface

1. Jerome Hines, quoted in Paul F. Driscoll, "The Tucker Review," *Opera News,* January 21, 1995. Courtesy *Opera News,* © The Metropolitan Opera Guild 1995.

Notes to the Prologue

1. In *The Glory Road,* Tibbett says he was assigned the role because the Spanish baritone Vincente Ballester had become ill and Gatti needed a replacement. (Tibbett, in fact, had replaced Ballester as Valentin earlier in the season.) See Tibbett, *The Glory Road,* in *Lawrence Tibbett: Singing Actor,* ed. Andrew Farkas (Portland, Ore.: Amadeus Press, 1989), 76. However, Tibbett may have been confused. In speaking of the event in his memoirs, Gatti makes no mention of Ballester or anyone, for that matter, being ill, and says he wanted to try Tibbett from the beginning. (In fact, Gatti even disputes Tibbett's description of the rehearsals, though other accounts corroborate it.) Moreover, since Ballester sang the first of five Alfios on December 29, 1924, and a concert the following January 4, he could not have been very ill, or certainly not so ill management would go to such lengths to prepare Tibbett for the role.

2. Quoted in Farkas, ed., *Lawrence Tibbett: Singing Actor,* 76, 77.

3. Quoted in Hertzel Weinstat and Bert Wechsler, *Dear Rogue: A Biography of the American Baritone Lawrence Tibbett* (Portland, Ore.: Amadeus Press, 1996), 67.

4. Farkas, ed., *Lawrence Tibbett: Singing Actor,* 77.

5. Oscar Thompson, *The American Singer: A Hundred Years of Success in Opera* (New York: Dial Press, 1937), 365.

6. Lawrence Gilman, *New York Herald Tribune,* January 3, 1925, quoted in promotional ad in *Musical America,* January 24, 1925.

7. Obituary of Olin Downes, *New York Times,* August 23, 1955.

8. "Kahn Congratulates Lawrence Tibbett," *New York Times,* January 4, 1925.

9. Olin Downes, "American Baritone Stirs Opera House," *New York Times,* January 3, 1925.

10. Quoted in Olin Downes, "Kahn Congratulates Lawrence Tibbett," *New York Times,* January 4, 1925.

11. "Mephisto's Musings," *Musical America,* January 10, 1925.

Notes to Chapter One

1. Marcia Davenport based the funeral service of the fictional singer in *Of Lena Geyer* on this same service.

2. H. Goddard Owen, *A Recollection of Marcella Sembrich* (New York: DaCapo Press, 1982), 18.

3. Other Americans who studied with Sembrich at one time or another and had notable careers were Alma Gluck, Sophie Braslau, Hulda Lashanska, Lucielle Browning, Polyna Stoska, Margaret Halstead, Anna Hamlin, Charlotte Symons, Maxine Stellman, Pearl Besuner, Edith Piper, Natalie Bodanya, Winifred Cecil, and Florence Page Kimball. Sembrich did not teach men.

4. This was, in fact, the first time Toscanini had returned to the Met since leaving in 1915, when he was disgusted with Gatti for letting financial considerations take priority over artistic values.

5. So great, in fact, was America's passion for Wagner that nine of the thirty-seven operas offered in Gatti's final season were by the German titan, compared to six by Verdi, three by Puccini, three by Donizetti, two by Gounod, and one each by Mascagni, Leoncavallo, Ponchielli, Humperdink, Delibes, Massenet, Thomas, Richard Strauss, Bellini, Pergolesi, Debussy, Seymour, Taylor, and, astoundingly, Mozart.

6. Gatti would die there in 1940, a few months after Galli.

7. "Timely Topics," *Musical Digest*, April 1935.

8. Leonard Liebling, review, *New York American,* December 15, 1935.

9. Howard Taubman, review, *New York Times,* December 31, 1935.

10. Quoted in Herbert Kupferberg, *Tanglewood* (New York: McGraw-Hill, 1976), 31.

11. Helen Noble, *Life with the Met* (New York: G. P. Putnam's Sons, 1954), 135.

12. In his book *The American Opera Singer* (New York: Doubleday, 1997), Peter Davis suggests that Mary Moore had connections to the Met, which probably helped.

13. Review, *New York Times,* March 18, 1935.

14. Review, *Musical Courier,* June 15, 1935.

15. Quoted in "Edward Johnson Announces," *Musical Leader,* June 8, 1935.

Notes to Chapter Two

1. The next night, January 2, 1925, Bori would sing Alice Ford in the historic performance of *Falstaff* described in the prologue.

2. "Famous Stars Sing First Time by Radio," *New York Times,* January 2, 1925.

3. Victor actually dropped the broadcasts after a few months primarily because managers were telling their artists not to provide this kind of publicity for the company without compensation.

4. Statistics are from *Variety Radio Directory, 1937–38* (New York: Variety, 1937), 17–27.

5. Lotte Lehmann, *Midway in My Song* (Indianapolis: Bobbs-Merrill, 1938), 224–25.

6. Eileen Farrell and Brian Kellow, *Can't Help Singing: The Life of Eileen Farrell* (Boston: Northeastern University Press, 1999), 39.

7. Gladys Swarthout, "The American Singer's Opportunities," *Etude,* December 1934.

8. "'Crooning' Caustically Stigmatized by Majority of Twenty Musical Notables in Lively Symposium," *Musical America,* May 25, 1932.

9. Jessica Dragonette, *Faith Is a Song: The Odyssey of an American Artist* (New York: David McKay, 1951), 71, 47, 70.

10. Eileen Farrell, "After the Studio," *Etude,* July 1952.

11. Giovanni Martinelli, "Can't Ask Met to Accomplish Miracles," *Variety,* March 5, 1941.

12. Ernestine Schumann-Heink, Charles Hackett, Richard Bonelli, Beniamino Gigli, Giuseppe de Luca, and John Charles Thomas all appeared in subsequent Vitaphone shorts, helping to pave the way, if not for opera, at least for opera singers.

13. Tibbett, *The Glory Road,* in *Lawrence Tibbett: Singing Actor,* ed. Farkas, 78.

14. Grace Moore, *You're Only Human Once* (Garden City, N.Y.: Doubleday, Doran, 1944), 197.

15. Flagstad, who confessed to being fascinated by Hollywood, sang a Wagner excerpt in *The Big Broadcast of 1938* but did not have a role.

16. *Daily News,* April 1935, quoted in Edward Baron Turk, *Hollywood Diva: A Biography of Jeanette MacDonald* (Berkeley and Los Angeles: University of California Press, 1998), 153.

17. Quoted in Robert Sabin, "Nelson Eddy—Story-Teller in Song," *Musical America,* January 15, 1951.

18. *New York Sun,* February 15, 1936, as quoted in Turk, *Hollywood Diva,* 173.

19. Quoted in Sharon Rich, *Sweethearts* (New York: Donald I. Fine, 1994), 320.

20. Eleanor Steber with Martha Sloat, *Eleanor Steber: An Autobiography* (Ridgewood, N.J.: Wordsworth, 1992), 12.

21. Quoted in an editorial by Deems Taylor, *Musical America,* April 10, 1929.

22. Moore, *You're Only Human Once,* 2.

23. Quoted by Douglas Gilbert, "Socializing a Tougher Racket These Days, Says Blonde, Soon to Make Met Debut," *New York World Telegram* (date illegible, but Jepson's Metropolitan Opera debut was January 24, 1935). "Westian" is a reference to the voluptuous film star Mae West.

24. Ronald L. Davis, *Opera in Chicago* (New York: Appleton-Century, 1966), 220.

Notes to Chapter Three

1. Michel Mok, "Filling Gatti-Casazza's Shoes, but Not His Chair," *New York Post,* December 14, 1935.

2. Noble, *Life with the Met,* 130.

3. Quoted in Ruby Mercer, *The Tenor of His Time: Edward Johnson of the Met* (Toronto: Clarke, Irwin, 1976), 274.

4. No reference seems clear as to whether Johnson ever actually became a U.S. citizen. Much of the contemporary press seems to assume he had. In her biography, however, Mercer relates the steps Johnson took toward citizenship in detail and seems convinced the process was never completed. The *Times* obituary concurs.

5. Quoted in Mercer, *The Tenor of His Time,* 171.

6. Ibid., 174.

7. Giulio Gatti-Casazza, *Memories of the Opera* (New York: Charles Scribner's Sons, 1941), 21.

8. Ibid.

9. Grace Goldini (Golden), who sang three performances of the Page in *Rigoletto,* was the other.

10. Emma Eames (about to retire), Geraldine Farrar, Bessie Abbott, Ellen Yaw, Marie Rappold, Josephine Jacoby, Louise Homer, Marion Weed, and one male, Riccardo Martin. If one includes the Swedish-born Olive Fremstad, the number is ten.

11. It is difficult to be sure of all the nationalities on any of these early rosters, especially of those who sang small roles, because we have less information on them and Americans often changed their names to sound European.

12. Though not on Gatti's final roster, Mario Chamlee had sung with him earlier and returned under Johnson.

13. Quoted in Mary Mellish, *Sometimes I Reminisce: An Autobiography* (New York: G. Putnam's Sons, 1941), 154. Mellish was a comprimario soprano at the Met for six seasons.

14. W. H. Henderson, review, *New York Sun,* March 20, 1913.

15. *Il Secolo* (Genoa), quoted in *Musical Courier,* December 15, 1916.

16. Quoted in Lawrence F. Holdridge, "Charles Hackett," *The Record Collector* 22, nos. 8 and 9 (February 1975), 182.

17. H.H., "Ovation to Bonelli at New York Debut," *New York Times,* December 2, 1932.

18. Quoted in Edward C. Moore, "War Has Set Women Free, Says Mary Garden, Back from France," *Musical America,* December 8, 1918.

19. Carmela, a mezzo-soprano, was not engaged until 1925.

20. Rosa Ponselle and James A. Drake, *Ponselle: A Singer's Life* (Garden City, N.Y.: Doubleday, 1982), 42. Though there are several versions of this comment, they all closely resemble this one.

21. Ibid., 43.

22. H. Maurice Jacquet, "Grace Moore's Career Was Inspiration to Young Singers," *Musical Courier,* March 15, 1947. Jacquet was one of Moore's pianists.

23. Later, under her real name of Marion Tillotson, Mario would publish three mystery novels, including *Murder at the Opera House.*

24. Quoted in "Scaling the Song-Ladder from Verdi to Honegger," *Musical America,* November 21, 1925.

25. Francis D. Perkins, "Rose Bampton Makes Debut at Metropolitan," *Herald Tribune,* November 29, 1932.

26. Ponselle and Drake, *Ponselle,* 156.

27. Marjorie M. Fisher, "New Singers Lend Interest to San Francisco Opera," *Musical America,* November 10, 1941.

28. Helen Jepson, interview with author, June 11, 1994. Jepson described the problem as a slow and insidious thickening of the cords that she believed began as far back as her high school years, when she performed Nedda in *Pagliacci* and soon after contracted scarlet fever.

29. In *Dear Rogue* (174–79), Weinstat and Wechsler make the case that Tibbett's sudden vocal decline was first and foremost the result of a throat ailment, possibly strep.

30. Cecil Smith, "Lawrence Tibbett, American Pioneer at the Metropolitan," *Musical America,* February 10, 1949.

Notes to Chapter Four

1. Mok, "Filling Gatti-Casazza's Shoes."

2. Ibid.

3. Quoted in Mercer, *The Tenor of His Time,* 179.

4. Steber, *Eleanor Steber,* 96.

5. Ibid., 95. Though here Steber is speaking specifically of the Auditions winners, in light of the fact that Stevens has said the young Americans were called "Johnson's babies" (see Mercer, *The Tenor of His Time,* 211), the general use of the phrase seems appropriate.

6. Nadine Conner, interview with author, October 11, 1997.

7. "Opera Auditions on Air," *New York Times,* December 19, 1935. (© The New York Times Co., 1935. Reprinted with permission.) There are various versions as to where the idea of the Auditions of the Air originated, but an unpublished account compiled and written by Theodore T. C. Bijou, Daniel F. Tritter, and Rita Shane Tritter (no date given, but revised in 1968, and obtained by the author from Howard Hook, its director under Rudolf Bing) suggests the president of Sherwin-Williams proposed it with the idea that it would be good advertising for his paint company. Virtually all versions, however, credit Pelletier as its actual founder and first director.

8. Patrice Munsel, interview with author, January 5, 1995.

9. Review, *Musical America,* December 22, 1928.

10. Noble, *Life at the Met,* 186.

11. Howard Taubman, review, *New York Times,* December 20, 1935.

12. Samuel Chotzinoff, review, *New York Post,* December 27, 1935.

13. Olin Downes, review, *New York Times,* December 27, 1935.

14. Olin Downes, review, *New York Times,* December 28, 1935.

15. Samuel Chotzinoff, review, *New York Post,* January 6, 1936.

16. "Aïda from Philadelphia," *Time,* February 24, 1936.

17. Olin Downes, "Metropolitan Review," *New York Times,* March 22, 1936.

18. Robert Lawrence, "Among the Missing," *New York Herald Tribune,* March 22, 1942.

19. Downes, "Metropolitan Review," March 22, 1936.
20. Bruna Castagna, Armand Tokatyan, and Carlo Morelli.
21. Martinelli, Jagel, Kullman, René Maison, and Tokatyan were all regularly in service; Carron was being primed; Crooks occasionally dropped by; Bentonelli, Chamlee, and Hackett, though neglected, were on the roster; Bruno Landi and Jussi Björling were on the horizon.
22. Quoted in Voytek Matushevski, "Bidù Sayāo: The Last Pupil of Jean de Reszke," *Opera Quarterly*, Winter 1995/96, 66.
23. Horace Johnson, review, *Musical Courier*, May 15, 1937.
24. Review, *Musical America*, March 25, 1937.
25. Anna M. Hamlin, *Father Was a Tenor* (Hicksville, N.Y.: Exposition Press, 1978), 60.
26. Quoted in *New York Times*, April 8, 1938.
27. According to Carol Poppenger, a student and close friend of Galli-Campi.

Notes to Chapter Five

1. Reinald Werrenrath, "New Aspects of the Art of Singing in America," *Etude*, June 1921.
2. Frida Leider, *Playing My Part* (New York: Meredith Press, 1966), 117.
3. William Brady, "Operatic Opportunities in America," *The Musician*, April 1937.
4. Nicholas deVore, "Operatic Futures Rest with Bush-League Houses," *The Musician*, January 1936.
5. Quoted in "Mezzo from Ohio," *Time*, February 12, 1945.
6. Beverly Sills and Lawrence Linderman, *Beverly: An Autobiography* (New York: Bantam Books, 1987), 54.
7. "Chicago's Worst," *Time*, December 16, 1935.
8. Editorial, *The Musician*, November 1945.
9. Review, *Musical America*, May 1949.
10. Arthur Bloomfield, *50 Years of the San Francisco Opera* (San Francisco: San Francisco Book Co., 1972), 10.
11. Virgil Thomson, *New York Herald Tribune*, February 20, 1941, as quoted on a promotional brochure found in clippings file at the New York Public Library for the Performing Arts.
12. Quoted in Arthur Bronson, "Pelosi Still Seeks a New Caruso," *Philadelphia Record*, December 15, 1940.
13. "Americans Preferred in Opera Casts Here," *Philadelphia Evening Bulletin*, October 4, 1934.
14. From an ad the company took out, *Musical America*, May 10, 1939.
15. Henry Pleasants, review, *Philadelphia Bulletin*, January 20, 1939.
16. Brenda Lewis, interview with author, September 15, 1998.
17. Quoted in Mary Jane Matz, "The Voice of Crooks," *Opera News*, April 9, 1966.

18. "Poor Man's Impresario," *Time,* March 1, 1943.

19. Guido Salmaggi, interview with author, August 9, 1995.

20. Alfredo Salmaggi's obituary, *Opera News,* November 1975.

21. In addition to Guido, another son, Felix, a brother, Valentino, and a nephew, Ugo, also founded companies.

22. Fortune T. Gallo, *Lucky Rooster: The Autobiography of an Impresario* (New York: Exposition Press, 1967), 44, 45.

23. Ibid., 112.

24. Tom Durrie, "San Carlo Souvenir," *Opera News,* January 20, 1973.

25. Cardell Bishop, *San Carlo Opera Company, 1913–1955: Grand Opera for Profit* (Santa Monica, Calif.: Cardell Bishop, 1978), 171.

26. "Opera in Review," *Theater Arts,* August 1947.

27. Claudia Cassidy, review, *Chicago Daily Tribune,* October 13, 1945.

28. Durrie, "San Carlo Souvenir."

29. Gary Diedrichs, "Coe, the Eternal Gypsy," *Opera News,* January 12, 1974.

30. Oscar Thompson, review, *Musical America,* September 25, 1926, as quoted in Bishop, *San Carlo Opera,* 101.

31. Dorothy Kirsten with Lanfranco Rasponi, *A Time to Sing* (Garden City, N.Y.: Doubleday, 1982), 37.

32. Edward Moore, *Chicago Daily Tribune,* used in a promotional ad in *Musical America,* February 2, 1929.

33. Quoted in Paul Kempf, "How Fortune Gallo Saved an Opera Season," *The Musician,* September 1934.

34. It should be noted that in addition to running a solvent touring opera company, Gallo juggled a myriad of other ventures. They include managing tours for Eleanora Duse, Anna Pavlova, and a Gilbert and Sullivan company; producing an al fresco *Aida* for fifty-five thousand to benefit flood victims in Italy; building his own theater in Manhattan (selling it just before the Depression); serving as director of a bank; managing the Chicago Grand Opera for two years; and, in 1931—the only year he canceled the San Carlo tour—producing the first full-length sound motion picture of an opera, *Pagliacci.*

Notes to Chapter Six

1. "Aïda without Makeup," *Time,* July 31, 1933.

2. Virgil Thomson, review, *New York Herald Tribune,* January 17, 1941.

3. *Time,* July 31, 1933.

4. Because Bledsoe was the only black singer in this performance and because the year was 1932, the point could be made that it was the first time in America a black singer sang opera with whites. However, because it was only a pickup performance and there was no specific company involved, it did not carry nearly the same significance as Jarboro's debut for Salmaggi's established Chicago Opera Company (as he then called his strictly New York company).

5. Review, *Times* (Amsterdam), April 5, 1937, used in a promotional ad in *Musical Courier,* May 15, 1937.

6. Quoted in Alan Rich, "A Bouncy Seventy-five," *New York Times,* clipping in the New York Public Library for the Performing Arts; no date given.

7. "Hayes Sings American Songs at Wigmore Hall," *Musical America,* November 27, 1920.

8. Review, *London Daily Express,* September 29, 1943, used in a promotional ad in *Musical America,* February 10, 1944.

9. *New York Times,* March 12, 1920, quoted in Raoul Abdul, *Blacks in Classical Music* (New York: Dodd, Mead, 1977), 77.

10. Vincent Sheean, *Between the Thunder and the Sun* (New York: Random House, 1943), 26.

11. Marian Anderson, *My Lord, What a Morning: An Autobiography* (New York: Viking, 1943), 158. The words have been repeated in various ways. Though this is the version Anderson herself gave, in his memoirs of Anderson, Vehanen, who thought Toscanini was referring to her whole art and not the voice alone, reported the remark as "What I heard today one is privileged to hear only once in a hundred years."

12. Anderson, *My Lord,* 189.

13. "Salt at Stockbridge," *Time,* August 21, 1939.

14. "The Talk of the Town," *New Yorker,* November 18, 1939.

15. *Time,* August 21, 1939.

16. "Talk of the Town," *New Yorker,* November 18, 1939.

17. Quoted in Virgil Thomson, *Virgil Thomson* (New York: Alfred A. Knopf, 1966), 325. The original appeared in the *New York Herald Tribune,* October 24, 1940.

18. Thomson, *Virgil Thomson,* 217

19. Steven Watson, *Prepare for Saints: Gertrude Stein, Virgil Thomson, and the Mainstreaming of American Modernism* (New York: Random House, 1998), 288.

20. Review, *Musical America,* October 25, 1937.

21. Hollis Alpert, *The Life and Times of Porgy and Bess: The Story of an American Classic* (New York: Alfred A. Knopf, 1990), 94.

22. Anne Wiggins Brown, interview by Barry Singer, "On Hearing Her Sing, Gershwin Made 'Porgy,' 'Porgy and Bess,'" *New York Times,* March 29, 1998.

23. W. J. Henderson, review, *New York Sun,* no date given; quoted in promotional material found in clippings file in the New York Public Library for the Performing Arts.

Notes to Chapter Seven

1. Leonard Stocker, "Reminiscence and Warning," *NATS Bulletin,* September/October 1978.

2. Quoted in Albert Fuller, *Alice Tully: An Intimate Portrait* (Urbana and Chicago: University of Illinois Press, 1999), 43.

3. "Debs," *Time,* December 26, 1938.

4. In addition to Stevens and Warren, they included Jan Peerce, Richard Tucker, Robert Merrill, Regina Resnik, Roberta Peters, and Beverly Sills.

5. Review, *New York Times,* November 28, 1938.

6. Though it has been routinely written that Warren never sang a solo at Radio City, I found his name on a Radio City program dated May 16, 1935, as the Sultan of Shariar in Rimsky-Korsakov's *Sheherazade,* which was part of the stage show that accompanied the movie *Break of Hearts.* There may be other instances.

7. Lanfranco Rasponi, interview with Maria Caniglia, in *The Last Prima Donnas,* 243.

8. "Opera Season Opens Gayly Despite Shadow of War," *New York Times,* November 28, 1939.

9. Editorial, "Orderly Progress of America's Opera in a War-Torn World," *Musical America,* December 10, 1939.

10. Editorial, *Musical Courier,* April 1, 1938.

11. Laholm was the name of the town in Sweden his family came from.

12. *Time,* January 8, 1940, as quoted in promotional material for Traubel in *Musical American,* February 10, 1940.

13. Editorial, *Musical Courier,* December 12, 1940.

14. Review, *Musical Courier,* January 1, 1941.

15. Noel Strauss, review, *New York Times,* January 6, 1940.

16. Rasponi, *The Last Prima Donnas,* 47.

17. "Met-Trained Heldentenor," *Newsweek,* April 10, 1944.

18. Quoted in Spike Hughes, *A History of the Opera Festival Glyndebourne* (London: Methuen, 1965), 126.

19. Howard Taubman, review, *New York Times,* December 10, 1940.

20. Quoted in Judith Buffington et al., *He Loves Me When I Sing: Remembering Eleanor Steber* (n.p.: Judith Buffington, 1993), 1.

21. Steber, *Eleanor Steber,* 36.

22. Ibid., 42.

23. B. H. Haggin, review, *Nation,* February 12, 1944, in B. H. Haggin, *Music in the Nation* (New York: William Sloane, 1949), 170.

24. Steber, *Eleanor Steber,* 45.

Notes to Chapter Eight

1. Editorial, *Musical Courier,* December 1, 1941.

2. "Formulas for Fame," *Opera News,* November 21, 1949.

3. William Warfield with Alton Miller, *William Warfield: My Music & My Life* (Champaign, Ill.: Sagamore, 1991), 67.

4. "Operatic USO," *Opera News,* October 5, 1942.

5. Ibid.

6. "Opera in the Theaters of War," *Opera News,* October 2, 1944.

7. Ibid.

8. Quoted in "USO Log," *Musical Courier,* November 15, 1944.

9. Helen Traubel and Richard G. Hubler, *St. Louis Woman* (New York: Duell, Sloan and Pearce, 1959), 154.

10. Pauline Pierce, Andzia Kuzak, Waldemar Schroeder, Perry Askam, and Robert Marshall.

11. Yolanda Merö-Irion, "The New Opera," *Opera News,* February 16, 1959.

12. *Musical America,* November 10, 1941.

13. The amusing article, "Red, Purple Dress Starts Opera Feud," in the *New York Times,* December 6, 1942, describes in detail the feud that led to the cancellation.

14. Review, *Variety,* January 6, 1943.

15. In addition to those already mentioned, Americans who sang with the New Opera Company include James Pease, Winifred Heidt, Jeanne Palmer, Christine Johnson, Alice Howland, Thelma Altman, John Baker, Donald Dame, Hugh Thompson, George Rasely, Ruby Mercer, Kenneth Schon, Selma Kaye, Wilma Spence, Mimi Benzell, and Brenda Lewis.

16. According to John Pennino in "The New Opera Company: What Did It Accomplish," *Opera Quarterly* 16, no. 4 (Autumn 2000), 608, a single performance of Marcel Pagnol's play *Topaze* marked its demise in December 1947.

17. Jan Peerce and Alan Levy, *The Bluebird of Happiness: The Memoirs of Jan Peerce* (New York: Harper & Row, 1976), 170.

18. Astrid Varnay with Donald Arthur, *55 Years in Five Acts* (Boston: Northeastern University Press, 2000), 15.

19. John Reardon, as quoted by Robert Jacobson in "Varnay Revisited," *Opera News,* December 21, 1974.

20. Review, *Musical America,* April 10, 1939.

21. Quoted in James A. Van Sant, "Miss Margaret's Way," *Opera News,* March 2, 1996.

22. Conner was misleading about her age for most of her life. She was not twenty-eight, as was reported.

23. Howard Taubman, review, *New York Times,* December 23, 1941.

24. Brian Sullivan, Mona Paulee, Nan Merriman, and George London would also get early experience with the company, which was founded by the English conductor Albert Coates.

25. Quoted in Quaintance Eaton, "James Melton," *Musical America,* February 10, 1951.

26. Howard Taubman, review, *New York Times,* December 8, 1942.

27. Quoted in "Looking toward the Future: An Interview with Edward Johnson," *Musical Courier,* November 20, 1943.

28. "Soprano from Spokane," *Time,* December 3, 1951.

29. Olin Downes, review, *New York Times,* December 5, 1943.

30. Patrice Munsel, interview with author, January 5, 1995.

31. Ibid.

32. Quoted in George Jellinek, "On the Home Front," *Opera News,* July 1995.

Notes to Chapter Nine

1. "Con Spirito," *Newsweek,* March 6, 1944.

2. "Rhinestone Horseshoe," *Time,* March 6, 1944.

3. Martin L. Sokol, *The New York City Opera: An American Adventure* (New York: Macmillan, 1981), 34.

4. Simi Horwitz, "New York City Opera Founder Laszlo Halasz," *Opera Monthly,* September/October 1993.

5. Olin Downes, review, *New York Times,* February 22, 1944.

6. *Newsweek,* March 6, 1944.

7. "City Center Opera Makes Promising Beginning," editorial, *Musical America,* March 10, 1944.

8. Basil Walsh, Catherine Hayes's biographer, says Kirsten's claim was not possible. E-mail to author, October 9, 2002.

9. Kirsten, *A Time to Sing,* 13.

10. "A Star Is Born," *Newsweek,* May 25, 1942.

11. Review, *Musical America,* November 25, 1944.

12. Kirsten, *A Time to Sing,* 145.

13. Edward Johnson, "Opera Sells Out on Tour," *Variety,* March 5, 1941.

14. Exceptions were Britain's Richard Manning and the Mexican-born Frederick Gynrod, whose parents were German.

15. "4th War Season Opened by Opera," *New York Times,* November 28, 1944.

16. "Karin Branzell to quit Metropolitan Opera," *Musical America,* January 15, 1944.

17. Thebom's official company debut was as Brangäne in Philadelphia two weeks prior to her New York debut.

18. Jerome D. Bohm, review, *New York Herald Tribune,* December 16, 1944.

19. Noel Strauss, review, *New York Times,* December 15, 1944.

20. "Conquering Tensions: A Conference with Blanche Thebom," *Etude,* July 1948.

21. Olin Downes, *New York Times,* December 2, 1944.

22. Quoted in Irving Kolodin, *The Metropolitan Opera 1883–1966: A Candid History* (New York: Alfred A. Knopf, 1966), 454.

23. Virgil Thomson, review, *New York Herald Tribune,* November 30, 1944.

24. Olin Downes, review, *New York Times,* November 30, 1944.

25. Review, *Musical America,* February 10, 1940.

26. Philip Miller, *The Guide to Long-Playing Records: Vocal Music* (New York: Alfred A. Knopf, 1955), 349.

27. Quoted in John Ardoin, "Vivat Regina," *Opera Quarterly* 9, no. 3 (Spring 1993), 85.

28. Quoted in "Presenting Regina Resnik," *Musical America,* May 5, 1944.

29. Review, *New York Times,* May 8, 1944.

30. Review, *New York Times,* December 7, 1944.

31. Quoted in Robert Jacobson, "Regina Reflects," *Opera News,* December 8, 1984.

32. Quoted in James A. Drake, *Richard Tucker: A Biography* (New York: E. P. Dutton, 1984), 76.

Notes to Chapter Ten

1. This account of New Year's Eve 1944 is from the *New York Times*, December 31, 1944, January 1, 1945, and January 2, 1945.

2. Review, *Musical America*, January 25, 1945.

3. Review, *Musical America*, February 10, 1945.

4. Olin Downes, review, *New York Times*, January 5, 1945.

5. Thomas A. DeLong, *The Mighty Music Box: The Golden Age of Musical Radio* (Los Angeles: Amber Crest, 1980), 145.

6. Review, *Musical Courier*, April 1, 1945.

7. Herbert F. Peyser, "Two Verdicts on a Controversial 'Fidelio,'" *Musical America*, March 25, 1945.

8. "Radio: Music a Mainstay in Tribute to President," *Musical America*, April 25, 1945.

9. Steber, *Eleanor Steber*, 70.

10. Mary Craig, "Silhouettes: New Singers and the Year of Opportunity," *Musical Courier*, January 1, 1945.

11. Margaret Truman and Margaret Cousins, *Souvenir: Margaret Truman's Own Story* (New York: McGraw-Hill, 1956), 75.

12. Tito Gobbi, *My Life* (Garden City, N.Y.: Doubleday, 1980), 63.

13. "Schipa's Return," *Time*, July 1, 1946.

14. "Yankee Invasion," *Time*, August 30, 1943.

15. Review, *Musical America*, September 1945.

16. "Duncan to Sing Tonio," *New York Times*, September 9, 1945.

17. Sheryl Flatow, "Premiere Porgy," *Opera News*, March 16, 1985.

18. Review, *Musical America*, October 1945.

19. Review, *Musical Courier*, October 15, 1945.

20. "Porgi to Pagli," *Newsweek*, October 8, 1945.

21. Review, *Musical America*, April 25, 1945.

22. Review, *Musical Courier*, October 15, 1945.

23. Lois White Eck, "I Thought My Life Was Over," *Ladies' Home Journal*, April 1945.

24. Review, *Musical America*, October 1945.

25. Editorial, *Musical Leader*, November 1945.

26. Ronald F. Eyer, "Metropolitan Opera Opens with *Lohengrin*," *Musical America*, December 10, 1945.

Notes to Chapter Eleven

1. Mary Craig, "Silhouettes: Opera, Hardy and Perennial Art," *Musical Courier*, March 1, 1945.

2. "Opera Climbs across the Country," *Opera News,* November 1945.

3. Richard Torigi, interview with author, May 14, 1996.

4. "Touring Opera Sees Increased Demand," *Musical America,* February 10, 1946.

5. Quoted by Florence Stevenson in "A Place in the Sun," *Opera News,* March 13, 1971.

6. Francis D. Perkins, *New York Herald Tribune,* May 16, 1937; Robert Lawrence, *New York Herald Tribune,* February 28, 1941.

7. *New York Herald Tribune,* no date given, found in *Current Biography Yearbook 1957.*

8. Quoted in Irving Kolodin, "From Tonio to Tony (In Twenty Hard Years)," *Saturday Review of Literature,* May 5, 1956.

9. Vivian Della Chiesa, interview with author, June 1, 1999.

10. "Met Opera Named 'Co-respondent' in Detroit Divorce Suit," *Variety,* October 15, 1941.

11. Robert Bagar, *New York World-Telegram,* as quoted in a promotional ad in *Musical America,* February 1948.

12. Noel Strauss, *New York Times,* as quoted in a promotional ad in *Musical America,* February 10, 1950.

13. Harold Rosenthal, *Two Centuries of Opera at Covent Garden* (London: Putnam, 1958), 667.

14. Sherrill Milnes, *American Aria: From Farm Boy to Opera Star* (New York: Schirmer Books, 1998), 53.

15. Torigi interview.

16. Quoted in Ruth Glean Rosing, *Val Rosing: Musical Genius* (Manhattan, Kans.: Sunflower University Press, 1993), 132.

17. Quoted in ibid., 137.

18. Virgil Thomson, review, *New York Herald Tribune,* date missing (found in Nine O'Clock Opera clippings file, New York Public Library for the Performing Arts at Lincoln Center).

19. Amato is impressive in the role of Remendado on a recording of the Act 2 quintet from *Carmen* on the recording *Metropolitan Opera Artists in "Carmen."*

20. Editorial, "The Production of Opera Catches Up with the Times," *Musical America,* August 1949.

21. Ruth Kobart, interview with author, October 9, 1998.

22. Review, *New York Times,* February 24, 1950.

Notes to Chapter Twelve

1. Mattiwilda Dobbs, quoted in Ernest Dunbar, *Black Expatriates* (New York: E. P. Dutton, 1968), 210.

2. Bethany Beardslee, interview with author, August 8, 1999.

3. Quoted in Brian Kellow, "Notebook," *Opera News,* December 10, 1994.

4. Steber, *Eleanor Steber,* 64.

5. Quoted in Gerald Fitzgerald, "The Chapmans of Florence," *Opera News,* November 19, 1960.

6. Quoted in Gerald Fitzgerald, "Birth of a Tradition," *Opera News,* March 25, 1957.

7. Nan Merriman, "A Singer's View of Toscanini," *Saturday Review of Literature,* March 25, 1967.

8. With Gertrude Ribla, Jan Peerce, Frank Valentino, and Nicola Moscona.

9. Quoted in Albert Goldberg, "Nan Merriman," *Musical America,* January 1, 1959.

10. Quoted in William R. Trotter, *Priest of Music: The Life of Dimitri Mitropoulos* (Portland, Ore.: Amadeus Press, 1995), 17.

11. "Pioneer in the Fight on Vocal Chaos," *The Musician,* June 1933.

12. Founded by Mme. Anna E. Ziegler, Geraldine Farrar, and Enrico Caruso gave their names as charter members.

13. "National Association of Teachers of Singing Founded," *Musical America,* May 1944.

14. Gladys Swarthout, "The American Singer's Opportunities," *Etude,* December 1934.

15. Steber, *Eleanor Steber,* xii.

16. Patrice Munsel, interview with author, January 5, 1995.

17. Herbert Graf, *Opera for the People* (Minneapolis: University of Minnesota Press, 1951), 187.

18. Ibid.

19. Hans W. Heinsheimer, "The Grass Roots of Opera in America," *Etude,* December 1951.

20. F. J. Freeman, "Torch Bearers of Opera," *Opera News,* December 4, 1950.

21. Quoted in Foster Hirsch, *Kurt Weill on Stage: From Berlin to Broadway* (New York: Alfred A. Knopf, 2002), 292.

22. Graf, *Opera for the People,* 198.

23. Boris Goldovsky, as told to Curtis Cate, *My Road to Opera: The Recollections of Boris Goldovsky* (Boston: Houghton Mifflin, 1979), 348. The company would become the Goldovsky Opera Theater, which toured extensively in the late 1950s.

24. Quoted in Anthony Tommasini, "Reclaiming a Rich History of New Opera," *New York Times,* November 8, 1998.

25. A notable example was at Syracuse University, where Ruth Ives, a singing teacher, and the composer Ernst Bacon presided over a virtual operatic laboratory, which tested new works in productions reflecting contemporary theatrical developments.

26. Years later, when Guido turned to stage direction as a career, La Puma mounted whatever operas she needed to practice.

27. "From the Mail Pouch: Opportunities for Singers," *New York Times,* November 4, 1951.

Notes to Chapter Thirteen

1. This story of Conley, Vinay, and Carroll meeting Ruffo was reported in *Musical Courier,* November 1, 1947, and in *Opera News,* November 3, 1947. The accounts are very similar except that *Opera News* says it was D'Andria's birthday and there are small differences in Ruffo's remarks. As Vinay was born on August 31, I have used the *Courier* version.

2. Dorothy Speare, "My Adventures with the Opera Pirates," "The Gallery of Blasted Reputations," and "Mouth of the Wolf," *Cosmopolitan,* May, June, July 1928. Speare, who at one point studied with Jean de Reszke, performed on both sides of the ocean through 1930. She is best known, however, as the author of several novels, including a bestseller, *Dancers in the Dark,* and the play *Prima Donna,* which inspired the movie *One Night of Love.*

3. "For Major Leaguers," *Time,* June 8, 1936.

4. "Dickstein Bill: Musicians Battle over Immigration Ban," *Newsweek,* February 27, 1937.

5. Dorothy Dow, interview with author, March 11, 1997.

6. Howard Taubman, review, *New York Times,* November 16, 1951.

7. Dow interview.

8. Quoted in Dunbar, *Black Expatriates,* 178.

9. Mary Craig, "Silhouettes: Ellabelle Davis Reports on a 'Short Tour' of Europe," *Musical Courier,* June 1950.

10. One reference says Davis actually sang Aida at La Scala in 1949, but I found nothing to verify that claim.

11. Thomas Stewart, "George London," *Opera News,* July 1985.

12. Quoted in "'Very Remarkable,'" *Time,* January 9, 1950.

13. Quoted in Henry Pleasants, "From London to Vienna with Love: The Stunning Launch of a Great Career as Told by George London in His Letters Home, 1949–1952," *Opera Quarterly* 9, no. 3 (Spring 1993), 51.

14. Quoted in "'Very Remarkable,'" *Time,* January 9, 1950.

15. J. J. Vincent, quoted in "Assays Chances for U.S. Singers in Italy," *Musical Courier,* June 1, 1948.

16. Quoted in "Shortage at La Scala," *Time,* January 23, 1950.

17. Quoted in Peter Elvins, "Americans in Italy," *Opera News,* March 9, 1968. Kelston actually sang one performance of Leonora in *Forza del Destino* at La Scala, apparently as a reward for coming in on short notice to replace an ailing soprano as the *Trovatore* Leonora, but not singing the actual performance because the soprano recovered at the last minute.

18. Max de Schauensee, review, *Philadelphia Bulletin,* February 9, 1954.

19. "Lady with a Future," *Time,* January 28, 1946.

20. Review, *Il Popolo,* September 4, 1949, quoted in *Musical Courier,* January 1, 1950.

21. Mary Curtis-Verna, interview with author, November 1, 1998.

22. Renamed the Royal Opera Company in 1969.

23. Quoted in William Saunders, "The Edinburgh Opera Festival," *Opera News,* October 6, 1947.

Notes to Chapter Fourteen

1. Quoted in "Civic Concerts Mark 25th Birthday," *Musical America,* January 25, 1946.

2. Editorial, *Musical America,* January 25, 1946.

3. Ward French, "Community Concert Service," *Musical America,* February 10, 1945.

4. "Story behind the Scenes," *Variety,* January 7, 1942.

5. "Eddy No. 1 Concert Giver," *Variety,* February 11, 1942.

6. Steber, *Eleanor Steber,* 86.

7. Truman, *Souvenir,* 265.

8. "Recital Mill," *Time,* November 2, 1942.

9. Quoted in Faubion Bowers, "Amazin' Albert—II," *Opera News,* February 18, 1989. This quote appears with slightly different wording in other accounts.

10. Frieda Hempel, *My Golden Age of Singing* (Portland, Ore.: Amadeus Press, 1998), 111.

11. Review, *Musical Courier,* December 1, 1941.

12. Earl Wilson, review, *New York Post,* date not given, as quoted in *The Record Collector,* September, 1953.

13. "Lady Florence's Triumph," *Newsweek,* November 3, 1944.

14. "Recital Mill," *Time,* November 2, 1942.

15. Quoted in Kari Paulson, "Conversations with Inez Matthews," *Journal of Singing,* May/June 1997.

16. Quoted in Voytek Matushevski, "Jean de Reszke as Pedagogue," *Opera Quarterly* 12, no. 1 (Autumn 1995), 60.

17. Robeson was not a member and refused to sign on principle, but his passport was not restored until 1958.

18. Both the Koussevitzky and the Reiner remarks are quoted in David Ewen, *Living Musicians, First Supplement* (New York: H. W. Wilson, 1957), 29.

19. Virgil Thomson, review, *New York Herald Tribune,* used in a promotional ad in *Musical America,* February 1947.

20. Virgil Thomson, review, *New York Herald Tribune,* November 17, 1949, quoted in a promotional ad in *Musical Courier,* February 15, 1950.

21. Cecil Smith, review, *Musical America,* December 1, 1948.

22. "Harrell, the Versatile," *Newsweek,* November 17, 1952.

23. "The Music Mart," *Newsweek,* November 29, 1948.

24. Ned Rorem, *Setting the Tone: Essays and a Diary* (New York: Coward-McCann, 1983), 263.

25. Ned Rorem, *Knowing When to Stop* (New York: Simon & Schuster, 1994), 466.

26. "Such B's as Buxtehude," *Saturday Review of Literature,* December 25, 1954.

27. Bethany Beardslee, interview with author, August 8, 1999.

28. Andrew Derhen, review, *High Fidelity/Musical America,* May 1970.

29. "Song Plugger," *Time,* December 16, 1946. Copyright 1946 by Time Inc., reprinted by permission.

30. In addition, Fairbank's aunt Margaret Ayer Barnes was the author of the 1931 Pulitzer Prize–winning novel, *Years of Grace.*

31. Review, *New York Times,* November 17, 1944.

32. Cecil Smith, "Singers of Songs," *Theater Arts,* April 1947, 40.

Notes to Chapter Fifteen

1. Brooks Atkinson, review, *New York Times,* January 10, 1947.

2. Marc Blitzstein, "Notes on the Musical Theater," *Theater Arts,* June 1950.

3. Kurt Weill, liner notes to original recording of *Street Scene* (Columbia 4139, 1947).

4. Richard Rodgers, *Musical Stages: An Autobiography* (New York: Random House, 1975), 266.

5. Ned Rorem, *Knowing When to Stop,* 230, 170.

6. Review, *Musical America,* December 10, 1943.

7. Mary Craig, "Found in the Stars," *Musical Courier,* August 1954. Though this account is from an interview with the singer, it differs a little from another one she gave in 1994, which was published in *NATS Journal of Singing,* May/June 1997.

8. Symonette began in a small role, but later replaced Cordon.

9. Foster Hirsch, *Kurt Weill on Stage,* 262.

10. Brenda Lewis, interview with author, September 15, 1998.

11. *Amelia al Ballo* (1938) and *Ilo e Zeus* (1942).

12. Quoted in John Gruen, *Menotti: A Biography* (New York: Macmillan, 1978), 64.

13. Quoted in "Contralto on Broadway," *Time,* June 30, 1947.

14. Olin Downes, review, *New York Times,* February 19, 1947.

15. One interesting exception happened when Powers was performing in *The Consul* and Zelma George, a large black dramatic soprano who had already performed the role some sixty-seven times in her native Cleveland, played it in a theater-in-the-round production in New York. George, in real life a social worker, was uncomfortable with mistreating the deaf-mute Toby, and so Menotti had her play it as though crippled from the waist down in a wheelchair, which apparently was powerful theater.

16. Quoted in Gruen, *Menotti,* 79.

17. Quoted in Mary Braggiotti, "A Butterfly from Dixie," *New York Post,* October 3, 1946.

18. Camilla Williams, interview with author, May 21, 1997.

19. The Puccini opera was not performed in the United States after the attack on Pearl Harbor.

20. Noel Strauss, review, *New York Times,* May 16, 1946.

21. "New Butterfly," *Newsweek,* May 27, 1946.

22. "Ariadne auf New York," *Newsweek,* October 21, 1946.

23. Quoted in "30-Year Sleeper," *Time,* October 21, 1946.

24. Howard Taubman, review, *New York Times,* October 10, 1947.

25. Review, *Musical America,* May 1948.

26. Cecil Smith, review, *Theater Arts,* June 1947.

27. Howard Taubman, review, *New York Times,* September 26, 1947.

28. Rorem, *Knowing When to Stop,* 170.

29. Julius Rudel, "Ellen Faull: An Appreciation," liner notes to *Ellen Faull: An American Soprano* (VAI 1173, 1998).

30. Cecil Smith, review, *Musical America,* May 1948.

31. Adelaide Bishop, interview with author, April 23, 1999.

32. Teyte's first performances at the New York City Opera had, in fact, been the previous spring, when she sang the role opposite, among others, Theodor Uppman.

33. Olin Downes, review, *New York Times,* April 7, 1949.

34. Review, *Musical America,* April 1948.

35. "Black and White Aida," *Time,* November 8, 1948. Despite the title, the magazine made no mention of the Jarboro and Bledsoe father-and-daughter casting of more than a decade before, which it had written about at such length.

36. "Troubled Opera," *Time,* April 11, 1949.

37. Bible, however, regretted that she never sang at the Metropolitan, and in an interview with the author (May 24, 1999) explained that after she auditioned there in 1950, Bing issued her a contract, which her manager signed for her, overlooking the fact that he had already signed one for her with Halasz for the same period. Halasz would not release her, and Bing, she said, never forgave her.

38. Bible interview.

39. Bishop interview.

40. "A Five-Year Record of Lively Opera Production," editorial, *Musical America,* December 1, 1948.

41. "New York City Opera: Handsome Young Troupe Brightens U.S. Music Scene," *Life,* April 11, 1949.

Notes to Chapter Sixteen

1. "A New Kind of Opera," *Newsweek,* February 24, 1947.

2. Louis Biancolli, review, *New York World Telegram,* December 3, 1945.

3. Review, *Musical America,* December 25, 1945.

4. Robert Merrill and Sanford Dody, *Once More from the Beginning* (New York: Macmillan, 1965), 35, 122, 124.

5. Hayward would, however, essay more major roles than most comprimarios. Under Johnson he would sing several Rinuccios (*Gianni Schicchi*) and, under Bing, a Pinkerton, a Duke, an Alfredo, and several Fausts and Alfreds (*Fledermaus*), though primarily on tour.

6. Merrill, *Once More from the Beginning,* 168.

7. Jerome Hines, interview with author, April 11, 1995.

8. Howard Taubman, review, *New York Times,* January 19, 1946.

9. Howard Taubman, review, *New York Times,* February 8, 1946.

10. Howard Taubman, review, *New York Times,* January 30, 1947. Quartararo also sang her only Pamina on short notice.

11. Max de Schauensee, review, *Evening Bulletin,* February 28, 1951.

12. Quoted in Richard Michael Caniell, *Florence Quartararo: A Memorial,* a publication of the Immortal Performances Recorded Music Society, British Columbia, Canada, 1995.

13. Noel Straus, review, *New York Times,* December 5, 1948.

14. Review (translated), *Osterholzer Kreisblatt,* October 7, 1953.

15. Marilyn Cotlow, interview with author, March 6, 1996.

16. Edward Johnson, "Opera Faces the Peace," *Opera News,* October 15, 1945.

17. Irving Kolodin, review, *New York Sun,* December 5, 1946, used in a promotional ad in *Musical America,* February 10, 1947. That the review continued with the quote about "a good provider" was found in a story about the mezzo, "Many Mediums," *Opera News,* April 7, 1962.

18. "Preparing for Opera: A Conference with Polyna Stoska," *Etude,* May 1949.

19. Cecil Smith, review, *Musical America,* March 15, 1948.

20. Ribla was the soprano who had just sung "Pace, pace, mio Dio" under Toscanini when the news came that Mussolini had been overthrown. Later in the program she was the Gilda in the last act of *Rigoletto.*

21. Cecil Smith, review, *Musical America,* January 15, 1949.

22. Steber, *Eleanor Steber,* 199.

23. Lois Hunt, interview with author, August 17, 1999.

24. "Met Opens," *Newsweek,* December 5, 1949.

25. Review, *Musical America,* December 1, 1949.

26. Kolodin, *The Metropolitan Opera,* 496.

27. Martin Mayer, *The Met: One Hundred Years of Grand Opera* (New York: Simon and Schuster and the Metropolitan Opera Guild, 1983), 213.

28. Kolodin, *The Metropolitan Opera,* 493.

Notes to Chapter Seventeen

1. Quaintance Eaton, "Two Television Networks Give Opera," *Musical America,* January 15, 1950.

2. Quaintance Eaton, review, *Musical America,* March 15, 1950.

3. Louis Biancolli, *New York World Telegram,* no date given, quoted in *Operatic Fanatic,* April 1993.

4. Quoted in Quaintance Eaton, "Great Opera Houses: NBC-TV," *Opera News,* February 8, 1964.

5. Quoted in Cecil Smith, "The Metropolitan Has a New Manager," *Musical America,* February 1950.

6. Olin Downes, review, *New York Times,* March 16, 1950.

7. Robert Sabin, review, *Musical America,* March 15, 1950.

8. Jerome D. Bohm, review, *New York Herald Tribune,* March 20, 1950, used in promotional ad in *Musical Courier,* April 15, 1950.

9. Warfield, *William Warfield,* 124.

10. Steber, *Eleanor Steber,* 103.

11. Arthur Jacobs, "A British Music Critic in New York," *Musical America,* April 1, 1951.

12. Quoted in Bloomfield, *50 Years of the San Francisco Opera,* 119.

13. David Lloyd, interview with author, May 8, 1998.

14. Rudolf Bing, *5000 Nights at the Opera: The Memoirs of Sir Rudolf Bing* (Garden City, N.Y.: Doubleday, 1972), 142. Bing, in fact, engaged thirteen foreigners for the same season, but nothing was ever made of the discrepancy.

15. "The Dutchman Cometh," *Time,* November 20, 1950.

16. Cecil Smith, review, *Musical America,* December 15, 1950.

17. Margaret Truman, *Harry S. Truman* (New York: William Morrow, 1973), 502.

18. Cecil Smith, review, *Musical America,* January 15, 1951.

19. "Met Forming Separate Troupe to Tour U.S. with Fledermaus," *New York Times,* March 15, 1951.

20. *Quick,* March 12, 1951.

Notes to Chapter Eighteen

1. Quoted in Douglas T. Miller and Marion Nowak, *The Fifties* (Garden City, N.Y.: Doubleday, 1975), 9.

2. Warfield, *William Warfield,* 83.

3. Todd Duncan, "To Sing . . . But Where?" *Opera and Concert,* August 1950.

4. Others who made the historic tour of the Robert Breen production include Gloria Davy, Irene Williams, Martha Flowers, Vern LeHutcheson, Cab Calloway, and Martha Thigpen.

5. This phrase could be found on much of the promotional material.

6. "Ambassador Porgy," *Newsweek,* September 22, 1952.

7. "TV Tosca," *Time,* January 31, 1955.

8. Anderson, *My Lord, What a Morning,* 302.

9. "Marian Anderson Wins Ovation in First Opera Role at the 'Met,'" *New York Times,* January 8, 1955.

10. Walter Ducloux, "Return to Paradise," *Opera News,* May 4, 1963.

11. James Hinton, "The Opera Scene in America," in Harold Rosenthal, *Opera Annual: 1954/55* (New York: Lantern Press, 1955), 122.

12. Lawrence Kelley and Nicola Rescigno founded the company with Fox but abandoned it in 1956 to launch their own company in Dallas.

13. Howard Taubman, review, *New York Times,* May 21, 1955.

14. Frank Merkling, "The Grass Is Greener," *Opera News,* November 19, 1960.

15. Frederic V. Grunfeld, *Music and Recordings, 1955* (New York: Oxford University Press, 1955), 7.

16. *New York Herald Tribune,* August 26, 1956, quoted in "Elaine Malbin" in *Current Biography Yearbook, 1959,* 285.

17. Bing, *5,000 Nights at the Opera,* 189.

18. As quoted in an editorial, "Miss Traubel, Mr. Bing, and the Night-Club Issue," *Musical America,* October 1953.

19. "Traubel's Met Exit," *Newsweek,* October 5, 1953.

20. Vincent Sheean, introduction to Traubel, *St. Louis Woman,* p. xiii.

21. "Marguerite Piazza Finds Television a Steppingstone to Success in Music," *Musical America,* November 15, 1952.

22. Sills, *Beverly,* 101.

23. Ronald Eyer, "Moving in on Bach's Territory—A Different Kind of Entertainer," *New York Herald Tribune,* April 20, 1963.

24. Quoted in David Halberstam, *The Fifties* (New York: Villard Books, 1993), 456.

25. Interview with Rudolf Bing, *Agmazine* 10, no. 5 (April 1958).

26. Thomas Hayward, interview with author, May 11, 1994. Ironically, it was Bing, however, not Johnson, who would ultimately give the comprimario tenor his only chance at leading roles with the company.

27. Steber, *Eleanor Steber,* 96, 99.

28. Bing, *5000 Nights at the Opera,* 147.

29. George Martin, *Opera Annual 1958–1959* (London: John Calder, 1959), 76.

30. Sills, as quoted by Elise K. Kirk, *American Opera* (Urbana: University of Illinois Press, 2001), 272.

31. Ernest J. M. Lert, "Operatic Horizons in the U.S.," *Opera News,* January 1, 1945.

32. Lawrence Tibbett, "Shaking Off the Inferiority Complex," selections from an address on changing standards in American music that Tibbett gave at the Waldorf-Astoria on September 26, 1935, and published in *Musical America,* November 9, 1935.

33. Quoted in F. Paul Driscoll, *Opera News,* January 21, 1995.

34. Rudolf Bing, quoted in Frank Merkling, "Rudolf Bing Discusses the Met," *Musical America,* February 10, 1954.

Select Bibliography

Abdul, Raoul. *Blacks in Classical Music: A Personal History.* New York: Dodd, Mead, 1977.

Alpert, Hollis. *The Life and Times of Porgy and Bess: The Story of an American Classic.* New York: Alfred A. Knopf, 1990.

Anderson, Marian. *My Lord, What a Morning: An Autobiography.* New York: Viking, 1956.

Angelou, Maya. *Singin' and Swingin' and Gettin' Merry Like Christmas.* New York: Random House, 1976.

Belmont, Eleanor Robson. *The Fabric of Memory.* New York: Farrar, Straus and Cudahy, 1957.

Benton, Joseph. *Oklahoma Tenor: Musical Memories of Giuseppe Bentonelli.* Norman: University of Oklahoma Press, 1973.

Bessette, Roland L. *Mario Lanza: Tenor in Exile.* Portland, Ore: Amadeus Press, 1999.

Bijou, Theodore T. C., Daniel F. Tritter, and Rita Shane Tritter. "Regional Auditions History," revised 1968; unpublished.

Bing, Rudolf. *5000 Nights at the Opera.* Garden City, N.Y.: Doubleday, 1972.

Bishop, Cardell. *Opera in the Hippodrome in New York City: 1933–1939.* Santa Monica, Calif.: Cardell Bishop, 1979.

———. *San Carlo Opera Company, 1913–1955: Grand Opera for Profit.* Santa Monica, Calif.: Cardell Bishop, 1978.

Bloomfield, Arthur. *50 Years of the San Francisco Opera.* San Francisco: San Francisco Book Co., 1972.

Briggs, John. *Requiem for a Yellow Brick Brewery: A History of the Metropolitan Opera.* Boston: Little, Brown, 1969.

Buckland, Michel, and John Henken, eds. *The Hollywood Bowl: Tales of Summer Nights.* Los Angeles: Balcony Press, 1996.

Crichton, Kyle. *Subway to the Met; Risë Stevens' Story.* Garden City, N.Y.: Doubleday, 1959.

Cuney-Hare, Maud. *Negro Musicians and Their Music.* Washington, D.C.: Associated Publishers, 1936.

Davis, Peter G. *The American Opera Singer: The Lives & Adventures of America's Great Singers in Opera and Concert, from 1825 to the Present.* New York: Doubleday, 1997.

Davis, Ronald L. *Opera in Chicago.* New York: Appleton-Century, 1966.

DeLong, Thomas A. *The Mighty Music Box: The Golden Age of Musical Radio.* Los Angeles: Amber Crest, 1980.

Dizikes, John. *Opera in America: A Cultural History.* New Haven: Yale University Press, 1993.

Dragonette, Jessica. *Faith Is a Song: The Odyssey of an American Artist.* New York: David McKay, 1951.

Drake, James A. *Richard Tucker: A Biography.* New York: E. P. Dutton, 1984.

Duberman, Martin Bauml. *Paul Robeson: A Biography.* New York: Alfred A. Knopf, 1988.

Dunbar, Ernest. *The Black Expatriates.* New York: E. P. Dutton, 1968.

Dunning, John. *On the Air: The Encyclopedia of Old-Time Radio.* New York and Oxford: Oxford University Press, 1998.

Eaton, Quaintance. *The Miracle of the Met: An Informal History of the Metropolitan Opera, 1883–1967.* New York: Meredith, 1968.

Ewen, David. *Living Musicians.* New York: H. W. Wilson, 1940.

———. *Living Musicians, First Supplement.* New York: H. W. Wilson, 1957.

———. *Music Comes to America.* New York: Allen, Towne & Heath, 1947.

———. *New Encyclopedia of the Opera.* New York: Hill and Wang, 1973.

Farkas, Andrew, ed. *Lawrence Tibbett: Singing Actor.* Portland, Ore.: Amadeus Press, 1989.

Farrar, Rowena Rutherford. *Grace Moore and Her Many Worlds.* New York: Cornwall Books, 1982.

Farrell, Eileen, and Brian Kellow. *Can't Help Singing: The Life of Eileen Farrell.* Boston: Northeastern University Press, 1999.

Fawkes, Richard. *Opera on Film.* London: Gerald Duckworth, 2000.

Fitzgerald, Gerald, and Jean Sward Uppman, eds. *Annals of the Metropolitan Opera: The Complete Chronicle of Performances and Artists: Chronology 1883–1985,* 2 vols. Boston: G. K. Hall, 1989.

Fordin, Hugh. *Getting to Know Him: A Biography of Oscar Hammerstein II.* New York: Random House, 1977.

Fuller, Albert. *Alice Tully: An Intimate Portrait.* Urbana and Chicago: University of Illinois Press, 1999.

Gallo, Fortune T. *Lucky Rooster: The Autobiography of an Impresario.* New York: Exposition Press, 1967.

Gatti-Casazza, Giulio. *Memories of the Opera.* New York: Charles Scribner's Sons, 1941.

Gobbi, Tito. *My Life.* Garden City, N.Y.: Doubleday, 1980.

Goldovsky, Boris, as told to Curtis Cate. *My Road to Opera: The Recollections of Boris Goldovsky.* Boston: Houghton Mifflin, 1979.

Graf, Herbert. *Opera for the People.* Minneapolis: University of Minnesota Press, 1951.

Gruen, John. *Menotti: A Biography.* New York: Macmillan, 1978.

Haggin, B. H. *Music in the Nation.* New York: William Sloane, 1949.

Hamlin, Anna M. *Father Was a Tenor.* Hicksville, N.Y.: Exposition Press, 1978.

Helm, MacKinley. *Angel Mo' and Her Son, Roland Hayes.* Boston: Little, Brown, 1942.

Herman, Robert, as told to Mary Voelz Chandler. *The Greater Miami Opera: From Shoestring to Showpiece 1941–1985.* Miami: Miami Opera Guild, 1985.

Hines, Jerome. *This Is My Story, This Is My Song.* Westwood N.J.: Fleming H. Revell, 1968.

Hirsch, Foster. *Kurt Weill on Stage: From Berlin to Broadway.* New York: Alfred A. Knopf, 2002.

Hughes, Spike. *A History of the Opera Festival Glyndebourne.* London: Methuen, 1965.

Jackson, Paul. *Saturday Afternoons at the Old Met: The Metropolitan Opera Broadcasts, 1931–1950.* Portland, Ore: Amadeus Press, 1992.

———. *Sign-Off for the Old Met: The Metropolitan Opera Broadcasts, 1950–1966.* Portland, Ore.: Amadeus Press, 1997.

Keiler, Allan. *Marian Anderson: A Singer's Journey.* New York: Scribner, 2000.

Key, Pierre V. R. *Pierre Key's Music Year Book: The Standard Music Annual.* 1935 ed. New York: Pierre Key, 1934.

———. *Pierre Key's Music Year Book.* 1938 ed. New York: Pierre Key, 1938.

Kirk, Elise K. *American Opera.* Urbana and Chicago: University of Illinois Press, 2001.

Kirsten, Dorothy, with Lanfranco Rasponi. *A Time to Sing.* Garden City, N.Y.: Doubleday, 1982.

Kolodin, Irving. *The Metropolitan Opera: 1883–1966: A Candid History.* New York: Alfred A. Knopf, 1966.

Kupferberg, Herbert. *Tanglewood.* New York: McGraw-Hill, 1976.

Lehmann, Lotte. *Midway in My Song.* Indianapolis: Bobbs-Merrill, 1938.

Leider, Frida. *Playing My Part.* Trans. Charles Osborne. New York: Meredith Press, 1966.

London, Nora. *Aria for George.* New York: E. P. Dutton, 1987.

Mayer, Martin. *The Met: One Hundred Years of Grand Opera.* New York: Simon and Schuster and the Metropolitan Opera Guild, 1983.

McGovern, Dennis, and Deborah Grace Winer. *I Remember Too Much: 89 Opera Stars Speak Candidly of Their Work, Their Lives, and Their Colleagues.* New York: William Morrow, 1990.

Mercer, Ruby. *The Tenor of His Time: Edward Johnson of the Met.* Toronto: Clarke, Irwin, 1976.

Merrill, Robert, and Sandford Dody. *Once More from the Beginning.* New York: Macmillan, 1965.

Milnes, Sherrill. *American Aria: From Farm Boy to Opera Star.* New York: Schirmer, 1998.

Moore, Grace. *You're Only Human Once.* Garden City, N.Y.: Doubleday, Doran, 1944.

Noble, Helen. *Life with the Met.* New York: G. P. Putnam's Sons, 1954.

O'Connell, Charles. *The Other Side of the Record.* New York: Alfred A. Knopf, 1947.

Owen, H. Goddard. *A Recollection of Marcella Sembrich.* New York: Da Capo Press, 1982.

Peerce, Jan, and Alan Levy. *The Bluebird of Happiness: The Memoirs of Jan Peerce.* New York: Harper & Row, 1976.

Peters, Roberta, and Louis Biancolli. *A Debut at the Met.* New York: Meredith, 1967.

Phillips-Matz (Matz), Mary Jane. *Leonard Warren: American Baritone.* Portland, Ore: Amadeus, 2000.

———. *Opera: Grand and Not So Grand.* New York: William Morrow, 1966.

———. *Rosa Ponselle: American Diva.* Boston: Northeastern University Press, 1997.

Ponselle, Rosa, and James A. Drake. *Ponselle: A Singer's Life.* Garden City, N.Y.: Doubleday, 1982.

Rasponi, Lanfranco. *The Last Prima Donnas.* New York: Alfred A. Knopf, 1982.

Rorem, Ned. *Knowing When to Stop: A Memoir.* New York: Simon & Schuster, 1994.

———. *Setting the Tone: Essays and a Diary.* New York: Coward-McCann, 1983.

Rosing, Ruth Glean. *Val Rosing: Musical Genius, an Intimate Biography.* Manhattan, Kans.: Sunflower University Press, 1993.

Schoen-René, Anna Eugénie. *America's Musical Inheritance: Memories and Reminiscences.* New York: G. P. Putnam's Sons, 1941.

Sheean, Vincent. *Between the Thunder and the Sun.* New York: Random House, 1943.

———. *First and Last Love.* New York: Random House, 1956.

Sills, Beverly, and Lawrence Linderman. *Beverly: An Autobiography.* New York: Bantam Books, 1987.

Smith, Cecil. *Worlds of Music.* Philadelphia and New York: J. B. Lippincott, 1952.

Sokol, Martin L. *The New York City Opera: An American Adventure.* New York: Macmillan, 1981.

Southern, Eileen. *The Music of Black Americans: A History.* 3d ed. New York: W. W. Norton, 1997.

Steber, Eleanor, with Martha Sloat. *Eleanor Steber: An Autobiography.* Ridgewood, N.J.: Wordsworth, 1992.

Story, Rosalyn M. *And So I Sing: African-American Divas of Opera and Concert.* New York: Warner Books, 1990.

Thierstein, Eldred A. *Cincinnati Opera: From the Zoo to Music Hall.* Hillsdale, Mich.: Deerstone Books, 1995.

Thompson, Oscar. *The American Singer: A Hundred Years of Success in Opera.* New York: Dial Press, 1937.

Tommasini, Anthony. *Virgil Thomson: Composer on the Aisle.* New York: W. W. Norton, 1997.

Traubel, Helen, and Richard G. Hubler. *St. Louis Woman.* New York: Duell, Sloan and Pearce, 1959.

Truman, Margaret, and Margaret Cousins. *Souvenir: Margaret Truman's Own Story.* New York: McGraw-Hill, 1956.

Turk, Edward Baron. *Hollywood Diva: A Biography of Jeanette MacDonald.* Berkeley and Los Angeles: University of California Press, 1998.

Varnay, Astrid, and Donald Arthur. *55 Years in Five Acts: My Life in Opera.* Boston: Northeastern University Press, 2000.

Warfield, William, and Alton Miller. *William Warfield: My Music & My Life.* Champaign, Ill.: Sagamore, 1991.

Watson, Steven. *Prepare for Saints: Gertrude Stein, Virgil Thomson, and the Mainstreaming of American Modernism.* New York: Random House, 1998.

Wayner, Robert J., ed. *What Did They Sing at the Met?* 2d ed. New York: Wayner, 1976.

Weinstat, Hertzel, and Bert Wechsler. *Dear Rogue: A Biography of the American Baritone Lawrence Tibbett.* Portland, Ore.: Amadeus Press, 1996.

Who Is Who in Music: 1941 Edition. Chicago and New York: Lee Stern Press. 1940.

Wlaschin, Ken. *Opera on Screen.* Los Angeles: Beechwood, 1997.

Young, Allen. *Opera in Central City.* Denver, Colo.: Spectographics, 1993.

Index

Page references given in *italics* indicate illustrations.
For references to individual pieces of music, see under titles of works.